Kawasaki ZX900, 1000 & 1100 Liquid-cooled Fours Owners Workshop Manual

W9-CPR-011

by Mark Coombs
with an additional Chapter on the ZX1100 D
by Penny Cox

Models covered
ZX900 A (GPZ900R). 908cc. UK April 1984 to 1994
ZX900 A (Ninja). 908cc. US November 1983 to 1986
ZX1000 A (GPZ1000RX). 997cc. UK November 1985 to September 1989
ZX1000 A (Ninja 1000R). 997cc. US September 1985 to 1987
ZX1000 B (ZX-10). 997cc. UK December 1987 to April 1991
ZX1000 B (Ninja ZX-10). 997cc. US April 1988 to 1990
ZX1100 C (ZZ-R1100). 1052cc. UK March 1990 to December 1992
ZX1100 C (Ninja ZX-11C). 1052cc. US 1990 to 1993
ZX1100 D (ZZ-R1100). 1052cc. UK December 1992 to 1994
ZX1100 D (Ninja ZX-11D). 1052cc. US 1993 to 1994

(1681-3T1)

ABCDE
FGHIJ
KL

Haynes Publishing
Sparkford Nr Yeovil
Somerset BA22 7JJ England

Haynes Publications, Inc
861 Lawrence Drive
Newbury Park
California 91320 USA

Acknowledgements

Our thanks are due to CW Motorcycles of Dorchester and TVM Motorcycles of Newton Abbot who supplied the machines featured in the photographs throughout this manual. Thanks are also due to Kawasaki Motors (UK) Ltd for supply of technical information and permission to use some of the line drawings featured. The Avon Rubber Company supplied information on tyre care and fitting, and NGK Spark Plugs (UK) Ltd provided information on plug maintenance and electrode conditions.

© **Haynes Publishing 1994**

A book in the **Haynes Owners Workshop Manual Series**

Printed by J. H. Haynes & Co. Ltd., Sparkford, Nr Yeovil, Somerset BA22 7JJ, England

ISBN 1 85010 848 X

Library of Congress Catalog Card Number 94-75590

British Library Cataloguing in Publication Data
A catalogue record for this book is available from the British Library

Contents

Kawasaki ZX900 A

Kawasaki ZX1000 A

Kawasaki ZX1000 B

Kawasaki ZX1100 C

About this manual

The purpose of this manual is to present the owner with a concise and graphic guide which will enable him to tackle any operation from basic routine maintenance to a major overhaul. It has been assumed that any work would be undertaken without the luxury of a well-equipped workshop and a range of manufacturer's service tools.

To this end, the machine featured in the manual was stripped and rebuilt in our own workshop, by a team comprising a mechanic, a photographer and the author. The resulting photographic sequence depicts events as they took place, the hands shown being those of the mechanic and the author.

The use of specialised, and expensive, service tools was avoided unless their use was considered to be essential due to risk of breakage or injury. There is usually some way of improvising a method of removing a stubborn component, providing that a suitable degree of care is exercised.

The author learnt his motorcycle mechanics over a number of years, faced with the same difficulties and using similar facilities to those encountered by most owners. It is hoped that this practical experience can be passed on through the pages of this manual.

Armed with a working knowledge of the machine, the author undertakes a considerable amount of research in order that the maximum amount of data can be included in the manual. A comprehensive section, preceding the main part of the manual, describes procedures for carrying out the routine maintenance of the machine at intervals of time and mileage. This section is included particularly for those owners who wish to ensure the efficient day-to-day running of their motorcycle, but who choose not to undertake overhaul or renovation work.

Each chapter is divided into numbered sections. Within these sections are numbered paragraphs. All photographs in the main chapters are captioned with a section/paragraph number to which they refer. Figures (line illustrations) appear in a numerical but logical order, within a given chapter. Fig. 1.1 therefore refers to the first figure in Chapter 1.

Left-hand and right-hand descriptions of the machine and its components refer to the left and right of a given machine when the rider is seated in the normal riding position.

Motorcycle manufacturers continually make changes to specifications and recommendations, and these, when notified, are incorporated into our manuals at the earliest opportunity.

Introduction to the Kawasaki ZX900, 1000 and 1100 Liquid-cooled Fours

In 1981 Kawasaki first introduced its GPz range of motorcycles with a 550 and 1100 cc model. These machines were widely acclaimed throughout the motorcycle world and sold well. In 1982 a 750 cc model was introduced, and was followed up by a 305 cc twin in 1983. In late 1983 a turbocharged version of the 750 cc model was also added to the range. All of the above models, with the exception of the 305 which was a twin, used an air-cooled in-line four cylinder engine with two valves per cylinder.

Kawasaki further enhanced the range with the introduction of the GPZ900R, known as the Ninja in the US. Although cosmetically similar to the other GPzs, the GPZ900R was technically a new machine with very little in common with the older models. By far the biggest change was that the old air-cooled engine of earlier models was replaced with a new liquid-cooled 16-valve in-line four engine; the first ever to be fitted to a production motorcycle. Although closely based on the air-cooled engine, major differences included mounting the alternator behind the cylinder block instead of on the crankshaft end, and the fitting of a balancer shaft to dampen out vibration. Other modifications included running the camchain down the left-hand side of the cylinders (making it possible to remove the chain without separating the crankcase halves), and using screw and locknuts to adjust the valve clearances. Chassis changes included the old full cradle frame being replaced by a new lightweight 'Diamond' type frame which used the engine as a stressed member, and the fitting of a 16 inch front wheel.

In late 1985 Kawasaki introduced the GPZ1000RX (Ninja 1000 R) model which used an uprated 900 engine which had been bored and stroked to take the capacity out to 997 cc. The main design change was that the 'Diamond' frame of the 900 was replaced with a full cradle frame constructed in square section steel. The fairing and bodywork were also redesigned to update the styling of the machine.

For 1988 Kawasaki introduced the ZX-10 (Ninja). The engine is similar to that which is fitted to the GPZ1000RX but with a redesigned top end. The main difference here is that the valve clearances are now adjusted using shims rather than screw and locknut adjusters; the shims are fitted on the top of each valve and can be changed without removing the cams. Other changes include the fitting of downdraught carburettors and an electric fuel pump. On the chassis side a new full cradle type frame was fitted, constructed totally in an aluminium alloy. The brake calipers were uprated to the dual-piston type.

In early 1990 the ZZ-R1100 (ZX-11 Ninja) was introduced. This model is very similar to the ZX-10, the engine being basically an uprated ZX-10 unit which has been bored out by 2mm. The other mechanical change was the fitting of a new air filter housing. This air filter housing has its intake situated in the upper fairing section and uses the forward motion of the machine to force air into the air filter housing and through the carburettors, so increasing the power output of the engine. As far as the chassis is concerned, new four-piston calipers were fitted to uprate the front braking system.

Apart from the usual colour and graphic changes all models remained largely unchanged throughout their production run, the exception being the long running GPZ900R, which for 1990 (A7 model) has been fitted with a 17 inch front wheel, new forks and the same brakes as the ZZ-R1100. The ZZ-R1100 (ZX-11) underwent change in 1993 when the D model was introduced. Whilst mechanical changes were few, the intake system benefited from a twin Ram Air system, and the fairing and frame were redesigned.

It will be noted that throughout this Manual machines are identified by their full Kawasaki code and not by their popular name. The actual model of machine can be identified by its engine and frame number using the accompanying list. Note that the dates given refer to the year of production by Kawasaki which is not necessarily the same as the date of sale or registration.

Year	Model code	Frame number	Engine number
UK GPZ900R:			
1984	ZX900 A1	ZX900A-000001 - 015000	ZX900AE000001 on
		ZX900A-015004 - 015500	ZX900AE000001 on
1985	ZX900 A2	ZX900A-015001 - 015003	ZX900AE019001 on
		ZX900A-015501 on	ZX900AE019001 on
1986	ZX900 A3	ZX900A-031001 on	ZX900AE040001 on
1987	ZX900 A4	ZX900A-035101 on	ZX900AE046001 on
1988	ZX900 A5/A5A	ZX900A-038501 on	ZX900AE048501 on
1989	ZX900 A6	ZX900A-042001 on	ZX900AE048501 on
1990	ZX900 A7	ZX900A-048001 on	ZX900AE048501 on
1991-94	ZX900 A8	ZX900A-056001 on	ZX900AE048501 on
UK GPZ1000RX:			
1986	ZX1000 A1	ZXT00A-000001 on	ZXT00AE000001 on
1987	ZX1000 A2	ZXT00A-014801 on	ZXT00AE021001 on
1988	ZX1000 A3/A3A	ZXT00A-022401 on	ZXT00AE028501 on
UK ZX-10:			
1988	ZX1000 B1	ZXT00B-000001- 012000	ZXT00AE027801 on
		ZXT00B-012452- 017000	ZXT00AE028501 on
1989	ZX1000 B2	ZXT00B-012001- 012451	ZXT00AE028501 on
		ZXT00B-017001- 028000	ZXT00AE028501 on
1990-91	ZX1000 B3	ZXT00B-028001 on	ZXT00AE028501 on
UK ZZ-R1100:			
1990	ZX1100 C1	ZXT10C-000001- 013000	ZXT10CE000001 on
1991	ZX1100 C2	ZXT10C-013001 on	ZXT10CE000001 on
1992	ZX1100 C3	ZXT10C-024001 on	ZXT10CE000001 on
1993	ZX1100 D1	ZXT10D-000001- 020000	ZXT10CE000001 on
1994	ZX1100 D2	ZXT10D-020001 on	ZXT10CE000001 on
US Ninja:			
1984	ZX900 A1 - Made in Japan	JKAZX2A1-EA000001 on	ZX900AE000001 on
	ZX900 A1 - Made in US	JKAZX2A1-EB000001 on	ZX900AE000001 on
1985	ZX900 A2 - Made in Japan	JKAZX2A1-FA015001 on	ZX900AE019001 on
	ZX900 A2 - Made in US	JKAZX2A1-FB505301 on	ZX900AE019001 on
1986	ZX900 A3 - Made in Japan	JKAZX2A1-GA031001 on	ZX900AE040001 on
	ZX900 A3 - Made in US	JKAZX2A1-GB512701 on	ZX900AE040001 on
US Ninja 1000R:			
1986	ZX1000 A1 - Made in Japan	JKAZXCA1-GA000001 on	ZXT00AE000001 on
	ZX1000 A1 - Made in US	JKAZXCA1-GB500001 on	ZXT00AE000001 on
1987	ZX1000 A2 - Made in Japan	JKAZXCA1-HA014801 on	ZXT00AE021001 on
	ZX1000 A2 - Made in US	JKAZXCA1-HB508401 on	ZXT00AE021001 on
US Ninja ZX-10:			
1988	ZX1000 B1	JKAZXCB1-JA000001 on	ZXT00AE028501 on
1989	ZX1000 B2	JKAZXCB1-KA012001 on	ZXT00AE040301 on
1990	ZX1000 B3	JKAZXCB1-LA028001 on	N/A
US Ninja ZX-11:			
1990	ZX1100 C1 - Made in Japan	JKAZXBC1-LA000001 on	ZXT10CE000001 on
	ZX1100 C1 - Made in US	JKAZXBC1-LB000001 on	ZXT10CE000001 on
1991	ZX1100 C2 - Made in Japan	JKAZXBC1-MA013001-024000	ZXT10CE000001 on
	ZX1100 C2 - Made in US	JKAZXBC1-MB501701-504600	ZXT10CE000001 on
1992	ZX1100 C3 - Made in Japan	JKAZXBC1-NA024001 on	ZXT10CE000001 on
	ZX1100 C3 - Made in US	JKAZXBC1-NB504601 on	ZXT10CE000001 on
1993	ZX1100 C4 - Made in US	JKAZXBC1-PB508201 on	ZXT10CE000001 on
1993	ZX1100 D1 - Made in Japan	JKAZXBD1-PA000001 on	ZXT10CE000001 on
	ZX1100 D1 - Made in US	JKAZXBD1-PB500001 on	ZXT10CE000001 on
1994	ZX1100 D2 - Made in Japan	JKAZXBD1-RA020001 on	ZXT10CE000001 on
	ZX1100 D2 - Made in US	JKAZXBD1-RB502701 on	ZXT10CE000001 on

Model dimensions and weights

	ZX900 A1 to A6	ZX900 A7-on	ZX1000 A
Overall length:			
UK models	2200 mm (86.6 in)	2200 mm (86.6 in)	2230 mm (88.0 in)
US models	2150 mm (84.6 in)	2150 mm (84.6 in)	2180 mm (85.8 in)
Overall width	750 mm (29.5 in)	730 mm (27.8 in)	725 mm (28.5 in)
Overall height	1215 mm (47.8 in)	1220 mm (48.0 in)	1215 mm (47.8 in)
Seat height	780 mm (30.7 in)	Not available	805 mm (31.7 in)
Wheelbase:			
UK models	1495 mm (58.9 in)	1500 mm (59.1 in)	1505 mm (59.3 in)
US models	1495 mm (58.9 in)	1500 mm (59.1 in)	1500 mm (59.0 in)
Ground clearance	140 mm (5.5 in)	140 mm (5.5 in)	140 mm (5.5 in)
Dry weight*	228 kg (503 lb)	234 kg (516 lb)	238 kg (525 lb)

	ZX1000 B	ZX1100 C	ZX1100 D
Overall length	2170 mm (85.4 in)	2165 mm (85.2 in)	2165 mm (85.2 in)
Overall width	715 mm (28.1 in)	720 mm (28.4 in)	730 mm (28.7 in)
Overall height	1240 mm (48.8 in)	1210 mm (47.6 in)	1205 mm (47.4 in)
Seat height	790 mm (31.1 in)	780 mm (30.7 in)	780 mm (30.7 in)
Wheelbase	1490 mm (58.7 in)	1480 mm (58.3 in)	1495 mm (58.9 in)
Ground clearance	125 mm (4.9 in)	110 mm (4.3 in)	110 mm (4.3 in)
Dry weight*	222 kg (490 lb)	228 kg (503 lb)	233 kg (514 lbs)

* Add 0.5 kg (1 lb) for California models

Ordering spare parts

Before attempting any overhaul or maintenance work it is important to ensure that any parts likely to be required are at hand. Many of the more common items such as gaskets and seals will be available off the shelf but it will often prove necessary to order any specialised parts in advance. It is therefore well worth running through the operation to be undertaken by referring to the appropriate Chapter and Section of this Manual, and making a note of the items that are likely to be required. In some cases it will, of course, be necessary to dismantle the assembly in question so that the components can be measured for wear. If this is the case it must be remembered that the machine may have to be left dismantled whilst the replacement parts are obtained.

During the initial warranty period and as a general rule, make sure that only genuine Kawasaki parts are used. Retain any worn or broken parts until the replacements are at hand; they may be needed as a pattern to help identify the correct replacement when design changes have taken place during a model run. Be wary of using "pattern" parts. Whilst in most cases these will be of acceptable quality, there is no guarantee of their standard. Although they may be cheaper, it is often false economy to purchase them as some of the more important parts have been known to fail causing extensive damage to the machine and even the rider. When ordering spare parts, always quote the engine and frame numbers in full. The engine number is stamped in the crankcase top surface, on the right-hand side, just below number 4 carburettor. The frame number is stamped in the steering head.

Some of the more expendable items such as oils, spark plugs, tyres and bulbs can be obtained from accessory shops and motor factors who have more convenient opening hours and can usually be found closer to home. It is also possible to obtain parts on a mail order basis from a number of specialists who advertise regularly in the motorcycle press.

Engine number location

Frame number location

Safety first!

Professional motor mechanics are trained in safe working procedures. However enthusiastic you may be about getting on with the job in hand, do take the time to ensure that your safety is not put at risk. A moment's lack of attention can result in an accident, as can failure to observe certain elementary precautions.

There will always be new ways of having accidents, and the following points do not pretend to be a comprehensive list of all dangers; they are intended rather to make you aware of the risks and to encourage a safety-conscious approach to all work you carry out on your vehicle.

Essential DOs and DON'Ts

DON'T start the engine without first ascertaining that the transmission is in neutral.

DON'T suddenly remove the filler cap from a hot cooling system – cover it with a cloth and release the pressure gradually first, or you may get scalded by escaping coolant.

DON'T attempt to drain oil until you are sure it has cooled sufficiently to avoid scalding you.

DON'T grasp any part of the engine, exhaust or silencer without first ascertaining that it is sufficiently cool to avoid burning you.

DON'T allow brake fluid or antifreeze to contact the machine's paintwork or plastic components.

DON'T syphon toxic liquids such as fuel, brake fluid or antifreeze by mouth, or allow them to remain on your skin.

DON'T inhale dust – it may be injurious to health (see *Asbestos* heading).

DON'T allow any spilt oil or grease to remain on the floor – wipe it up straight away, before someone slips on it.

DON'T use ill-fitting spanners or other tools which may slip and cause injury.

DON'T attempt to lift a heavy component which may be beyond your capability – get assistance.

DON'T rush to finish a job, or take unverified short cuts.

DON'T allow children or animals in or around an unattended vehicle.

DON'T inflate a tyre to a pressure above the recommended maximum. Apart from overstressing the carcase and wheel rim, in extreme cases the tyre may blow off forcibly.

DO ensure that the machine is supported securely at all times. This is especially important when the machine is blocked up to aid wheel or fork removal.

DO take care when attempting to slacken a stubborn nut or bolt. It is generally better to pull on a spanner, rather than push, so that if slippage occurs you fall away from the machine rather than on to it.

DO wear eye protection when using power tools such as drill, sander, bench grinder etc.

DO use a barrier cream on your hands prior to undertaking dirty jobs – it will protect your skin from infection as well as making the dirt easier to remove afterwards; but make sure your hands aren't left slippery. Note that long-term contact with used engine oil can be a health hazard.

DO keep loose clothing (cuffs, tie etc) and long hair well out of the way of moving mechanical parts.

DO remove rings, wristwatch etc, before working on the vehicle – especially the electrical system.

DO keep your work area tidy – it is only too easy to fall over articles left lying around.

DO exercise caution when compressing springs for removal or installation. Ensure that the tension is applied and released in a controlled manner, using suitable tools which preclude the possibility of the spring escaping violently.

DO ensure that any lifting tackle used has a safe working load rating adequate for the job.

DO get someone to check periodically that all is well, when working alone on the vehicle.

DO carry out work in a logical sequence and check that everything is correctly assembled and tightened afterwards.

DO remember that your vehicle's safety affects that of yourself and others. If in doubt on any point, get specialist advice.

IF, in spite of following these precautions, you are unfortunate enough to injure yourself, seek medical attention as soon as possible.

Asbestos

Certain friction, insulating, sealing, and other products – such as brake linings, clutch linings, gaskets, etc – contain asbestos. *Extreme care must be taken to avoid inhalation of dust from such products since it is hazardous to health.* If in doubt, assume that they *do* contain asbestos.

Fire

Remember at all times that petrol (gasoline) is highly flammable. Never smoke, or have any kind of naked flame around, when working on the vehicle. But the risk does not end there – a spark caused by an electrical short-circuit, by two metal surfaces contacting each other, by careless use of tools, or even by static electricity built up in your body under certain conditions, can ignite petrol vapour, which in a confined space is highly explosive.

Always disconnect the battery earth (ground) terminal before working on any part of the fuel or electrical system, and never risk spilling fuel on to a hot engine or exhaust.

It is recommended that a fire extinguisher of a type suitable for fuel and electrical fires is kept handy in the garage or workplace at all times. Never try to extinguish a fuel or electrical fire with water.

Note: *Any reference to a 'torch' appearing in this manual should always be taken to mean a hand-held battery-operated electric lamp or flashlight. It does **not** mean a welding/gas torch or blowlamp.*

Fumes

Certain fumes are highly toxic and can quickly cause unconsciousness and even death if inhaled to any extent. Petrol (gasoline) vapour comes into this category, as do the vapours from certain solvents such as trichloroethylene. Any draining or pouring of such volatile fluids should be done in a well ventilated area.

When using cleaning fluids and solvents, read the instructions carefully. Never use materials from unmarked containers – they may give off poisonous vapours.

Never run the engine of a motor vehicle in an enclosed space such as a garage. Exhaust fumes contain carbon monoxide which is extremely poisonous; if you need to run the engine, always do so in the open air or at least have the rear of the vehicle outside the workplace.

The battery

Never cause a spark, or allow a naked light, near the vehicle's battery. It will normally be giving off a certain amount of hydrogen gas, which is highly explosive.

Always disconnect the battery earth (ground) terminal before working on the fuel or electrical systems.

If possible, loosen the filler plugs or cover when charging the battery from an external source. Do not charge at an excessive rate or the battery may burst.

Take care when topping up and when carrying the battery. The acid electrolyte, even when diluted, is very corrosive and should not be allowed to contact the eyes or skin.

If you ever need to prepare electrolyte yourself, always add the acid slowly to the water, and never the other way round. Protect against splashes by wearing rubber gloves and goggles.

Mains electricity and electrical equipment

When using an electric power tool, inspection light etc, always ensure that the appliance is correctly connected to its plug and that, where necessary, it is properly earthed (grounded). Do not use such appliances in damp conditions and, again, beware of creating a spark or applying excessive heat in the vicinity of fuel or fuel vapour. Also ensure that the appliances meet the relevant national safety standards.

Ignition HT voltage

A severe electric shock can result from touching certain parts of the ignition system, such as the HT leads, when the engine is running or being cranked, particularly if components are damp or the insulation is defective. Where an electronic ignition system is fitted, the HT voltage is much higher and could prove fatal.

Tools and working facilities

The first priority when undertaking maintenance or repair work of any sort on a motorcycle is to have a clean, dry, well-lit working area. Work carried out in peace and quiet in the well-ordered atmosphere of a good workshop will give more satisfaction and much better results than can usually be achieved in poor working conditions. A good workshop must have a clean flat workbench or a solidly constructed table of convenient working height. The workbench or table should be equipped with a vice which has a jaw opening of at least 4 in (100 mm). A set of jaw covers should be made from soft metal such as aluminium alloy or copper, or from wood. These covers will minimise the marking or damaging of soft or delicate components which may be clamped in the vice. Some clean, dry, storage space will be required for tools, lubricants and dismantled components. It will be necessary during a major overhaul to lay out engine/gearbox components for examination and to keep them where they will remain undisturbed for as long as is necessary. To this end it is recommended that a supply of metal or plastic containers of suitable size is collected. A supply of clean, lint-free, rags for cleaning purposes and some newspapers, other rags, or paper towels for mopping up spillages should also be kept. If working on a hard concrete floor note that both the floor and one's knees can be protected from oil spillages and wear by cutting open a large cardboard box and spreading it flat on the floor under the machine or workbench. This also helps to provide some warmth in winter and to prevent the loss of nuts, washers, and other tiny components which have a tendency to disappear when dropped on anything other than a perfectly clean, flat, surface.

Unfortunately, such working conditions are not always available to the home mechanic. When working in poor conditions it is essential to take extra time and care to ensure that the components being worked on are kept scrupulously clean and to ensure that no components or tools are lost or damaged.

A selection of good tools is a fundamental requirement for anyone contemplating the maintenance and repair of a motor vehicle. For the owner who does not possess any, their purchase will prove a considerable expense, offsetting some of the savings made by doing-it-yourself. However, provided that the tools purchased meet the relevant national safety standards and are of good quality, they will last for many years and prove an extremely worthwhile investment.

To help the average owner to decide which tools are needed to carry out the various tasks detailed in this manual, we have compiled three lists of tools under the following headings: *Maintenance and minor repair, Repair and overhaul,* and *Specialized.* The newcomer to practical mechanics should start off with the simpler jobs around the vehicle. Then, as his confidence and experience grow, he can undertake more difficult tasks, buying extra tools as and when they are needed. In this way, a *Maintenance and minor repair* tool kit can be built-up into a *Repair and overhaul* tool kit over a considerable period of time without any major cash outlays. The experienced home mechanic will have a tool kit good enough for most repair and overhaul procedures and will add tools from the specialized category when he feels the expense is justified by the amount of use these tools will be put to.

It is obviously not possible to cover the subject of tools fully here. For those who wish to learn more about tools and their use there is a book entitled *Motorcycle Workshop Practice Manual* (Book no 1454) available from the publishers of this manual.

As a general rule, it is better to buy the more expensive, good quality tools. Given reasonable use, such tools will last for a very long time, whereas the cheaper, poor quality, items will wear out faster and need to be renewed more often, thus nullifying the original saving. There is also the risk of a poor quality tool breaking while in use, causing personal injury or expensive damage to the component being worked on.

For practically all tools, a tool factor is the best source since he will have a very comprehensive range compared with the average garage or accessory shop. Having said that, accessory shops often offer excellent quality tools at discount prices, so it pays to shop around. There are plenty of tools around at reasonable prices, but always aim to purchase items which meet the relevant national safety standards. If in doubt, seek the advice of the shop proprietor or manager before making a purchase.

The basis of any toolkit is a set of spanners. While open-ended spanners with their slim jaws, are useful for working on awkwardly-positioned nuts, ring spanners have advantages in that they grip the nut far more positively. There is less risk of the spanner slipping off the nut and damaging it, for this reason alone ring spanners are to be preferred. Ideally, the home mechanic should acquire a set of each, but if expense rules this out a set of combination spanners (open-ended at one end and with a ring of the same size at the other) will provide a good compromise. Another item which is so useful it should be considered an essential requirement for any home mechanic is a set of socket spanners. These are available in a variety of drive sizes. It is recommended that the ½-inch drive type is purchased to begin with as although bulkier and more expensive than the ⅜-inch type, the larger size is far more common and will accept a greater variety of torque wrenches, extension pieces and socket sizes. The socket set should comprise sockets of sizes between 8 and 24 mm, a reversible ratchet drive, an extension bar of about 10 inches in length, a spark plug socket with a rubber insert, and a universal joint. Other attachments can be added to the set at a later date.

Maintenance and minor repair tool kit

Set of spanners 8 – 24 mm
Set of sockets and attachments
Spark plug spanner with rubber insert – 10, 12, or 14 mm as appropriate
Adjustable spanner
C-spanner/pin spanner
Torque wrench (same size drive as sockets)
Set of screwdrivers (flat blade)
Set of screwdrivers (cross-head)
Set of Allen keys 4 – 10 mm
Impact screwdriver and bits
Ball pein hammer – 2 lb
Hacksaw (junior)
Self-locking pliers – Mole grips or vice grips
Pliers – combination
Pliers – needle nose
Wire brush (small)
Soft-bristled brush
Tyre pump
Tyre pressure gauge
Tyre tread depth gauge
Oil can
Fine emery cloth
Funnel (medium size)
Drip tray
Grease gun
Set of feeler gauges
Brake bleeding kit
Strobe timing light
Continuity tester (dry battery and bulb)
Soldering iron and solder
Wire stripper or craft knife
PVC insulating tape
Assortment of split pins, nuts, bolts, and washers

Repair and overhaul toolkit

The tools in this list are virtually essential for anyone undertaking major repairs to a motorcycle and are additional to the tools listed above.

Plastic or rubber soft-faced mallet
Pliers – electrician's side cutters
Circlip pliers – internal (straight or right-angled tips are available)
Circlip pliers – external
Cold chisel
Centre punch
Pin punch
Scriber
Scraper (made from soft metal such as aluminium or copper)
Soft metal drift
Steel rule/straightedge
Assortment of files
Electric drill and bits
Wire brush (large)
Soft wire brush (similar to those used for cleaning suede shoes)
Sheet of plate glass
Hacksaw (large)
Valve grinding tool
Valve grinding compound (coarse and fine)
Stud extractor set (E-Z out)

Specialized tools

This is not a list of the tools made by the machine's manufacturer to carry out a specific task on a limited range of models. Occasional references are made to such tools in the text of this manual and, in general, an alternative method of carrying out the task without the manufacturer's tool is given where possible. The tools mentioned in this list are those which are not used regularly and are expensive to buy in view of their infrequent use. Where this is the case it may be possible to hire or borrow the tools against a deposit from a local dealer or tool hire shop. An alternative is for a group of friends or a motorcycle club to join in the purchase.

Valve spring compressor
Piston ring compressor
Universal bearing puller
Cylinder bore honing attachment (for electric drill)
Micrometer set
Vernier calipers
Dial gauge set
Cylinder compression gauge
Vacuum gauge set
Multimeter
Dwell meter/tachometer

Care and maintenance of tools

Whatever the quality of the tools purchased, they will last much longer if cared for. This means in practice ensuring that a tool is used for its intended purpose; for example screwdrivers should not be used as a substitute for a centre punch, or as chisels. Always remove dirt or grease and any metal particles but remember that a light film of oil will prevent rusting if the tools are infrequently used. The common tools can be kept together in a large box or tray but the more delicate, and more expensive, items should be stored separately where they cannot be damaged. When a tool is damaged or worn out, be sure to renew it immediately. It is false economy to continue to use a worn spanner or screwdriver which may slip and cause expensive damage to the component being worked on.

Fastening systems

Fasteners, basically, are nuts, bolts and screws used to hold two or more parts together. There are a few things to keep in mind when working with fasteners. Almost all of them use a locking device of some type; either a lock washer, locknut, locking tab or thread adhesive. All threaded fasteners should be clean, straight, have undamaged threads and undamaged corners on the hexagon head where the spanner fits. Develop the habit of replacing all damaged nuts and bolts with new ones.

Rusted nuts and bolts should be treated with a rust penetrating fluid to ease removal and prevent breakage. After applying the rust penetrant, let it 'work' for a few minutes before trying to loosen the nut or bolt. Badly rusted fasteners may have to be chiselled off or removed with a special nut breaker, available at tool shops.

Flat washers and lock washers, when removed from an assembly should always be replaced exactly as removed. Replace any damaged washers with new ones. Always use a flat washer between a lock washer and any soft metal surface (such as aluminium), thin sheet metal or plastic. Special locknuts can only be used once or twice before they lose their locking ability and must be renewed.

If a bolt or stud breaks off in an assembly, it can be drilled out and removed with a special tool called an E-Z out. Most dealer service departments and motorcycle repair shops can perform this task, as well as others (such as the repair of threaded holes that have been stripped out).

Spanner size comparison

Jaw gap (in)	Spanner size	Jaw gap (in)	Spanner size
0.250	$\frac{1}{4}$ in AF	0.945	24 mm
0.276	7 mm	1.000	1 in AF
0.313	$\frac{5}{16}$ in AF	1.010	$\frac{9}{16}$ in Whitworth; $\frac{5}{8}$ in BSF
0.315	8 mm	1.024	26 mm
0.344	$\frac{11}{32}$ in AF; $\frac{1}{8}$ in Whitworth	1.063	$1\frac{1}{16}$ in AF; 27 mm
0.354	9 mm	1.100	$\frac{5}{8}$ in Whitworth; $\frac{11}{16}$ in BSF
0.375	$\frac{3}{8}$ in AF	1.125	$1\frac{1}{8}$ in AF
0.394	10 mm	1.181	30 mm
0.433	11 mm	1.200	$\frac{11}{16}$ in Whitworth; $\frac{3}{4}$ in BSF
0.438	$\frac{7}{16}$ in AF	1.250	$1\frac{1}{4}$ in AF
0.445	$\frac{3}{16}$ in Whitworth; $\frac{1}{4}$ in BSF	1.260	32 mm
0.472	12 mm	1.300	$\frac{3}{4}$ in Whitworth; $\frac{7}{8}$ in BSF
0.500	$\frac{1}{2}$ in AF	1.313	$1\frac{5}{16}$ in AF
0.512	13 mm	1.390	$1\frac{3}{16}$ in Whitworth; $1\frac{5}{16}$ in BSF
0.525	$\frac{1}{4}$ in Whitworth; $\frac{5}{16}$ in BSF	1.417	36 mm
0.551	14 mm	1.438	$1\frac{7}{16}$ in AF
0.563	$\frac{9}{16}$ in AF	1.480	$\frac{7}{8}$ in Whitworth; 1 in BSF
0.591	15 mm	1.500	$1\frac{1}{2}$ in AF
0.600	$\frac{5}{16}$ in Whitworth; $\frac{3}{8}$ in BSF	1.575	40 mm; $1\frac{5}{16}$ in Whitworth
0.625	$\frac{5}{8}$ in AF	1.614	41 mm
0.630	16 mm	1.625	$1\frac{5}{8}$ in AF
0.669	17 mm	1.670	1 in Whitworth; $1\frac{1}{8}$ in BSF
0.686	$\frac{11}{16}$ in AF	1.688	$1\frac{11}{16}$ in AF
0.709	18 mm	1.811	46 mm
0.710	$\frac{3}{8}$ in Whitworth; $\frac{7}{16}$ in BSF	1.813	$1\frac{13}{16}$ in AF
0.748	19 mm	1.860	$1\frac{1}{8}$ in Whitworth; $1\frac{1}{4}$ in BSF
0.750	$\frac{3}{4}$ in AF	1.875	$1\frac{7}{8}$ in AF
0.813	$1\frac{3}{16}$ in AF	1.969	50 mm
0.820	$\frac{7}{16}$ in Whitworth; $\frac{1}{2}$ in BSF	2.000	2 in AF
0.866	22 mm	2.050	$1\frac{1}{4}$ in Whitworth; $1\frac{3}{8}$ in BSF
0.875	$\frac{7}{8}$ in AF	2.165	55 mm
0.920	$\frac{1}{2}$ in Whitworth; $\frac{9}{16}$ in BSF	2.362	60 mm
0.938	$1\frac{5}{16}$ in AF		

Standard torque settings

Specific torque settings will be found at the end of the specifications section of each chapter. Where no figure is given, it should be secured according to the table below.

Fastener type (thread diameter)	kgf m	lbf ft
5 mm bolt or nut	0.45 – 0.6	3.5 – 4.5
6 mm bolt or nut	0.8 – 1.2	6 – 9
8 mm bolt or nut	1.8 – 2.5	13 – 18
10 mm bolt or nut	3.0 – 4.0	22 – 29
12 mm bolt or nut	5.0 – 6.0	36 – 43
5 mm screw	0.35 – 0.5	2.5 – 3.6
6 mm screw	0.7 – 1.1	5 – 8
6 mm flange bolt	1.0 – 1.4	7 – 10
8 mm flange bolt	2.4 – 3.0	17 – 22
10 mm flange bolt	3.5 – 4.5	25 – 33

Choosing and fitting accessories

The range of accessories available to the modern motorcyclist is almost as varied and bewildering as the range of motorcycles. This Section is intended to help the owner in choosing the correct equipment for his needs and to avoid some of the mistakes made by many riders when adding accessories to their machines. It will be evident that the Section can only cover the subject in the most general terms and so it is recommended that the owner, having decided that he wants to fit, for example, a luggage rack or carrier, seeks the advice of several local dealers and the owners of similar machines. This will give a good idea of what makes of carrier are easily available, and at what price. Talking to other owners will give some insight into the drawbacks or good points of any one make. A walk round the motorcycles in car parks or outside a dealer will often reveal the same sort of information.

The first priority when choosing accessories is to assess exactly what one needs. It is, for example, pointless to buy a large heavy-duty carrier which is designed to take the weight of fully laden panniers and topbox when all you need is a place to strap on a set of waterproofs and a lunchbox when going to work. Many accessory manufacturers have ranges of equipment to cater for the individual needs of different riders and this point should be borne in mind when looking through a dealer's catalogues. Having decided exactly what is required and the use to which the accessories are going to be put, the owner will need a few hints on what to look for when making the final choice. To this end the Section is now sub-divided to cover the more popular accessories fitted. Note that it is in no way a customizing guide, but merely seeks to outline the practical considerations to be taken into account when adding aftermarket equipment to a motorcycle.

Luggage racks or carriers

Carriers are possibly the commonest item to be fitted to modern motorcycles. They vary enormously in size, carrying capacity, and durability. When selecting a carrier, always look for one which is made specifically for your machine and which is bolted on with as few separate brackets as possible. The universal-type carrier, with its mass of brackets and adaptor pieces, will generally prove too weak to be of any real use. A good carrier should bolt to the main frame and have its luggage platform as low and as far forward as possible to minimise the effect of any load on the machine's stability. Look for good quality, heavy gauge tubing, good welding and good finish. Also ensure that the carrier does not prevent opening of the seat, sidepanels or tail compartment, as appropriate. When using a carrier, be very careful not to overload it. Excessive weight placed so high and so far to the rear of any motorcycle will have an adverse effect on the machine's steering and stability.

Luggage

Motorcycle luggage can be grouped under two headings: soft and hard. Both types are available in many sizes and styles and have advantages and disadvantages in use.

Soft luggage is now becoming very popular because of its lower cost and its versatility. Whether in the form of tankbags, panniers, or strap-on bags, soft luggage requires in general no brackets and no modification to the motorcycle. Equipment can be swapped easily from one motorcycle to another and can be fitted and removed in seconds. Awkwardly shaped loads can easily be carried. The disadvantages of soft luggage are that the contents cannot be secure against the casual thief, very little protection is afforded in the event of a crash, and waterproofing is generally poor. Also, in the case of panniers, carrying capacity is restricted to approximately 10 lb, although this amount will vary considerably depending on the manufacturer's recommendation.

When purchasing soft luggage, look for good quality material, generally vinyl or nylon, with strong, well-stitched attachment points. It is always useful to have separate pockets, especially on tank bags, for items which will be needed on the journey. When purchasing a tank bag, look for one which has a separate, well-padded, base. This will protect the tank's paintwork and permit easy access to the filler cap at petrol stations.

Hard luggage is confined to two types: panniers, and top boxes or tail trunks. Most hard luggage manufacturers produce matching sets of these items, the basis of which is generally that manufacturer's own heavy-duty luggage rack. Variations on this theme occur in the form of separate frames for the better quality panniers, fixed or quickly-detachable luggage, and in size and carrying capacity. Hard luggage offers a reasonable degree of security against theft and good protection against weather and accident damage. Carrying capacity is greater than that of soft luggage, around 15 – 20 lb in the case of panniers, although top boxes should never be loaded as much as their apparent capacity might imply. A top box should only be used for lightweight items, because one that is heavily laden can have a serious effect on the stability of the machine. When purchasing hard luggage look for the same good points as mentioned under fairings and windscreens, ie good quality mounting brackets and fittings, and well-finished fibreglass or ABS plastic cases. Again as with fairings, always purchase luggage made specifically for your motorcycle, using as few separate brackets as possible, to ensure that everything remains securely bolted in place. When fitting hard luggage, be careful to check that the rear suspension and brake operation will not be impaired in any way and remember that many pannier kits require re-siting of the indicators. Remember also that a non-standard exhaust system may make fitting extremely difficult.

Handlebars

The occupation of fitting alternative types of handlebar is extremely popular with modern motorcyclists, whose motives may vary from the purely practical, wishing to improve the comfort of their machines, to the purely aesthetic, where form is more important than function. Whatever the reason, there are several considerations to be borne in mind when changing the handlebars of your machine. If fitting lower bars, check carefully that the switches and cables do not foul the petrol tank on full lock and that the surplus length of cable, brake pipe, and electrical wiring are smoothly and tidily disposed of. Avoid tight kinks in cable or brake pipes which will produce stiff controls or the premature and disastrous failure of an overstressed component. If necessary, remove the petrol tank and re-route the cable from the engine/gearbox unit upwards, ensuring smooth gentle curves are produced. In extreme cases, it will be necessary to purchase a shorter brake pipe to overcome this problem. In the case of higher handlebars than standard it will almost certainly be necessary to purchase extended cables and brake pipes. Fortunately, many standard motorcycles have a custom version which will be equipped with higher handlebars and, therefore, factory-built extended components will be available from your local dealer. It is not usually necessary to extend electrical wiring, as switch clusters may be used on several different motorcycles, some being custom versions. This point should be borne in mind however when fitting extremely high or wide handlebars.

When fitting different types of handlebar, ensure that the mounting clamps are correctly tightened to the manufacturer's specifications and that cables and wiring, as previously mentioned, have smooth easy runs and do not snag on any part of the motorcycle throughout the full steering lock. Ensure that the fluid level in the front brake master cylinder remains level to avoid any chance of air entering the hydraulic system. Also check that the cables are adjusted correctly and that all handlebar controls operate correctly and can be easily reached when riding.

Exhaust systems

The fitting of aftermarket exhaust systems is another extremely popular pastime amongst motorcyclists. The usual motive is to gain more performance from the engine but other considerations are to gain more ground clearance, to lose weight from the motorcycle, to obtain a more distinctive exhaust note or to find a cheaper alternative to the manufacturer's original equipment exhaust system. Original equipment exhaust systems often cost more and may well have a relatively short life. It should be noted that it is rare for an aftermarket exhaust system alone to give a noticeable increase in the engine's power output. Modern motorcycles are designed to give the highest power output possible allowing for factors such as quietness, fuel economy, spread of power, and long-term reliability. If there were a magic formula which allowed the exhaust system to produce more power without affecting these other considerations you can be sure that the manufacturers, with their large research and development facilities, would have found it and made use of it. Performance increases of a worthwhile and noticeable nature only come from well-tried and properly matched modifications to the entire engine, from the air filter, through the carburettors, port timing or camshaft and valve design, combustion chamber shape, compression ratio, and the exhaust system. Such modifications are well outside the scope of this manual but interested owners might refer to specialist books produced by the publisher of this manual which go into the whole subject in great detail.

Whatever your motive for wishing to fit an alternative exhaust system, be sure to seek expert advice before doing so. Changes to the carburettor jetting will almost certainly be required for which you must consult the exhaust system manufacturer. If he cannot supply adequately specific information it is reasonable to assume that insufficient development work has been carried out, and that particular make should be avoided. Other factors to be borne in mind are whether the exhaust system allows the use of both centre and side stands, whether it allows sufficient access to permit oil and filter changing and whether modifications are necessary to the standard exhaust system. Many two-stroke expansion chamber systems require the use of the standard exhaust pipe; this is all very well if the standard exhaust pipe and silencer are separate units but can cause problems if the two, with so many modern two-strokes, are a one-piece unit. While the exhaust pipe can be removed easily by means of a hacksaw it is not so easy to refit the original silencer should you at any time wish to return the machine to standard trim. The same applies to several four-stroke systems.

On the subject of the finish of aftermarket exhausts, avoid black-painted systems unless you enjoy painting. As any trail-bike owner will tell you, rust has a great affinity for black exhausts and re-painting or rust removal becomes a task which must be carried out with monotonous regularity. A bright chrome finish is, as a general rule, a far better proposition as it is much easier to keep clean and to prevent rusting. Although the general finish of aftermarket exhaust systems is not always up to the standard of the original equipment the lower cost of such systems does at least reflect this fact.

When fitting an alternative system always purchase a full set of new exhaust gaskets, to prevent leaks. Fit the exhaust first to the cylinder head or barrel, as appropriate, tightening the retaining nuts or bolts by hand only and then line up the exhaust rear mountings. If the new system is a one-piece unit and the rear mountings do not line up exactly, spacers must be fabricated to take up the difference. Do not force the system into place as the stress thus imposed will rapidly cause cracks and splits to appear. Once all the mountings are loosely fixed, tighten the retaining nuts or bolts securely, being careful not to overtighten them. Where the motorcycle manufacturer's torque settings are available, these should be used. Do not forget to carry out any carburation changes recommended by the exhaust system's manufacturer.

Electrical equipment

The vast range of electrical equipment available to motorcyclists is so large and so diverse that only the most general outline can be given here. Electrical accessories vary from electronic ignition kits fitted to replace contact breaker points, to additional lighting at the front and rear, more powerful horns, various instruments and gauges, clocks, anti-theft systems, heated clothing, CB radios, radio-cassette players, and intercom systems, to name but a few of the more popular items of equipment.

As will be evident, it would require a separate manual to cover this subject alone and this section is therefore restricted to outlining a few basic rules which must be borne in mind when fitting electrical equipment. The first consideration is whether your machine's electrical system has enough reserve capacity to cope with the added demand of the accessories you wish to fit. The motorcycle's manufacturer or importer should be able to furnish this sort of information and may also be able to offer advice on uprating the electrical system. Failing this, a good dealer or the accessory manufacturer may be able to help. In some cases, more powerful generator components may be available, perhaps from another motorcycle in the manufacturer's range. The second consideration is the legal requirements in force in your area. The local police may be prepared to help with this point. In the UK for example, there are strict regulations governing the position and use of auxiliary riding lamps and fog lamps.

When fitting electrical equipment always disconnect the battery first to prevent the risk of a short-circuit, and be careful to ensure that all connections are properly made and that they are waterproof. Remember that many electrical accessories are designed primarily for use in cars and that they cannot easily withstand the exposure to vibration and to the weather. Delicate components must be rubber-mounted to insulate them from vibration, and sealed carefully to prevent the entry of rainwater and dirt. Be careful to follow exactly the accessory manufacturer's instructions in conjunction with the wiring diagram at the back of this manual.

Accessories – general

Accessories fitted to your motorcycle will rapidly deteriorate if not cared for. Regular washing and polishing will maintain the finish and will provide an opportunity to check that all mounting bolts and nuts are securely fastened. Any signs of chafing or wear should be watched for, and the cause cured as soon as possible before serious damage occurs.

As a general rule, do not expect the re-sale value of your motorcycle to increase by an amount proportional to the amount of money and effort put into fitting accessories. It is usually the case that an absolutely standard motorcycle will sell more easily at a better price than one that has been modified. If you are in the habit of exchanging your machine for another at frequent intervals, this factor should be borne in mind to avoid loss of money.

Fault diagnosis

Contents

1 Introduction

This Section provides an easy reference-guide to the more common faults that are likely to afflict your machine. Obviously, the opportunities are almost limitless for faults to occur as a result of obscure failures, and to try and cover all eventualities would require a book. Indeed, a number have been written on the subject.

Successful fault diagnosis is not a mysterious 'black art' but the application of a bit of knowledge combined with a systematic and logical approach to the problem. Approach any fault diagnosis by first accurately identifying the symptom and then checking through the list of possible causes, starting with the simplest or most obvious and progressing in stages to the most complex. Take nothing for granted, but above all apply liberal quantities of common sense.

The main symptom of a fault is given in the text as a major heading below which are listed, as Section headings, the various systems or areas which may contain the fault. Details of each possible cause for a fault and the remedial action to be taken are given, in brief, in the paragraphs below each Section heading. Further information should be sought in the relevant Chapter.

Starter motor problems

2 Starter motor not rotating

● Engine stop switch off.
● Fuse blown. Check the main fuse located behind the battery side cover.
● Battery voltage low. Switching on the headlamp and operating the horn will give a good indication of the charge level. If necessary recharge the battery from an external source.
● Neutral gear not selected. Where a neutral indicator switch is fitted.
● Faulty neutral indicator switch or clutch interlock switch (where fitted). Check the switch wiring and switches for correct operation.
● Ignition switch defective. Check switch for continuity and connections for security.
● Engine stop switch defective. Check switch for continuity in 'Run' position. Fault will be caused by broken, wet or corroded switch contacts. Clean or renew as necessary.
● Starter button switch faulty. Check continuity of switch. Faults as for engine stop switch.
● Starter relay (solenoid) faulty. If the switch is functioning correctly a pronounced click should be heard when the starter button is depressed. This presupposes that current is flowing to the solenoid when the button is depressed.
● Wiring open or shorted. Check first that the battery terminal connections are tight and corrosion free. Follow this by checking that all wiring connections are dry, tight and corrosion free. Check also for frayed or broken wiring. Occasionally a wire may become trapped between two moving components, particularly in the vicinity of the steering head, leading to breakage of the internal core but leaving the softer but more resilient outer cover intact. This can cause mysterious intermittent or total power loss.
● Starter motor defective. A badly worn starter motor may cause high current drain from a battery without the motor rotating. If current is found to be reaching the motor, after checking the starter button and starter relay, suspect a damaged motor. The motor should be removed for inspection.

3 Starter motor rotates but engine does not turn over

● Starter motor clutch defective. Suspect jammed or worn engagement rollers, plungers and springs.
● Damaged starter motor drive train. Inspect and renew component where necessary. Failure in this area is unlikely.

4 Starter motor and clutch function but engine will not turn over

● Engine seized. Seizure of the engine is always a result of damage to internal components due to lubrication failure, or component breakage resulting from abuse, neglect or old age. A seizing or partially seized component may go un-noticed until the engine has cooled down and an attempt is made to restart the engine. Suspect first seizure of the valves, valve gear and the pistons. Instantaneous seizure whilst the engine is running indicates component breakage. In either case major dismantling and inspection will be required.

Engine does not start when turned over

5 No fuel flow to carburettor

● No fuel or insufficient fuel in tank.
● Fuel tap lever position incorrectly selected.
● Float chambers require priming after running dry (vacuum taps only).
● Tank filler cap air vent obstructed. Usually caused by dirt or water. Clean the vent orifice.
● Fuel tap or filter blocked. Blockage may be due to accumulation of rust or paint flakes from the tank's inner surface or of foreign matter from contaminated fuel. Remove the tap and clean it and the filter. Look also for water droplets in the fuel.
● Fuel line blocked. Blockage of the fuel line is more likely to result from a kink in the line rather than the accumulation of debris.
● Faulty fuel pump (where fitted).

6 Fuel not reaching cylinder

● Float chamber not filling. Caused by float needle or floats sticking in up position. This may occur after the machine has been left standing for an extended length of time allowing the fuel to evaporate. When this occurs a gummy residue is often left which hardens to a varnish-like substance. This condition may be worsened by corrosion and crystaline deposits produced prior to the total evaporation of contaminated fuel. Sticking of the float needle may also be caused by wear. In any case removal of the float chamber will be necessary for inspection and cleaning.
● Blockage in starting circuit, slow running circuit or jets. Blockage of these items may be attributable to debris from the fuel tank by-passing the filter system or to gumming up as described in paragraph 1. Water droplets in the fuel will also lock jets and passages. The carburettor should be dismantled for cleaning.
● Fuel level too low. The fuel level in the float chamber is controlled by float height. The float height may increase with wear or damage but will never reduce, thus a low float height is an inherent rather than developing condition. Check the float height and make any necessary adjustment.

7 Engine flooding

● Float valve needle worn or stuck open. A piece of rust or other debris can prevent correct seating of the needle against the valve seat thereby permitting an uncontrolled flow of fuel. Similarly, a worn needle or needle seat will prevent valve closure. Dismantle the carburettor float bowl for cleaning and, if necessary, renewal of the worn components.
● Fuel level too high. The fuel level is controlled by the float height which may increase due to wear of the float needle, pivot pin or operating tang. Check the float height, and make any necessary adjustment. A leaking float will cause an increase in fuel level, and thus should be renewed.
● Cold starting mechanism. Check the choke (starter mechanism) for correct operation. If the mechanism jams in the 'On' position subsequent starting of a hot engine will be difficult.
● Blocked air filter. A badly restricted air filter will cause flooding. Check

the filter and clean or renew as required. A collapsed inlet hose will have a similar effect.

8 No spark at plug

● Ignition switch not on.
● Engine stop switch off.
● Fuse blown. Check fuse for ignition circuit. See wiring diagram.
● Battery voltage low. The current draw required by a starter motor is sufficiently high that an under-charged battery may not have enough spare capacity to provide power for the ignition circuit during starting.
● Starter motor inefficient. A starter motor with worn brushes and a worn or dirty commutator will draw excessive amounts of current causing power starvation in the ignition system. See the preceding paragraph. Starter motor overhaul will be required.
● Spark plug failure. Clean the spark plug thoroughly and reset the electrode gap. Refer to the spark plug section and the colour condition guide in Routine maintenance. If the spark plug shorts internally or has sustained visible damage to the electrodes, core or ceramic insulator it should be renewed. On rare occasions a plug that appears to spark vigorously will fail to do so when refitted to the engine and subjected to the compression pressure in the cylinder.
● Spark plug cap or high tension (HT) lead faulty. Check condition and security. Replace if deterioration is evident.
● Spark plug cap loose. Check that the spark plug cap fits securely over the plug and, where fitted, the screwed terminal on the plug end is secure.
● Shorting due to moisture. Certain parts of the ignition system are susceptible to shorting when the machine is ridden or parked in wet weather. Check particularly the area from the spark plug cap back to the ignition coil. A water dispersant spray may be used to dry out water-logged components. Recurrence of the problem can be prevented by using an ignition sealant spray after drying out and cleaning.
● Ignition or stop switch shorted. May be caused by water, corrosion or wear. Water dispersant and contact cleaning sprays may be used. If this fails to overcome the problem dismantling and visual inspection of the switches will be required.
● Shorting or open circuit in wiring. Failure in any wire connecting any of the ignition components will cause ignition malfunction. Check also that all connections are clean, dry and tight.
● Ignition coil failure. Check the coil, referring to Chapter 4.
● Pulser coil failure. Check the coil(s), referring to Chapter 4.
● IC ignitor unit failure. Check the unit as described in Chapter 4.

9 Weak spark at plug

● Feeble sparking at the plug may be caused by any of the faults mentioned in the preceding Section other than those items in paragraphs 1 to 3. Check first the spark plugs, these being the most likely culprits.

10 Compression low

● Spark plug loose. This will be self-evident on inspection, and may be accompanied by a hissing noise when the engine is turned over. Remove the plug and check that the threads in the cylinder head are not damaged. Check also that the plug sealing washer is in good condition.
● Cylinder head gasket leaking. This condition is often accompanied by a high pitched squeak from around the cylinder head and oil loss, and may be caused by insufficiently tightened cylinder head fasteners, a warped cylinder head or mechanical failure of the gasket material. Re-torqueing the fasteners to the correct specification may seal the leak in some instances but if damage has occurred this course of action will provide, at best, only a temporary cure.
● Valve not seating correctly. The failure of a valve to seat may be caused by insufficient valve clearance, pitting of the valve seat or face, carbon deposits on the valve seat or seizure of the valve stem or valve gear components. Valve spring breakage will also prevent correct valve closure. The valve clearances should be checked first and then, if these are found to be in order, further dismantling will be required to inspect the relevant components for failure.

● Cylinder, piston and ring wear. Compression pressure will be lost if any of these components are badly worn. Wear in one component is invariably accompanied by wear in another. A top end overhaul will be required.
● Piston rings sticking or broken. Sticking of the piston rings may be caused by seizure due to lack of lubrication or heating as a result of poor carburation or incorrect fuel type. Gumming of the rings may result from lack of use, or carbon deposits in the ring grooves. Broken rings result from over-revving, overheating or general wear. In either case a top-end overhaul will be required.

Engine stalls after starting

11 General causes

● Improper cold start mechanism operation. Check that the operating controls function smoothly and, where applicable, are correctly adjusted. A cold engine may not require application of an enriched mixture to start initially but may baulk without choke once firing. Likewise a hot engine may start with an enriched mixture but will stop almost immediately if the choke is inadvertently in operation.
● Ignition malfunction. See Section 9, 'Weak spark at plug'.
● Carburettor incorrectly adjusted. Maladjustment of the mixture strength or idle speed may cause the engine to stop immediately after starting. See Chapter 3.
● Fuel contamination. Check for filter blockage by debris or water which reduces, but does not completely stop, fuel flow or blockage of the slow speed circuit in the carburettor by the same agents. If water is present it can often be seen as droplets in the bottom of the float bowl. Clean the filter and, where water is in evidence, drain and flush the fuel tank and float bowl.
● Intake air leak. Check for security of the carburettor mounting and hose connections, and for cracks or splits in the hoses. Check also that the carburettor top is secure and that the vacuum gauge adaptor plug (where fitted) is tight.
● Air filter blocked or omitted. A blocked filter will cause an over-rich mixture; the omission of a filter will cause an excessively weak mixture. Both conditions will have a detrimental effect on carburation. Clean or renew the filter as necessary.
● Fuel filler cap air vent blocked. Usually caused by dirt or water. Clean the vent orifice.

Poor running at idle and low speed

12 Weak spark at plug or erratic firing

● Battery voltage low. In certain conditions low battery charge, especially when coupled with a badly sulphated battery, may result in misfiring. If the battery is in good general condition it should be recharged; an old battery suffering from sulphated plates should be renewed.
● Spark plug fouled, faulty or incorrectly adjusted. See Section 8 or refer to Routine maintenance.
● Spark plug cap or high tension lead shorting. Check the condition of both these items ensuring that they are in good condition and dry and that the cap is fitted correctly.
● Spark plug type incorrect. Fit plug of correct type and heat range as given in Specifications. In certain conditions a plug of hotter or colder type may be required for normal running.
● Faulty ignition coil. Partial failure of the coil internal insulation will diminish the performance of the coil. No repair is possible, a new component must be fitted.

13 Fuel/air mixture incorrect

● Intake air leak. See Section 11.
● Mixture strength incorrect. Adjust slow running mixture strength using pilot adjustment screw.

● Carburettor synchronisation.
● Pilot jet or slow running circuit blocked. The carburettor should be removed and dismantled for thorough cleaning. Blow through all jets and air passages with compressed air to clear obstructions.
● Air cleaner clogged or omitted. Clean or fit air cleaner element as necessary. Check also that the element and air filter cover are correctly seated.
● Cold start mechanism in operation. Check that the choke has not been left on inadvertently and the operation is correct. Check the operating cable free play as described in Routine maintenance.
● Fuel level too high or too low. Check the float height and adjust as necessary. See Section 7.
● Fuel tank air vent obstructed. Obstruction usually caused by dirt or water. Clean vent orifice.
● Valve clearance incorrect. Check, and if necessary, adjust, the clearances.

14 Compression low

● See Section 10.

Acceleration poor

15 General causes

● All items as for previous Section.
● Sticking throttle vacuum piston. Examine carburettors, referring to Chapter 3.
● Brakes binding. Usually caused by maladjustment or partial seizure of the operating mechanism due to poor maintenance. Check brake adjustment (where applicable). A bent wheel spindle or warped brake disc can produce similar symptoms.

Poor running or lack of power at high speeds

16 Weak spark at plug or erratic firing

● All items as for Section 12.
● HT lead insulation failure. Insulation failure of the HT lead and spark plug cap due to old age or damage can cause shorting when the engine is driven hard. This condition may be less noticeable, or not noticeable at all at lower engine speeds.

17 Fuel/air mixture incorrect

● All items as for Section 13, with the exception of items 2 and 4.
● Main jet blocked. Debris from contaminated fuel, or from the fuel tank, and water in the fuel can block the main jet. Clean the fuel filter, the float bowl area, and if water is present, flush and refill the fuel tank.
● Main jet is the wrong size. The standard carburettor jetting is for sea level atmospheric pressure. For high altitudes, usually above 5000 ft, a smaller main jet will be required.
● Jet needle and needle jet worn. These can be renewed individually but should be renewed as a pair. Renewal of both items requires partial dismantling of the carburettor.
● Air bleed holes blocked. Dismantle carburettor and use compressed air to blow out all air passages.
● Reduced fuel flow. A reduction in the maximum fuel flow from the fuel tank to the carburettor will cause fuel starvation, proportionate to

the engine speed. Check for blockages through debris or a kinked fuel line.
● Vacuum diaphragm split. Renew.

18 Compression low

● See Section 10.

Knocking or pinking

19 General causes

● Carbon build-up in combustion chamber. After high mileages have been covered a large accumulation of carbon may occur. This may glow red hot and cause premature ignition of the fuel/air mixture, in advance of normal firing by the spark plug. Cylinder head removal will be required to allow inspection and cleaning.
● Fuel incorrect. A low grade fuel, or one of poor quality may result in compression induced detonation of the fuel resulting in knocking and pinking noises. Old fuel can cause similar problems. A too highly leaded fuel will reduce detonation but will accelerate deposit formation in the combustion chamber and may lead to early pre-ignition as described in item 1.
● Spark plug heat range incorrect. Uncontrolled pre-ignition can result from the use of a spark plug the heat range of which is too hot.
● Weak mixture. Overheating of the engine due to a weak mixture can result in pre-ignition occurring where it would not occur when engine temperature was within normal limits. Maladjustment, blocked jets or passages and air leaks can cause this condition.

Overheating

20 Firing incorrect

● Spark plug fouled, defective or maladjusted. See Section 8.
● Spark plug type incorrect. Refer to the Specifications and ensure that the correct plug type is fitted.

21 Fuel/air mixture incorrect

● Slow speed mixture strength incorrect. Adjust pilot air screw.
● Main jet wrong size. The carburettor is jetted for sea level atmospheric conditions. For high altitudes, usually above 5000 ft, a smaller main jet will be required.
● Air filter badly fitted or omitted. Check that the filter element is in place and that it and the air filter box cover are sealing correctly. Any leaks will cause a weak mixture.
● Induction air leaks. Check the security of the carburettor mountings and hose connections, and for cracks and splits in the hoses. Check also that the carburettor top is secure and that the vacuum gauge adaptor plug (where fitted) is tight.
● Fuel level too low. See Section 6.
● Fuel tank filler cap air vent obstructed. Clear blockage.

22 Lubrication inadequate

● Engine oil too low. Not only does the oil serve as a lubricant by preventing friction between moving components, but it also acts as a coolant. Check the oil level and replenish.
● Engine oil overworked. The lubricating properties of oil are lost slowly during use as a result of changes resulting from heat and also contamination. Always change the oil at the recommended interval.
● Engine oil of incorrect viscosity or poor quality. Always use the recommended viscosity and type of oil.

● Oil filter and filter by-pass valve blocked. Renew filter and clean the by-pass valve.

23 Miscellaneous causes

● Radiator clogged. A build-up of mud in the radiator matrix will decrease the cooling capabilities of the fins. Clean the radiator as described in Chapter 2.

Clutch operating problems

24 Clutch slip

● Excess fluid in reservoir. Check fluid level as described in Routine maintenance.
● Friction plates worn or warped. Overhaul clutch assembly, replacing plates out of specification.
● Steel plates worn or warped. Overhaul clutch assembly, replacing plates out of specification.
● Clutch springs broken or worn. Old or heat-damaged (from slipping clutch) springs should be replaced with new ones.
● Clutch centre and outer drum worn. Severe indentation by the clutch plate tangs of the channels in the centre and drum will cause snagging of the plates preventing correct engagement. If this damage occurs, renewal of the worn components is required.
● Lubricant incorrect. Use of a transmission lubricant other than that specified may allow the plates to slip.

25 Clutch drag

● Insufficient fluid in reservoir. Top up as described in Routine maintenance.
● Air in hydraulic fluid. Bleed the system as described in Chapter 6.
● Clutch plates warped or damaged. This will cause a drag on the clutch, causing the machine to creep. Overhaul clutch assembly (Chapter 1).
● Clutch spring tension uneven. Usually caused by a sagged or broken spring. Check and replace springs (Chapter 1).
● Engine oil deteriorated. Badly contaminated engine oil and a heavy deposit of oil sludge and carbon on the plates will cause plate sticking. The oil recommended for this machine is of the detergent type, therefore it is unlikely that this problem will arise unless regular oil changes are neglected.
● Engine oil viscosity too high. Drag in the plates will result from the use of an oil with too high a viscosity. In very cold weather clutch drag may occur until the engine has reached operating temperature.
● Clutch centre and outer drum worn. Indentation by the clutch plate tangs of the channels in the centre and drum will prevent easy plate disengagement. If the damage is light the affected areas may be dressed with a fine file. More pronounced damage will necessitate renewal of the components.
● Clutch drum seized to shaft. Lack of lubrication, severe wear or damage can cause the drum to seize to the shaft. Overhaul of the clutch, and perhaps the transmission, may be necessary to repair damage (Chapter 1).
● Clutch slave cylinder defective. Worn or damaged piston can stick and fail to return correctly. Overhaul clutch cylinder components (Chapter 1).
● Loose clutch nut. Causes drum and hub misalignment, putting a drag on the engine. Engagement adjustment continually varies. Overhaul clutch assembly (Chapter 1).

Gear selection problems

26 Gear lever does not return

● Weak or broken return spring. Renew the spring.
● Gearchange shaft bent or seized. Distortion of the gearchange shaft

often occurs if the machine is dropped heavily on the gear lever. Provided that damage is not severe straightening of the shaft is permissible.

27 Gear selection difficult or impossible

● Clutch not disengaging fully. See Section 25.
● Gearchange shaft bent. This often occurs if the machine is dropped heavily on the gear lever. Straightening of the shaft is permissible if the damage is not too great.
● Gearchange arms, pawls or pins worn or damaged. Wear or breakage of any of these items may cause difficulty in selecting one or more gears. Overhaul the selector mechanism.
● Gearchange arm spring broken. Renew spring.
● Gearchange drum stopper cam or detent arm damage. Failure, rather than wear, of these items may jam the drum thereby preventing gearchanging. The damaged items must be renewed.
● Selector forks bent or seized. This can be caused by dropping the machine heavily on the gearchange lever or as a result of lack of lubrication. Though rare, bending of a shaft can result from a missed gearchange or false selection at high speed.
● Selector fork end and pin wear. Pronounced wear of these items and the grooves in the gearchange drum can lead to imprecise selection and, eventually, no selection. Renewal of the worn components will be required.
● Structural failure. Failure of any one component of the selector rod and change mechanism will result in improper or fouled gear selection.

28 Jumping out of gear

● Detent assembly worn or damaged. Wear of the arms and the cam with which they locate or breakage of the detent springs can cause imprecise gear selection resulting in jumping out of gear. Renew the damaged components.
● Gear pinion dogs worn or damaged. Rounding off the dog edges and the mating recesses in adjacent pinion can lead to jumping out of gear when under load. The gears should be inspected and renewed. Attempting to reprofile the dogs is not recommended.
● Selector forks, gearchange drum and pinion grooves worn. Extreme wear of these interconnected items can occur after high mileages especially when lubrication has been neglected. The worn components must be renewed.
● Gear pinions, bushes and shafts worn. Renew the worn components.
● Bent gearchange shaft. Often caused by dropping the machine on the gear lever.
● Gear pinion tooth broken. Chipped teeth are unlikely to cause jumping out of gear once the gear has been selected fully; a tooth which is completely broken off, however, may cause problems in this respect and in any event will cause transmission noise.

29 Overselection

● Pawl spring weak or broken. Renew the spring.
● Detent arm assemblies worn or broken. Renew the damaged items.
● Selector limiter claw components (where fitted) worn or damaged. Renew the damaged items.

Abnormal engine noise.

30 Knocking or pinking

● See Section 19.

31 Piston slap or rattling from cylinder

● Cylinder bore/piston clearance excessive. Resulting from wear, partial seizure or improper boring during overhaul. This condition can often be heard as a high, rapid tapping noise when the engine is under little or no load, particularly when power is just beginning to be applied. Reboring to the next correct oversize should be carried out and a new oversize piston fitted.

● Connecting rod bent. This can be caused by over-revving, trying to start a very badly flooded engine (resulting in a hydraulic lock in the cylinder) or by earlier mechanical failure such as a dropped valve. Attempts at straightening a bent connecting rod from a high performance engine are not recommended. Careful inspection of the crankshaft should be made before renewing the damaged connecting rod.

● Gudgeon pin, piston boss bore or small-end bearing wear or seizure. Excess clearance or partial seizure between normal moving parts of these items can cause continuous or intermittent tapping noises. Rapid wear or seizure is caused by lubrication starvation resulting from an insufficient engine oil level or oilway blockage.

● Piston rings worn, broken or sticking. Renew the rings after careful inspection of the piston and bore.

32 Valve noise or tapping from the cylinder head

● Valve clearance incorrect. Adjust the clearances with the engine cold.
● Valve spring broken or weak. Renew the spring set.
● Camshaft or cylinder head worn or damaged. The camshaft lobes are the most highly stressed of all components in the engine and are subject to high wear if lubrication becomes inadequate. The bearing surfaces on the camshaft and cylinder head are also sensitive to a lack of lubrication. Lubrication failure due to blocked oilways can occur, but over-enthusiastic revving before engine warm-up is complete is the usual cause.

● Rocker arm or spindle wear. Rapid wear of a rocker arm, and the resulting need for frequent valve clearance adjustment, indicates break-through or failure of the surface hardening on the rocker arm tips. Similar wear in the cam lobes can be expected. Renew the worn components after checking for lubrication failure.

● Worn camshaft drive components. A rustling noise or light tapping which is not improved by correct re-adjustment of the cam chain tension can be emitted by a worn cam chain or worn sprockets and chain. If uncorrected, subsequent cam chain breakage may cause extensive damage. The worn components must be renewed before wear becomes too far advanced.

33 Other noises

● Big-end bearing wear. A pronounced knock from within the crankcase which worsens rapidly is indicative of big-end bearing failure as a result of extreme normal wear or lubrication failure. Remedial action in the form of a bottom end overhaul should be taken; continuing to run the engine will lead to further damage including the possibility of connecting rod breakage.

● Main bearing failure. Extreme normal wear or failure of the main bearings is characteristically accompanied by a rumble from the crankcase and vibration felt through the frame and footrests. Renew the worn bearings and carry out a very careful examination of the crankshaft.

● Crankshaft excessively out of true. A bent crank may result from over-revving or damage from an upper cylinder component or gearbox failure. Damage can also result from dropping the machine on either crankshaft end. Straightening of the crankshaft is not possible in normal circumstances; a replacement item should be fitted.

● Engine mounting loose. Tighten all the engine mounting nuts and bolts.

● Cylinder head gasket leaking. The noise most often associated with a leaking head gasket is a high pitched squeaking, although any other noise consistent with gas being forced out under pressure from a small orifice can also be emitted. Gasket leakage is often accompanied by oil seepage from around the mating joint or from the cylinder head holding down bolts and nuts. Leakage into the cam chain tunnel or oil return passages will increase crankcase pressure and may cause oil leakage at joints and oil seals. Also, oil contamination will be accelerated. Leakage results from insufficient or uneven tightening of the cylinder head fasteners, or from random mechanical failure. Retightening to the

correct torque figure will, at best, only provide a temporary cure. The gasket should be renewed at the earliest opportunity.

● Exhaust system leakage. Popping or crackling in the exhaust system, particularly when it occurs with the engine on the overrun, indicates a poor joint either at the cylinder port or at the exhaust pipe/silencer connection. Failure of the gasket or looseness of the clamp should be looked for.

Abnormal transmission noise

34 Clutch noise

● Clutch outer drum/friction plate tang clearance excessive.
● Clutch outer drum/spacer clearance excessive.
● Clutch outer drum/thrust washer clearance excessive.
● Primary drive gear teeth worn or damaged.
● Clutch shock absorber assembly worn or damaged.
● Balancer shaft incorrectly adjusted. Adjust as described in Chapter 1.

35 Transmission noise

● Bearing or bushes worn or damaged. Renew the affected components.
● Gear pinions worn or chipped. Renew the gear pinions.
● Metal chips jammed in gear teeth. This can occur when pieces of metal from any failed component are picked up by a meshing pinion. The condition will lead to rapid bearing wear or early gear failure.
● Engine/transmission oil level too low. Top up immediately to prevent damage to gearbox and engine.
● Gearchange mechanism worn or damaged. Wear or failure of certain items in the selection and change components can induce mis-selection of gears (see Section 27) where incipient engagement of more than one gear set is promoted. Remedial action, by the overhaul of the gearbox, should be taken without delay.
● Loose gearbox chain sprocket. Remove the sprocket and check for impact damage to the splines of the sprocket and shaft. Excessive slack between the splines will promote loosening of the securing nut; renewal of the worn components is required. When retightening the nut ensure that it is tightened fully and that the lock washer is bent up against one flat of the nut.
● Chain snagging on cases or cycle parts. A badly worn chain or one that is excessively loose may snag or smack against adjacent components.

Exhaust smokes excessively

36 White/blue smoke (caused by oil burning)

● Piston rings worn or broken. Breakage or wear of any ring, but particularly the oil control ring, will allow engine oil past the piston into the combustion chamber. Overhaul the cylinder barrel and piston.
● Cylinder cracked, worn or scored. These conditions may be caused by overheating, lack of lubrication, component failure or advanced normal wear. The cylinder barrel should be renewed or rebored and the next oversize piston fitted.
● Valve oil seal damaged or worn. This can occur as a result of valve guide failure or old age. The emission of smoke is likely to occur when the throttle is closed rapidly after acceleration, for instance, when changing gear. Renew the valve oil seals and, if necessary, the valve guides.
● Valve guides worn. See the preceding paragraph.
● Engine oil level too high. This increases the crankcase pressure and allows oil to be forced past the piston rings. Often accompanied by seepage of oil at joints and oil seals.
● Cylinder head gasket blown between cam chain tunnel or oil return passage. Renew the cylinder head gasket.
● Abnormal crankcase pressure. This may be caused by blocked

breather passages or hoses causing back-pressure at high engine revolutions.

37 Black smoke (caused by over-rich mixture)

● Air filter element clogged. Clean or renew the element.
● Main jet loose or too large. Remove the float chamber to check for tightness of the jet. If the machine is used at high altitudes rejetting will be required to compensate for the lower atmospheric pressure.
● Cold start mechanism jammed on. Check that the mechanism works smoothly and correctly and that, where fitted, the operating cable is lubricated and not snagged.
● Fuel level too high. The fuel level is controlled by the float height which can increase as a result of wear or damage. Remove the float bowl and check the float height. Check also that floats have not punctured; a punctured float will loose buoyancy and allow an increased fuel level.
● Float valve needle stuck open. Caused by dirt or a worn valve. Clean the float chamber or renew the needle and, if necessary, the valve seat.

Oil pressure indicator lamp goes on

38 Engine lubrication system failure

● Engine oil defective. Oil pump shaft or locating pin sheared off from ingesting debris or seizing from lack of lubrication (low oil level) (Chapter 3).
● Engine oil screen clogged. Change oil and filter and service pickup screen (Chapter 3 and Routine maintenance).
● Engine oil level too low. Inspect for leak or other problem causing low oil level and add recommended lubricant (Chapters 3 and Routine maintenance).
● Engine oil viscosity too low. Very old, thin oil, or an improper weight of oil used in engine. Change to correct lubricant (Routine maintenance).
● Camshaft or journals worn. High wear causing drop in oil pressure. Replace camshaft and/or head. Abnormal wear could be caused by oil starvation at high rpm from low oil level, improper oil weight or type, or loose oil fitting on upper cylinder oil line (Chapters 1 and 3).
● Crankshaft and/or bearings worn. Same problems as paragraph 5. Overhaul lower end (Chapter 1).
● Relief valve stuck open. This causes the oil to be dumped back into the sump. Repair or renew (Chapter 3).

39 Electrical system failure

● Oil pressure switch defective. Check switch according to the procedures in Chapter 7. Replace if defective.
● Oil pressure indicator lamp wiring system defective. Check for pinched, shorted, disconnected or damaged wiring (Chapter 7).

Poor handling or roadholding

40 Directional instability

● Suspension settings incorrect. Check and adjust as described in Routine maintenance.
● Steering head bearing adjustment too tight. This will cause rolling or weaving at low speeds. Re-adjust the bearings.
● Steering head bearings worn or damaged. Correct adjustment of the bearing will prove impossible to achieve if wear or damage has occurred. Inconsistent handling will occur including rolling or weaving at low speed and poor directional control at indeterminate higher speeds. The steering head bearing should be dismantled for inspection and renewed if required. Lubrication should also be carried out.

● Bearing races pitted or dented. Impact damage caused, perhaps, by an accident or riding over a pot-hole can cause indentation of the bearing, usually in one position. This should be noted as notchiness when the handlebars are turned. Renew and lubricate the bearings.
● Steering stem bent. This will occur only if the machine is subjected to a high impact such as hitting a kerb or a pot-hole. The lower yoke/stem should be renewed; do not attempt to straighten the stem.
● Front or rear tyre pressures too low.
● Front or rear tyre worn. General instability, high speed wobbles and skipping over white lines indicates that tyre renewal may be required. Tyre induced problems, in some machine /tyre combinations, can occur even when the tyre in question is by no means fully worn.
● Swinging arm or linkage bearings worn. Difficulty in holding line, particularly when cornering or when changing power settings indicates wear in the swinging arm bearings. The swinging arm should be removed from the machine and the bearings renewed.
● Swinging arm flexing. The symptoms given in the preceding paragraph will also occur if the swinging arm fork flexes badly. This can be caused by structural weakness as a result of corrosion, fatigue or impact damage, or because the rear wheel spindle is slack.
● Wheel bearings worn. Renew the worn bearings.
● Tyres unsuitable for machine. Not all available tyres will suit the characteristics of the frame and suspension, indeed, some tyres or tyre combinations may cause a transformation in the handling characteristics. If handling problems occur immediately after changing to a new tyre type or make, revert to the original tyres to see whether an improvement can be noted. In some instances a change to what are, in fact, suitable tyres may give rise to handling deficiencies. In this case a thorough check should be made of all frame and suspension items which affect stability.

41 Steering bias to left or right

● Rear wheel out of alignment. Caused by uneven adjustment of chain tensioner adjusters allowing the wheel to be askew in the fork ends. A bent rear wheel spindle will also misalign the wheel in the swinging arm.
● Wheels out of alignment. This can be caused by impact damage to the frame, swinging arm, wheel spindles or front forks. Although occasionally a result of material failure or corrosion it is usually as a result of a crash.
● Front forks twisted in the steering yokes. A light impact, for instance with a pot-hole or low curb, can twist the fork legs in the steering yokes without causing structural damage to the fork legs or the yokes themselves. Re-alignment can be made by loosening the yoke pinch bolts, wheel spindle and mudguard bolts. Re-align the wheel with the handlebars and tighten the bolts working upwards from the wheel spindle. This action should be carried out only when there is no chance that structural damage has occurred.

42 Handlebar vibrates or oscillates

● Tyres worn or out of balance. Either condition, particularly in the front tyre, will promote shaking of the fork assembly and thus the handlebars. A sudden onset of shaking can result if a balance weight is displaced during use.
● Tyres badly positioned on the wheel rims. A moulded line on each wall of a tyre is provided to allow visual verification that the tyre is correctly positioned on the rim. A check can be made by rotating the tyre; any misalignment will be immediately obvious.
● Wheel rims warped or damaged. Inspect the wheels for runout as described in Routine maintenance.
● Swinging arm bearings worn. Renew the bearings.
● Wheel bearings worn. Renew the bearings.
● Steering head bearings incorrectly adjusted. Vibration is more likely to result from bearings which are too loose rather than too tight. Re-adjust the bearings.
● Loose fork component fasteners. Loose nuts and bolts holding the fork legs, wheel spindle, mudguards or steering stem can promote shaking at the handlebars. Fasteners on running gear such as the forks

and suspension should be check tightened occasionally to prevent dangerous looseness of components occurring.
● Engine mounting bolts loose. Tighten all fasteners.

43   Poor front fork performance

● Suspension settings incorrect. Check and adjust front fork settings (as applicable) as described in Routine maintenance.
● Damping fluid level incorrect. If the fluid level is too low poor suspension control will occur resulting in a general impairment of roadholding and early loss of tyre adhesion when cornering and braking. Too much oil is unlikely to change the fork characteristics unless severe overfilling occurs when the fork action will become stiffer and oil seal failure may occur.
● Damping oil viscosity incorrect. The damping action of the fork is directly related to the viscosity of the damping oil. The lighter the oil used, the less will be the damping action imparted. For general use, use the recommended viscosity of oil, changing to a slightly higher or heavier oil only when a change in damping characteristic is required. Overworked oil, or oil contaminated with water which has found its way past the seals, should be renewed to restore the correct damping performance and to prevent bottoming of the forks.
● Damping components worn or corroded. Advanced normal wear of the fork internals is unlikely to occur until a very high mileage has been covered. Continual use of the machine with damaged oil seals which allows the ingress of water, or neglect, will lead to rapid corrosion and wear. Dismantle the forks for inspection and overhaul. See Chapter 5.
● Weak fork springs. Progressive fatigue of the fork springs, resulting in a reduced spring free length, will occur after extensive use. This condition will promote excessive fork dive under braking, and in its advanced form will reduce the at-rest extended length of the forks and thus the fork geometry. Renewal of the springs as a pair is the only satisfactory course of action.
● Bent stanchions or corroded stanchions. Both conditions will prevent correct telescoping of the fork legs, and in an advanced state can cause sticking of the fork in one position. In a mild form corrosion will cause stiction of the fork thereby increasing the time the suspension takes to react to an uneven road surface. Bent fork stanchions should be attended to immediately because they indicate that impact damage has occurred, and there is a danger that the forks will fail with disastrous consequences.

44   Front fork judder when braking (see also Section 52)

● Wear between the fork stanchions and the fork legs. Renewal of the affected components is required.
● Slack steering head bearings. Re-adjust the bearings.
● Warped brake disc. If irregular braking action occurs fork judder can be induced in what are normally serviceable forks. Renew the damaged brake components.

45   Poor rear suspension performance

● Suspension settings incorrect. Check and adjust rear suspension settings as described in Routine maintenance.
● Rear suspension unit damper worn out or leaking. The damping performance of most rear suspension units falls off with age. This is a gradual process, and thus may not be immediately obvious. Indications of poor damping include hopping of the rear end when cornering or braking, and a general loss of positive stability. See Chapter 5.
● Weak rear spring. If the suspension unit spring fatigues it will promote excessive pitching of the machine and reduce the ground clearance when cornering. If spring fatigue has occurred the suspension unit must be renewed.
● Swinging arm flexing or bearings worn. See Sections 40 and 41.
● Bent suspension unit damper rod. This is likely to occur only if the

machine is dropped or if seizure of the piston occurs. If either happens the suspension unit should be renewed.

Abnormal frame and suspension noise

46   Front end noise

● Oil level low or too thin. This can cause a 'spurting' sound and is usually accompanied by irregular fork action. Change fork oil as described in Routine maintenance.
● Spring weak or broken. Makes a clicking or scraping sound. Fork oil will have a lot of metal particles in it (Chapter 5).
● Steering head bearings loose or damaged. Clicks when braking. Check, adjust or replace (Chapter 5).
● Fork clamps loose. Make sure all fork clamp pinch bolts are tight (Chapter 5).
● Fork stanchion bent. Good possibility if machine has been dropped. Repair or replace tube (Chapter 5).

47   Rear suspension noise

● Fluid level too low. Leakage of a suspension unit, usually evident by oil on the outer surfaces, can cause a spurting noise. The suspension unit should be renewed.
● Defective rear suspension unit with internal damage. Renew the suspension unit.

Brake problems

48   Brakes are spongy or ineffective

● Air in brake circuit. This is only likely to happen in service due to neglect in checking the fluid level or because a leak has developed. The problem should be identified and the brake system bled of air.
● Pads worn. Check the pad wear as described in Routine maintenance and renew the pads if necessary.
● Contaminated pads. Cleaning pads which have been contaminated with oil, grease or brake fluid is unlikely to prove successful; the pads should be renewed.
● Pads glazed. This is usually caused by overheating. The surface of the pads may be roughened using glass-paper or a fine file.
● Brake fluid deterioration. A brake which on initial operation is firm but rapidly becomes spongy in use may be failing due to water contamination of the fluid. The fluid should be drained and then the system refilled and bled.
● Master cylinder seal failure. Wear or damage of master cylinder internal parts will prevent pressurisation of the brake fluid. Overhaul the master cylinder unit.
● Caliper seal failure. This will almost certainly be obvious by loss of fluid, a lowering of fluid in the master cylinder reservoir and contamination of the brake pads and caliper. Overhaul the caliper assembly.
● Rear brake pedal height incorrect. Adjust as described in Routine maintenance.

49   Brakes drag

● Disc warped. The disc must be renewed.
● Caliper piston, caliper or pads corroded. The brake caliper assembly is vulnerable to corrosion due to water and dirt, and unless cleaned at regular intervals and lubricated in the recommended manner, will become sticky in operation.
● Piston seal deteriorated. The seal is designed to return the piston in the caliper to the retracted position when the brake is released. Wear or old age can affect this function. The caliper should be overhauled if this occurs.
● Brake pad damaged. Pad material separating from the backing plate

due to wear or faulty manufacture. Renew the pads. Faulty installation of a pad also will cause dragging.
● Wheel spindle bent. The spindle may be straightened if no structural damage has occurred.
● Brake lever or pedal not returning. Check that the lever or pedal works smoothly throughout its operating range and does not snag on any adjacent cycle parts. Lubricate the pivot if necessary.
● Twisted caliper support bracket. This is likely to occur only after impact in an accident. No attempt should be made to re-align the caliper; the bracket should be renewed.

50 Brake lever or pedal pulsates in operation

● Disc warped or irregularly worn. The disc must be renewed.
● Wheel spindle bent. The spindle may be straightened provided no structural damage has occurred.

51 Disc brake noise

● Brake squeal. Squealing can be caused by dust on the pads, usually in combination with glazed pads, or other contamination from oil, grease, brake fluid or corrosion. Persistent squealing which,cannot be traced to any of the normal causes can often be cured by applying a thin layer of high temperature silicone grease to the rear of the pads. Make absolutely certain that no grease is allowed to contaminate the braking surface of the pads.
● Glazed pads. This is usually caused by high temperatures or contamination. The pad surfaces may be roughened using glass-paper or a fine file. If this approach does not effect a cure the pads should be renewed.
● Disc warped. This can cause a chattering, clicking or intermittent squeal and is usually accompanied by a pulsating brake lever or pedal or uneven braking. The disc must be renewed.
● Brake pads fitted incorrectly or undersize. Longitudinal play in the pads due to omission of the locating springs (where fitted) or because pads of the wrong size have been fitted will cause a single tapping noise every time the brake is operated. Inspect the pads for correct installation and security.

52 Brake induced fork judder

● Worn front fork stanchions and legs, or worn or badly adjusted steering head bearings. These conditions, combined with uneven or pulsating braking as described in Section 50 will induce more or less judder when the brakes are applied, dependent on the degree of wear and poor brake operation. Attention should be given to both areas of malfunction. See the relevant Sections.

Electrical problems

53 Battery dead or weak

● Battery faulty. Battery life should not be expected to exceed 3 to 4 years, particularly where a starter motor is used regularly. Gradual sulphation of the plates and sediment deposits will reduce the battery performance. Plate and insulator damage can often occur as a result of vibration. Complete power failure, or intermittent failure, may be due to a broken battery terminal. Lack of electrolyte will prevent the battery maintaining charge.
● Battery leads making poor contact. Remove the battery leads and clean them and the terminals, removing all traces of corrosion and

tarnish. Reconnect the leads and apply a coating of petroleum jelly to the terminals.
● Load excessive. If additional items such as spot lamps, are fitted, which increase the total electrical load above the maximum alternator output, the battery will fail to maintain full charge. Reduce the electrical load to suit the electrical capacity.
● Regulator/rectifier failure.
● Alternator generating coils open-circuit or shorted.
● Charging circuit shorting or open circuit. This may be caused by frayed or broken wiring, dirty connectors or a faulty ignition switch. The system should be tested in a logical manner. See Section 56.

54 Battery overcharged

● Rectifier/regulator faulty. Overcharging is indicated if the battery becomes hot or it is noticed that the electrolyte level falls repeatedly between checks. In extreme cases the battery will boil causing corrosive gases and electrolyte to be emitted through the vent pipes.
● Battery wrongly matched to the electrical circuit. Ensure that the specified battery is fitted to the machine.

55 Total electrical failure

● Fuse blown. Check the main fuse. If a fault has occurred, it must be rectified before a new fuse is fitted.
● Battery faulty. See Section 53.
● Earth failure. Check that the earth strap from the battery is securely affixed to the engine and is making a good contact.
● Ignition switch or power circuit failure. Check for current flow through the battery positive lead to the ignition switch. Check the ignition switch for continuity.

56 Circuit failure

● Wiring failure. Refer to the machine's wiring diagram and check the circuit for continuity. Open circuits are a result of loose or corroded connections, either at terminals or in-line connectors, or because of broken wires. Occasionally, the core of a wire will break without there being any apparent damage to the outer plastic cover.
● Switch failure. All switches may be checked for continuity in each switch position, after referring to the switch position boxes incorporated in the wiring diagram for the machine. Switch failure may be a result of mechanical breakage, corrosion or water.
● Fuse blown. Refer to the wiring diagram to check whether or not a circuit fuse is fitted. Replace the fuse, if blown, only after the fault has been identified and rectified.

57 Bulbs blowing repeatedly

● Vibration failure. This is often an inherent fault related to the natural vibration characteristics of the engine and frame and is, thus, difficult to resolve. Modifications of the lamp mounting, to change the damping characteristics may help.
● Intermittent earth. Repeated failure of one bulb, particularly where the bulb is fed directly from the generator, indicates that a poor earth exists somewhere in the circuit. Check that a good contact is available at each earthing point in the circuit.
● Reduced voltage. Where a quartz-halogen bulb is fitted the voltage to the bulb should be maintained or early failure of the bulb will occur. Do not overload the system with additional electrical equipment in excess of the system's power capacity and ensure that all circuit connections are maintained clean and tight.

Routine maintenance

Refer to Chapter 8 for information on the ZX1100 D model

Specifications

Engine

Oil capacity:

At oil change:

ZX1100 C .... 3.2 lit (5.7 Imp pt/3.4 US qt)

All other models .... 2.7 lit (4.8 Imp pt/2.9 US qt)

At oil and filter change:

ZX1100 C models .... 3.5 lit (6.2 Imp pt/3.7 US qt)

All other models .... 3.0 lit (5.3 Imp pt/3.2 US qt)

Spark plug type:	NGK	Nippon-denso
ZX900 and ZX1000 A models:		
UK models	DR8ES	X27ESR-U
US models	D8EA	X24ES-U
ZX1000 B and ZX1100 C models:		
UK models	CR9E	U27ESR-N
US models	C9E	U27ES-N

Spark plug gap:

ZX900 and ZX1000 A models .... 0.6 – 0.7 mm (0.024 – 0.028 in)

ZX1000 B and ZX1100 C models .... 0.7 – 0.8 mm (0.028 – 0.032 in)

Valve clearances – engine cold:

Inlet:

ZX900 and ZX1000 A models .... 0.13 – 0.18 mm (0.005 – 0.007 in)

ZX1000 B and ZX1100 C models .... 0.13 – 0.19 mm (0.005 – 0.007 in)

Exhaust:

ZX900 and ZX1000 A models .... 0.18 – 0.23 mm (0.007 – 0.009 in)

ZX1000 B and ZX1100 C models .... 0.18 – 0.24 mm (0.007 – 0.009 in)

Idle speed:

ZX1000 A California models .... 1150 – 1250 rpm

All other models .... 950 – 1050 rpm

Throttle cable free play – measured at twistgrip .... 2 – 3 mm (0.08 – 0.12 in)

Choke lever free play – measured at the base of lever .... 2 – 3 mm (0.08 – 0.12 in)

Cycle parts

Brake pad friction material thickness:

ZX900 A1 to A6 and ZX1000 A models .... 4.85 mm (0.191 in)

ZX1000 B models .... 4.50 mm (0.177 in)

ZX900 A7-on and ZX1100 C models:

Front .... 4.00 mm (0.157 in)

Rear .... 4.50 mm (0.177 in)

Service limit – all models .... 1.00 mm (0.039 in)

Rear brake pedal height (below top of footrest):

ZX900 models .... 29 – 39 mm (1.14 – 1.54 in)

ZX1000 A models .... Approx 37 mm (1.46 in)

ZX1000 B and ZX1100 C models .... Approx 45 mm (1.77 in)

Drive chain free play:

ZX1000 B models .... 30 – 40 mm (1.18 – 1.57 in)

All other models .... 35 – 40 mm (1.38 – 1.57 in)

Drive chain length – 20 link length:

ZX1000 A models .... 381.0 – 381.8 mm (15.00 – 15.04 in)

Service limit .... 389.0 mm (15.31 in)

All other models .... 317.5 – 318.4 mm (12.50 – 12.54 in)

Service limit .... 323.0 mm (12.72 in)

Front forks:

	cc	Imp fl oz	US fl oz
Oil capacity (approx) per leg – at oil change:			
ZX900 A1 to A6 models	270	9.5	9.1
ZX900 A7-on models	420	14.8	14.2
ZX1000 A models	295	10.4	10.0
ZX1000 B models	360	12.7	12.2
ZX1100 C models	390	13.7	13.2

Fork oil level:*
ZX900 A1 to A6 models	357 ± 2 mm (14.1 ± 0.08 in)
ZX900 A7-on models	110 ± 2 mm (4.3 ± 0.08 in)
ZX1000 A models	348 ± 4 mm (13.7 ± 0.16 in)
ZX1000 B models	130 ± 2 mm (5.1 ± 0.08 in)
ZX1100 C models	149 ± 2 mm (5.9 ± 0.08 in)

* Oil level is measured from the top of the stanchion with the fork spring removed. Measurement is taken with fork leg either fully compressed or extended – see text.

Tyre pressures – tyres cold:

	Front	Rear
UK ZX900 A1 to A6 models:		
Up to 97.5 kg (215 lb) load, below 130 mph (210 kmh)	2.25 kg/cm² (32psi)	2.50 kg/cm² (36psi)
97.5 – 181 kg (215 – 399 lb) load, below 130 mph (210 kmh)	2.50 kg/cm² (36psi)	2.50 kg/cm² (36psi)
Above 130 mph (210 kmh)	2.50 kg/cm² (36psi)	2.90 kg/cm² (41psi)
UK ZX900 A7-on models	2.50 kg/cm² (36psi)	2.90 kg/cm² (41psi)
US ZX900 A1 to A3 models:		
Up to 97.5 kg (215 lb) load	2.25 kg/cm² (36psi)	2.50 kg/cm² (36psi)
97.5 – 180 kg (215 – 397 lb) load	2.50 kg/cm² (36psi)	2.50 kg/cm² (36psi)
UK ZX1000 A models:		
Below 130 mph (210 kmh)	2.50 kg/cm² (36psi)	2.50 kg/cm² (36psi)
Above 130 mph (210 kmh)	2.50 kg/cm² (36psi)	2.90 kg/cm² (41psi)
UK ZX1000 B models:		
Up to 97.5 kg (215 lb) load, below 130 mph (210 kmh)	2.50 kg/cm² (36psi)	2.50 kg/cm² (36psi)
97.5 – 181 kg (215 – 399 lb) load, below 130 mph (210 kmh)	2.50 kg/cm² (36psi)	2.90 kg/cm² (41psi)
Above 130 mph (210 kmh)	2.50 kg/cm² (36psi)	2.90 kg/cm² (41psi)
US ZX1000 A and ZX1000 B models	2.50 kg/cm² (36psi)	2.90 kg/cm² (41psi)
ZX1100 C models	2.90 kg/cm² (41psi)	2.90 kg/cm² (41psi)

Recommended fluids and lubricants

Engine:	
Recommended oil	SAE 10W/40, 10W/50, 20W/40 or 20W/50 SE or SF class
Fuel grade	Unleaded or leaded. Minimum octane rating 91 (Research method/RON)
Air filter	SAE 30 engine oil, SE class
Front forks:	
ZX900 A1 to A6 and ZX1000 A models	SAE 10W fork oil
ZX900 A7-on, ZX1000 B and ZX1100 C models	SAE 10W/20 fork oil
Brake and clutch fluid	DOT 4 specification
Final drive chain	SAE 90 gear oil
Wheel bearings and speedometer drive gearbox	High melting-point grease
Steering head bearings	General purpose grease
Swinging arm and suspension linkage pivots	Molybdenum-disulphide grease
All control pivots, stand, stand pivots and throttle twistgrip	Good quality general purpose grease
Control cables	Engine oil

Introduction

Periodic routine maintenance is a continuous process which should commence immediately the machine is used. The object is to maintain all adjustments and to diagnose and rectify minor defects before they develop into more extensive, and often more expensive, problems.

It follows that if the machine is maintained properly, it will both run and perform with optimum efficiency, and be less prone to unexpected breakdowns. Regular inspection of the machine will show up any parts which are wearing, and with a little experience, it is possible to obtain the maximum life from any one component, renewing it when it becomes so worn that it is liable to fail.

Regular cleaning can be considered as important as mechanical maintenance. This will ensure that all the cycle parts are inspected regularly and are kept free from accumulations of road dirt and grime. Cleaning is especially important during the winter months, despite its appearance of being a thankless task which very soon seems pointless. On the contrary, it is during these months that the paintwork, chromium plating, and the alloy casings suffer the ravages of abrasive grit, rain and road salt. A couple of hours spent weekly on cleaning the machine will maintain its appearance and value, and highlight small points, such as chipped paint, before they become a serious problem.

It should be noted that the intervals between each maintenance task serve only as a guide. As the machine gets older, or if it is used under particularly arduous conditions, it is advisable to reduce the period between each check.

For ease of reference, most service operations are described in detail under the relevant heading. However, if further general information is required, this can be found under the pertinent section heading and chapter in the main text.

Although no special tools are required for routine maintenance, a good selection of general workshop tools is essential; refer to the Maintenance and minor repair toolkit section of Tools and working facilities.

It will also be noted that Allen screws are used extensively on these machines, and it follows that a selection of metric Allen keys (wrenches) will be required. These are available from most auto accessory shops and are not expensive.

Daily (pre-ride) checks

It is recommended that the following items are checked whenever the machine is about to be used. This is important to prevent the risk of unexpected failure of any component while riding the machine, and with experience, can be reduced to a simple checklist which will only take a few moments to complete. For those owners who are not inclined to check all items with such frequency, it is suggested that the best course of action is to carry out the checks in the form of a service which can be undertaken each week or before any long journey. It is essential that all items are checked and serviced with reasonable frequency.

1 Check the engine oil level

The level of the engine oil is quickly checked by way of the oil sight glass set in the left-hand outer casing. With the machine standing upright on level ground, the oil should be visible half way up the plastic window. Marks are provided on the rim of the window, indicating the maximum and minimum oil levels. If necessary, top up using the recommended oil by way of the filler cap at the top of the casing. Should too much oil have been added, it should be removed, using a syringe or an empty plastic squeeze pack such as that used for gear oils. Note that it is best to check the level with the machine at normal operating temperature so that the oil level is accurate; wait a few minutes for the oil to settle before checking the level if the machine has just been run.

2 Check the coolant level

Although the cooling system is semi-sealed and should not require frequent topping up, it is still necessary to check the coolant level at regular intervals. A separate expansion tank is fitted to allow for expansion of the coolant when the engine is hot, the displaced liquid being drawn back into the system when it cools. It is therefore the level of coolant in the expansion tank which is to be checked; the tank is constructed of translucent plastic so that the coolant level can be easily seen in relation to the upper and lower level lines.

The location of the tank varies from model to model. On ZX900 models the tank is situated behind the right-hand sidepanel, which must be removed to gain access to it. On ZX1000 A models the expansion tank is located behind the lower fairing section, the coolant level marks being on the fairing section rather than the expansion tank itself. The ZX1000 B and ZX1100 C models have the expansion tank mounted in the right-hand side of the upper fairing, the coolant level marks being

visible from the inside of the fairing.

The coolant level should be checked with the machine positioned on its centre stand on level ground, when the engine is cold. The coolant level must be between the higher ('Full', 'Hi' or 'U') and lower ('Low', 'Lo' or 'L') level marks at all times. If the level is below the lower mark, it should be topped right up to the higher mark using a coolant mixture of the required strength, and using only the specified ingredients as described in Chapter 2. In emergency cases distilled water alone may be used, but remember that this will dilute the coolant and reduce its degree of protection against freezing. If the coolant is significantly above the higher mark at any time, the surplus coolant should be siphoned off to prevent it from being expelled out of the breather hose once the engine has warmed up.

If the coolant level falls steadily, check the system for leaks as described in Chapter 2. If no leaks are found and the level still continues to fall, it is recommended that the machine be taken to an authorized Kawasaki dealer who will pressure test the system.

3 Check the fuel level

Checking the fuel level may seem obvious, but it is all too easy to forget. Ensure that you have enough fuel to complete your journey, or at least to get you to the nearest filling station.

4 Check the tyres

Check the tyre pressures with a pressure gauge that is known to be accurate. Always check the pressures when the tyres are cold. If the machine has travelled a number of miles, the tyres will have become hot and consequently the pressure will have increased – a false reading will therefore result.

It is well worth purchasing a small pocket gauge which can be relied on to give consistent readings, and which will remove any reliance on garage forecourt gauges which tend to be less dependable.

At the same time as the tyre pressures are checked, examine the tyres themselves. Check them for damage, especially splitting of the sidewalls. Remove any small stones or other road debris caught between the treads. When checking the tyres for damage, they should be examined for tread depth in view of both the legal and safety aspects. It

Oil level is checked via the sightglass – level must be between the lines (arrowed) cast in casing ...

... if not, top up via the filler cap at top of casing

On ZX1000 B and ZX1100 C models expansion tank is situated below the right-hand inner fairing section

If level is low, top up to the higher mark using only the specified coolant

Check tyre pressures with an accurate gauge

Lubricating the final drive chain

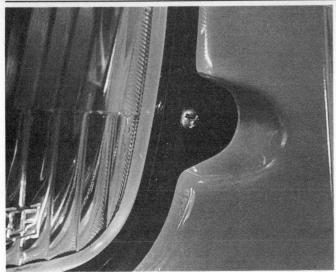

On ZX900 models headlamp horizontal adjustment is made with screw situated in rim ...

... and vertical adjustment by slackening bolt situated behind headlamp cover

On ZX1000 and ZX1100 C models both the vertical ...

... and horizontal adjusters are situated on the back of the headlamp unit – ZX1100 C shown

is vital to keep the tread depth within the UK legal limits of 1 mm of depth over three-quarters of the tread breadth around the entire circumference with no bald patches in evidence. Many riders, however, consider nearer 2 mm to be the limit for secure roadholding, traction and braking, especially in adverse weather conditions, and it should be noted that Kawasaki recommend a minimum tread depth of 1 mm for the front tyre, 2 mm for the rear tyre when used at low speed (under 130 kmh, 80 mph), or 3 mm for the rear tyre when used at speeds above 130 kmh (80 mph).

5 Lubricate the final drive chain

Although the chain fitted as standard equipment is of the O-ring type, grease being sealed into the internal bearing surfaces by O-rings at each end of the rollers, lubrication is still required to prevent the rollers from wearing on the sprocket teeth and to prevent the O-rings from drying up. A heavy (SAE 90) gear oil is best; it will stay on the rollers longer than a lighter engine oil. Whilst spinning the back wheel, allow oil to dribble onto the rollers until all are oily, then apply a small amount to the O-rings on each side.

The only alternative to this is to use one of the proprietary aerosol-applied chain lubricants. **Warning:** some propellants used in aerosols cause the O-rings to deteriorate very rapidly, so make certain that the product is marked as being suitable for use with O-ring type chains.

6 Check the brakes

Check that both brakes function correctly and that their control lever (front) or pedal (rear) operates smoothly. Check the level of fluid in both brake master cylinder reservoirs. Check that the stop lamp illuminates when the brakes are applied.

7 General check

Check that all control levers and switches are working smoothly and that the throttle cable is correctly adjusted. Also check that the steering has no freeplay, and can move from lock to lock without fouling on any cables or cycle components. Check that the stands pivot smoothly and are held securely in their raised positions by the return springs. Check the security of all nuts and bolts on the cycle components.

8 Legal check

Check that the lights, turn signals, horn and speedometer function correctly to make sure the machine complies with all legal requirements in this respect. Also check that the headlamp beam is correctly aimed to comply with local legislation. In the UK lighting regulations stipulate that the headlamp must be set so that the beam does not dazzle a person standing same horizontal plane as the vehicle, at a distance greater than 25 feet from the lamp, whose eye level is not less than 3 feet 6 inches above that plane. It is easy to approximate this setting by placing the

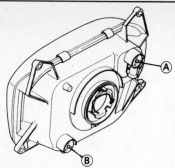

Headlamp beam adjuster locations – ZX1000 models

A   Horizontal adjustment   B   Vertical adjustment

machine 25 feet away from a wall, on its centre stand on a level surface, and setting the beam height so that it is concentrated at the same height as the distance from the centre of the headlamp to the ground. In addition, the headlamp must be capable of being dipped. If required, the beam can be adjusted as follows.

On ZX900 models, the horizontal adjustment is altered by rotating the spring-loaded screw situated in the right-hand side of the headlamp rim (when viewed from the front of the machine). To make vertical adjustment, it is first necessary to remove the small headlamp cover which is situated on the underside of the upper fairing. Once the cover has been removed, slacken the headlamp retaining bolt situated at the bottom of the headlamp, and move the headlamp to the required position. When the headlamp is correctly aligned, tighten the bolt and refit the cover.

Both headlamp beam adjusters on ZX1000 models are situated on the back of the headlamp unit and are adjusted from underneath. On ZX1000 B models these can be reached using the holes provided in the fairing, whereas on ZX1000 A models it is first necessary to remove the cover situated on the underside of the upper fairing to gain access to the adjusters. The adjusters can be rotated using a crosshead screwdriver; the upper right-hand adjuster alters the horizontal aim, and the lower left-hand one alters the vertical aim. On ZX1000 A models refit the headlamp cover once the headlamp is correctly adjusted.

The headlamp unit which is fitted to ZX1100 C models is similar to that used on the ZX1000 models, the only differences being that the upper (horizontal) adjuster is fitted with an adjusting knob and both adjusters are accessed from inside the fairing.

Monthly, or every 500 miles (800 km)

---

1 Check and adjust the final drive chain

The exact interval at which the final drive chain will require adjustment and renewal is entirely dependent on the usage to which the machine is put. However, Kawasaki do recommend that the chain freeplay is checked, and if necessary adjusted, every 500 miles (800 km) and checked for wear every 3000 miles (5000 km).

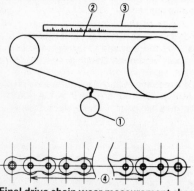

Final drive chain wear measurement check

1   10 kg weight   3   Ruler
2   Top run of chain   4   Distance between 1st and 21st pins

The amount of wear in the chain can be assessed by measuring a 20 link length of the chain, ie the distance from any one pin to the 21st pin along. Note that the distance measured should be from the centre of the first pin to the centre of the other (21st) pin. This can be done with the chain in place on the machine as follows.

Remove the chainguard and hang a weight of approximately 10 kg (22 lbs) on the bottom run of the chain to keep the chain taut, then measure the specified length of the chain along the top run of the chain. Since the chain is likely to wear unevenly, measure several different sections of the chain. If any one measurement exceeds the limit given in the Specifications, the chain is worn out and must be renewed.

Chain renewal will require the removal of the swinging arm, unless a chain with a connecting link has been fitted previously. Refer to the relevant Sections of Chapter 5 for details of swinging arm removal. If the chain is to be renewed, this must always be done in conjunction with both sprockets to prevent the increased wear that would result from the running together of new and part-worn components. If a connecting link is fitted, the spring clip must be refitted with its closed end facing the normal direction of chain travel.

Before the chain tension can be checked it is necessary to ensure that the wheel alignment is correct. This can be checked using the notches on the outside of the chain adjusters. Identify which notch aligns with, or is closest to the mark on the swinging arm and ensure that the corresponding notch on the opposite adjuster is in the same position. A more accurate check of wheel alignment can be made by laying a plank of wood or drawing a length of string parallel to the machine so that it touches both walls of the rear tyre. Wheel alignment is correct when the plank or string is equidistant from both walls of the front tyre when tested on both sides of the machine, as shown in the accompanying illustration. If the wheel alignment is found to be incorrect, it can be adjusted as follows.

Place the machine on its centre stand and slacken the rear brake caliper and collar fixing bolts on ZX900 models, or the caliper to torque arm mounting bolt on all other models. Remove either the left or right-hand side wheel spindle retaining circlip and slacken the wheel spindle and chain adjuster pinch bolts. Rotate the adjusters until the same notch on each one is aligned with the mark on the swinging arm, then tighten both the chain adjuster pinch bolts. Check that the notches on the chain adjusters are still aligned and then tighten the wheel spindle to the specified torque setting, and refit its retaining circlip. Once the wheel alignment is correct proceed to check the chain tension as follows before securing the caliper bolts.

Chain tension is adjusted with the machine on its centre stand and with the rear wheel clear of the ground. Find the tightest spot of the chain by rotating the rear wheel and feeling the amount of freeplay present on the bottom run of the chain, midway between the sprockets, testing along the complete length of the chain. When the tightest spot has been found, measure the total amount of up and down movement available. This measurement should be within the limits given in the Specifications.

To adjust the chain, slacken the rear brake caliper and collar fixing bolts on ZX900 models, and the caliper to torque arm mounting bolt on all other models. Slacken the chain adjuster pinch bolts and rotate the adjusters by an equal amount until the correct amount of freeplay required is obtained. Once the chain is correctly adjusted tighten the chain adjuster pinch bolts to their specified torque setting, followed by

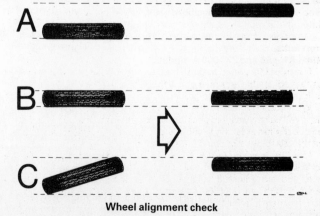

Wheel alignment check

A and C – Incorrect   B – Correct

Set wheel alignment using the notches in the adjusters ...

... then tighten spindle to the specified torque setting and refit circlip

Rotate both chain adjusters until chain tension is correct ...

... then tighten both chain adjuster pinch bolts to specified torque setting ...

... followed by the rear brake caliper and collar fixing bolts on ZX900 models ...

... or the torque arm mounting bolt on ZX1000 and ZX1100 C models

the rear brake caliper and collar fixing bolts or the caliper to torque arm mounting bolt (as applicable). Finally lubricate the chain as described in the Daily (pre-ride) checks section and check the operation of the rear brake before taking the machine out on the road.

2 Check the suspension settings

To ensure the machine handles well and is safe to ride, it is essential that both front and rear suspension settings (as applicable) are regularly checked. **Note:** *when checking the air pressures do not use a tyre pressure gauge as they are not accurate enough and lose too much air when disconnected. Kawasaki produce a suitable gauge under Part Number 52005-1003. When adding air to the suspension components NEVER use an air line, because they operate at far too high a pressure and could damage the seals.* It is recommended that only a bicycle pump or one of the specialist aftermarket kits is used to add air, the latter usually comes equipped with its own built in gauge and is extremely accurate in use. Note that the standard settings given are recommended for solo riding with a rider of average build, weighing approximately 68 kg (150 lb).

Front forks
ZX900 A1 – A6 and ZX1000 A models

The front forks fitted to these models are air-assisted and feature a 3 position adjustable anti-dive unit. When checking the air pressure raise the front wheel clear of the ground to prevent the pressure in the fork being artificially increased due to the weight of the machine. To achieve this, it will be necessary to position the machine on its centre stand, then remove the lower fairing section as described in Chapter 5, and place a suitably-sized block or stand underneath the crankcases.

The fork legs on ZX900 A1 to A6 models and early ZX1000 A1 models are linked by an air balance pipe, fitted just above the bottom yoke, and are adjusted via the valve at the top of the right-hand stanchion. On later ZX1000 A1 and all A2, A3 models, the pressure in each fork leg is adjusted separately via a valve at the top of each stanchion; it is essential to ensure that equal pressure exists in each fork leg. Take the pressure reading when the forks are cold. The standard air pressure is 0.5 kg/cm² (7 psi), with a usable range of 0.4 – 0.6 kg/cm² (5.7

– 8.5 psi). On no account should the air pressure in the forks ever exceed 2.5 kg/cm² (36 psi) as this will almost certainly damage the fork seals. Refit the valve dust cap when complete.

On both models ensure that the anti-dive units, fitted on the front of each lower fork leg, are set to the same position. They are adjusted using the thumb-wheel situated at the bottom of the unit. The present position is indicated by the index mark on the front of the unit which aligns with a number on the thumb-wheel. Position 1 is the softest setting and position 3 the strongest. To make adjustment, turn the thumb-wheel until it clicks and the required number (setting) is aligned with the index mark on the front of the unit. Set each unit to the same position.

ZX1100 C models

The front forks feature an 8 position spring preload adjuster and a 4 position damping adjuster. Both the preload and damping adjusters are an integral part of the fork top bolts.

Preload is adjusted by turning the large hexagon-headed bolt that protrudes out of the top bolt. The position in which the adjuster is set is indicated by the marks on the side of the adjuster, ie the number of marks or lines visible above the surface of the top bolt. Position 8 (adjuster fully extended) is the softest setting and position 1 (adjuster fully in) is the hardest. The standard setting is position 6 (6th mark from the top).

The damping adjuster is situated in the centre of the preload adjuster and is adjusted using a flat-bladed screwdriver. As there are no marks on the preload adjuster to indicate the four positions, the only way to

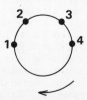
Front fork damping adjuster position – ZX1100 C model

Adjusting the front fork preload – ZX1100 C models

Adjusting the front fork damping – ZX1100 C models

Remove plastic cover to gain access to rear suspension damping adjuster on ZX1100 C models

identify its present position is to count the number of clicks the adjuster makes whilst being rotated. The 4 adjuster positions are all situated within 180° (half a turn) of the adjuster (see accompanying illustration). Therefore, whilst rotating the adjuster it should click 4 times in 180° and not at all for another 180°. The first click after the 180° break is position 1. *Note: always turn the damping adjuster clockwise and never anticlockwise (counterclockwise).*

Once position 1 has been identified the other positions will click into place with further turning of the adjuster in a clockwise direction. After position 4 there should be an 180° break after which the adjuster will click back into the number 1 position. Set the adjuster to the required position noting that position 1 is the softest setting and position 4 the hardest. The standard recommended setting is position 2.

Once both preload and damping adjusters are set to the required settings, repeat the procedure on the other fork leg, ensuring that both fork legs are set to identical positions; failure to do so will lead to the machine's handling being impaired.

Rear suspension unit
ZX900 and ZX1000 models
The rear suspension unit is air-assisted and has a 4 position remote damping adjuster. The air pressure valve and damping adjuster are situated behind the right-hand sidepanel, with the exception of the damping adjuster on ZX1000 B models, which is located in the right-hand frame member.

Air pressure should be checked with the machine on its centre stand and the suspension unit cold, ie at room temperature. Remove the right-hand sidepanel and check the air pressure in the unit via the frame mounted valve. Take note of the figures given in the table below, and adjust as necessary. Note that on no account must the pressure in the suspension unit ever exceed 5 kg/cm² (71 psi) as this will almost certainly damage the seals.

	Standard pressure	Usable range
ZX900	0.5 kg/cm² (7 psi)	0.5 – 1.5 kg/cm² (7 – 21 psi)
ZX1000 A	0.5 kg/cm² (7 psi)	0 – 1.5 kg/cm² (0 – 21 psi)
ZX1000 B	Atmospheric	0 – 1 kg/cm² (0 – 14 psi)

Damping is adjusted using the frame-mounted remote adjuster. The unit has 4 positions, position 1 being the softest and position 4 the hardest. The recommended position to comply with the standard air pressure is No.3 for ZX900 models and No.2 for ZX1000 models.

On ZX900 models the adjuster positions are indicated by the numbers on the top surface of the knob, the highest number visible being the present position. The settings are adjusted either by pushing or pulling the knob until the desired setting is reached. Position 4 is when the knob is fully extended and position 1 when the knob is fully pushed in. Positions 2 and 3 are the two click stops in between.

On ZX1000 models the damping setting is adjusted by rotating the knob until the required number aligns with the triangular indicator mark. On ZX1000 A models the indicator mark is situated at the bottom of the adjuster mounting bracket and the numbers are on the wheel, whereas on ZX1000 B models the indicator mark is on the knob and the numbers are situated on the outer edge. *Note that on ZX1000 A models the adjusting knob will only rotate in an anticlockwise (counterclockwise) direction. Do not attempt to turn it in a clockwise direction.*

Ensure both the damping and air pressure are set to the required settings and refit the sidepanel.

ZX1100 C models
The rear suspension unit is linked to a pressurised remote oil reservoir and features a 4 position damping adjuster. The spring preload can also be adjusted but this is a complicated and time-consuming job which requires the removal of the suspension unit from the frame (see below). Therefore, it is recommended that it should only be carried out if absolutely necessary.

The damping adjuster is situated on the lower end of the suspension unit, and can be adjusted from underneath the machine. Position the machine on its centre stand. Access to the adjuster wheel can be gained from the right-hand side of the machine after removing the plastic cover situated just above the suspension unit lower mounting bolt. The present position is indicated by the Roman numeral visible on the edge of the adjuster wheel. Position I is the softest setting and position IIII the hardest; the standard setting being position II. If necessary, adjust the setting by turning the wheel until it clicks into the required position. Note that the adjuster wheel will turn in one direction only, towards the front of the machine. *Do not attempt to force it in the opposite direction.* Once the adjuster is correctly set, refit the plastic cover to prevent the entry of dirt and water.

As mentioned previously, it is not necessary to check the spring preload adjustment unless handling problems have occurred. Remove the rear suspension unit from the machine as described in Chapter 5. Accurately measure the length of the suspension unit spring and note this measurement down. Slacken the large locknut and spring adjusting nut, using a suitable C-spanner, until all spring pressure acting on the adjusting nut is released. Measure the free length of the spring at this point. Subtract the first measurement (compressed length) from the second measurement (free length) to obtain the present spring preload distance; this can then be compared with the standard setting and, if necessary, adjusted.

The recommended standard setting for the spring preload is 18 mm (0.71 in), although a tolerance of 14 – 30 mm (0.55 – 1.18 in) is allowed for further adjustment. The actual amount of preload will depend very much on the use to which the machine is put. To increase the preload and stiffen the ride the spring preload distance should be increased, and to decrease the preload and soften the ride the preload should be decreased. The extent of adjustment is very much a case of trial and error, and it may be worth seeking the advise of an authorised Kawasaki dealer in this respect.

Set the spring compression to the required distance using the adjusting nut, and then tighten the large locknut securely. Refit the suspension unit to the machine as described in Chapter 5.

3 Check the clutch and brake fluid levels
Note: brake fluid is an excellent paint stripper and will attack painted and plastic components. Wash away any spilt fluid immediately with copious quantities of water.

To check the fluid level in the front brake and clutch master cylinders, turn the handlebars until the reservoir is horizontal and check that the fluid level, as seen through the sightglass in the reservoir body,

Front brake and clutch fluid level is checked via the sightglass – level must be above cast mark on reservoir body ...

... if not, top up fluid level to the upper mark cast on the front inside face of reservoir

Electrolyte level must be between marks on casing

is not below the lower level mark. The mark is in the form of a raised line cast into the reservoir body.

On the rear brake reservoir, located behind the right-hand sidepanel (ZX900 and 1000 models) or under the seat (ZX1100 models), the fluid level is visible through the translucent material of the reservoir; it should be between the upper and lower level marks on the side of the reservoir.

In all cases, if the fluid level is on or below the lower level mark, there is a risk of air entering the hydraulic system and the level should be topped up immediately. Wipe the reservoir clean of any dirt and remove both the retaining screws. Lift off the cover or unscrew the reservoir cap (as applicable) and remove the diaphragm; note that later models have a plate fitted above the diaphragm on the front reservoir. Using a good quality brake fluid of the recommended type, from a freshly opened container, top up the reservoir to the upper level mark. On the front brake and clutch reservoirs, the upper level mark is in the form of a line, cast on the inside of the front face of the reservoir.

When the fluid level is correct, clean and dry the diaphragm, fold it into its compressed state and refit it, together with the plate (later models), to the reservoir. Refit the reservoir cover and retaining screws or the reservoir cap and tighten it securely. Check the operation of the clutch and braking system before taking the machine out on the road; if there is evidence of air in the system, it must be bled as described in Chapter 6.

4 Check the battery

The battery is situated under the seat, which must be removed to gain access to it. Due to its location, it will be necessary to remove the battery from the machine to check the electrolyte level. On the ZX1100 C model the seat hook bracket must first be removed. Release the rubber retaining strap, disconnect the leads from the battery terminals and lift the battery out of the machine. Note that whenever the battery leads are disconnected, always disconnect the negative (-) terminal first to prevent the possibility of short circuits.

The electrolyte level, visible through the translucent casing, should be between the two level marks on the battery casing. If not, remove the cell caps and top up to the upper level mark using only distilled water. Check that the terminals are clean and apply a thin smear of petroleum jelly (not grease) to them to prevent corrosion.

Check the battery for any signs of pale grey sediment at the bottom of the casing. This is caused by sulphation of the plates as a result of re-charging at too high a rate or as a result of the battery being left discharged for long periods. A good battery should have little or no sediment visible and its plates should be straight and pale grey or brown in colour. If sediment deposits are deep enough to reach the bottom of the plates, or if the plates are buckled and have whitish deposits on them, the battery is faulty and must be renewed. Remember that a poor battery will give rise to a large number of minor electrical faults.

On refitting, check that the breather hose is not blocked and is correctly routed, and secure the battery with its retaining strap. Connect up the battery terminals, remembering to connect the negative (-) terminal last. Ensure the terminals are tight and that the rubber cover is correctly fitted over the positive (+) terminal. Check the junction box fuses are of the correct ratings and in good condition, and that spare fuses of both ratings (10 and 30A) are available on the machine should the need arise.

If the machine is not in regular use, disconnect the battery and give it a refresher charge every month to six weeks, as described in Chapter 7.

Every 3000 miles (5000 km)

Carry out all the checks given under the previous headings, then carry out the following:

1 Check the spark plugs

Remove the fuel tank as described in Chapter 3. On ZX1100 C models remove the front section of the air filter housing and on ZX1000 A models the top section of the air filter housing, each being retained by four screws. Carefully pull off the spark plug caps and remove any dirt or other foreign matter from the spark plug channels. Using only the correct tool, unscrew and remove the spark plugs whilst keeping them clearly defined by their cylinder number.

Using feeler gauges, preferably of the wire type for greater accuracy, measure the gap between the electrodes and compare it with the figure given in the Specifications. If adjustment is required this can be carried out as described below, assuming that the plug is otherwise un-damaged. In the event that any plug is heavily fouled or damaged in any way renewal is required; renew the plugs as a set. On UK models always ensure that the plugs are of the resistor type (indicated by the letter R) so that its resistance value is correct for the ignition system. The same applies to the suppressor caps if these are ever renewed.

If the spark plugs are still serviceable, carefully compare the appearance of their electrodes with the accompanying colour section and note any information which can be obtained from this. If any plug appears to show a fault, seek expert advice as soon as possible. The standard grade of spark plug should prove adequate in all normal use and a change of specification (such as fitting a hotter or colder grade of plug) should not be made without expert advice from an authorized Kawasaki dealer.

Spark plugs can be removed using plug spanner supplied in machine's tool kit

Clean the plug electrodes by carefully scraping away the accumulated carbon deposits using a small knife blade or small files and abrasive paper; take care not to bend the centre electrode or to chip or damage the ceramic insulator. The cleaning of spark plugs on commercial sand-blasting equipment is **not** recommended due to the risk of abrasive particles being jammed in the gap between the insulator and the plug metal body, only to fall clear later and drop into the engine; any plug that is so heavily fouled should be renewed.

Once clean, file the opposing faces of the electrodes flat using a small fine file. A magneto file or even a nail file can be used for this purpose. Whichever method is chosen, make sure that every trace of abrasive and loose carbon is removed before the plug is refitted. If this is not done, the debris will enter the engine and cause damage or rapid wear.

Whether a cleaned or new plug is to be fitted, always check the electrode gap before it is installed. Use a spark plug adjusting tool or feeler gauges to measure the gap, and if adjustment is required, bend the outer, earth electrode only. *Never bend the centre electrode or the ceramic insulator nose will be damaged.*

Before the plugs are fitted, apply a fine coat of PBC or molybdenum disulphide grease to their threads. This will help prevent thread wear and damage on refitting and make their subsequent removal easier. Fit each plug finger-tight, then tighten it by a further ¼ turn only, to ensure a gas-tight seal. Beware of overtightening, and always use a plug spanner or socket of the correct size; tighten all plugs to the specified torque setting, where possible.

Never overtighten a spark plug otherwise there is a risk of stripping the thread from the cylinder head, especially as it is cast in light alloy. A stripped thread can be repaired without having to scrap the cylinder head by using a 'Helicoil' thread insert. This is a low-cost service, operated by a number of dealers.

When refitting the spark plug suppressor caps, ensure that the HT leads are correctly routed; note that the leads are numbered as an aid to identification.

2 Check the fuel and oil lines

Give all the fuel hoses a close visual examination checking for cracks or any sign of leakage. In time, the synthetic rubber pipe will tend to deteriorate, and will eventually leak. Apart from the obvious fire risk, the leaking fuel will affect fuel economy. The pipe will usually split only at the ends; if there is sufficient spare length the damaged portion can be cut off and the pipe refitted. The seal is effected by the interference fit of the pipe on the spigot; although the wire clips are only an additional security measure they should always be refitted correctly and should be renewed if damaged, twisted or no longer effective. If the pipe is to be renewed, always use the correct replacement type and size of neoprene tubing to ensure a good leak-proof fit. Never use natural rubber tubing, as this tends to break up when in contact with petrol (gasoline) and will obstruct carburettor jets, or clear plastic tubing which stiffens to the point of being brittle when in contact with petrol and will produce leaks that are difficult to cure.

Also give the oil cooler hoses a close inspection for signs of deterioration or leakage. If any hose is damaged it must be renewed as described in Chapter 3.

Owners of US machines should also examine the clean air system hoses, and on California models, the emission control system. Any faulty component must be renewed using only genuine Kawasaki replacement parts. Refer to Chapter 3 for further information on the clean air and emission control systems.

3 Check the air suction valves – US models

In order to gain access to the valves it is necessary to remove the lower and side fairing sections and the fuel tank as described for cylinder head cover removal in Chapter 1, Section 6.

Slacken their spring clips and pull the vacuum valve switch pipes off the air suction valve covers. Remove each air suction valve after releasing its two bolts. Inspect the reeds for distortion, cracks or any other damage and their contact surface on the cover for scratches or deterioration; if found, the assembly should be renewed. If carbon deposits have built up in the assembly, these must be cleaned off with a high flash-point solvent.

On reassembly install a new gasket between the air suction valve cover and cylinder head cover and tighten the bolts securely.

4 Check and synchronise the carburettors

Start by ensuring that the throttle cable(s) operate smoothly and are correctly adjusted. There should be 2 – 3 mm (0.08 – 0.12 in) of free play which is measured in terms of twistgrip rotation.

As ZX900 A1 and A2 models only use one throttle cable the freeplay is adjusted simply by slackening the locknut on the handlebar mounted adjuster and turning the adjuster until the required amount of freeplay is obtained. If there is insufficient adjustment at the handlebar adjuster it will be necessary to use the lower adjuster situated midway along the cable's length. This adjuster should be accessible from the left-hand front edge of the fuel tank, if not it will be necessary to remove the fuel tank as described in Chapter 3. Screw the handlebar adjuster fully in and tighten its locknut. Loosen the locknut on the lower cable adjuster and rotate the adjuster until the required amount of free play is obtained, then tighten its locknut securely.

All other models use two throttle cables, an accelerator and decelerator cable. If adjustment is needed, first try to obtain the required amount of free play by slackening the locknut and turning the handlebar-mounted adjuster on the accelerator cable. If this fails to give enough free play it will be necessary to remove the fuel tank, as described in Chapter 3, and adjust the cables using the lower adjusters. Note that on ZX1000 A models access to the adjusters will be greatly improved if the top section of the air filter housing is also removed. On ZX900 A3 onwards and ZX1000 models these adjusters are at the bottom of the cables and are located on the carburettor mounting brackets, the rear adjuster is for the accelerator cable and the front one for the decelerator cable. On ZX1100 C models the adjusters are situated midway along the length of the cables and are accessible from the front of the air filter housing, the right-hand adjuster is for the accelerator cable and the centre one for the decelerator cable.

Release their locknuts and fully slacken all the cable adjusters to obtain the maximum free play possible. Whilst holding the twistgrip closed, slowly turn the decelerator cable adjuster until all the slack has been removed and the cable is just becoming tight, then tighten its locknut securely. Rotate the lower accelerator cable adjuster until the correct amount of free play is obtained at the twistgrip, and securely tighten both the lower and handlebar adjuster locknuts. On ZX1000 A models refit the air filter top cover.

Throttle cable freeplay is measured in terms of twistgrip rotation

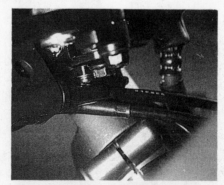
Handlebar-mounted upper throttle cable adjuster

On ZX1100 C models lower throttle and choke cable adjusters are situated just in front of air filter housing

Spark plug maintenance: Checking plug gap with feeler gauges

Altering the plug gap. Note use of correct tool

Spark plug conditions: A brown, tan or grey firing end is indicative of correct engine running conditions and the selection of the appropriate heat rating plug

White deposits have accumulated from excessive amounts of oil in the combustion chamber or through the use of low quality oil. Remove deposits or a hot spot may form

Black sooty deposits indicate an over-rich fuel/air mixture, or a malfunctioning ignition system. If no improvement is obtained, try one grade hotter plug

Wet, oily carbon deposits form an electrical leakage path along the insulator nose, resulting in a misfire. The cause may be a badly worn engine or a malfunctioning ignition system

A blistered white insulator or melted electrode indicates over-advanced ignition timing or a malfunctioning cooling system. If correction does not prove effective, try a colder grade plug

A worn spark plug not only wastes fuel but also overloads the whole ignition system because the increased gap requires higher voltage to initiate the spark. This condition can also affect air pollution

Choke mechanism is situated on the left-hand side of carburettor
bank – plunger must operate smoothly

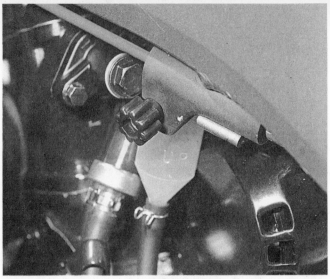

Idle speed adjuster is situated on left-hand side carburettors – ZX1100
C shown

On all models start the engine and allow it to idle, then move the
handlebars from lock to lock. If the idle speed rises and falls as the
handlebars are turned the throttle cable(s) are incorrectly routed. To
remedy, remove the retaining screws from the right-hand handlebar
switch and separate the two halves of the switch. Disconnect the
cable(s) from the twistgrip and reroute them along the smoothest
possible route, ensuring that they are not kinked or could foul any other
component. Before connecting the throttle cable(s) lubricate them as
described in operation 8 of this service interval, then reconnect the
cable(s) and check the free play, adjusting again if necessary.

Once the throttle cable adjustment is correctly set, go on to check
the operation of the choke mechanism, especially if the machine has
been difficult to start when cold, or a rich fuel mixture is indicated. This
can be checked by operating the handlebar mounted choke lever whilst
observing the choke mechanism of the left-hand carburettor. The choke
mechanism should extend smoothly when the lever is pulled, and
return fully home when the lever is returned. If the choke does not
operate smoothly this is probably due to a cable fault. Remove the
retaining screws from the left-hand handlebar switch and disconnect
the cable at its upper end. Reroute the cable so it takes the smoothest
route possible and lubricate it as described in operation 7 of this service.
Reconnect the cable and tighten the handlebar switch screws securely.
If this fails to improve the operation of the choke the cable must be
renewed. Note that in very extreme cases the fault could be in the
carburettors rather than the cable, necessitating the removal of the
carburettors and examination of the choke plungers as described in
Chapter 3.

Once the choke is operating smoothly it is necessary to check the
amount of cable free play. The free play is measured at the base of the
operating lever where there should be 2 – 3 mm (0.08 – 0.12 in) of travel

in the lever before the choke mechanism on the left-hand carburettor
begins to move. The cable is adjusted by slackening the locknut and
turning the adjuster until the correct amount of free play is obtained. On
most models the adjuster is situated at the mid-point of the cable,
although on some early ZX900 A1 models it is situated on the underside
of the left-hand handlebar switch. Once the cable is correctly adjusted
securely tighten the adjuster locknut.

When both the throttle and choke cables are correctly adjusted and
operating smoothly check that the carburettors are correctly synchronised, as described in Chapter 3, and then check the idle speed.

Idle speed should be checked with the engine at its normal running
temperature, preferably after the machine has been on a short run.
Allow the engine to idle and check that it runs at the specified speed
given in the Specifications. Make any adjustment to the idle speed using
the adjuster knob situated on the left-hand side of the carburettors.
Open and close the throttle a few times to check that the setting has not
changed.

5 Check the brake pads

The hydraulic brake requires no regular adjustment as pad wear is
compensated for by the entry of more fluid into the system from the
fluid reservoir. All that is necessary is to keep a regular check on the fluid
level (see 500 mile service) and the degree of pad wear. To check the
condition of the brake pads it is necessary to remove the caliper from
the machine.

Front brake

On all models except the ZX900 A1 to A6, the front brake calipers
can be removed by simply removing their mounting bolts and lifting
them off the discs. On ZX900 A1 to A6 models, however, it is first
necessary to remove the front wheel, as described in Chapter 6. Once
the caliper is free from its mountings note that it is not necessary to
disconnect the hydraulic hose if care is taken not to place any strain on
the hose, such as allowing the caliper to hang by its hose without
support.

To remove the brake pads on ZX900 A1 to A6 and ZX1000 models,
first detach the piston-side pad and remove it from the caliper mounting
bracket. Remove both the small pad springs that are fitted to the bracket
on each side of the brake pad. Make a note of the way these springs are
fitted to ensure they are positioned correctly on reassembly. Push the
caliper bracket towards the caliper itself and manoeuvre the second
brake pad off the pins of the caliper bracket.

On ZX900 A7-on and ZX1100 C models, release both the pad spring
retaining screws from the top of the caliper and lift off the pad spring.
Remove the R-clip from the pad retaining pin and withdraw the pin from
the caliper. The pads can then be slid out of the caliper body for
inspection.

On all models, inspect the surface of each pad for contamination and
measure the thickness of the friction material. If either pad is worn to or
beyond the service limit at any point, fouled with oil or grease, or heavily

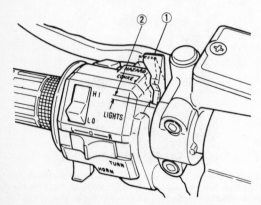

Choke lever free play measurement

1 Choke lever   *2   2 – 3 mm free play*

Front brake calipers are retained by two bolts

On ZX900 A7 and ZX1100 C models, remove its screws and lift off pad spring ...

... withdraw R-clip and slide out pad retaining pin ...

... pads can then be removed from caliper

Remove rear caliper mounting bolts and slide caliper off disc

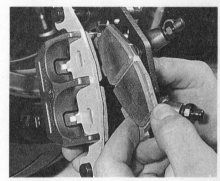

Remove the piston side pad ...

... followed by the larger inner pad

On refitting ensure pad springs are correctly fitted. Do not omit the piston insulators (where fitted)

On ZX900 models it is necessary to remove the footrest bracket to adjust the brake pedal and stop lamp switch

scored or damaged by dirt and debris, they must be renewed as a set. Note that it is not possible to degrease the friction material; if the pads are contaminated in any way they must be renewed. If the pads are in good condition clean them carefully, using a fine wire brush which is completely free of oil or grease, to remove all traces of road dirt and corrosion. *Take great care not to inhale any brake dust during the operation, and read the notes given in 'Safety first!' concerning asbestos.* Use a pointed instrument to clean out the grooves in the friction material and to dig out any embedded particles of foreign matter (as applicable). Any areas of glazing may be removed using emery cloth.

On ZX900 A1 to A6 and ZX1000 models, before refitting the pads check that the caliper slides easily along its mounting bracket and that the rubber dust boots are in a good condition. If not, separate the caliper and mounting bracket, remove any traces of old grease or corrosion from the sliding pins of the bracket and examine them for wear. If the pins are bent or damaged in any way the mounting bracket must be renewed. If necessary, also renew the dust boots. On reassembly apply PBC (Poly Butyl Cuprysil) grease to all sliding surfaces and refit the bracket to the caliper, ensuring that the rubber dust boots are correctly

seated and the large pad spring fitted to the roof of the caliper is in position. Refit the pad springs to the caliper bracket, using the notes made on dismantling to position them correctly, and push the caliper bracket towards the caliper. Push the piston(s) as far back into the caliper as possible by hand only; this is especially important if new pads are being fitted, due to the increased friction material thickness. Fit the larger pad over the pins of the bracket (friction material facing the piston) and then fit the smaller pad into the bracket whilst ensuring the pad springs remain in position.

On ZX900 A7-on and ZX1100 C models, remove all traces of corrosion from the pad retaining pin and smear a small amount of PBC grease along it. Slide the pads back into the caliper, noting that if new pads are being fitted the pistons must be pushed back into their bores to provide sufficient room. Insert the pad retaining pin and secure it with the R-clip. Ensure that the pin is fitted with the small hole for the R-clip facing the outside edge of the caliper and that the R-clip does not trap the outside pad when in position. Check that both pads move freely along the retaining pin, then refit the pad spring and tighten its retaining screws securely.

On all models, refit the calipers to the machine and tighten the mounting bolts to the specified torque setting. On ZX900 A1 to A6 models refit the wheel as described in Chapter 6. Pump the brake lever repeatedly until the pads are pushed back against the discs and normal operation of the brake lever has returned. Check the fluid level in the reservoir as described in the 500 mile service, noting that if new brake pads have been fitted it may be necessary to remove fluid from the reservoir.

Before taking the machine on the road, check the hydraulic system for leaks and ensure that the braking system is operating correctly. Remember that new pads, and to a lesser extent, cleaned pads will not function at peak efficiency until they have bedded in. Where new pads have been fitted, use the brake gently but firmly for the first 50 – 100 miles.

Rear brake

On all models it is necessary to remove the brake caliper to gain access to the pads, although the hydraulic hose can be left attached if care is taken not to place any strain on it. On ZX900 and ZX1000 A models, it will first be necessary to remove the right-hand silencer. On all models, remove the caliper mounting bolts and slide the caliper off the disc.

The rear caliper fitted to ZX900 A1 to A6 and ZX1000 models is identical to the front caliper, and the rear caliper fitted to ZX900 A7-on and ZX1100 C models is identical to that fitted to the ZX1000 B model. Therefore the rear brake pads can be removed and inspected as described above for the ZX900 A1 to A6 and ZX1000 front brake caliper.

After the pads have been examined and the caliper is refitted to the machine it will be necessary to check the rear brake pedal height and the operation of the rear stop lamp switch.

Measure the vertical distance between the top of the footrest and the tip of the brake pedal. If this measurement differs greatly from the figure given in the Specifications, it should be adjusted. The pedal height is adjusted by altering the length of the rod which connects the pedal and master cylinder.

On ZX900 models, due to the location of the rod it will be necessary to remove the right-hand footrest bracket assembly to gain sufficient access. To remove the bracket, remove the right-hand sidepanel, slacken and remove the rear brake master cylinder and reservoir bolts and right-hand silencer mounting bolts, and disconnect the rear stop lamp switch wires. Then remove all the footrest bracket mounting bolts, including the swinging arm pivot nut, and remove the bracket assembly from the machine. Make adjustment by slackening the locknut (situated at the pedal end of the rod) and turning the adjusting nut, situated at the master cylinder end of the rod, until the correct pedal height is obtained. Once the pedal height is correct tighten the locknut securely and adjust the stop lamp switch as described below. Refit the footrest bracket to the machine, tightening all mounting nuts and bolts to the specified torque settings, where given, and reconnect the stop lamp switch wires.

On all other models the task is simplified because the adjuster is accessible without removing the footrest bracket. Remove the split pin from the clevis pin at the end of the master cylinder rod and withdraw the clevis pin to disconnect the rod from the brake pedal. Slacken the locknut which secures the forked end of the master cylinder rod, remove the master cylinder mounting bolts and partially remove the master cylinder. The rod length is adjusted by screwing the forked end of the rod either in or out to obtain the correct pedal height. On ZX1000 B and ZX1100 C models Kawasaki actually specify a measurement for the length of the rod. This measurement is taken parallel to the rod itself from the centre of the hole in the forked end of the rod to the centre of the first mounting bolt hole on the master cylinder, and should be 119 ± 1 mm (4.68 ± 0.04 in). On ZX1000 A models it is simply a case of trial and error to find the correct length, temporarily installing the master cylinder mounting bolts and clevis pin and rechecking after each adjustment until the pedal height is correct. Once the pedal height or rod length is correct, refit the master cylinder mounting bolts and install the clevis pin. Tighten the master cylinder mounting bolts and the connecting rod locknut securely, and secure the clevis pin with a new split pin.

On all models, once the brake pedal height is known to be correct it is necessary to check that the rear stop lamp switch is functioning correctly. This is done by measuring the amount of travel there is at the brake pedal tip before the stop lamp is illuminated. The stop lamp should come on after the brake pedal travels approximately 10 mm (0.4 in). The stop lamp is altered by turning the adjusting nut which is fitted to the switch whilst holding the body of the switch to prevent it from turning.

6 Check the final drive chain for wear

The manufacturer recommends that the chain be checked for wear at this interval. Refer to the Monthly service operations for details.

7 Check the steering

Place the machine on its centre stand and remove the lower fairing section (see Chapter 5). Raise the front wheel clear of the ground by placing a stand or some suitably sized blocks beneath the crankcase. Grasp the front fork legs near the wheel spindle and push and pull them firmly in a fore and aft direction to check for any free play in the steering head bearings. Check for overtightened bearings by placing the forks in the straight ahead position and tapping lightly on one end of the handlebars. The forks should move smoothly and easily to the opposite lock, taking into account the effect of the cables and wiring, with no trace of notchiness. If adjustment is required proceed as follows:

Remove the fuel tank as described in Chapter 3. On ZX900 A7-on and ZX1100 C models, prise out the large circular cap which covers the top yoke retaining nut, and on all other models remove the top yoke cover retaining screws and lift off the cover. On all models, slacken the top yoke retaining nut and all the bottom yoke pinch bolts.

Tighten or slacken (as applicable) the steering stem adjuster nut situated under the top yoke, using a suitable C-spanner, by approximately $\frac{1}{8}$ of a turn at a time until the handlebars turn freely from lock to lock and no free play can be felt when pushing and pulling the fork legs. Once the steering head bearings are correctly adjusted, tighten the top yoke retaining nut and all the bottom yoke pinch bolts to their specified torque settings. Refit the top yoke cover or cap (as applicable), and refit the fuel tank as described in Chapter 3. Finally remove the stand from beneath the crankcases and refit the lower fairing section.

8 Lubricate the cables, stands and controls

Check the outer cables for signs of damage, then examine the exposed portions of the inner cables. Any signs of kinking or fraying will indicate that renewal is required. To obtain maximum life and reliability from the cables they should be thoroughly lubricated. To do the job properly and quickly use one of the hydraulic cable oilers available from most motorcycle shops. Free one end of the cable and assemble the cable oiler as described by the manufacturer's instructions. Operate the oiler until oil emerges from the lower end, indicating that the cable is lubricated throughout its length. This process will expel any dirt or moisture and will prevent its subsequent ingress.

If a cable oiler is not available, an alternative is to remove the cable from the machine. Hang the cable upright and make up a small funnel arrangement using plasticine or by taping a plastic bag around the upper end as shown in the accompanying illustration. Fill the funnel with oil and leave it overnight to drain through. Note that where nylon-lined cables are fitted, they should be used dry or lubricated with a silicone-based lubricant suitable for this application. On no account use ordinary engine oil because this will cause the liner to swell, pinching the cable.

When refitting the cables, ensure that they are routed in easy curves and that full use is made of any guides or clamps that have been provided to secure the cable out of harm's way. Adjustment of the individual cables is described under the relevant routine maintenance headings.

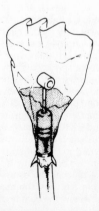

Method of oiling a control cable

The speedometer cable should be removed for examination and lubrication as described in Chapter 5.

Check all pivots and the control levers, cleaning and lubricating them to prevent wear and corrosion. Where necessary, dismantle and clean any moving part which may have become stiff in operation. Similarly clean and check both the centre and side stand pivot bolts for security and signs of wear, renewing them if necessary. Thoroughly grease the pivot bolts and ensure that the return springs hold both stands securely in the up positions when retracted.

Lubricate the handlebar, ignition and stop lamp switches with WD40 or a similar water dispersant spray. This will keep the switches working properly and prolong their life, especially if the machine is used in adverse weather conditions.

Every 6000 miles (10 000 km)

1 Change the engine/transmission oil and filter

It is important that the engine/transmission oil is changed at this interval to ensure adequate lubrication of the engine and transmission components. If regular oil changes are overlooked the prolonged use of degraded and contaminated oil will lead to premature engine wear. The oil should be changed with the engine at its normal operating temperature, after a short run. This ensures that the oil is relatively thin and will therefore drain quicker and more completely, also any impurities will be held in suspension.

Place the machine on its centre stand and remove the lower fairing section (see Chapter 5). Place a suitably-sized container, of at least 4.0 litres (7.1 Imp pint/4.2 US qt) capacity, beneath the engine unit and remove both drain plugs from the sump. As the engine will be hot, take great care to avoid scalding your hands on the escaping oil or on the exhaust system. Remove the oil filler plug to assist draining. Once the oil has drained from the engine unit slacken the single central bolt which retains the oil filter cover, noting that approximately another 0.5 litre of oil will be released as soon as the bolt is loosened, then lower the cover

away from the engine. Remove the element baffle, element, flat washer and spring from the filter cover and separate the cover and centre bolt. Clean all the filter components, except the element which should be discarded, and check both the sealing O-rings for signs of damage, renewing them if necessary.

Refit the centre bolt to the filter cover and fit the coil spring and flat washer over the centre bolt. Fit the new oil filter element by carefully screwing it onto the centre bolt to prevent damaging its sealing grommets; apply a smear of oil to the element seals to ease the operation. Place the element baffle over the top of the element and refit the filter assembly in the engine unit, ensuring that the large sealing O-ring on the cover is correctly positioned. Check the condition of the sealing washers on both the drain plugs, renewing them if damaged, then refit them in the sump. Tighten both drain plugs and the oil filter centre bolt to their specified torque settings.

Remove the filler plug from the top of the left-hand engine casing and fill the crankcases with the specified amount and grade of oil. Refit the filler plug and start the engine, allowing it to idle for a few minutes to distribute the new oil through the lubrication system. Switch off the engine and wait a few minutes to allow the oil level to settle. Check that the oil level is between the marks on the sightglass set in the left-hand casing and top up if necessary (see Daily/pre ride checks).

Although not specified as a regular maintenance item, the two filter screens situated in the sump should be removed and cleaned of any deposits with reasonable frequency. Access can be gained to the filters by removing the sump as described in Chapter 1. Information on cleaning will be found in Chapter 3, Section 17.

2 Clean the air filter element

The air filter element on ZX900 models is situated behind the left-hand sidepanel. With the sidepanel removed, release the two screws which retain the filter housing end cover and lift it clear. Pull out the plastic wedge which holds the element in place, and then withdraw the element from the housing.

On ZX1000 and ZX1100 models it will first be necessary to remove the fuel tank, as described in Chapter 3. On ZX1000 A models, remove the four screws that secure the top of the filter housing and lift it away.

Engine oil drain plugs are situated in the sump (front plug shown)

Renew its O-ring and refit centre bolt to filter cover

Refit the spring and flat washer ...

... and carefully screw on the new element

Fit the baffle plate over the element and a new O-ring to the cover ...

... and refit the filter assembly to the sump

On ZX900 models remove end cover from left-hand side of filter housing ...

... pull out the plastic wedge ...

... and withdraw the air filter element

On ZX1000 and ZX1100 C models ensure the element is refitted with the gauze on the carburettor side of the element ...

... and tighten all housing screws securely – ZX1100 C shown

On ZX1100 C models do not forget to clean the vent filter ...

The element can then be removed from the housing. On ZX1000 B models, slacken and remove the four Allen bolts from the top of the air filter housing and on ZX1100 C models remove the two screws which secure the rear section of the air filter housing to the rest of the assembly. Partially separate the air filter housing until the element can be withdrawn from the gap.

Check that the element is not split, hardened or severely clogged, renewing it if necessary. To clean the element, soak it in a high flash-point solvent such as white spirit (stoddard solvent); petrol (gasoline) is not recommended due to the fire risk. Squeeze it gently to remove any old oil and dirt, taking care not to break or deform the frame. Dry the element with compressed air or by shaking it and place the

element to one side to allow any remaining solvent to evaporate.

When it is completely dry, soak the element in a clean SE class SAE 30 motor oil and carefully squeeze out the excess oil. Wrap it in a clean rag and continue squeezing the element until it is as dry as possible and only slightly oily to the touch.

On refitting, check that the element is correctly seated and is secured by the plastic wedge (ZX900 models only). Note that on ZX1000 and ZX1100 models, ensure the element is positioned so that the gauze which supports the foam is on the carburettor side of the element. On all models reassemble the air filter housing, ensuring that all disturbed sections or covers are correctly seated, then tighten the retaining screws securely.

... and drain the filter housing reservoir ...

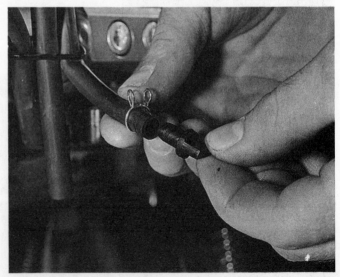

... by removing the plug from the bottom of its drain hose

Remember it is essential that the filter element and housing sections or covers are correctly positioned and seat well to prevent unfiltered air from entering and damaging the engine. The carburettor is jetted to compensate for the presence of the air filter element; if the element is damaged, severely blocked or bypassed in any way or omitted, serious engine damage could result. Owners of US machines should also note that the air filter is subject to the anti-tampering legislation currently in force (see Chapter 3). For this reason the engine should never be run with the air filter element removed or disconnected.

Note that this interval is the maximum for filter cleaning. If the machine is used in wet weather or very dirty or dusty conditions, the filter must be removed for cleaning more frequently.

On ZX1100 C models it will also be necessary to clean the small vent filter, located underneath the left-hand inner fairing section. Remove the inner fairing section (see Chapter 5) and disconnect the vent filter from its hose on the right-hand side of the main air duct. Before removing the filter, mark it in some way to ensure that it can be returned to its original position on refitting. Clean the filter by directing a jet of compressed air from the clean to the dirty side of the filter. Note that if the filter is damaged in any way it must be renewed. Refit the filter to the hose, using the mark made on removal to align it correctly, and secure with the hose clips. Also check the transparent oil reservoir, situated on the left-hand side of the engine next to the alternator, for any sign of oil. If oil is present in the reservoir it must be drained off by removing the plug from the bottom of the drain hose and draining the oil into a suitable container. When all oil has drained from the reservoir, refit the plug to the drain hose.

3 Renew the spark plugs

The spark plugs should be renewed at this interval regardless of their apparent condition as they will have passed peak efficiency. Check that the new plugs are of the correct type and heat range and are gapped correctly before fitting them.

4 Check and adjust the valve clearances

The valve clearances must be checked and adjusted with the engine cold, preferably after the machine has been left overnight. Remove the fuel tank, pulser coil cover and the cylinder head cover using the information given in the appropriate Chapters.

Using a spanner on the large hexagon nut on the left-hand end of the crankshaft, turn the crankshaft anticlockwise until the 1.4 T mark on the ignition rotor aligns with the index mark on the crankcase and number 4 cylinder is at TDC on its compression stroke (ie inlet valve has just closed). The index mark on the crankcase is in the form of a straight line which is situated just above the right-hand pulser coil. With the engine in this position check the inlet valve clearances of numbers 2 and 4 cylinders and the exhaust valve clearances of cylinders 3 and 4. Using feeler gauges, measure the clearance between the valve and adjusting screw tip or follower (as applicable). Turn the crankshaft through one complete turn (360°) so that number 1 cylinder is at TDC on its compression stroke, and check the inlet valve clearances on numbers 1 and 3 cylinders and the exhaust valve clearances on cylinders 1 and 2.

All clearances must be within the specified limits given in the Specifications. If any are less than specified, action must be taken immediately to prevent damage to the valve and valve seat. If any are larger than specified the error must still be corrected but the problem is not quite as serious. If necessary adjust the clearances using the relevant procedure given below.

On ZX900 and ZX1000 A models the valve clearances are adjusted via the screw and locknuts which are fitted to the cam followers. Slacken the locknut and turn the adjusting screw in or out until a feeler gauge of the appropriate size is a light sliding fit between the adjusting screw tip and valve. Hold the screw and tighten the locknut to the specified torque setting. Recheck the clearance after the locknut has been tightened and readjust if necessary. Repeat the above procedure for the second screw and locknut on the cam follower noting that it is essential that the clearance on both screws is identical.

The method of adjustment is slightly more complicated on ZX1000 B and ZX1100 C models due to the fact that the clearances are

VALVE CLEARANCE (mm)	PRESENT SHIM																				
PART NUMBER (92025–)	1870	1871	1872	1873	1874	1875	1876	1877	1878	1879	1880	1881	1882	1883	1884	1885	1886	1887	1888	1889	1890
THICKNESS (mm)	2.00	2.05	2.10	2.15	2.20	2.25	2.30	2.35	2.40	2.45	2.50	2.55	2.60	2.65	2.70	2.75	2.80	2.85	2.90	2.95	3.00
0.00 – 0.03				2.00	2.05	2.10	2.15	2.20	2.25	2.30	2.35	2.40	2.45	2.50	2.55	2.60	2.65	2.70	2.75	2.80	2.85
0.04 – 0.08			2.00	2.05	2.10	2.15	2.20	2.25	2.30	2.35	2.40	2.45	2.50	2.55	2.60	2.65	2.70	2.75	2.80	2.85	2.90
0.09 – 0.12		2.00	2.05	2.10	2.15	2.20	2.25	2.30	2.35	2.40	2.45	2.50	2.55	2.60	2.65	2.70	2.75	2.80	2.85	2.90	2.95
0.13 – 0.18	SPECIFIED CLEARANCE / NO CHANGE REQUIRED																				
0.19 – 0.23	2.05	2.10	2.15	2.20	2.25	2.30	2.35	2.40	2.45	2.50	2.55	2.60	2.65	2.70	2.75	2.80	2.85	2.90	2.95	3.00	
0.24 – 0.28	2.10	2.15	2.20	2.25	2.30	2.35	2.40	2.45	2.50	2.55	2.60	2.65	2.70	2.75	2.80	2.85	2.90	2.95	3.00		
0.29 – 0.33	2.15	2.20	2.25	2.30	2.35	2.40	2.45	2.50	2.55	2.60	2.65	2.70	2.75	2.80	2.85	2.90	2.95	3.00			
0.34 – 0.38	2.20	2.25	2.30	2.35	2.40	2.45	2.50	2.55	2.60	2.65	2.70	2.75	2.80	2.85	2.90	2.95	3.00				
0.39 – 0.43	2.25	2.30	2.35	2.40	2.45	2.50	2.55	2.60	2.65	2.70	2.75	2.80	2.85	2.90	2.95	3.00					
0.44 – 0.48	2.30	2.35	2.40	2.45	2.50	2.55	2.60	2.65	2.70	2.75	2.80	2.85	2.90	2.95	3.00						
0.49 – 0.53	2.35	2.40	2.45	2.50	2.55	2.60	2.65	2.70	2.75	2.80	2.85	2.90	2.95	3.00							
0.54 – 0.58	2.40	2.45	2.50	2.55	2.60	2.65	2.70	2.75	2.80	2.85	2.90	2.95	3.00								
0.59 – 0.63	2.45	2.50	2.55	2.60	2.65	2.70	2.75	2.80	2.85	2.90	2.95	3.00									
0.64 – 0.68	2.50	2.55	2.60	2.65	2.70	2.75	2.80	2.85	2.90	2.95	3.00										
0.69 – 0.73	2.55	2.60	2.65	2.70	2.75	2.80	2.85	2.90	2.95	3.00											
0.74 – 0.78	2.60	2.65	2.70	2.75	2.80	2.85	2.90	2.95	3.00												
0.79 – 0.83	2.65	2.70	2.75	2.80	2.85	2.90	2.95	3.00													
0.84 – 0.88	2.70	2.75	2.80	2.85	2.90	2.95	3.00														
0.89 – 0.93	2.75	2.80	2.85	2.90	2.95	3.00															
0.94 – 0.98	2.80	2.85	2.90	2.95	3.00																
0.99 – 1.03	2.85	2.90	2.95	3.00																	
1.04 – 1.08	2.90	2.95	3.00																		
1.09 – 1.13	2.95	3.00																			
1.14 – 1.18	3.00																				

INSTALL THE SHIM OF THIS THICKNESS (mm)

Inlet valve shim selection table

									PRESENT SHIM												
PART NUMBER (92025–)	1870	1871	1872	1873	1874	1875	1876	1877	1878	1879	1880	1881	1882	1883	1884	1885	1886	1887	1888	1889	1890
THICKNESS (mm)	2.00	2.05	2.10	2.15	2.20	2.25	2.30	2.35	2.40	2.45	2.50	2.55	2.60	2.65	2.70	2.75	2.80	2.85	2.90	2.95	3.00

VALVE CLEARANCE (mm)

Clearance	1870	1871	1872	1873	1874	1875	1876	1877	1878	1879	1880	1881	1882	1883	1884	1885	1886	1887	1888	1889	1890
0.00 – 0.03	░	░	░	░	2.00	2.05	2.10	2.15	2.20	2.25	2.30	2.35	2.40	2.45	2.50	2.55	2.60	2.65	2.70	2.75	2.80
0.04 – 0.08	░	░	░	2.00	2.05	2.10	2.15	2.20	2.25	2.30	2.35	2.40	2.45	2.50	2.55	2.60	2.65	2.70	2.75	2.80	2.85
0.09 – 0.13	░	░	2.00	2.05	2.10	2.15	2.20	2.25	2.30	2.35	2.40	2.45	2.50	2.55	2.60	2.65	2.70	2.75	2.80	2.85	2.90
0.14 – 0.17	░	2.00	2.05	2.10	2.15	2.20	2.25	2.30	2.35	2.40	2.45	2.50	2.55	2.60	2.65	2.70	2.75	2.80	2.85	2.90	2.95
0.18 – 0.23	SPECIFIED CLEARANCE / NO CHANGE REQUIRED																				
0.24 – 0.28	2.05	2.10	2.15	2.20	2.25	2.30	2.35	2.40	2.45	2.50	2.55	2.60	2.65	2.70	2.75	2.80	2.85	2.90	2.95	3.00	
0.29 – 0.33	2.10	2.15	2.20	2.25	2.30	2.35	2.40	2.45	2.50	2.55	2.60	2.65	2.70	2.75	2.80	2.85	2.90	2.95	3.00		
0.34 – 0.38	2.15	2.20	2.25	2.30	2.35	2.40	2.45	2.50	2.55	2.60	2.65	2.70	2.75	2.80	2.85	2.90	2.95	3.00			
0.39 – 0.43	2.20	2.25	2.30	2.35	2.40	2.45	2.50	2.55	2.60	2.65	2.70	2.75	2.80	2.85	2.90	2.95	3.00				
0.44 – 0.48	2.25	2.30	2.35	2.40	2.45	2.50	2.55	2.60	2.65	2.70	2.75	2.80	2.85	2.90	2.95	3.00					
0.49 – 0.53	2.30	2.35	2.40	2.45	2.50	2.55	2.60	2.65	2.70	2.75	2.80	2.85	2.90	2.95	3.00						
0.54 – 0.58	2.35	2.40	2.45	2.50	2.55	2.60	2.65	2.70	2.75	2.80	2.85	2.90	2.95	3.00							
0.59 – 0.63	2.40	2.45	2.50	2.55	2.60	2.65	2.70	2.75	2.80	2.85	2.90	2.95	3.00								
0.64 – 0.68	2.45	2.50	2.55	2.60	2.65	2.70	2.75	2.80	2.85	2.90	2.95	3.00									
0.69 – 0.73	2.50	2.55	2.60	2.65	2.70	2.75	2.80	2.85	2.90	2.95	3.00										
0.74 – 0.78	2.55	2.60	2.65	2.70	2.75	2.80	2.85	2.90	2.95	3.00											
0.79 – 0.83	2.60	2.65	2.70	2.75	2.80	2.85	2.90	2.95	3.00												
0.84 – 0.88	2.65	2.70	2.75	2.80	2.85	2.90	2.95	3.00													
0.89 – 0.93	2.70	2.75	2.80	2.85	2.90	2.95	3.00														
0.94 – 0.98	2.75	2.80	2.85	2.90	2.95	3.00															
0.99 – 1.03	2.80	2.85	2.90	2.95	3.00																
1.04 – 1.08	2.85	2.90	2.95	3.00																	
1.09 – 1.13	2.90	2.95	3.00																		
1.14 – 1.18	2.95	3.00																			
1.19 – 1.23	3.00																				

INSTALL THE SHIM OF THIS THICKNESS (mm)

Exhaust valve shim selection table

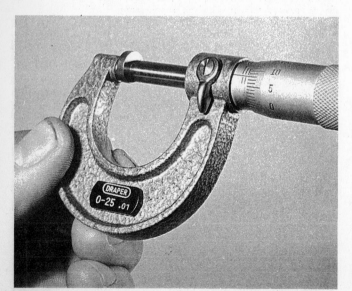

Shim thickness can be determined using a micrometer or vernier if numbers are illegible

altered by using shims of varying thicknesses. Measure the clearance between the valve and cam follower and make a note of this exact distance. Slide the cam follower to one side of the valve and carefully remove the shim from the top of the valve, using a magnet or pair of tweezers. The thickness of the shim should be printed on one side of it, if however the numbers are illegible the size of the shim can be determined by direct measurement using a micrometer or vernier caliper. Refer to the relevant accompanying table (inlet or exhaust), follow the vertical column down until the measured clearance is found (given in millimetres), then follow the top column across until the existing shim thickness is found. Where the two columns intersect the size of the required shim is given.

The shims can be purchased from an authorized Kawasaki dealer, but note that it may be possible to swap shims between the valves to reduce the cost. On no account use more than one shim on any valve, or grind the surface of a larger shim to make it smaller. Attempting to do either will almost certainly lead to extensive engine damage. Once the correct shim has been obtained, install it on the top of the valve (size marking facing downwards), ensuring that it is correctly seated in the valve spring retaining collar, then slide the cam follower back into position.

On all models recheck the valve clearances before refitting the cylinder head cover as described in Chapter 1.

Fortunately the valve clearances, once properly set, will not go out of adjustment for thousands of miles and the adjusting procedure will not be required very often. However they should still be checked at this interval to preserve engine performance and prevent the risk of engine damage. Always record all the information (original clearance and shim thickness, new clearance and shim thickness) so that an accurate picture of the valve gear and its rate of wear can be built up. This information will also greatly assist any future adjustments which are needed.

On ZX1100 C models fuel filter is separate from the fuel tap and is a screw fit in the tank

5 Clean or renew the fuel filter

Note: *Petrol (gasoline) is extremely flammable, especially when in the form of vapour. Take all precautions to prevent the risk of fire and read the Safety first! section of this manual before starting work.*

Prior to cleaning the fuel filters drain a small amount of fuel from the carburettor float chambers and check for contamination. Set the fuel tap to the PRI position and, dealing with one carburettor at a time, attach a short length of hose to the stub on the bottom of the float chamber and place the end in a clear glass container. Unscrew the drain screw on the float chamber by a few turns and allow a small amount of fuel to drain into the container. Tighten the drain screw. Note that if difficulty is experienced in gaining access to the drain screws on ZX1000 B and ZX1100 C models, a service tool is available under Part no. 57001-1269. If the drained fuel shows signs of water contamination or dirt, the fuel system components must be dismantled and thoroughly cleaned as described in Chapter 3.

On ZX900 and ZX1000 models remove the fuel tap, as described in Chapter 3, and remove the gauze filter(s) from the tap assembly. On ZX1100 C models the fuel tap filter is situated on the underside of the tank and is separate from the tap assembly. The filter is a screw fit into the tank and is joined to the tap by a short length of hose.

These filters can be cleaned by washing them in clean petrol (gasoline). If the filter is cracked or badly clogged it should be renewed. Check that the sealing O-ring is in good condition and then refit the filter or fuel tap assembly to the tank. Do not overtighten the filter or tap components as they are easily damaged.

The ZX1000 B and ZX1100 C models are fitted with a second fuel filter which filters the fuel before entering the fuel pump. It is not possible to clean the filter; it should be renewed at this interval as described in Chapter 3.

6 Change the front fork oil

The fork oil should be changed at regular intervals to prevent the inevitable reduction in fork performance which results as the oil deteriorates in service.

ZX900 A1 to A6 and ZX1000 A models

Place the machine on its centre stand and release the fork air pressure by depressing the air valve(s). On ZX900 A2 to A6 models, unscrew the large top bolts from the top of each fork leg.

With the forks fully extended unscrew the top plug from one of the fork legs, noting that the plug may be expelled forcibly as the last threads are released. Lift out the fork spring. Remove the drain plug from the lower leg and allow the oil to drain into a suitable container; pump the fork legs up and down to assist draining. It is advisable to place a large piece of card against the wheel to prevent oil running onto the tyre. Once all the oil has drained clean the threads of the drain plug and its threaded hole. Apply a

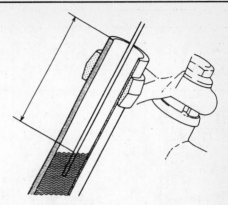

Front fork oil level check

small amount of liquid gasket to the threads of the drain plug, to ensure an oil-tight seal, and tighten it securely.

Pour in the specified amount of oil and then gently pump the forks to expel any air which may be trapped. Remove the lower fairing section (see Chapter 5) and raise the front wheel clear of the ground by placing blocks or a suitable stand beneath the crankcase so that the forks are fully extended. Using a dipstick (a length of welding rod or a steel rule is ideal) check the level of the oil below the top of the stanchion as shown in the accompanying illustration. If necessary, add or subtract oil until the level is correct, then refit the fork spring and top plug and tighten the top plug to the specified torque setting. On ZX900 A2 to A6 models, refit the top bolt and tighten it to the specified torque setting.

Repeat the above procedure on the other fork leg, then set the air pressure as described in the Monthly interval. Remove the stand from beneath the crankcase and refit the lower fairing section.

ZX900 A7-on and ZX1000 B models

On ZX1000 B models first remove the two screws which retain the top yoke cover and lift it clear of the machine. On both models, unscrew the handlebar casting mounting bolts and remove the bars from the top yoke. Support the handlebars to avoid placing any strain on the hydraulic hoses and to prevent the possible spillage of fluid from the master cylinder reservoirs. Remove the lower fairing section (see Chapter 5) and raise the front wheel clear of the ground by placing blocks or a suitable stand beneath the crankcase. With the forks fully extended, remove the fork top plugs, noting that they may be expelled forcibly as the last threads are released. Withdraw the fork spring from each leg. Place a large piece of card against the wheel to prevent oil running onto the tyre and remove the drain plugs from the lower legs, catching the oil in a suitable container. Pump the forks up and down to assist the draining of the oil. When all the oil has drained clean the drain plug and its threaded hole. Apply a liquid gasket to the threads of the drain plug, to ensure an oil tight seal, and tighten it securely.

Add the specified amount of oil to each fork leg (where given) and pump the forks gently to expel air which may be trapped. Measure the level of the fork oil from the top of the stanchion, using a steel ruler or a dipstick fabricated from a length of welding rod; note that the fork legs must be fully compressed when the measurement is taken. The easiest way to achieve this is to remove the stand from under the crankcase and allow the weight of the machine to compress them. If necessary, add or subtract oil until the level is correct. Reposition the stand beneath the crankcase and refit the fork spring and top plug to each leg; tighten the top plugs to the specified torque setting. Remount the handlebars onto the top yoke, tightening their mounting bolts to the specified torque setting, and on ZX1000 B models refit the top yoke cover.

ZX1100 C models

Due to the lack of a drain plug on the lower fork legs, it is necessary to remove the fork legs from the machine, as described in Chapter 5, and invert them to change the front fork oil. After refilling with the specified quantity of oil, check the oil level as described above; note that the forks must be fully compressed when the level check is made.

7 Check the cooling system and clean the coolant filter

With reference to Chapter 2, check the cooling system for leaks or any damaged components. Pay particular attention to the hoses and check that all hose clips are correctly positioned and securely fastened.

Coolant filter (UK models) is located on the right-hand side of the carburettors – ZX900 shown

Where provided, lubricate swinging arm and suspension linkage via the grease nipples

On UK models, the carburettor warmer (coolant) hose filter (if fitted) should also be removed and cleaned at this service interval. The filter is located on the front right-hand side of the carburettors. On ZX1000 B and ZX1100 C models it will be necessary to remove the right-hand lower fairing section to gain access to it (see Chapter 5).

Mark the filter as an aid to reassembly and disconnect it from the coolant hoses. Swiftly plug the ends of the hoses with a suitably-sized clean screw or bolt to prevent the coolant from escaping and mop up any spilt coolant immediately. The filter can be cleaned by directing a jet of compressed air through it from the carburettor side of the filter to dislodge and remove any particles of foreign matter. If the filter is severely blocked or damaged in any way it must be renewed.

Refit the filter to the coolant hoses, using the mark made on dismantling to return it to its original position, and secure it with the hose clips. Refit the lower fairing section (if removed) and top up the cooling system if necessary.

8 Lubricate the swinging arm and suspension linkage bearings

To ensure the rear suspension functions correctly and that the bearings in the swinging arm and suspension linkage do not fail prematurely it is essential to lubricate all the swinging arm and rear suspension pivots regularly. On ZX1000 B and ZX1100 C models this task is simplified by the fitting of grease nipples at all the pivot points. A grease gun can be used to force molybdenum disulphide grease into the bearings until grease is expelled from both ends of the bearing. On ZX1000 A models, a grease nipple is fitted to the relay arm pivot.

All the pivot points on ZX900 models, and the remaining pivot points on ZX1000 A models are not equipped with grease nipples. Therefore the suspension linkage and swinging arm must be removed from the machine to lubricate the bearings. Refer to Chapter 5 for information on all operations involving the swinging arm and rear suspension linkage.

9 General check

Work around the machine checking all nuts and bolts for tightness. Pay particular attention to the engine mountings, exhaust mountings, rear suspension and swinging arm bolts, top and bottom yoke pinch bolts, rear sprocket nuts, footrest bolts, front wheel spindle nut and all the brake caliper bolts. Where possible, use a torque wrench to check that all fasteners are tightened to their specified torque settings. Note that the cylinder head bolts must also be check tightened at this interval – refer to Chapter 1.

Every 12 000 miles (20 000 km)

1 Renew the air filter element

The air filter element should be renewed at this interval or every five cleanings, whichever comes first. Details of element removal can be

found under the 6000 mile (10 000 km) service interval.

2 Renew the brake and clutch fluid

Note: *brake fluid is an excellent paint stripper and will attack painted and plastic components. Wash away any spilt fluid immediately with copious quantities of water.*

The hydraulic fluid must be renewed at this interval or every two years to preserve maximum brake/clutch efficiency by ensuring the fluid has not been contaminated and deteriorated to an unsafe level.

Before starting work, obtain a new, sealed can of the recommended hydraulic fluid and carefully read the Section on bleeding in Chapter 6. Prepare the clear plastic tube and glass jar in the same way as for bleeding, then open the bleed nipple and apply the lever or pedal (as applicable) repeatedly. This will pump out the old fluid. **Note:** keep the master cylinder reservoir topped up at all times, otherwise air will enter the system and greatly lengthen the operation. The old hydraulic fluid is invariably darker in colour than the new, making it easier to see when it is pumped out and the new fluid has replaced it.

When the new fluid appears in the clear plastic tubing completely uncontaminated by traces of old brake fluid, close the bleed nipple and remove the plastic tubing. Refit the bleed nipple cap. Top up the master cylinder reservoir as described under the Monthly interval, and wash off any spilt fluid immediately. Finally check that the clutch/braking system is operating correctly before taking the machine on the road.

3 Grease the steering head bearings

The steering head bearings must be lubricated at this interval or every two years, whichever comes first.

Refer to the relevant Sections of Chapter 5 and dismantle the steering head. Clean all the components and examine them for wear, renewing any worn items. Reassemble the steering head and lubricate the bearings with fresh grease.

Every 24 000 miles (30 000 km)

1 Renew the coolant

The coolant must be renewed at this interval or every two years, whichever comes first.

To minimise the build-up of deposits in the cooling system and to ensure the maximum protection against freezing, the cooling system should be checked for leakage and damage, drained completely, flushed out and filled with fresh coolant as described in Chapter 2.

Additional routine maintenance

1 Overhaul the hydraulic brake and clutch components

At intervals of every two years, the master cylinders, brake calipers and clutch slave cylinder should be dismantled and checked. This is because their seals will deteriorate whether the machine is ridden regularly or hardly at all. The seals should be renewed regardless of their apparent condition and the master cylinder, slave cylinder and caliper bores checked carefully for wear or damage. Refer to Chapter 6 for further information.

2 Renew all hydraulic hoses and fuel lines

The hydraulic hoses and fuel lines should be renewed every four years regardless of their external appearance. After this period of time the synthetic material of the hoses is likely to have deteriorated significantly and for reasons of safety they should be renewed. Refer to Chapter 2 for further information on the fuel lines and Chapter 6 for information on the brake hoses.

3 Renew the anti-dive unit seals – ZX900 A1 to A6 and ZX1000 A models

Every two years the anti-dive units should be dismantled and the seals, plungers and O-rings renewed, regardless of their apparent condition. Information on overhaul can be found in Chapter 5. Note that a test is also given for testing the units, should there be any doubt about their correct operation. At the same time as the seals are renewed, check the condition of the metal pipe; if corroded this should be renewed.

4 Check the wheels

Periodically check the complete wheel for cracks and chipping, particularly at the spoke roots and the edge of the rim. As a general rule a damaged wheel must be renewed as cracks will cause stress points which may lead to sudden failure under heavy load. Small nicks may be radiused carefully with a fine file and emery paper (No 600 – No 1000) to relieve the stress. If there is any doubt as to the condition of a wheel, advice should be sought from a reputable dealer or specialist repairer.

Each wheel is covered with a coating of lacquer, to prevent corrosion. If damage occurs to the wheel and the lacquer finish is penetrated, the bared aluminium alloy will soon start to corrode. A whitish grey oxide will form over the damaged area, which in itself is a protective coating. This deposit however, should be removed carefully as soon as possible and a new protective coating of lacquer applied.

Check the lateral runout at the rim by spinning the wheel and placing a fixed pointer close to the rim edge. If the maximum runout is greater than 0.5 mm (0.020 in) axially or 0.8 mm (0.032 in) radially, Kawasaki recommend that the wheel be renewed. This is, however, a counsel of perfection; a runout somewhat greater than this can probably be accommodated without noticeable effect on steering. No means is available for straightening a warped wheel without resorting to the expense of having the wheel skimmed on all faces. If warpage was caused by impact during an accident, the safest measure is to renew the wheel complete. Worn wheel bearings may cause rim runout. These should be renewed.

Note that impact damage or serious corrosion on models fitted with tubeless tyres has wider implications in that it could lead to a loss of pressure from the tubeless tyres. If in any doubt as to the wheel's condition, seek professional advice.

5 Cleaning the machine

Keeping the motorcycle clean should be considered as an important part of routine maintenance, to be carried out whenever the need arises. A machine cleaned regularly will not only succumb less speedily to the inevitable corrosion of external surfaces, and hence maintain its market value, but will be far more approachable when the time comes for maintenance or service work. Furthermore, loose or failing components are more readily spotted when not partially obscured by a mantle of road grime and oil.

Surface dirt should be removed using a sponge and warm, soapy water; the latter being applied copiously to remove the particles of grit which might otherwise cause damage to the paintwork and polished surfaces.

Use a wax polish on the painted and plastic parts, applied with a soft cloth. The windshield is best cleaned with a chamois leather.

If the engine parts are particularly oily, use a cleaning compound such as 'Gunk' or 'Jizer'. Apply the compound whilst the parts are dry and work it in with a brush so that it has the opportunity to penetrate the film of grease and oil. Finish off by washing down liberally with plenty of water, taking care that it does not enter the carburettor, air filter or the electrics.

Whenever possible, the machine should be wiped down after it has been used in the wet, so that it is not garaged under damp conditions which will promote rusting. Remember there is little chance of water entering the control cables and causing stiffness of operation if they are lubricated regularly as recommended in the preceding sections.

While it is realised that cleaning a machine is quickest and most effective if carried out using a pressure washer, steam cleaner or even a very powerful hose, the very real disadvantages of such usage should be pointed out. Quite apart from the rapid deterioration of the finish of plastic components caused by the scouring action of caked-on dirt being blasted off, the operating pressure of such machines is high enough to force a mixture of dirt and water past oil seals etc and into the bearings, brakes, forks and suspension unit, causing their premature failure unless great care is taken to dismantle, clean and lubricate all cycle parts after cleaning. Note that the manufacturer specifically advises against using such cleaning equipment. If cleaning must be carried out in this way, be very careful both when cleaning and afterwards; check that the jet is directed away from the fuel tank filler cap, the engine breather, the open ends of the exhausts, the handlebar switches and other electrical components.

Chapter 1 Engine, clutch and gearbox

Refer to Chapter 8 for information on the ZX1100 D model

Contents

Specifications

Engine

Type..	DOHC, 16 valve, 4-cylinder, liquid-cooled
Capacity:	
ZX900 models...	908 cc (55 cu in)
ZX1000 models	997 cc (60 cu in)
ZX1100 C models...	1052 cc (64 cu in)
Bore:	
ZX900 models...	72.5 mm (2.85 in)
ZX1000 models	74.0 mm (2.91 in)
ZX1100 C models...	76.0 mm (2.99 in)
Stroke:	
ZX900 models...	55.0 mm (2.17 in)
ZX1000 and ZX1100 C models..............................	58.0 mm (2.28 in)
Compression ratio:	
ZX1000 A models...	10.2:1
All other models	11.0:1

Engine output – UK models:	Maximum power bhp @ rpm	Maximum torque kgf m (lbf ft) @ rpm
ZX900 models	115 @ 9500	8.7 (62.9) @ 8500
ZX1000 A models	125 @ 9500	10.1 (73.1) @ 8500
ZX1000 B models	125 @ 10000	Not available
ZX1100 C models	125 @ 9500	Not available
Engine output – US models:		
ZX900 models	110 @ 9500	8.7 (62.9) @ 8500
ZX1000 A models	125 @ 9500	10.1 (73.1) @ 8500
ZX1000 B models	137 @ 10000	10.5 (76.0) @ 9000
ZX1100 C models	147 @ 10500	9.0 (81.0) @ 8500
Cylinder identification	Left to right, 1-2-3-4	
Firing order	1-2-4-3	

Compression pressure – at cranking speed with engine fully warmed up:

ZX900 models	9.4 – 14.5 kg/cm² (134 – 206 psi)
ZX1000 A models	8.4 – 13.0 kg/cm² (119 – 185 psi)
ZX1000 B models	8.8 – 13.5 kg/cm² (125 – 192 psi)
ZX1100 C models	9.0 – 13.8 kg/cm² (128 – 196 psi)

Note: *compression pressure must not vary excessively between any two cylinders*

Camshafts, followers and cam chain

Cam lobe height:	
ZX900 and ZX1000 A models	35.824 – 35.940 mm (1.410 – 1.414 in)
Service limit	35.710 mm (1.406 in)
ZX1000 B models	21.687 – 21.787 mm (0.854 – 0.858 in)
Service limit	21.590 mm (0.850 in)
ZX1100 C models:	
Inlet	36.872 – 36.972 mm (1.452 – 1.456 in)
Service limit	36.770 mm (1.448 in)
Exhaust	36.687 – 36.787 mm (1.444 – 1.448 in)
Service limit	36.590 mm (1.441 in)
Camshaft journal OD	24.900 – 24.922 mm (0.980 – 0.981 in)
Service limit	24.870 mm (0.979 in)
Camshaft bearing ID	25.000 – 25.021 mm (0.984 – 0.985 in)
Service limit	25.080 mm (0.987 in)
Camshaft journal/cylinder head bearing clearance	0.078 – 0.121 mm (0.003 – 0.005 in)
Service limit	0.210 mm (0.008 in)
Camshaft standard runout	Less than 0.02 mm (0.001 in)
Service limit	0.1 mm (0.004 in)
Cam follower ID:	
ZX900 and ZX1000 A models	12.500 – 12.518 mm (0.492 – 0.493 in)
Service limit	12.550 mm (0.494 in)
ZX1000 B and ZX1100 C models	12.000 – 12.018 mm (0.472 – 0.473 in)
Service limit	12.050 mm (0.474 in)
Cam follower shaft ID:	
ZX900 and ZX1000 A models	12.466 – 12.484 mm (0.490 – 0.491 in)
Service limit	12.440 mm (0.489 in)
ZX1000 B models	11.976 – 11.994 mm (0.471 – 0.472 in)
Service limit	11.950 mm (0.470 in)
ZX1100 C models	11.966 – 11.984 mm (0.470 – 0.471 in)
Service limit	11.940 mm (0.469 in)
Camchain – standard length of 20 links	158.8 – 159.2 mm (6.252 – 6.268 in)
Service limit	161.5 mm (6.358 in)

Cylinder head

Maximum warpage	0.050 mm (0.002 in)

Valves guides and springs

Inlet valve clearances:	
ZX900 and ZX1000 A models	0.13 – 0.18 mm (0.005 – 0.007 in)
ZX1000 B and ZX1100 C models	0.13 – 0.19 mm (0.005 – 0.007 in)
Exhaust valve clearances:	
ZX900 and ZX1000 A models	0.18 – 0.23 mm (0.007 – 0.009 in)
ZX1000 B and ZX1100 C models	0.18 – 0.24 mm (0.007 – 0.009 in)
Valve head thickness:	
Inlet	0.50 mm (0.20 in)
Service limit	0.25 mm (0.10 in)
Exhaust:	
ZX900 and ZX1000 A models	1.00 mm (0.40 in)
Service limit	0.70 mm (0.28 in)
ZX1000 B and ZX1100 C models	0.80 mm (0.31 in)
Service limit	0.50 mm (0.20 in)

Valve stem maximum runout .... 0.05 mm (0.002 in)
Inlet valve stem OD:
    ZX900 and ZX1000 A models... 5.475 – 5.490 mm (0.215 – 0.216 in)
    Service limit .... 5.460 mm (0.214 in)
    ZX1000 B and ZX1100 C models .... 4.975 – 4.990 mm (0.195 – 0.196 in)
    Service limit .... 4.960 mm (0.194 in)
Exhaust valve stem OD:
    ZX900 and ZX1000 A models... 5.455 – 5.470 mm (0.214 – 0.215 in)
    Service limit .... 5.440 mm (0.213 in)
    ZX1000 B and ZX1100 C models .... 4.955 – 4.970 mm (0.194 – 0.195 in)
    Service limit .... 4.940 mm (0.193 in)
Valve seat width.. 0.5 – 1.0 mm (0.02 – 0.04 in)
Valve seat OD:
    ZX900 and ZX1000 A models – inlet .... 28.3 – 28.5 mm (1.114 – 1.122 in)
    ZX900 and ZX1000 A models – exhaust .... 24.0 – 24.2 mm (0.945 – 0.953 in)
    ZX1000 B model – inlet .... 29.3 – 29.5 mm (1.154 – 1.161 in)
    ZX1000 B model – exhaust .... 25.3 – 25.5 mm (0.996 – 1.004 in)
    ZX1100 C model – inlet .... 30.8 – 31.0 mm (1.213 – 1.220 in)
    ZX1100 C model – exhaust .... 26.3 – 26.5 mm (1.035 – 1.043 in)
Valve guide ID:
    ZX900 and ZX1000 A models... 5.500 – 5.512 mm (0.216 – 0.217 in)
    Service limit .... 5.580 mm (0.219 in)
    ZX1000 B and ZX1100 C models .... 5.000 – 5.012 mm (0.197 – 0.198 in)
    Service limit .... 5.080 mm (0.200 in)
Inlet valve/guide clearance – valve installed, using dial gauge:
    ZX900 and ZX1000 A models... 0.02 – 0.08 mm (0.001 – 0.003 in)
    Service limit .... 0.22 mm (0.008 in)
    ZX1000 B and ZX1100 C models .... 0.02 – 0.07 mm (0.001 – 0.003 in)
    Service limit .... 0.18 mm (0.007 in)
Exhaust valve/guide clearance – valve installed, using dial gauge:
    ZX900 and ZX1000 A models... 0.07 – 0.14 mm (0.003 – 0.006 in)
    Service limit .... 0.27 mm (0.011 in)
    ZX1000 B and ZX1100 C models .... 0.06 – 0.11 mm (0.002 – 0.004 in)
    Service limit .... 0.21 mm (0.008 in)
Inner valve spring free length:
    ZX900 and ZX1000 A models... 37.2 mm (1.46 in)
    Service limit .... 36.0 mm (1.42 in)
    ZX1000 B and ZX1100 C models .... 35.5 mm (1.40 in)
    Service limit .... 33.6 mm (1.32 in)
Outer valve spring free length:
    ZX900 and ZX1000 A models... 40.4 mm (1.58 in)
    Service limit .... 39.0 mm (1.54 in)
    ZX1000 B and ZX1100 C models .... 40.5 mm (1.59 in)
    Service limit .... 38.6 mm (1.52 in)

Cylinder block

Cylinder bore ID:
    ZX900 models.. 72.494 – 72.506 mm (2.854 – 2.855 in)
    Service limit .... 72.600 mm (2.858 in)
    ZX1000 models .... 73.994 – 74.006 mm (2.913 – 2.914 in)
    Service limit .... 74.110 mm (2.918 in)
    ZX1100 C models .... 75.994 – 76.006 mm (2.991 – 2.992 in)
    Service limit .... 76.100 mm (2.996 in)
Piston/cylinder clearance:
    ZX900 and ZX1000 models.. 0.044 – 0.071 mm (0.002 – 0.003 in)
    ZX1100 C models.. 0.056 – 0.088 mm (0.002 – 0.004 in)

Pistons

Piston OD:
    ZX900 models.. 72.435 – 72.450 mm (2.851 – 2.852 in)
    Service limit .... 72.300 mm (2.846 in)
    ZX1000 models .... 73.935 – 73.964 mm (2.911 – 2.912 in)
    Service limit .... 73.790 mm (2.905 in)
    ZX1100 C models .... 75.918 – 75.938 mm (2.988 – 2.989 in)
    Service limit .... 75.770 mm (2.983 in)
Top compression ring groove width:
    ZX900 and ZX1000 A models... 1.02 – 1.04 mm (0.040 – 0.041 in)
    Service limit .... 1.12 mm (0.044 in)
    ZX1000 B models .... 0.82 – 0.84 mm (0.032 – 0.033 in)
    Service limit .... 0.92 mm (0.036 in)
    ZX1100 C models .... 0.84 – 0.86 mm (0.033 – 0.034 in)
    Service limit .... 0.94 mm (0.037 in)

Second compression ring groove width:
   ZX900 and ZX1000 models .... 1.01 – 1.03 mm (0.039 – 0.040 in)
   ZX1100 C models .... 1.02 – 1.04 mm (0.040 – 0.041 in)
   Service limit – all models .... 1.12 mm (0.044 in)
Oil scraper ring groove width .... 2.51 – 2.53 mm (0.098 – 0.099 in)
Service limit .... 2.60 mm (0.102 in)
Top compression ring/groove clearance .... 0.03 – 0.07 mm (0.001 – 0.003 in)
Service limit .... 0.17 mm (0.007 in)
Second compression ring/groove clearance .... 0.02 – 0.06 mm (0.001 – 0.002 in)
Service limit .... 0.16 mm (0.006 in)

Piston rings

Top compression ring thickness:
   ZX900 and ZX1000 A models .... 0.97 – 0.99 mm (0.038 – 0.039 in)
   Service limit .... 0.90 mm (0.035 in)
   ZX1000 B and ZX1100 C models .... 0.77 – 0.79 mm (0.030 – 0.031 in)
   Service limit .... 0.70 mm (0.027 in)
Second compression ring thickness .... 0.97 – 0.99 mm (0.038 – 0.039 in)
Service limit .... 0.90 mm (0.035 in)
Top compression ring end gap – installed:
   ZX900 and ZX1000 models .... 0.20 – 0.35 mm (0.007 – 0.013 in)
   ZX1100 C models .... 0.20 – 0.32 mm (0.007 – 0.012 in)
   Service limit – all models .... 0.70 mm (0.027 in)
Second compression ring end gap – installed .... 0.20 – 0.35 mm (0.007 – 0.013 in)
Service limit .... 0.70 mm (0.027 in)
Oil scraper ring end gap – installed:
   ZX900 and ZX1000 models .... 0.20 – 0.70 mm (0.007 – 0.027 in)
   Service limit .... 1.00 mm (0.039 in)
   ZX1100 C models .... Not available

Connecting rod and bearings

Connecting rod maximum distortion .... 0.2/100 mm (0.008/3.94 in)
Big-end bearing standard ID:
   ZX900 and ZX1000 models .... 38.000 – 38.016 mm (1.4961 – 1.4967 in)
   ZX1100 C models .... 39.000 – 39.016 mm (1.5354 – 1.5361 in)
Size groups – ZX900 and ZX1000 models:
   Connecting rod unmarked .... 38.000 – 38.008 mm (1.4961 – 1.4963 in)
   Connecting rod marked 'O' .... 38.009 – 38.016 mm (1.4964 – 1.4967 in)
Size groups – ZX1100 C models:
   Connecting rod unmarked .... 39.000 – 39.008 mm (1.5354 – 1.5357 in)
   Connecting rod marked 'O' .... 39.009 – 39.016 mm (1.5358 – 1.5361 in)
Crankpin standard OD:
   ZX900 and ZX1000 models .... 34.984 – 35.000 mm (1.3773 – 1.3779 in)
   Service limit .... 34.970 mm (1.3767 in)
   ZX1100 C models .... 35.984 – 36.000 mm (1.4167 – 1.4173 in)
   Service limit .... 35.970 mm (1.4161 in)
Size groups – ZX900 and ZX1000 models:
   Crankshaft unmarked .... 34.984 – 34.992 mm (1.3773 – 1.3776 in)
   Crankshaft marked 'O' .... 34.993 – 35.000 mm (1.3777 – 1.3780 in)
Size groups – ZX1100 C models:
   Crankshaft unmarked .... 35.984 – 35.992 mm (1.4167 – 1.4170 in)
   Crankshaft marked 'O' .... 35.993 – 36.000 mm (1.4171 – 1.4173 in)

Big-end rod bearing insert size:	Thickness	Colour code
ZX900 models:		
Thin	1.475 – 1.480 mm (0.0581 – 0.0583 in)	Brown
Medium	1.480 – 1.485 mm (0.0583 – 0.0585 in)	Black
Thick	1.485 – 1.490 mm (0.0585 – 0.0587 in)	Blue
ZX1000 A models:		
Thin	1.470 – 1.475 mm (0.0579 – 0.0581 in)	Brown
Medium	1.475 – 1.480 mm (0.0581 – 0.0583 in)	Black
Thick	1.480 – 1.485 mm (0.0583 – 0.0585 in)	Blue
ZX1000 B and ZX1100 C models:		
Thin	1.475 – 1.480 mm (0.0581 – 0.0583 in)	Black
Medium	1.480 – 1.485 mm (0.0583 – 0.0585 in)	Blue
Thick	1.485 – 1.490 mm (0.0585 – 0.0587 in)	White

Bearing insert/crankpin clearance:
   ZX900 and ZX1000 B models .... 0.036 – 0.066 mm (0.0014 – 0.0026 in)
   Service limit .... 0.10 mm (0.0039 in)
   ZX1000 A models .... 0.046 – 0.076 mm (0.0018 – 0.0030 in)
   Service limit .... 0.11 mm (0.0043 in)
   ZX1100 C models .... 0.037 – 0.065 mm (0.0015 – 0.0025 in)
   Service limit .... 0.10 mm (0.0039 in)

Big-end bearing side clearance:
    ZX900 and ZX1000 models .... 0.13 – 0.33 mm (0.0051 – 0.0130 in)
    Service limit .... 0.50 mm (0.0197 in)
    ZX1100 C models .... 0.13 – 0.38 mm (0.0051 – 0.0150 in)
    Service limit .... 0.60 mm (0.0236 in)
Crankshaft runout .... Less than 0.05 mm (0.0020 in)
Crankshaft endfloat .... 0.05 – 0.20 mm (0.0020 – 0.0079 in)
Service limit .... 0.40 mm (0.0157 in)
Crankcase main bearing ID .... 39.000 – 39.016 mm (1.5354 – 1.5361 in)
Size groups:
    Crankcase marked 'O' .... 39.000 – 39.008 mm (1.5354 – 1.5357 in)
    Crankcase unmarked .... 39.009 – 39.016 mm (1.5358 – 1.5361 in)
Crankshaft journal OD .... 35.984 – 36.000 mm (1.4167 – 1.4173 in)
Service limit .... 35.960 mm (1.4157 in)
Size groups:
    Crankshaft unmarked .... 35.984 – 35.992 mm (1.4167 – 1.4170 in)
    Crankshaft marked '1' .... 35.993 – 36.000 mm (1.4171 – 1.4173 in)
Main bearing insert size: **Thickness**   **Colour code**
    Thin .... 1.490 – 1.494 mm (0.0587 – 0.0588 in)   Brown
    Medium .... 1.494 – 1.498 mm (0.0588 – 0.0590 in)   Black
    Thick .... 1.498 – 1.502 mm (0.0590 – 0.0591 in)   Blue
Bearing insert/journal clearance .... 0.020 – 0.044 mm (0.0008 – 0.0017 in)
Service limit:
    ZX900 and ZX1000 models .... 0.080 mm (0.0031 in)
    ZX1100 C models .... 0.070 mm (0.0027 in)

Clutch

Type .... Wet, multi-plate
Friction plates:
    Number:
        ZX900 models 8
        ZX1000 and ZX1100 C models 9
    Thickness:
        ZX900 and ZX1000 B models .... 2.9 – 3.1 mm (0.114 – 0.122 in)
        Service limit .... 2.75 mm (0.108 in)
        ZX1000 A models .... 2.9 – 3.1 mm (0.114 – 0.122 in)
        Service limit .... 2.8 mm (0.110 in)
        ZX1100 C models .... 2.7 – 3.0 mm (0.106 – 0.118 in)
        Service limit .... 2.5 mm (0.098 in)
Plain plates:
    Number:
        ZX900 models 7
        ZX1000 and ZX1100 C models 8
Friction and plain plate warpage .... Less than 0.2 mm (0.008 in)
Service limit .... 0.3 mm (0.012 in)
Clutch springs:
    Number:
        ZX900 models 5
        ZX1000 and ZX1100 C models 6
    Free length:
        ZX900 models .... 33.0 – 34.2 mm (1.30 – 1.35 in)
        Service limit .... 32.1 mm (1.26 in)
        ZX1000 models .... 33.2 mm (1.31 in)
        Service limit .... 32.1 mm (1.26 in)
        ZX1100 C models .... 46.3 mm (1.82 in)
        Service limit .... 42.7 mm (1.68 in)
Primary gear/clutch drum backlash .... 0.03 – 0.10 mm (0.0011 – 0.0039 in)
Service limit .... 0.14 mm (0.0055 in)

Alternator/starter clutch

Drive chain - 20 link length .... 158.8 – 159.2 mm (6.25 – 6.27 in)
Service limit .... 161.5 mm (6.36 in)

Gearbox

Type .... 6 speed, constant mesh
Ratios:
    1st .... 2.800:1 (42/15 T)
    2nd (except ZX1100 C4) .... 2.000:1 (38/19 T)
    2nd (ZX1100 C4) .... 2.055:1 (37/18 T)
    3rd .... 1.590:1 (35/22 T)
    4th .... 1.333:1 (32/24 T)
    5th .... 1.153:1 (30/26 T)
    6th .... 1.035:1 (29/28 T)
Gear backlash - all pinions .... 0.06 – 0.23 mm (0.0024 – 0.0091 in)
Service limit .... 0.30 mm (0.0118 in)
Gear pinion selector fork groove width .... 5.05 – 5.15 mm (0.199 – 0.203 in)
Service limit .... 5.3 mm (0.209 in)

Selector fork end thickness	4.9 – 5.0 mm (0.193 – 0.197 in)
Service limit	4.8 mm (0.189 in)
Selector fork guide pin thickness	7.9 – 8.0 mm (0.311 – 0.315 in)
Service limit	7.8 mm (0.307 in)
Selector drum groove width	8.05 – 8.20 mm (0.317 – 0.323 in)
Service limit	8.30 mm (0.327 in)

Final drive

Type	Chain and sprockets
Ratio:	
ZX900 models:	
UK models	2.882:1 (49/17 T)
US models	2.941:1 (50/17 T)
ZX1000 A models:	
UK models	2.666:1 (40/15 T)
US models	2.733:1 (41/15 T)
ZX1000 B and ZX1100 C models	2.647:1 (45/17 T)

Torque settings

Component	kgf m	lbf ft
Cylinder head cover bolts	1.0	7.0
Top camchain guide bolts:		
ZX900 and ZX1000 A models	1.0	7.0
ZX1000 B and ZX1100 C models	Not available	
Cam follower shaft retaining bolts – ZX900 and ZX1000 A models only	1.0	7.0
Camshaft cap bolts	1.2	9.0
Camshaft sprocket retaining bolts	1.5	11.0
Cam follower locknuts	2.5	18.0
Cylinder head oil pipe union bolts – ZX900 and ZX1000 A models only	1.0	7.0
Main cylinder head oil pipe union bolts	2.5	18.0
Sump to crankcase metal oil pipe union bolts:		
ZX900 and ZX1100 C models	2.5	18.0
ZX1000 models	1.8	13.0
Cylinder head bolts:		
ZX900 and ZX1000 A models:*		
New head bolt and washer:		
Flat-headed bolts	4.0	29.0
Taper-headed bolts	5.2	38.0
Old head bolt and washer:		
Flat-headed bolts	3.7	27.0
Taper-headed bolts	4.9	35.0
ZX1000 B and ZX1100 C models:		
Initial torque setting	2.0	14.5
Final torque setting:		
Flat-headed bolts	4.0	29.0
Taper-headed bolts	5.2	38.0
6 mm cylinder head/block retaining bolt	1.0	7.0
7 mm block/crankcase retaining bolts	1.5	11.0
Camchain tensioner mounting bolts	1.0	7.0
Camchain blade mounting bolt	2.0	14.5
Clutch spring retaining bolts:		
ZX900 and ZX1000 models	1.0	7.0
ZX1100 C model	1.1	8.0
Clutch centre nut	13.5	98.0
Ignition rotor retaining bolt	2.5	18.0
Alternator mounting bolts	2.5	18.0
Alternator/starter clutch drive sprocket bolt	2.5	18.0
Alternator/starter clutch shaft cush drive coupling nut	6.0	43.0
Alternator drive coupling/shaft retaining bolt	1.0	7.0
Starter clutch bolts:		
ZX900 and ZX1000 A models	3.5	25.0
ZX1000 B and ZX1100 C models	1.2	9.0
Engine sprocket nut	10.0	72.0
Gearchange mechanism cover bolts – ZX1100 C model	1.0	7.0
Crankcase fastening bolts:		
6 mm	1.5	11.0
7 mm – ZX1100 C and late ZX900 A7-on models only	1.8	13.0
8 mm	2.8	20.0
8 mm main bearing bolts – ZX900 and ZX1000 models:		
Initial setting	1.4	10.0
Final setting	2.8	20.0
9 mm main bearing bolts – ZX1100 C and late ZX900 A7-on models:		
Initial setting	1.0	7.0
Final setting	3.3	24.0

	kgf m	lbf ft
Connecting rod bolts (see text):		
ZX900 models	3.7	27.0
ZX1000 A models:		
With new nuts	3.0	22.0
With old nuts	2.7	19.5
ZX1000 B models:		
New connecting rod and new nuts	2.0	14.5
New connecting rod and old nuts	1.8	13.0
Old connecting rod and new nuts	2.6	18.8
Old connecting rod and old nuts	2.4	17.4
ZX1100 C models	1.5	11.0
Oil drain plugs in sump	3.0	22.0
Oil filter mounting bolt	2.0	14.5
Engine mounting bolts:		
ZX900 models	6.0	43.0
ZX1000 A models:		
Front mounting bolts	4.5	33.0
Rear mounting bolts	5.3	38.0
ZX1000 B and ZX1100 C models	4.5	33.0
Frame cradle retaining bolts:		
ZX1000 A models	5.3	38.0
ZX1000 B and ZX1100 C models	4.5	33.0

On ZX900 and 1000 A models initial torque setting is approximately half of the final torque settings which are given overleaf.

1 General description

The engine/gearbox unit is of water-cooled four cylinder in-line design, fitted transversely across the frame. The sixteen valves are operated by double overhead camshafts which are chain driven off the crankshaft. The engine/gearbox unit is constructed in aluminium alloy with the crankcase being divided horizontally.

The crankcase incorporates a wet sump, pressure fed lubrication system which incorporates a gear driven dual rotor oil pump, an oil filter and by-pass valve assembly, a relief valve and an oil pressure switch. Also contained in the crankcase is the balancer shaft and starter clutch.

Power from the crankshaft is transmitted to the gearbox via the clutch, which is of the wet multi-plate type and is gear driven off the crankshaft. The starter motor and alternator assemblies are also linked to the crankshaft via a chain and tensioner mechanism on the right-hand end of the crankshaft. The water pump is mounted on the left-hand side of the crankcase and is driven off the oil pump shaft.

Final drive to the rear wheel is by chain and sprockets. The engine sprocket being externally mounted on the output shaft.

2 Operations with the engine/gearbox unit in the frame

The components and assemblies listed below can be removed without having to remove the engine unit from the frame. If, however a number of areas require attention at the same time, removal of the engine is recommended:

(a) Clutch slave cylinder
(b) Engine sprocket
(c) Neutral switch
(d) Gear selector mechanism external components
(e) Water pump
(f) Ignition system components
(g) Starter motor
(h) Alternator
(i) Alternator/starter clutch drive components
(j) Clutch assembly
(k) Oil filter and bypass valve assembly
(l) Sump, oil screens, oil pump and relief valve assembly
(m) Cylinder head cover and camshafts
(n) Camchain and tensioner
(o) Cylinder head
(p) Cylinder block and pistons

3 Operations with the engine/gearbox unit removed from the frame

It is necessary to remove the engine/gearbox unit from the frame

and separate the crankcase halves to gain access to the following components:

(a) Crankshaft assembly
(b) Main and big-end bearings
(c) Connecting rods
(d) Gearbox shafts and pinions
(e) Gear selector drum and forks
(f) Balancer shaft
(g) Starter clutch

Note that if only removal of the gearbox components is required, the engine/gearbox unit can be removed from the frame and inverted so that the lower crankcase half can be withdrawn. This will permit the examination of the gearbox components without disturbing the top end of the engine or the clutch. This also applies to the balancer shaft and starter clutch components.

4 Removing the engine/gearbox unit from the frame

1   If the machine is dirty, wash it thoroughly before starting any major dismantling work. This will make work much easier and will rule out the possibility of caked on lumps of dirt falling into some vital component. If possible work can also be made easier by raising the machine to a suitable working height on a hydraulic ramp or a suitable platform.
2   Remove the fuel tank as described in Chapter 3, and the complete fairing as described in Chapter 5.
3   Place a suitably sized container beneath the engine/gearbox unit and drain the engine oil as described in Routine maintenance. Remove the oil filter assembly and discard the element, ensuring the baffle, spring and washer are retained. Disconnect the battery leads (negative lead first) and remove the battery from the machine. If the machine is to be left dismantled for some time, give the battery regular refresher charges as described in Chapter 7.
4   Drain the coolant and remove the radiator and cooling fan assembly, and the water pump as described in Chapter 2. Slacken and remove all the oil cooler hose union bolts which secure the hoses to the engine and the oil cooler mounting bolts, and remove the oil cooler and hose assembly from the machine. Make a note of the routes taken by the oil cooler hoses to use as a guide when refitting them to the machine.
5   Remove the carburettors from the machine as described in Chapter 3. Once the carburettors have been removed on ZX900 and ZX1000 A models slacken and remove the air filter housing mounting bolt(s) and manoeuvre it out of the frame. On ZX1100 C models remove the mounting bolts which retain the front section of the air filter housing (duct) noting the correct position of the shouldered spacer, situated behind the front mounting bolt. Disconnect the vent hose from the carburettors and lift the assembly clear of the machine. On US models disconnect and remove all the relevant clean air and emission control system components, referring to Chapter 3 for further information.
6   Remove the three bolts that secure the clutch slave cylinder to the

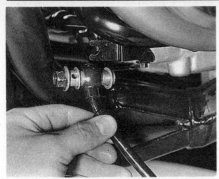

4.4a Remove all union bolts which secure the oil cooler hoses to the engine unit ...

4.4b ... release oil cooler mounting bolts and remove cooler and hoses as an assembly - ZX1100 C shown

4.8a ZX900 silencer mounting bolt ...

4.8b ... and clamp

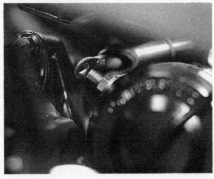

4.10a Remove the lead from the starter motor terminal

4.10b On ZX1000 B and ZX1100 C remove coolant hose which runs over cylinder head cover

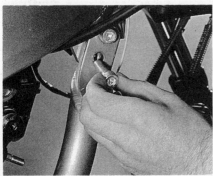

4.12a On ZX1000 and ZX1100 C remove the engine front and frame cradle mounting bolts ...

4.12b ... and lower the frame cradle away from the machine ...

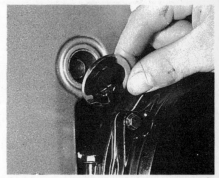

4.12c ... remove chrome caps to reveal engine rear mounting bolts

engine sprocket casing and withdraw the cylinder from the casing. Push the piston as far back as possible by hand and then slowly bring the clutch operating lever back to the handlebars and hold it there with a stout elastic band. This will prevent the slave cylinder piston from being accidentally expelled. Tie the slave cylinder to the frame so that it does not hamper engine removal.

7   Marking its shaft so that it can be refitted in the same position, slacken and remove the gearchange linkage pinch bolt and pull the linkage off the gearchange shaft splines. Release the engine sprocket casing retaining bolts and remove the casing from the machine, noting the two locating dowels fitted behind it. If these dowels are loose they should be removed and stored with the casing for safekeeping. The clutch pushrod should also be removed for safekeeping. Flatten the sprocket nut locking tab and slacken the sprocket nut whilst applying the rear brake hard to prevent it rotating. Pull the sprocket off the output shaft splines and disengage it from the chain, noting that it may be necessary to first slacken the drive chain to obtain the required amount of freeplay to enable this. Remove the sprocket and allow the chain to hang over the swinging arm.

8   On ZX900 models release the two bolts which secure the lower fairing mounting bracket to the bottom of the crankcase and remove the bracket from the machine. Mark the bracket in some way to use as a reference on refitting. Also remove all the mounting bolts from the lower front fairing mounting bracket. On ZX900 and ZX1000 A models, release the silencer mounting bolts and clamps and pull the left and right-hand silencers out of the exhaust pipes. Slacken the eight nuts which secure the exhaust pipes to the cylinder head and remove the exhaust pipe mounting clamps. Remove the two bolts that secure the exhaust pipe assembly to the frame and lower the exhaust pipe assembly and fairing bracket (ZX900 models) away from the machine.

9   On ZX1000 B and ZX1100 C models, release the eight nuts which secure the exhaust pipes to the cylinder head and remove the exhaust mounting clamps. Slacken the clamp situated beneath the engine which secures the left and right-hand exhaust sections together. Remove the right-hand silencer mounting bolt and then on ZX1100 C models remove the right-hand silencer. Remove the left-hand silencer mounting bolt, lower the exhaust system to the ground and manoeuvre it clear of the machine. Note that on ZX1000 B models removal may prove easier

if the left and right-hand sections of the exhaust are first separated.

10   On all models, disconnect the lead from the starter motor terminal and remove the earth strap from the top of the crankcase. Also disconnect the electrical connections from the pulser coil(s), neutral switch, sidestand switch and the oil pressure and temperature switch (as applicable) and release all wiring from any cable ties or hooks which secure it to the frame. Pull the suppressor caps off the spark plugs and position them clear of the engine. On ZX900 models slacken the HT ignition coil retaining nuts and remove the coils from the machine having first made a note of the correct location of the low tension leads. On ZX1000 B and ZX1100 C models slacken the hose clips on each end of the coolant hose which runs over the cylinder head cover and remove it from the machine. On all ZX1000 and ZX1100 C models remove the air baffle plate from the front of the cylinder head cover.

11   The engine/gearbox unit should now only be retained by its mounting bolts. Check carefully that all components which may hinder the removal of the unit have been removed and that all cables and leads are wedged or tied out of the way of the engine. Note at least two people will be required to remove the engine/gearbox from the frame safely.

12   On ZX1000 and ZX1100 C models remove the two front engine mounting bolts and then remove the eight bolts that retain the frame cradle and lower the cradle away from the engine. On ZX900 models remove the two upper engine mounting bolts which secure the cylinder head to the frame, noting that there may be a shim fitted between the frame and the cylinder head on the left-hand side. On all models, place some sort of support beneath the engine to take the weight of the engine then remove both the upper and lower rear mounting bolts. Take a firm hold of the engine and lift it off the support. Remove the support from below the engine and manoeuvre the engine out of the bottom of the frame.

5   Dismantling the engine/gearbox unit: preliminaries

1   Before any dismantling work is undertaken, the external surfaces of the unit should be thoroughly cleaned and degreased. This will prevent the contamination of the engine internals, and will also make working a lot easier and cleaner. A high flash-point solvent, such as paraffin (kerosene) can be used, or better still, a proprietary engine degreaser such as Gunk or Jizer. Use old paintbrushes and toothbrushes to work the solvent into the various recesses of the engine castings. Take care to exclude solvent or water from the electrical components and inlet and exhaust ports. The use of petrol (gasoline) as a cleaning medium should be avoided because of the fire risk.

2   When clean and dry, arrange the unit on the workbench, leaving a suitable clear area for working. Gather a selection of small containers and plastic bags so that parts can be grouped together in an easily identifiable manner. Some paper and a pen should be on hand to permit notes to be made and labels attached where necessary. A supply of clean rag is also required.

3   Before commencing work, read through the appropriate section so that some idea of the necessary procedure can be gained. When removing the various engine components it should be noted that great force is seldom required, unless specified. In many cases, a component's reluctance to be removed is indicative of an incorrect approach or removal method. If in any doubt, re-check with the text.

6   Dismantling the engine/gearbox: removing the cylinder head cover, camshafts and followers

1   These components can be removed with the engine/gearbox unit in or out of the frame. In the former case it will be necessary first to remove the fuel tank and the lower and side fairing sections as described in the relevant Sections of Chapters 3 and 5. On ZX900 models, the HT ignition coils should also be removed; make a note of how their low tension leads are arranged prior to removing them. On ZX1000 A models remove the four bolts which retain the top section of the air filter housing and lift it clear of the machine. On ZX1100 C models remove the rubber plugs from the back of the air filter housing and slacken the eight bolts which secure the housing to the carburettors. Slacken the clip which secures the air filter housing to the front section of the duct and lift the filter housing away from the machine. On both ZX1000 B and

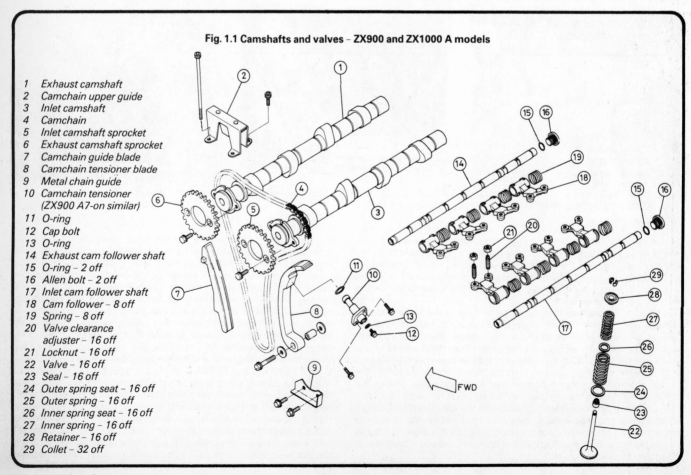

Fig. 1.1 Camshafts and valves – ZX900 and ZX1000 A models

1   Exhaust camshaft
2   Camchain upper guide
3   Inlet camshaft
4   Camchain
5   Inlet camshaft sprocket
6   Exhaust camshaft sprocket
7   Camchain guide blade
8   Camchain tensioner blade
9   Metal chain guide
10   Camchain tensioner (ZX900 A7-on similar)
11   O-ring
12   Cap bolt
13   O-ring
14   Exhaust cam follower shaft
15   O-ring – 2 off
16   Allen bolt – 2 off
17   Inlet cam follower shaft
18   Cam follower – 8 off
19   Spring – 8 off
20   Valve clearance adjuster – 16 off
21   Locknut – 16 off
22   Valve – 16 off
23   Seal – 16 off
24   Outer spring seat – 16 off
25   Outer spring – 16 off
26   Inner spring seat – 16 off
27   Inner spring – 16 off
28   Retainer – 16 off
29   Collet – 32 off

6.6a Withdraw cam follower shaft using a suitable 8 mm bolt ...

6.6b ... and remove springs ...

6.6c ... and followers as they are freed from the end of the shaft

ZX1100 C models drain at least 500 cc of coolant out of the cooling system, then remove the flexible coolant hose which runs over the cylinder head cover. On all US models disconnect the hoses from the air suction valves and carefully remove the reed valve assemblies from the cylinder head cover. On all models unplug the suppressor caps from the cylinder head and position them clear of the cover.

2   Slacken and remove the cylinder head cover retaining bolts and carefully lift the cover away from the engine. If possible remove all the dowels and store them with the cover for safekeeping. **Note:** *take care not to allow the cover locating dowels to drop into the engine.* If a dowel should drop into the engine do not turn the engine over until it has been retrieved. Failure to do so will lead to extensive engine damage. Carefully remove all the rubber gaskets from the top of the cylinder head.

3   If the camshafts are also to be removed, slacken the tensioner cap bolt and the two bolts which secure the camchain tensioner to the back left-hand side of the cylinder block. Remove the tensioner assembly from the engine. Remove the Allen bolts which retain the top camchain guide and lift the guide away from the cylinder head.

4   Slacken each of the camshaft bolts by about one turn at a time. The camshafts are under pressure from the valve springs and will be pushed clear of the bearing surfaces in the cylinder head. Once the valve spring pressure has been relieved remove the bolts and place them with the bearing caps in a safe place. Also remove all the bearing cap dowels and store these with the caps. Note that on ZX1000 B and ZX1100 C models,

if the engine is in the frame it may not be possible to remove the left-hand camshaft bearing cap due to there being insufficient clearance to lift the bolts out. If this is so and removal is necessary the cap can be removed with the cylinder head assembly as described in Section 9.

5   The camshafts can then be disengaged from the camchain and manoeuvred out of the cylinder head. The camshafts are marked on their shafts to avoid confusion (IN on the inlet shaft, EX on the exhaust shaft). *Do not remove the sprockets from the camshafts unless necessary.* On ZX1000 and ZX1100 C models each sprocket has two sets of holes, one for the inlet shaft and another for the exhaust. If the sprockets are ever removed make a note of which holes are used for each respective shaft, although as a rule the holes with a square indented area surrounding them are used for the inlet camshaft and those with a round surrounding area are used for the exhaust camshaft.

6   If necessary the cam followers can be removed as follows. Note that on ZX1000 B and ZX1100 C models, if the work is being carried out with the engine unit in the frame, it will first be necessary to remove the cylinder head if the inlet cam followers are to be removed. On ZX1000 B and ZX1100 C models remove the two union bolts from the oil delivery on the right-hand side of the cylinder head, remove it from the head, and withdraw the springs which are fitted behind it. On ZX900 and ZX1000 A models remove the two Allen headed bolts from the cylinder head. On all models the cam follower shafts can then be removed by screwing an 8 mm bolt of suitable length into the end of the shaft and

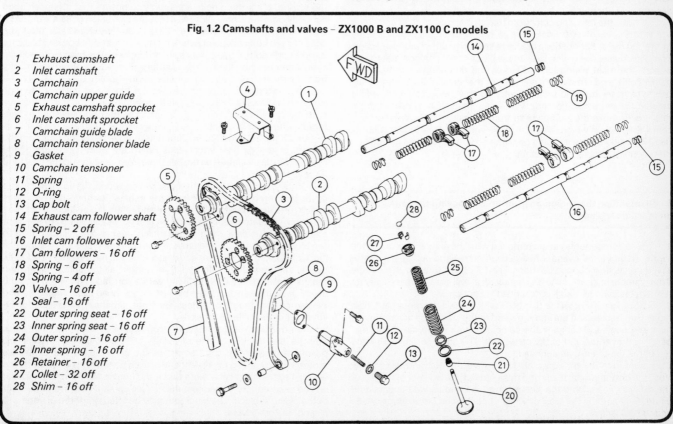

Fig. 1.2 Camshafts and valves – ZX1000 B and ZX1100 C models

1   Exhaust camshaft
2   Inlet camshaft
3   Camchain
4   Camchain upper guide
5   Exhaust camshaft sprocket
6   Inlet camshaft sprocket
7   Camchain guide blade
8   Camchain tensioner blade
9   Gasket
10 Camchain tensioner
11 Spring
12 O-ring
13 Cap bolt
14 Exhaust cam follower shaft
15 Spring – 2 off
16 Inlet cam follower shaft
17 Cam followers – 16 off
18 Spring – 6 off
19 Spring – 4 off
20 Valve – 16 off
21 Seal – 16 off
22 Outer spring seat – 16 off
23 Inner spring seat – 16 off
24 Outer spring – 16 off
25 Inner spring – 16 off
26 Retainer – 16 off
27 Collet – 32 off
28 Shim – 16 off

7.2 If loose, remove pin (arrowed) from crankshaft end

Fig. 1.3 Method of removing piston rings (Sec 9)

pulling it out with the bolt. Lift the followers and springs clear of the cylinder head as they are freed from the end of the shaft. Make a note of how the followers and springs are arranged to use as a reference on reassembly.

7 Dismantling the engine/gearbox unit: removing the ignition rotor assembly

1   The ignition rotor can be removed with the engine in or out of the frame. In the case of the former, the only preliminary dismantling required being that on ZX1000 and ZX1100 C models it will be necessary to remove the lower and left-hand side fairing sections as described in Chapter 5.
2   Remove the retaining bolts from the left-hand crankshaft end cover and lift the cover away from the engine, noting that if the engine is in the frame and the oil has not been drained a small amount of oil may escape. Trace the pulser coil wiring back to the block connector and disconnect it from the main wiring loom. Slacken the mounting bolts from the pulser coil(s) and remove the coil(s) from the engine. Slacken the Allen bolt which secures the ignition rotor to the crankshaft end, whilst holding the large hexagon nut with a ring spanner to prevent it from rotating. Remove the ignition rotor from the end of the crankshaft and check that the pin which is located in the end of the crankshaft is firmly fixed in position. If not it should be removed and stored with the ignition rotor components for safekeeping.

8 Dismantling the engine/gearbox unit: removing the camchain and tensioner blade

1   These components can be removed with the engine in or out of the frame. Remove the cylinder head cover, camshafts and ignition rotor assembly as described in Sections 6 and 7 of this Chapter. Note if the front camchain guide is to be removed it will also be necessary to remove the cylinder head as described in Section 9.
2   Slacken and remove the two bolts which retain the metal camchain guide (situated behind the ignition rotor) to the crankcase and remove it from the engine. Disengage the camchain from its sprocket and manoeuvre it over the end of the crankshaft. The chain can then be lifted out of the top of the cylinder head.
3   To remove the tensioner blade, remove the bolt and flat washer from the bottom of the blade and manoeuvre the blade out of the top of the cylinder head. Note the sleeve which is fitted inside the tensioner blade pivot and the flat washer which is positioned between the blade and the crankcase.

9 Dismantling the engine/gearbox unit: removing the cylinder head, block and pistons

1   These components can be removed with the engine in or out of the frame. However, if the engine is in the frame it will be necessary first to remove the radiator, oil cooler, carburettors and exhaust system as described in Section 4 of this Chapter, then carry out the work described in Section 6.
2   Before proceeding any further on ZX1000 B and ZX1100 C models, it is recommended that all the shims are removed from the tops of the valves. Make a note of where each shim is positioned and store the shims separately so that each shim can be refitted in its original position. On reassembly this will make the task of adjusting the valve clearances easier. If not already done during the coolant draining process, remove any residual coolant from the cylinder block by removing the drain plugs which are situated on the front face of the block.
3   On ZX900 and ZX1000 A models remove the two union bolts which retain the oil pipe to the inside of the cylinder head and lift the pipe out of the engine. Mark the pipe in some way to ensure that it is positioned correctly on reassembly. Note also that the two union bolts are different and it is essential that they are refitted correctly. Kawasaki mark the head of each bolt with paint (white for the exhaust side bolt and black for the inlet side bolt), if these marks are no longer visible mark both bolts to avoid interchanging them on reassembly. Remove the three union bolts from the main oil pipe which is situated at the front of the engine and the bolt that secures the pipe to the cylinder block and remove the pipe from the engine. On ZX900 models if the engine is in the frame, remove both the cylinder head to frame mounting bolts noting the shim (where fitted) between the left-hand side of the cylinder head and the frame.
4   On ZX1000 B and ZX1100 C models remove the union bolt from the bottom of the oil pipe which runs down the right-hand side of the cylinder block. Unscrew the flexible hose from its union on the head and remove the pipe.
5   On all models slacken the bolts which retain the ignition pickup cover and remove the cover from the engine. Remove the two bolts which pass up through the crankcase and retain the cylinder block, one of which is situated behind the cover, and the single bolt from the front underside of the cam chain tunnel which secures the cylinder head to the block. Working in the reverse of the tightening sequence shown in Fig.1.21 slacken by about one turn at a time the ten cylinder head bolts until all the pressure is released, then remove all the bolts. Tap around the joint faces of the cylinder head with a soft faced mallet to free the head. Once the seal has been broken, lift the head clear whilst feeding the camchain through the tunnel. The front camchain guide can then be lifted out of the cylinder block.
6   Remove any residual road dirt from the base of the cylinder block then lift the block a couple of inches off the crankcase. Before the pistons emerge from the bottom of the bores, pack the crankcase mouth with clean rag to prevent any broken piston rings or other debris falling into the crankcase. Note that if the engine unit is in the frame, it will be necessary to disconnect the flexible coolant hose from the front of the cylinder block. The block can now be lifted off of the pistons and clear of the crankcase.

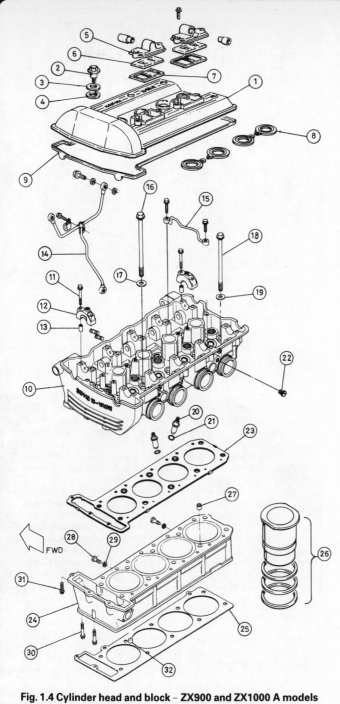

Fig. 1.4 Cylinder head and block – ZX900 and ZX1000 A models

1 Cylinder head cover	17 Washer – 6 off
2 Bolt – 6 off	18 Flat-headed bolt – 4 off
3 Washer – 6 off	19 Washer – 4 off
4 O-ring – 6 off	20 Valve guide – 16 off
5 Air suction valve cover △	21 O-ring – 16 off
6 Reed valve △	22 Plug – 2 off
7 Gasket △	23 Head gasket
8 Seal – 4 off	24 Cylinder block
9 Cover seal	25 Base gasket
10 Cylinder head	26 Bore liner – 4 off
11 Bolt – 20 off	27 Dowel – 2 off
12 Camshaft cap – 10 off	28 Coolant drain plug – 2 off
13 Dowel – 20 off	29 Sealing washer – 2 off
14 Main oil pipe	30 Bolt – 2 off
15 Inner oil pipe	31 Bolt
16 Tapered-headed bolt – 6 off	32 Dowel – 2 off
	△ US models only

Fig. 1.5 Cylinder head and block – ZX1000 B and ZX1100 C models

1 Bolt – 6 off	17 Bolt – 2 off
2 Sealing ring – 6 off	18 Left-hand inner camshaft cap
3 Cylinder head cover	19 Dowel – 2 off
4 Cover seal	20 Cylinder head
5 Seal – 4 off	21 Valve guides – 16 off
6 Dowel – 4 off	22 Oil pipe
7 Air suction valve cover △	23 Oil pipe union block
8 Reed valve △	24 Head gasket
9 Gasket △	25 Cylinder block
10 Tapered-headed bolt – 6 off	26 Dowel – 2 off
11 Washer – 10 off	27 Coolant drain plug – 2 off
12 Flat-headed bolt – 4 off	28 Sealing washer – 2 off
13 Camshaft cap – 8 off	29 Bore liner – 4 off
14 Bolt – 18 off	30 Bolt
15 Dowel – 18 off	31 Bolt – 2 off
16 Left-hand outer camshaft cap	△ US models only

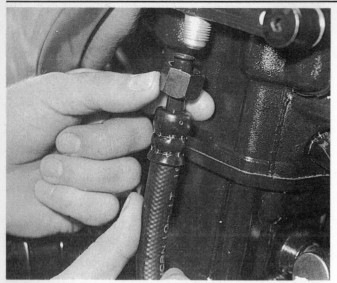

9.4 ZX1000 B and ZX1100 C models remove oil hose which runs down right-hand side of cylinder block

9.5 Do not forget to remove two bolts which pass up through the crankcase

7   Remove the circlips from the pistons by inserting a small flat-bladed screwdriver into the groove in the piston boss and levering them out of position. Discard all circlips regardless of their apparent condition and use new ones during the rebuild.

8   Press each gudgeon pin out of position, noting that if the pins are a tight fit in the piston bosses it is advisable to warm up the pistons before attempting to remove them. Do not use excessive force to remove the gudgeons pins, if necessary, make up a drawbolt arrangement to press them from position. Using a spirit-based marker or scriber, mark each piston inside the skirt so that it is refitted in the appropriate bore on reassembly.

9   The piston rings can be removed by holding the piston in both hands and gently prising the ring ends apart until they can be lifted out of their grooves and onto the piston lands, one side at a time. The rings can then be slipped off the piston and put to one side for examination. Store the rings in the exact order that they were fitted as a guide to reassembly. If the rings are stuck in their grooves by excessive carbon deposits use three strips of thin metal to remove them as shown in the accompanying illustration. Be careful as the rings are brittle and will break easily if overstressed.

10.5 Hold alternator/starter clutch cush drive with service tool (or equivalent) and slacken nut

crankshaft sprocket off their respective shafts and remove them along with the drive chain. Disengage the sprocket and cush drive from the chain, and dismantle the cush drive assembly.

10   Dismantling the engine/gearbox unit: removing the alternator/starter clutch drive components

1   The alternator/starter clutch drive components can be removed with the engine unit in or out of the frame. If the work is to be carried out with the engine in the frame it will first be necessary to drain the oil as described in Routine maintenance, and remove the lower and right-hand fairing sections as described in Chapter 5.

2   **Note:** *if it is necessary to remove the alternator/starter clutch shaft cush drive, a holding tool will be required.* Kawasaki produce a service tool, Part Number 57001-1189, for the job. Alternately a home made peg spanner could be fabricated.

3   Slacken and remove all the retaining bolts from the right-hand crankcase cover and remove the cover from the machine. Be prepared to catch any residual oil which may be released as the cover is removed.

4   Lock the alternator/starter clutch drive chain tensioner by pushing up the tensioner's locking plate. Slacken both its mounting bolts and lift the tensioner assembly clear of the engine. Release the bolt which retains the chain guide and lift the guide off its locating stud. Remove the sleeve from inside the chain guide and store it with the tensioner components for safekeeping.

5   Using the service tool or the home made alternative, hold the alternator/starter clutch shaft cush drive and slacken the cush drive assembly nut, followed by the bolt from the right-hand end of the crankshaft. Once loose, remove both the nut and bolt along with their flat washers. Simultaneously pull both the cush drive assembly and the

11   Dismantling the engine/gearbox unit: removing the clutch

1   The clutch can be removed for inspection or overhaul with the engine unit in or out of the frame. In the former case it will be necessary to drain the engine oil as described in Routine maintenance, and remove the lower and right-hand side fairing sections as described in Chapter 5.

2   **Note:** *if it is necessary to remove the clutch centre nut, a holding tool will be required to prevent the clutch centre from rotating.* Kawasaki produce a service tool, Part Number 57001-305 for ZX900 and ZX1000 A models, and 57001-1243 for ZX1000 B and ZX1100 C models, which is basically a self-locking wrench with blade-like jaws that are turned through 90° to engage with the splines in the clutch centre. In the absence of the correct tool a simple alternative, which is shown in the accompanying photograph, can be made. The tool was fabricated from 1/8 in steel strip and uses a nut and bolt as a pivot. The jaws should be filed or ground to suit the splines in the clutch centre and the handles should be about 2 – 3 feet in length to provide a secure grip.

3   Remove the retaining screws from the right-hand crankcase cover

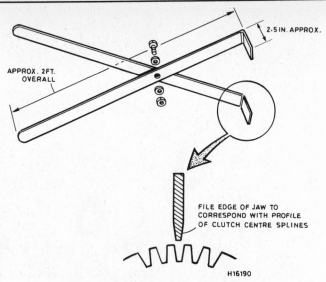

Fig. 1.6 Fabricated clutch holding tool (Sec 11)

11.5 Hold the clutch centre as shown whilst slackening centre nut

and detach the cover from the engine. Be prepared to catch any residual oil which may be released as the cover is removed. Progressively slacken the clutch spring retaining bolts until spring pressure is released, and remove the clutch springs and their retaining bolts. Lift off the clutch pressure plate.

4   On ZX1000 and ZX1100 C models withdraw the short mushroom-headed pushrod assembly from the centre of the input shaft. Remove the cup from the end of the pushrod and lift off the thrust washer and bearing. On ZX900 models pull out the pushrod from the centre of the input shaft and remove the shouldered spacer from the centre of the

pressure plate. On all models remove all the clutch plain and friction plates.

5   Using the Kawasaki service tool or home made substitute, securely hold the clutch centre whilst slackening the centre nut with a socket and extension bar. Once the nut has been slackened, remove it and the large plain or toothed washer beneath it. Pull off the clutch centre followed by the large plain thrust washer.

6   Withdraw the clutch drum centre collar by screwing one of the crankcase cover bolts into the holes provided and pulling it out with the bolt. The clutch drum can then be manoeuvred out of the crankcase

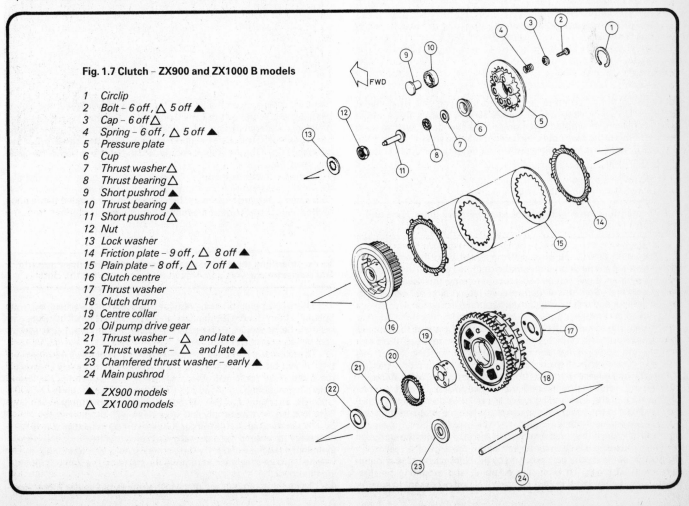

Fig. 1.7 Clutch – ZX900 and ZX1000 B models

1   Circlip
2   Bolt – 6 off , △ 5 off ▲
3   Cap – 6 off △
4   Spring – 6 off , △ 5 off ▲
5   Pressure plate
6   Cup
7   Thrust washer △
8   Thrust bearing △
9   Short pushrod ▲
10   Thrust bearing ▲
11   Short pushrod △
12   Nut
13   Lock washer
14   Friction plate – 9 off , △ 8 off ▲
15   Plain plate – 8 off , △ 7 off ▲
16   Clutch centre
17   Thrust washer
18   Clutch drum
19   Centre collar
20   Oil pump drive gear
21   Thrust washer – △ and late ▲
22   Thrust washer – △ and late ▲
23   Chamfered thrust washer – early ▲
24   Main pushrod

▲   ZX900 models
△   ZX1000 models

Fig. 1.8 Clutch ZX1000 A and ZX1100 C models

1   Cirlcip
2   Bolt – 6 off
3   Cap – 6 off
4   Spring – 6 off
5   Pressure plate
6   Cup
7   Thrust washer
8   Thrust bearing
9   Short pushrod
10   Nut
11   Lock washer
12   Friction plate – 9 off
13   Plain plate – 8 off
14   Clutch centre
15   Damper cam follower
16   Spacer
17   Spring seat
18   Spring – 12 off
19   Damper plate
20   Circlip
21   Clutch shaft
22   Thrust washer
23   Clutch drum
24   Needle roller bearing – ZX1100 only
25   Centre collar
26   Oil pump drive gear
27   Thrust washer – ZX1100 and late ZX1000 models
28   Thrust washer – ZX1100 and late ZX1000 models
29   Chamfered thrust washer – early ZX1000 models
30   Main pushrod

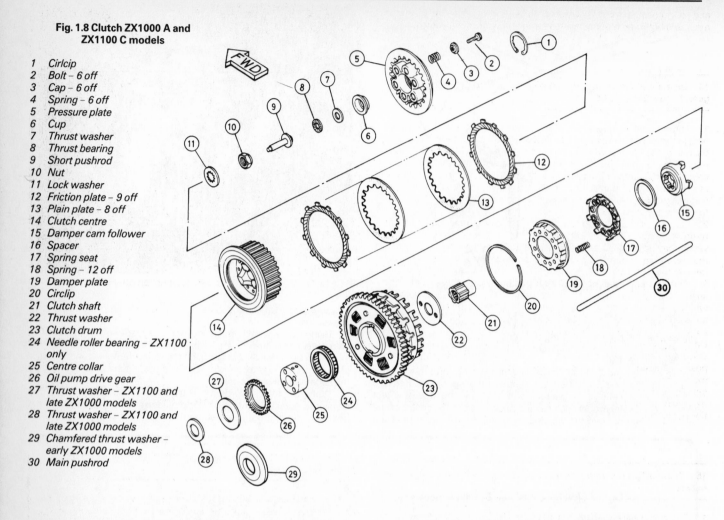

followed by the oil pump drive gear and the large and small thrust washers. On some early ZX900 and ZX1000 A models these thrust washers have been omitted and a single large chamfered washer used instead; if this is the case note which way round the washer is fitted. On ZX1100 C models remove the needle roller bearing from the centre of the clutch drum.

12   Dismantling the engine/gearbox unit: removing the sump and oil pump

1   The sump and oil pump can be removed with the engine unit installed in the frame or on the workbench. If the work is to be carried out in the frame, it will first be necessary to remove the lower and side fairing sections, drain the oil and remove the oil filter, oil cooler and hoses, radiator and exhaust system as described in Section 4.
2   Slacken and remove both the union bolts from the metal oil pipe which links the sump to the crankcase and lift it clear of the engine. Remove the union bolt which secures the main cylinder head oil pipe or hose to the sump, if not already having done so. Disconnect the electrical leads from both the oil pressure and temperature switches (as necessary) and release the lead(s) from any cable ties or guides. Remove all the sump retaining bolts and lower it away from the engine unit. Make a note of the correct position of any oil hose or electrical guides that are fitted to the sump bolts to use as a reference when refitting the sump to the engine. Note the large dowel which locates the sump on the oil pump bracket, if this is loose remove it and store it with the sump.
3   Once the sump has been removed, pull out the large oil screen from the bottom of the engine unit, followed by the black plastic pipe and the two metal oil pipes. To allow the oil pump and mounting bracket assembly to be removed from the engine it is first necessary to ensure

that the projections on the shaft of the pump are vertical. If the clutch has also been removed this can be done by simply turning the oil pump drive gear, situated behind the clutch. If not, it will be necessary to turn the crankshaft. This can be done by removing the cover from the left-hand end of the crankshaft and turning the ignition rotor with a large ring spanner.
4   Remove the three oil pump bracket mounting bolts and withdraw the bracket assembly from the engine noting the dowel, and the oil nozzle and O-ring that locate the bracket on the crankcase. Make a note of their correct positions and remove them if loose.

13   Dismantling the engine/gearbox unit: removing the alternator and starter motor

1   These components can be removed with the engine unit either in or out of the frame. In the former case on ZX1000 and ZX1100 C models, it will first be necessary to remove the lower and left-hand side fairing sections as described in Chapter 5.
2   The alternator is situated on the left-hand side of the engine, behind the cylinder block. Trace the alternator wiring back to its block connector and disconnect it from the main wiring loom. Remove the three alternator mounting bolts and pull the alternator away from the engine. Once the alternator has been lifted clear, remove the rubber dampers from its cush drive assembly and store them with the alternator.
3   To remove the starter motor Kawasaki recommend that it is first necessary to remove the external gearchange mechanism cover. However on the machine shown in the photographs, it was found that there was just enough clearance to remove the starter motor without removing this cover.
4   Slacken and remove the nut which secures the starter motor lead

and disconnect it from the motor. Release both the starter motor mounting bolts and manoeuvre the motor away from the engine.

14 Dismantling the engine/gearbox unit: removing the external gearchange components

1   The external gearchange mechanism components can be removed with the engine in or out of the frame. If the work is to be carried out with the unit in the frame it will first be necessary on ZX1000 and ZX1100 C models to remove the lower and left-hand side fairing sections as described in Chapter 5. On all models it is necessary to drain the oil and remove the water pump, clutch slave cylinder, gearchange linkage, engine sprocket casing and the sprocket itself. Refer to Section 4 for further information.
2   Slacken all the gearchange mechanism cover retaining bolts and remove the cover from the engine. Be prepared to catch any residual oil which may be released as the cover is removed. Note the two dowels that locate the cover on the crankcase. If these dowels are loose, remove them and store them with the cover for safekeeping.
3   Disengage the gearchange shaft from the selector drum and pull the shaft out of the crankcase. Remove the nuts and shouldered washers which retain the neutral and gear position detent arms and remove the arms along with their return springs. Note that although the detent arms are identical the return springs are different and are not interchangeable. On ZX900 and ZX1000 A models Kawasaki mark the neutral (upper) arm return spring with blue paint, and on ZX1000 B models the gear position (lower) arm spring is marked with white paint. On ZX1100 C models the gear position (lower) arm spring is yellow, and the neutral (upper) arm spring white. If these marks have worn off, it will be necessary to mark the springs in some way to ensure they are positioned correctly on refitting.

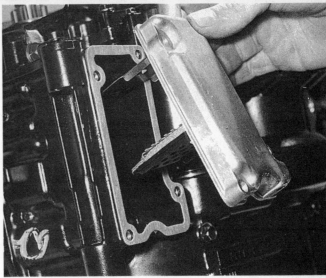

16.4 If necessary, breather cover can be removed for cleaning; use a new gasket on refitting

4   Separate the crankcase halves with the unit inverted on the bench, lifting the lower half off the upper half. The crankshaft and gearbox shafts will remain in position in the upper half but take care not to dislodge or lose any main bearing inserts from the lower casing. Note the two crankcase half locating dowels that are located on each side of the crankshaft; if loose, remove them for safekeeping.

15 Dismantling the engine/gearbox unit: separating the crankcase halves

1   The crankcase halves cannot be separated until the engine/gearbox unit has been removed from the frame as described in Section 4 of this Chapter, and all the preliminary dismantling has been carried out. If a full engine/gearbox strip is being performed, then all operations described in Sections 6 to 14 inclusive must be carried out first. If, however, it is wished only to examine the gearbox or starter clutch components, then the operations described in Sections 6, 7, 8, 9, 11 and 13 can be ignored. Note also that it is only necessary to remove the clutch if the gearbox input shaft is to be dismantled, otherwise it can be left in position.
2   The crankcase halves are secured by two 8 mm bolts and six 6 mm bolts fitted from the top side of the crankcase, and eleven 6 mm bolts and nine 8 mm bolts (which are situated around the main bearings) from the underside of the crankcase. Note on ZX1100 C models the nine main bearing bolts are 9 mm in diameter and one of the lower 6 mm bolts is replaced with a 7 mm item. With the unit upright, progressively slacken and remove first the 6 mm bolts, then the 8 mm bolts from the top side of the crankcase. Then invert the crankcase and repeat the process for the bolts on the underside of the crankcase. Slacken the main bearing bolts in the reverse order of their tightening sequence which is stamped on the lower crankcase half. Note that it is not necessary to remove the main bearing cap, situated behind the balancer shaft, to separate the crankcase halves. As each bolt is removed, store it in its relative position, along with any guides or washers, in a cardboard template of the crankcase halves so that it can be refitted in its original position on reassembly.
3   Leverage points are provided on the front left-hand side of the crankcase, inside the ignition rotor housing, and on the back right-hand side, inside the clutch housing. Insert a large flat-bladed screwdriver between these points and gently prise the crankcase halves apart. Alternately, a hammer and a block of wood can be used to jar the cases apart. Usually the joint will break fairly easily. If difficulty is encountered in breaking the seal on the crankcase halves, thoroughly check that all crankcase bolts and components have been removed before forcing the cases apart.

16 Dismantling the engine/gearbox unit: removing the upper crankcase components

1   Once the crankcase halves have been separated, both the input and output gearbox shaft assemblies can be lifted out of the upper casing, noting that these have half ring retainers fitted to the ball journal bearing grooves, and locating pins for the needle roller bearing outer races on the opposite ends of each shaft. Remove the half ring retainers from the casing and, if loose, the locating pins.
2   To remove the crankshaft, slacken the two bolts which retain the single main bearing cap and lift it clear. Note the direction of the arrow on the top surface of the bearing cap and take care not to lose the bearing insert or the dowels. The crankshaft can then be lifted out of position, taking care not to dislodge any of the bearing inserts.
3   Hold the alternator cush drive coupling, slacken its retaining bolt, and remove the coupling from the engine. If difficulty is encountered in holding the coupling, temporarily refit the alternator/starter clutch cush drive assembly to the opposite end of the shaft and hold it with the service tool whilst removing the bolt. The shaft can then be withdrawn from the casing and the starter clutch removed. If the starter motor idler gear is also to be removed, slacken and remove the bolt and washer that hold the idler gear shaft in position, remove the shaft itself and lift out the idler gear. Note that on ZX1100 C models, the idler shaft retaining bolt also retains an oil spray pipe. This should also be removed from the casing.
4   On all models the breather cover on the top surface of the crankcase, retained by four bolts, need not be removed except for cleaning purposes. If removed, renew the gasket when refitting the cover to the casing.

17 Dismantling the engine/gearbox unit: removing the lower crankcase components

1   Remove the bolts which secure the selector drum retaining plate to the side of the casing and remove the plate. Withdraw the selector fork

snaft from the lower crankcase and lift out the selector forks as they are freed from the end of the shaft. Make a note of how the three selector forks are positioned to use as a guide when reassembling the gear selector components. Once the selector shaft and forks are removed the selector drum can also be removed from the casing.

2   To remove the balancer shaft assembly, slacken and remove both the balancer shaft clamp pinch and mounting bolts and pull the clamp off its shaft. On ZX1000 B and ZX1100 C models, remove the balancer shaft guide pin retaining plate from inside the crankcase, and lift out the guide pin with a pair of sharp-nosed pliers. On all models tap or pull the balancer shaft out until the oil seal is displaced from the crankcase half. Remove the oil seal from the end of the shaft, followed by the thrust washer (ZX1000 B and ZX1100 C models only). Fully withdraw the balancer shaft, whilst holding the balancer weight, and remove both components from the casing.

18   Examination and renovation: general

1   Before any component is examined, it must be cleaned thoroughly. Being careful not to mark or damage the item in question, use a blunt-edged scraper (an old kitchen knife or a broken plastic ruler can be very useful) to remove any caked-on deposits of dirt or oil, followed by a good scrub with a soft wire brush (a brass wire brush of the type sold for cleaning suede shoes is best, with an assortment of bottle-cleaning brushes for ports, coolant passages etc). Take care not to remove any paint code marks from internal components.

2   Soak the component in a solvent to remove the bulk of the remaining dirt or oil. If one of the proprietary engine degreasers (such as Gunk or Jizer) is not available, a high flash-point solvent such as paraffin (kerosene) should be used. The use of petrol as a cleaning agent cannot be recommended because of the fire risk. With all of the above cleaning agents take great care to prevent any drops getting into the eyes and try to avoid prolonged skin contact. To finish off the cleaning procedure wash each component in hot soapy water (as hot as your hands can bear); this will remove a surprising amount of dirt on its own and the residual heat usually dries the component very effectively. Carefully scrape away any remaining traces of old gasket material from all joint faces.

3   If there is the slightest doubt about the lubrication system, for example if a fault appears to have been caused by a failure of the oil supply, all components should be dismantled so that the oilways can be checked and cleared of any possible obstructions. Always use clean, lint-free rag for cleaning and drying components to prevent the risk of small particles obstructing oilways.

4   Examine each part carefully to determine the extent of wear, checking with the tolerance figures listed in the Specifications section of this chapter. If there is any doubt about the condition of a particular component, play safe and renew it.

5   Various instruments for measuring wear are required, including an internal and external micrometer or vernier gauge, and a set of standard feeler gauges. Additionally, although not absolutely necessary, a dial gauge and mounting bracket are invaluable for accurate measurement of endfloat, and play between components of very low diameter bores – where a micrometer cannot reach. After some experience has been gained, the state of wear of many components can be determined visually, or by feel, and a decision on their suitability for re-use made without resorting to direct measurement.

6   The machine's manufacturer recommends the use of Plastigage for measuring radial clearance between working surfaces such as shell bearings and their journals. Plastigage consists of a fine strand of plastic material manufactured to an accurate diameter. A short length of Plastigage is placed between the two surfaces, the clearance of which is to be measured. The surfaces are assembled in their normal working positions and the securing nuts or bolts fastened to the correct torque setting; the surfaces are then separated. The amount of compression to which the gauge material is subjected and the resultant spreading indicates the clearance. This is measured directly, across the width of the Plastigage, using a pre-marked indicator supplied with the Plastigage kit. If Plastigage is not available, both an internal and external micrometer will be required to check wear limits.

19   Examination and renovation: engine cases and covers

1   Small cracks or holes in aluminium castings may be repaired with an epoxy resin adhesive, such as Araldite, as a temporary measure. Permanent repairs can only be effected by argon-arc welding, and only a specialist in this process is in a position to advise on the economics or practicability of such a repair.

2   Damaged threads can be economically reclaimed by using a diamond section wire insert, of the helicoil type, which is easily fitted after drilling and re-tapping the affected thread. Most motorcycle dealers and small engineering firms offer a service of this kind.

3   Sheared studs or screws can usually be removed with screw extractors, which consist of tapered, left-hand thread screws of very hard steel. These are inserted into a pre-drilled hole in the stud, and usually succeed in dislodging the most stubborn stud or screw. If a problem arises which seems beyond your scope, it is worth consulting a professional engineering firm before condemning an otherwise sound casing. Many of these firms advertise regularly in the motorcycle press.

20   Examination and renovation: bearings and oil seals

1   Ball bearings should be washed thoroughly to remove all traces of oil then tested as follows. Hold the outer race firmly and attempt to move the inner race up and down, then from side to side. Examine bearing balls, tracks and cages looking for signs of pitting or other damage. Finally spin the bearing and check that it rotates smoothly and with no sign of notchiness. If any free play, roughness or other damage is found the bearing must be renewed.

2   Roller bearings are checked in much the same way, except that free play can only be checked in the up and down direction with the components temporarily assembled. Remember that if a roller bearing fails it may well mean having to replace, as well as the bearing, one or two other components which form its inner and outer races. If in any doubt about the condition of a roller bearing, renew it.

3   Do not waste time checking oil seals. Discard all seals and O-rings disturbed during dismantling work and fit new ones on reassembly. Considering their habit of leaking once disturbed, and the amount of time and trouble necessary to replace them, they are relatively cheap if renewed as a matter of course whenever they are disturbed.

4   Oil seals can be levered out of the casings using a large flat-bladed screwdriver. Take care not to scratch or damage the casing whilst doing this. On refitting, use a hammer and suitably sized socket, which bears only on the hard outer race of the seal, to tap the seal into position. Ensure the seal enters the casing squarely and is flush with the casing once in position. Smear the lips of the seal with grease to prevent the seal being damaged on reassembly.

20.4a Carefully lever out old oil seals using a flat-bladed screwdriver ...

20.4b ... and tap new seals into position with a suitable drift

21   Examination and renovation: camshafts and camshaft drive mechanism

1   Examine the camshaft lobes for signs of wear or scoring. Wear is normally evident in the form of visual flats worn on the peak of the lobes, and this may be checked by measuring each lobe at its widest point. If any lobe is worn by a significant amount the camshaft must be renewed. Scoring or similar damage can usually be attributed to a partial failure of the lubrication system, possibly due to the oil and filter not having been renewed at the specified intervals, causing unfiltered oil to be circulated by way of the bypass valve. Before fitting a new camshaft, examine the bearing surfaces of the cylinder head and the cam followers.
2   If the cam lobes are scored it is likely that the surfaces of the cam followers are also damaged. If this is the case all the damaged followers must be renewed along with the camshaft. Also measure the inside diameter of each follower and the external diameter of the followers shaft. If any component is found to have worn beyond the service limits given in the Specifications at the start of this Chapter, it must be renewed.
3   If the camshaft bearing surfaces are scored or excessively worn, it is likely that renewal of both the cylinder head and camshafts will be necessary. This is because the camshafts run directly in the cylinder

21.1 Examine cam lobes for signs of scoring

head casting, using the alloy as a bearing surface. Note that it is not possible to purchase the camshaft bearing caps alone, as they are machined together with the cylinder head and are thus matched to it. It may however be possible for an expert to effect a repair. There are a number of engineering firms who specialise in this repair, usually involving the fitting of bearing inserts (shells), or needle roller bearings to the cylinder head and bearing caps. Due to the cost of a new cylinder head it is recommended that one of these firms, who regularly advertise in the motorcycle press, is consulted before condemning an otherwise sound cylinder head.
4   Measure the camshaft bearing journals, using a micrometer. If any journal has worn beyond the service limit, the camshaft(s) must be renewed. The clearance between the camshaft and its bearing cap can be checked using Plastigage or by direct measurement. The clearance must not exceed the specified limit.
5   Camshaft runout can be checked by supporting each end of the camshaft on V-blocks, and measuring any runout using a dial gauge. If the runout exceeds the service limit the camshaft must be renewed.
6   The camchain should also be checked for wear, particularly if chain noise has been noted when the engine is running, this is usually an indication that the chain is due for renewal. Lay the chain on a flat surface and get an assistant to stretch it taut. Using a vernier caliper, measure a 20 link length of the chain, ie from the centre of one pin to the centre of the 21st pin along. Repeat this check on several different sections of the chain and note the readings obtained. If any section of the chain has worn beyond the service limit it must be renewed.
7   The tensioner guide and blade should be examined for wear or damage, which will normally be fairly obvious, renewing it if necessary. The camchain tensioner can be checked for wear only by comparison with a new item. If any doubt exists as to the condition of the tensioner it should be renewed.

22   Examination and renovation: cylinder head

1   Remove all traces of carbon from the cylinder head using a blunt-ended scraper (the rounded end of an old steel rule will do). Finish by polishing with metal polish to give a smooth shiny surface.
2   Check the condition of the spark plug threads. If the threads are worn or cross-threaded they can be reclaimed by the fitting of a Helicoil insert. Most motorcycle dealers operate this service which is very simple, cheap and effective.
3   Lay the cylinder head on a sheet of $\frac{1}{4}$ inch plate glass to check for distortion. Aluminium alloy cylinder heads distort very easily, especially if the cylinder head bolts are tightened down unevenly. If the amount of distortion is only slight, it is permissible to rub the head down until it is flat again by wrapping a sheet of very fine emery cloth around the sheet of glass and rubbing with a rotary motion.
4   If the cylinder head is badly distorted (as shown by frequent blowing of the cylinder head gasket), the head will have to be skimmed by a competent engineer who is experienced in this kind of work. This will of course raise the compression of the engine and if too much is removed, the performance of the engine will be adversely affected. In extreme cases the valves might even strike the pistons, causing serious engine damage. If there is a risk of this happening, the only solution is to renew the cylinder head.
5   Refer to Sections 21 and 23 of this Chapter for information on the camshaft bearings and valves.

23   Examination and renovation: valves, valve seats and valve guides

1   Before removing the valves from the cylinder head, obtain a container and partition it off into 16 separate sections. Clearly label each section with the cylinder number and valve position and place the valve components in their respective sections as they are removed. This will prevent interchanging of valve components and ensure that they are refitted in their original positions. However, where possible, it is still recommended that work should be carried out on one valve assembly at a time.
2   Compress the valve springs with a suitable valve spring compressor, and remove both valve collets. Carefully remove the valve spring compressor and lift the spring retainer collar off the valve. Lift off both

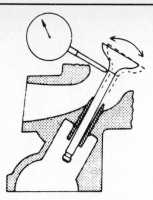

Fig. 1.9 Valve stem to guide wear check (Sec 23)

the valve springs, noting that they are fitted with the closer-pitched coils at the bottom, and then slide the valve out of the cylinder head. The oil seal can then be carefully levered off the valve guide and both the spring seats removed.

3   Inspect each valve for wear, overheating or burning and renew as a set if necessary. Normally, the exhaust valves will need attention or renewing more often than the inlet valves, as the latter run at relatively low temperatures. If any of the valve seats are badly pitted, do not attempt to cure this by grinding them, as this invariably causes the valve seats to become pocketed. It is permissible to have the valve(s) refaced by a motorcycle specialist or engineering firm. Measure the valve stem diameter, the valve head thickness (distance between the edge of the seating surface and the top of its head) and the valve stem runout. Renew the valve if any measurement obtained is outside the service limits given in the Specifications.

4   Check the valve stems and their guides for wear either by direct measurement or as follows using the 'wobble' method. Insert the valve into its guide and set up a dial test indicator perpendicular to it as shown in the accompanying figure. Rock the valve to and fro along the direction of the cam lobe, and then at right angles to it. Note the readings obtained. If either measurement is greater than the service limit and the valve stem diameter is known to be correct, the valve guide is worn and must be renewed. If a small bore gauge and micrometer are available, the two components can be measured at three or four points along their bearing surfaces, both in the direction of the cam lobe and at right angles to it. If any measurement obtained is beyond the service limit, one or both components must be renewed.

5   Valve guide renewal is not easy and will require that the valve seats be recut after the guide has been fitted and reamed. It is also remarkably easy to damage the cylinder head unless great care is taken during these operations. With this and the cost of the Kawasaki service tools needed for the job in mind, it is strongly recommended that the job be entrusted to an authorized Kawasaki dealer. However, for the more skilled and better equipped owner the procedure is as follows.

6   Heat the cylinder head slowly and evenly, in an oven to prevent warpage, to approximately 120 – 150°C (248 – 302°F). Using a stepped drift, tap the guide(s) lightly out of the head, taking care not to burn yourself on the hot casting. New guides are fitted in a similar manner, being tapped down lightly until they are correctly seated. If a valve guide is loose in the cylinder head, it may be possible to have an oversize guide machined and fitted by a competent engineering works.

7   After the guide has been fitted it must be reamed using a Kawasaki reamer (Part Number 57001-1079 on ZX900 and ZX1000 A models and 57001-1204 on ZX1000 B and ZX1100 C models). Make sure the reamer passes squarely through the valve guide, taking care not to gouge out too much material accidentally. The valve seat must now be recut as follows. This process requires the use of five cutters, 32° and 45° inlet valve cutter, 32° and 45° exhaust valve cutter and 60° cutter for both, along with a pilot bar and T-handle. All of which can be purchased from any Kawasaki dealer.

8   Fit the appropriate 45° cutter to the pilot bar, fit the T-handle and insert the pilot bar into the valve guide until the cutter makes contact with the valve seat. Using firm hand pressure, rotate the cutter through one or two full turns to clean the seat then withdraw the cutter and examine the seat. If the seat is continous and free from pitting proceed to the next step, but if pitting is still evident, refit the cutter and repeat the procedure until all pitting has been removed. Be very careful to

remove only the bare minimum of material necessary as valve seat inserts are not available. If the seat becomes sunken through over-cutting, the complete cylinder head assembly must be renewed.

9   Once the valve seating face is in good condition it is necessary to check the outside diameter of the seating face, using a vernier caliper, to ensure it is within the specified limits. If the outside diameter is too small, repeat the above procedure with the 45° cutter until it is within the specified range. However, if the outside diameter is too large proceed as follows.

10   Fit the appropriate 32° cutter to the pilot bar, fit the T-handle and insert the pilot bar into the valve guide until the cutter comes into contact with the valve seat. Noting that the 32° cutter removes material very quickly, press down lightly on the T-handle and rotate the cutter through one turn. Remove the cutter and recheck the valve seat diameter, repeat the above procedure until the outside diameter is within the specified range.

11   With the seating face outside diameter correct, it is now necessary to check the width of the valve seat (45° portion). If the valve seat width is below the specified limit, cut the seat using the 45° cutter until the seat width is slightly too wide, then trim the seat back to within the specified range using the 32° cutter. If the seat is too wide, fit the 60° cutter to the pilot bar and trim the seat until it is within the specified range. Once both the outside diameter and the width of the valve seat are correct the valves should be ground in as follows.

12   The valves should be ground in using oil-bound grinding paste to remove any light pitting or to finish off a newly cut seat. Note that it is not normally essential to resort to using the coarse grinding paste which is supplied in the dual-grade containers. Commence by smearing a trace of fine grinding compound (carborundum paste) on the valve seat and apply a suction tool to the head of the valve. Oil the valve stem and insert the valve into its guide so that the valve and valve seat make contact with each other. With a semi-rotary motion, grind in the valve head to the seat, using a backwards and forwards motion. Lift the valve occasionally to ensure the grinding paste is evenly distributed. Repeat the application until an unbroken ring of light grey matt finish is obtained on both the valve and valve seat. This denotes the grinding operation is now complete. Before moving on to the next valve, ensure that all traces of grinding compound are removed from both the valve and its seat and that none has entered the valve guide. If this precaution is not observed, rapid wear will take place due to the highly abrasive nature of the grinding compound.

13   Examine the spring retaining collars and collets, renewing any that are marked or damaged in any way. Measure the length of all the valve springs and renew any that are on or below the service limit given in the Specifications at the start of this Chapter. Although valve springs are available separately, it is considered good practice to renew them all as a set.

14   Place both the spring seats over the guides and press a new seal over each valve guide upper end. Liberally oil the guide bore and the valve stem before inserting the valves into the guides. Refit the valve springs, ensuring that the closer-pitched coils are at the bottom (next to the cylinder head), and fit the spring retaining collar. Check that both springs are correctly seated, compress them, and refit the collets.

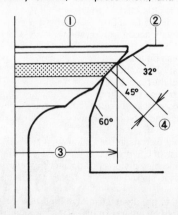

Fig. 1.10 Valve seat recutting angles (Sec 23)

1 Valve	3 Seating area outside
2 Cylinder head	diameter
	4 Seating area width

23.14a Fit a new oil seal (arrowed) to the valve guide and refit both the outer ...

23.14b ... and inner spring seats

23.14c Liberally oil the valve stem and insert it into the guide

23.14d Refit the valve springs, ensuring that their closer-pitched coils are at the bottom ...

23.14e ... followed by the spring retaining collar

23.14f Compress the valve springs and refit the collets

Remove the valve spring compressor and give the end of each valve a sharp tap with a hammer to ensure the collets are correctly seated.

24 Examination and renovation: cylinder block

1   The usual indication of badly worn cylinder bores and pistons is excessive smoking from the exhausts. This usually takes the form of a blue haze tending to develop into a white haze as the wear becomes more pronounced.

2   The other indication is piston slap, a form of metallic rattle which occurs when there is little load on the engine. If the top of the bore is examined carefully, it will be found that there is a ridge on the thrust side; the depth will vary according to the rate of wear which has taken place.

3   Cylinder wear can be assessed by measuring the bore diameter at the following points: 10 mm and 60 mm from the top of the bore, and 20 mm from the base of the bore. Measure both along the gudgeon pin axis and at right angles to it so that a total of six measurements are taken. If any of the readings obtained exceed the service limit given in the Specifications, the cylinder block will have to be rebored and fitted with oversize pistons.

4   Kawasaki supply pistons in only one oversize, + 0.5 mm (+ 0.020 in). If boring in excess of 0.5 mm becomes necessary, the cylinder liners must be renewed and new pistons fitted. Liner renewal is strictly a task for experts and the job should be entrusted to an authorised Kawasaki dealer.

5   If new rings are to be run in a used cylinder bore, the bore surface must first be prepared by honing, or glaze-busting. This process, which can also be used to remove marks caused by very light piston seizure, involves the use of a cylinder bore honing tool usually in conjunction with an electric drill to break down the glazed surface which forms on any bore during normal service. The prepared bore will have a very lightly roughened surface which will help the rings to bed in rapidly and

fully. This is normally done as a matter of course after reboring. It also has the advantage of removing the lip from the top of the bore which could otherwise damage the new top piston ring. Most motorcycle dealers have glaze-busting equipment and will carry out the work for a small charge.

25 Examination and renovation: pistons and piston rings

1   If the cylinders are rebored or new liners fitted, the existing pistons and rings can be disregarded as they will be replaced by new items. If, however, the bores have been cleaned and checked as described in the preceding Section and are to be reused, clean and check the pistons and rings as follows.

2   Remove all traces of carbon from the piston crowns using a blunt-ended scraper to avoid damaging the piston surface. Finish off by polishing the crowns of the pistons with metal polish to prevent carbon deposits adhering so rapidly in future. Never use emery cloth on the soft aluminium alloy of the piston.

3   Piston wear usually occurs at the skirt or lower end of the piston and takes the form of vertical streaks or score marks on the thrust side of the piston. Damage of this nature will necessitate renewal and is checked by measuring the outside diameter of the skirt at a point 5 mm (0.2 in) from the base of the skirt and at right angles to its gudgeon pin axis. If any piston has worn to or beyond its service limit, it must be renewed.

4   After the engine has covered a high mileage, it is possible that the ring grooves may have become enlarged. To check this, refit the rings to the piston and measure the clearance between the ring and groove using feeler gauges. If the gap exceeds the service limit, remove the rings from the piston and measure the thickness of the piston rings and the piston ring groove, renewing any component which exceeds its service limit.

5   To measure the piston ring end gap, insert the ring into its bore, using the crown of the bare piston to locate it approximately 10 mm

25.3 Measuring piston diameter

25.4 Checking piston ring to groove clearance

25.5 Measuring piston ring end gap

from the bottom of the bore. Ensure it is square in the bore and measure the end gap of the ring using feeler gauges. If the ring gap exceeds the limits given, the rings should be renewed as a set.

6   It is also necessary to check the end gap when fitting new rings. If there is insufficient clearance, the rings will break up in the bore whilst the engine is running causing extensive engine damage. If necessary the end gap can be increased by carefully filing the ends of the rings with a fine file. Support the ring on the end as much as possible to avoid breakage and ensure the ring ends are kept square. Remove only a small amount at a time and keep rechecking the end gap in the bore.

26 Examination and renovation: connecting rods and big-end bearings

1   Examine the connecting rods for signs of cracking or distortion, renewing any rod which is not in perfect condition. Check the connecting rod big-end side clearance, using feeler gauges. If the clearance exceeds the specified limit it will be necessary to renew the con-rod or crankshaft as necessary. Examine the gudgeon pin and small-end bore of the con-rod for scoring or signs of wear, renewing both components as a pair if any sign of damage is present. Connecting rod distortion can only be properly assessed with a great deal of specialised equipment and should therefore only be checked by an expert, otherwise if any doubt remains about the condition of a rod it should be renewed.

2   If a connecting rod is renewed, it is essential that it is of the correct weight group to minimise vibration. The weight is indicated by a letter which is marked across each rod and its big-end cap. This letter together with the crankpin diameter mark (see paragraph 6) should be quoted

when purchasing new con-rod(s). Ideally all rods should be of the same weight although it is permissible for the rods of cylinders 1 and 2 to be of one weight group and those of cylinders 3 and 4 of another.

3   To examine the big-end bearing inserts and the crankshaft journals it is necessary to remove the connecting rods from the crankshaft. Mark the rods with a spirit-based marker to ensure that they are refitted to their appropriate crankpin on reassembly. Note that on ZX1000 and ZX1100 C models the connecting rod bolts are designed to stretch when tightened and therefore whenever the bolts and nuts are disturbed they should be renewed on reassembly. *Never reuse them as this could lead to the big-end caps becoming loose while the engine is running, resulting in extensive engine damage.* The bolts are an extremely tight fit in the connecting rod and great care will be required to avoid marking the rod when tapping out the old bolts. Ensure the heads of the new bolts are fitted in the same position as the old ones and that

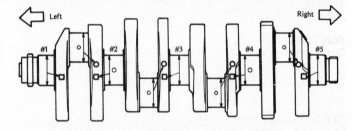

Fig. 1.11 Location of crankshaft size range marks (Sec 26)

○   *Crankpin diameter mark – O mark or unmarked*
□   *Main bearing journal diameter mark – 1 mark or unmarked*

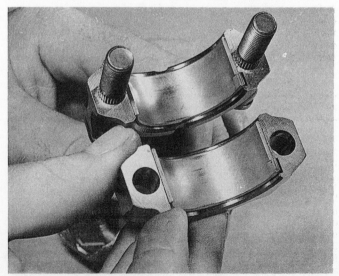

26.2 Connecting rod weight is indicated by the letter stamped on each rod

26.4 Examine bearing inserts for signs of wear, renewing if necessary

Fig. 1.12 Bearing insert (shell) colour code location (Sec 26)

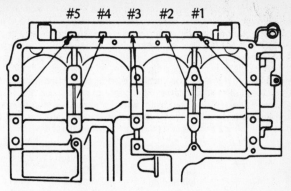

Fig. 1.13 Main bearing inserts journal number locations (Sec 27)

they do not rotate as their nuts are tightened. Wash the new nuts and bolts in a high flash-point solvent to remove the anti-rust solution which they are coated with at the factory. Dry the bolts immediately using a jet of compressed air.

4   Examine closely the big-end bearing inserts (shells). The bearing surface should be smooth and of even texture, with no signs of scoring or streaking on its surface. If any insert is in less than perfect condition, all bearing inserts should be renewed as a set. In practice, it is advisable to renew the bearing inserts during a major overhaul as a precautionary measure. The inserts are relatively cheap and it is false economy to reuse worn components.

5   The crankshaft journals should be given a close visual examination, paying particular attention where damaged bearing inserts were discovered. If the journals are scored or pitted in any way, a new crankshaft will be required. Note that undersize inserts are not available, thus precluding the option of re-grinding the crankshaft.

6   To select new inserts, use the manufacturers size code system. The standard crankpin outside diameter is divided into two size groups to allow for manufacturing tolerances. The size group of each crankpin can be determined by examining the crankshaft web which is immediately adjacent to it. The crank web will be marked with either an O or no mark at all. **Note:** *ignore 1 marks as these refer to main bearing journals.* The connecting rods are marked in a similar fashion with the mark, if applicable, being situated next to the weight mark. If the equipment is available, these marks can be checked by direct measurement. The bearing inserts can then be selected using the relevant table below.

ZX900 and ZX1000 A models

Connecting rod mark	Crankshaft mark	Insert colour
O	Unmarked	Blue
O	O	Black
Unmarked	Unmarked	Black
Unmarked	O	Brown

ZX1000 B and ZX1100 C models

Connecting rod mark	Crankshaft mark	Insert colour
O	Unmarked	White
O	O	Blue
Unmarked	Unmarked	Blue
Unmarked	O	Black

7   If the existing inserts are to be reused, use Plastigage to check the clearance as described in Section 17. If the clearance measured is within the specified limits, the existing shells can be reused. If the clearance is excessive, even with new shells (of the correct size code) the crankpin is worn and expert advice should be obtained.

27   Examination and renovation: crankshaft and main bearings

1   The crankshaft should be thoroughly cleaned using a high flash-point solvent. Be very careful to check that all the oilways are completely free from dirt and other foreign matter.

2   Examine the crankshaft closely. Any obvious signs of damage such as marked bearing surfaces or damaged threads will mean that it must be renewed. There are however engineering firms, who advertise in the motorcycle press, who can undertake major crankshaft repairs. In view of the expense of a new component it is worth trying such firms provided they are competent.

3   Temporarily refit the crankshaft in either crankcase half and use feeler gauges to measure the clearance between the crankcase pillars and their respective crank webs. Alternatively, a dial gauge can be mounted parallel to the crankshaft with its tip touching one end. Push the crankshaft fully away from the gauge, zero the gauge, then push the

crankshaft fully towards the gauge and note the reading obtained. If the crankshaft endfloat exceeds the specified service limit the crankcases must be renewed as a matched pair. Crankshaft runout is measured using a dial gauge with the crankshaft mounted on V-blocks at each outer main bearing journal. If crankshaft runout, measured at the centre main bearing journal, exceeds the service limit the crankshaft must be renewed.

4   Examine the camchain drive sprocket on the left-hand end of the crankshaft for signs of wear or damage. If necessary, the sprocket can be removed for renewal using a bearing puller tool.

5   Make a visual examination of the bearing crankshaft journals and inserts as described in paragraphs 4 and 5 of the preceding Section. New inserts can be selected as follows:

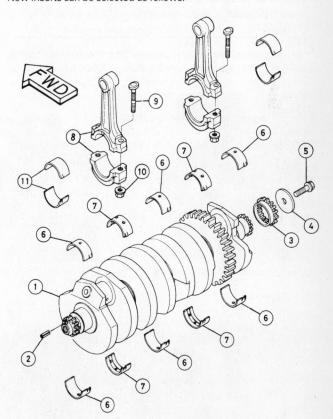

Fig. 1.14 Crankshaft and connecting rods

1 Crankshaft	7 Main bearing shells –
2 Locating pin	grooved – 4 off
3 Primary drive gear	8 Connecting rod – 4 off
4 Washer	9 Big-end bolt – 8 off
5 Bolt	10 Nut – 8 off
6 Main bearing shells – plain	11 Big-end bearing shells – 8
– 6 off	off

6   The standard crankshaft main bearing journal diameter is divided into two size groups to allow for manufacturing tolerances. The size group of each journal can be determined by examining its adjacent crank web. The crank web will be marked with either a 1 or no mark at all. Ignore O marks as these refer to big-end crankpin diameters. The upper crankcase is also marked along its front edge with either an O or no mark at all. Both marks can be checked by direct measurement if the necessary equipment is available. The bearing inserts can then be selected using the table below. Note: when ordering bearing inserts always state the journal number of the required insert (see Fig. 1.13), noting that numbers 2 and 4 inserts have an oil groove in them.

Crankcase mark	Crankshaft mark	Insert colour
O	1	Brown
Unmarked	Unmarked	Blue
O	Unmarked	Black
Unmarked	1	Black

7   If the existing inserts are to be reused, use Plastigage to check the clearance as described in Section 17, noting that it will be necessary to refit all the crankcase bolts and tighten them in the correct order progressively up to their specified torque settings. If the clearance measured is within the specified limits, the existing inserts can be reused. If the clearance is excessive, even with new inserts (of the correct size code), the main bearing journal is worn and expert advice should be obtained.

28 Examination and renovation: alternator/starter clutch drive components

1   The condition of the alternator/starter clutch drive chain can be assessed by measuring a section of the chain as follows. Lay the chain on a flat surface and get an assistant to stretch it taut. Using a vernier caliper, measure a 20 link length of the chain, ie from the centre of one pin to the centre of the 21st pin along. Repeat this check on several different sections of the chain and note the readings obtained. If any section of the chain measured has stretched beyond the service limit it must be renewed.

2   The tensioner blade and guide should be examined for wear or damage which will be fairly obvious, renewing it if necessary. The strength of the chain tensioner can only be tested in comparison with a new one. If any doubt exists as to the condition of the tensioner it should be renewed.

3   Wear of the shaft itself is unlikely unless a very high mileage has been covered. Check carefully its various threads and splines.

4   The two cush drives fitted on each end of the shaft consist of inner and outer parts with rubber segments to take up the transmission shocks. Any damage will be self-evident once they are dismantled and should normally be confined to the rubber segments. These will become compressed and rounded off, or may even start to break, but again only after a high mileage. Renew the rubbers as a set if in any doubt as to their condition.

5   Renew the starter idler gear and driven gear if their teeth are chipped or worn, or if their centre bearing surfaces have worn, making them a sloppy fit on their respective shafts.

6   Remove the circlip and washer from the starter clutch assembly, separate the starter clutch and driven gear, and remove the needle roller bearing from the clutch. Examine the needle roller bearing for any sign of wear together with the bearing surfaces of the driven gear and clutch. Also check that the outer bearing surface of the driven gear is smooth and unmarked by contact with the clutch rollers. The rollers themselves should also be undamaged with no signs of wear such as pitting or flat spots, and should be able to move freely. On ZX900 and early ZX1000 A models, check that the plungers and springs are in good condition. If any component is found to be worn or damaged, it must be renewed.

7   Liberally oil the needle roller bearing and fit it onto the starter clutch assembly. Refit the driven gear, followed by the washer and secure them both with the circlip. Check that the driven gear will spin freely in one direction, but not the other.

28.3 If worn, renew cush drive rubbers as a set

28.6 Renew starter clutch rollers if they are marked in any way

28.7a Refit the needle roller bearing ...

28.7b ... followed by the driven gear ...

28.7c ... and washer ...

28.7d ... and secure them with the circlip

Fig. 1.15 Alternator/starter clutch drive and balancer assembly

1   Nut
2   Washer
3   Cush drive outer section
4   Cush drive rubber – 4 off
5   Cush drive inner section
6   Drive chain
7   Alternator/starter clutch shaft
8   Needle roller bearing
9   Circlip
10 Washer – 2 off
11 Needle roller bearing
12 Starter clutch driven gear
13 Starter clutch body △
14 Plunger – 3 off △
15 Spring – 3 off △
16 Roller – 3 off △
17 Bolt – 3 off △
18 Washer – 3 off △
19 Starter clutch body ▲
20 Roller assembly ▲
21 Bolt – 6 off ▲
22 Starter clutch cover
23 Ball journal bearing
24 Cush drive inner section
25 Cush drive rubber – 4 off
26 Washer
27 Bolt
28 Bolt
29 Washer
30 Alternator coupling
31 Balancer
32 Thrust washer – 3 off
33 Needle roller bearing – 2 off
34 Shouldered thrust washer
35 Cush drive rubber – 6 off
36 Balancer weight
37 Thrust washer
38 Needle roller bearing
39 Shouldered thrust washer
40 Balancer shaft
41 Spacer
42 Oil seal
43 Adjusting lever

△ ZX900 and early ZX1000 A models
▲ ZX1000 B, ZX1100 C and late ZX1000 A models

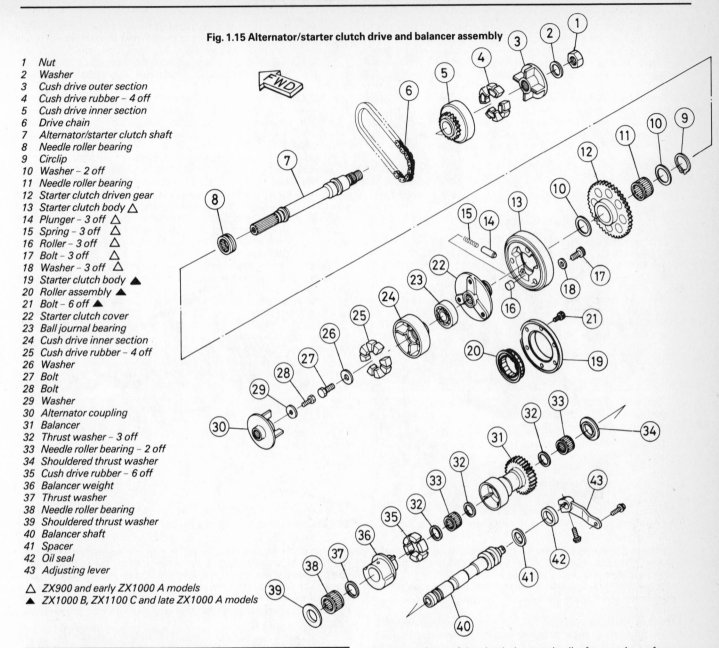

29 Examination and renovation: clutch

1   After an extended period of service the clutch friction plates will wear and promote clutch slip. Measure the thickness of each friction plate using a vernier caliper noting the readings obtained. If any plate has worn to or beyond the service limit given in the Specifications, the friction plates must be renewed as a set.
2   The plain plates should not show any signs of excess heating (blueing). Check the warpage of each plate using a flat surface and feeler gauges. If any plate exceeds the maximum permissible amount of warpage, or shows signs of blueing, all plain plates must be renewed as a set.
3   Examine the clutch assembly for burrs or indentations on the edges of the protruding tangs of the friction plates and/or slots in the edges of the clutch outer drum with which they engage. Similarly wear can occur between the inner tongues of the plain plates and the slots in the clutch centre. Wear of this nature will cause clutch drag and slow disengagement during gear changes, since the plates will snag and free fully when the pressure plate is lifted. With care a small amount of wear can be corrected by dressing with a fine file, but if this is excessive the worn components must be renewed.
4   On ZX1100 C models, examine the needle roller bearing and the

bearing surfaces of the clutch drum and collar for any signs of wear or damage, renewing any component as necessary.
5   Examine the pressure plate lifting bearing for wear. On ZX900 models ensure the ball journal bearing fitted in the pressure plate itself spins freely without any sign of notchiness and that there is no sign of freeplay between the inner and outer races. On all other models check the needle roller bearing, situated on the end of the mushroom-headed pushrod, and its relevant bearing surfaces for any signs of wear or damage. On all models, renew worn components as necessary.
6   On ZX1000 A and ZX1100 C models, the clutch centre is fitted with a damper mechanism which consists of twelve springs and a cam set up. If, after a high mileage, the clutch operation becomes harsh or excessive transmission slop has been noted, it is probably this which is at fault. Compress the damper plate, which has the pressure of the twelve damper springs on it, and remove the large circlip from the back of the clutch centre. Slowly release the damper plate and remove the springs and damper cam follower. Examine the bearing surface of the damper cam and follower and renew any worn component. The springs can only be tested by comparison with new items and should be renewed as a set if in any doubt as to their condition. Fit the springs, cam follower and damper plate to the clutch centre, compress the damper plate and refit the circlip.
7   On all models check that the teeth of the crankshaft drive gear and

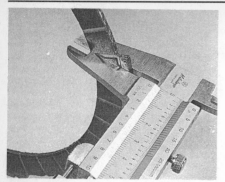

29.1 Measuring friction plate thickness

29.3a Examine the slots in the clutch drum ...

29.3b ... and centre for indentations or burrs and repair or renew as necessary

29.6 Clutch centre damper mechanism is retained by a circlip

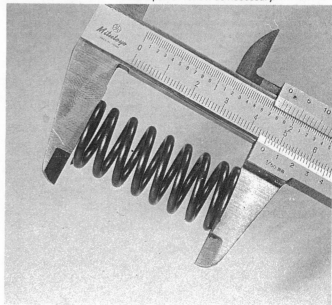

29.8 Measuring clutch spring free length

the clutch outer drum are unworn. If a dial gauge (DTI) is available the gear backlash can be measured. If the backlash exceeds the service limit, both components must be renewed as a pair.

8   Measure the free length of each clutch spring. If any one has settled to less than the service limit, the clutch springs must be renewed as a complete set.

9   The clutch pushrod should be rolled on a flat surface to check that it is not bent. If bent, it can be straightened but if its hardened ends are worn it must be renewed.

10   The clutch master cylinder is very similar to that which is used for the front brake and can be dismantled and overhauled as described in Section 10 of Chapter 6. The slave cylinder can be also be overhauled using the information given in Section 9 of Chapter 6. Ensure the new seal is fitted the correct way around and seats fully in its groove in the piston. On reassembly fill the master cylinder reservoir with new hydraulic fluid and bleed the system as described in Section 13 of Chapter 6.

30   Examination and renovation: gearbox components

1   Give the gearbox components a close visual inspection for signs of wear or damage such as broken or chipped teeth, worn dogs, damaged or worn splines and bent selector forks. Renew any parts found to be worn; there is no satisfactory way in which they can be reclaimed. The shaft assemblies can be dismantled and reassembled as described in the following section.

2   If a dial gauge is available the gear backlash can be checked to measure tooth wear, if any pair of gears is found to exceed the maximum permissible backlash both gears must be renewed as a pair.

3   The gearbox shafts are unlikely to sustain damage unless the engine

has seized, placing an unusually high loading on the gearbox, or unless the machine has covered a very high mileage. Check the surfaces of the shaft, especially where a pinion turns on it, and renew the shaft if it has scored or has picked up. Examine the threads of the shafts and check them for trueness by setting them up in V-blocks and measuring any runout with a dial gauge. Damage of any kind can only be cured by

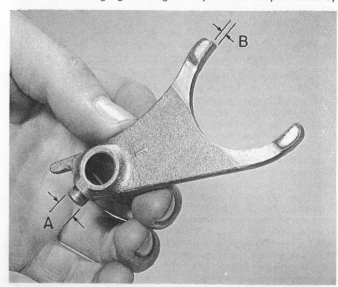

30.4 Measure the width of guide pin (A) and fork ends (B), renewing selector fork if necessary

compound to the threads of the screw and tighten it securely.
6   Check the gearchange shaft for signs of wear or damage especially at the splined end of the shaft. If the shaft is damaged in any way, the only satisfactory method of repair is renewal. The gearchange shaft and claw arm return spring tension can be checked only by comparison with new items. If in any doubt as to their condition, the springs should be renewed.

31   Gearbox input and output shafts: dismantling and reassembly

Dismantling – general
1   The gearbox shafts should not be disturbed unless damage is

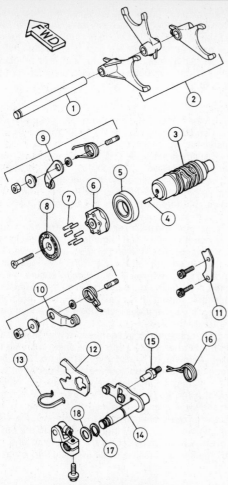

Fig. 1.16 Gearchange mechanism

1   Selector fork shaft
2   Selector forks
3   Selector drum
4   Camplate locating pin
5   Bearing
6   Camplate
7   Change pins
8   Pin retaining plate
9   Gear position detent arm assembly
10 Neutral detent arm assembly
11 Drum retaining plate
12 Selector claw
13 Spring
14 Gearchange shaft
15 Locating post
16 Return spring
17 Circlip
18 Washer

renewal of the shaft concerned. Renew any bushes that show signs of wear.
4   The selector forks should be examined closely to ensure that they are not badly damaged or worn. Measure the width of both fork ends and the diameter of its guide pin. If either fork end or the guide pin has worn to less than its service limit the selector fork(s) must be renewed. The selector fork shaft can be checked for trueness by rolling it along a flat surface. A bent shaft will cause difficulty in selecting gears and make the gearchange action heavy. The shaft must be renewed if it is bent.
5   Measure the width of the three grooves in the selector drum at several points along their length. If at any point the width of a groove exceeds the service limit the selector drum must be renewed. Check that the bearing fitted to the drum rotates freely and has no sign of freeplay between its inner and outer race. To renew the bearing, slacken the screw from the end of the drum and lift off the pin retaining plate. Remove the pins from the camplate, noting exactly which hole the longer pin is fitted in, and lift the camplate away from the drum. If loose, also remove the camplate locating pin, fitted to the selector drum. The bearing can then be removed from the drum. Fit the new bearing and reassemble the selector drum components ensuring the camplate locating pin is in position, and the longest pin is refitted in its original place as noted on dismantling. Apply a few drops of thread-locking

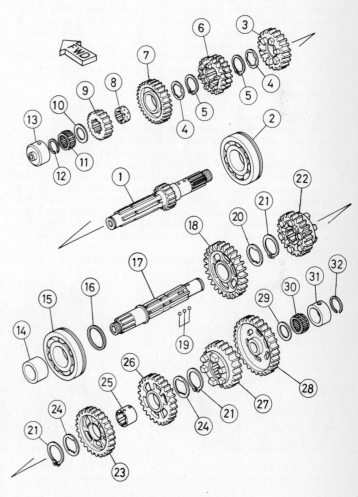

Fig. 1.17 Gearbox shafts

1   Input shaft
2   Ball journal bearing
3   Input shaft 5th gear
4   Splined thrust washer – 2 off
5   Circlip – 2 off
6   Input shaft 3rd/4th gear
7   Input shaft 6th gear
8   6th gear bush
9   Input shaft 2nd gear
10 Thrust washer
11 Needle roller bearing
12 Circlip
13 Bearing outer race
14 Spacer
15 Ball journal bearing
16 Thrust washer (where fitted)
17 Output shaft
18 Output shaft 2nd gear
19 Steel balls
20 Toothed washer
21 Circlip – 3 off
22 Output shaft 6th gear
23 Output shaft 4th gear
24 Toothed washer – 2 off
25 3rd/4th gear bush
26 Output shaft 3rd gear
27 Output shaft 5th gear
28 Output shaft 1st gear
29 Thrust washer
30 Needle roller bearing
31 Bearing outer race
32 Circlip

obvious, such as chipped or worn teeth, unless or course careful examination of the whole assembly fails to pinpoint the source of the problem.

2   Should either of the ball journal bearings require renewal, a bearing puller will be required to remove the oil seal collar from the output shaft and to extract both of the bearings. Note the position of the locating groove in the outer race of the bearing prior to removing it and ensure that the new bearing is fitted with the groove in the same position. Pull the bearing and collar (as necessary) off the shaft and fit the new bearing using a hammer and tubular drift which bears only on the inner race of the bearing.

3   The input and output shaft should be kept separate, to avoid confusion during reassembly, and if possible dismantled individually to avoid the risk of interchanging components. Dismantling the shafts should pose no problem providing a good pair of circlip pliers is available. As each component is removed, place it in order on a clean surface so that the reassembly sequence is self-evident and the risk of parts being fitted the wrong way around or in the wrong sequence is avoided. Note that the output shaft incorporates an ingenious neutral finder mechanism which consists of three steel balls running in radial drillings that are spaced 120° apart within the 5th gear pinion. Take care not to lose these balls as the 5th gear is slid off the shaft. Examine all thrust washers, renewing any which show signs of wear, and renew all circlips regardless of their apparent condition.

Reassembly – general

4   Having checked and renewed the gearbox components as required, reassemble each shaft, referring to the accompanying line drawing and photographs for guidance. The correct assembly sequence is detailed below. Oil the shafts and pinion bushes liberally during assembly. When fitting the circlips to the shafts take care not to expand them any larger than is necessary to slide them over the shaft. Also when fitting a circlip to a splined shaft ensure that the ends of the circlip are positioned in the middle of the splines (see accompanying photographs). These two simple precautions ensure that the circlips are as secure as possible on the shaft. Ensure that the bearing surfaces of each component are liberally oiled before fitting.

5   If problems arise in identifying the various gear pinions which cannot be solved by reference to the accompanying photographs or figures, the number of teeth on each pinion can be used to identify them. Reference to the gearbox specifications at the start of this chapter will show the number of teeth for each gear. The output shaft pinions are listed first, followed by those on the input shaft. The problem would not arise, however, if the instructions given in paragraph 3 of this Section are followed carefully.

Input shaft

6   The input shaft is easily identified by its integral 1st gear pinion. Although not strictly necessary, on the project bike it was found to be easier to install the input shaft and clutch drum in the upper crankcase half as one assembly. However, if wished, the clutch drum can be installed later as described in Section 40. If the input shaft and clutch drum are to be fitted together follow the sequence below, whereas if the clutch drum is to be installed later ignore the information (and the accompanying photographs) given in paragraph 7 and proceed as described in paragraph 8 onwards.

7   Holding the left-hand (plain) end of the shaft fit the following clutch components over the right-hand (threaded) end of the shaft. First fit the smaller thrust washer over the end of the shaft, followed by the larger thrust washer. On early ZX900 and ZX1000 A models where a single large chamfered thrust washer is used instead, ensure this is fitted with its chamfered edge facing the bearing. On all models install the clutch drum centre collar so that its flat face is against the thrust washer, then fit the oil pump drive gear (dogs facing right-hand end of the shaft) over the collar and turn the shaft around.

8   Holding the right-hand (threaded) end of the shaft fit the 5th gear pinion over the left-hand (plain) end of the shaft, ensuring that its dogs are facing left, followed by a splined thrust washer. Slide both the gear and washer along the shaft and secure them in position with a circlip. The double 3rd/4th gear pinion is fitted next with the smaller diameter 3rd gear towards the 5th gear pinion. Fit the second circlip to the groove in the shaft and slide on another splined thrust washer.

9   Fit the splined 6th gear bush on to the shaft ensuring that the hole in the bush aligns with the oilway in the shaft. Slide the 6th gear pinion onto the bush with its dogs facing the right-hand end of the shaft, followed by the 2nd gear pinion. Place the plain thrust washer over the

31.7a First fit the small thrust washer over the threaded end of the input shaft ...

31.7b ... followed by the large thrust washer ...

31.7c Fit the clutch drum centre collar with its flat surface facing the thrust washers ...

31.7d ... and the oil pump drive gear with its dogs facing away from the thrust washers

31.8a Turn the shaft around and slide on 5th gear pinion followed by splined thrust washer ...

31.8b ... and secure with circlip

31.8c Fit 3rd/4th gear with its smaller 3rd gear pinion facing 5th gear pinion ...

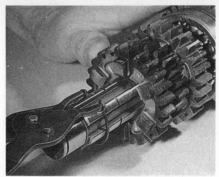

31.8d ... and fit the second circlip to the groove in the shaft ...

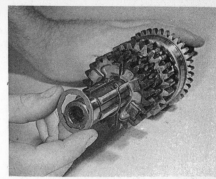

31.8e ... followed by splined thrust washer

31.9a Fit the splined 6th gear bush so that the hole in the bush aligns with the oilway in the shaft ...

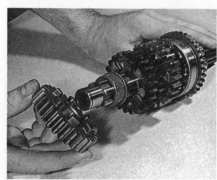

31.9b ... then fit the 6th gear pinion ...

31.9c ... followed by the 2nd gear pinion ...

31.9d ... and the plain thrust washer

31.9e Fit the needle roller bearing to the end of the shaft and secure with circlip

31.9f Liberally oil the bearing and fit its outer race

31.10a Output shaft - fit the 2nd gear pinion as shown ...

31.10b ... followed by the toothed washer ...

31.10c ... and secure them with a circlip as described in text

31.11a Slide on the 6th gear pinion and fit the second circlip to the shaft

31.11b Fit a splined thrust washer and the splined 3rd/4th gear bush - ensure holes in bush align with oilways in shaft

31.12a Fit the 4th gear pinion as shown ...

31.12b ... followed by the 3rd gear pinion

31.12c Slide another splined thrust washer along the shaft ...

31.12d ... and secure it with a circlip

31.13a Insert the three steel balls ...

31.13b ... into the closed-off drillings (arrowed) in 5th gear pinion

31.13c Refit the 5th gear pinion so that the balls in the pinion align with the recesses in the shaft

31.14a Slide on the 1st gear pinion followed by a plain thrust washer

31.14b Fit needle roller bearing and secure with circlip

31.14c Lubricate the bearing and fit the bearing outer race

shaft and fit the needle roller bearing. Secure the needle roller bearing with a circlip and slide the bearing outer race over the end of the shaft.

Output shaft

10   The output shaft is easily identified due to it having no integral pinions. Holding the shaft by its left-hand (threaded) end slide the 2nd gear pinion along the shaft so that its deeper recessed surface is facing the right, followed by the toothed washer and secure them with a circlip. Ensure the circlip is fitted so that the teeth of the washer are not positioned between the ends of the circlip.
11   The 6th gear pinion is then fitted with its selector fork groove facing the right-hand end of the shaft and is retained by another circlip. Slide a toothed washer along the shaft followed by the splined 3rd/4th gear pinion bush. Ensure both the holes in the bush align with the oilways in the output shaft.
12   Slide the 4th gear pinion onto the bush, with its recessed surface facing the 6th gear pinion, followed by the 3rd gear pinion with its recessed surface facing away from the 4th gear pinion, and a toothed washer. Secure the 3rd gear pinion and washer with a circlip.
13   Insert the three steel balls into the closed off drillings in the 5th gear pinion. Ensuring the balls remain in position, slide the 5th gear pinion on to the output shaft splines so that the steel balls in the pinion are aligned with the recesses in the shaft.
14   Fit the 1st gear pinion with its deeply recessed surface facing the 5th gear pinion, followed by the plain thrust washer and the needle roller bearing. Secure the needle roller bearing with the circlip and refit the outer bearing race.

32 Examination and renovation: balancer shaft

1   Dismantle the balancer shaft components, noting that the needle roller bearing and thrust washer fitted inside the balancer weight are a different size to the others. Check for wear as follows.
2   Examine the three needle roller bearings and thrust washers for signs of wear or damage, renewing them if necessary. Check the inside of the balancer gear/cush drive holder and the shaft itself for signs of scoring or flat spots. Such damage is only likely if the balancer shaft has been adjusted incorrectly or if a high mileage has been covered. Also check the balancer gear for wear or damage such as chipped teeth. If damage of any kind is discovered the only satisfactory means of repair is to renew the damaged components.
3   Examine the rubber segments of the cush drive for wear or deterioration. Any damage will be self evident and the rubbers must be renewed as a set. Renew the balancer shaft oil seal as a matter of course and reassemble the balancer as follows.
4   With the balancer gear/cush drive housing stood vertically on its gear, fit the first thrust washer to the inside of the housing followed by a needle roller bearing and a second thrust washer. Apply a small amount of grease to the backs of the cush drive rubbers and position them in the housing. Fit the balancer weight to the holder noting that the punch mark on the balancer weight must be positioned directly opposite the punch mark on the housing (see accompanying photo). Ensure the rubbers remain in position as the weight is fitted.
5   Place a thrust washer inside the balancer weight, followed by a

needle roller bearing and then fit the large shouldered thrust washer over the end of the weight. Turn the shaft around and fit the thrust washer, needle roller bearing and shouldered thrust washer to the gear end of the assembly. Ensure that both shouldered thrust washers are fitted with their shoulders facing the balancer assembly.

33 Engine reassembly: general

1   Before reassembly of the engine/gearbox unit is commenced, the various component parts should be cleaned thoroughly and placed on a sheet of clean paper, close to the working area.
2   Make sure all traces of old gaskets have been removed and that the mating surfaces are clean and undamaged. Great care should be taken when removing old gasket compound not to damage the mating surface. Most gasket compounds can be softened using a suitable solvent such as methylated spirits, acetone or cellulose thinner. The type of solvent required will depend on the type of compound used. Gasket compound of the non-hardening type can be removed using a soft brass-wire brush of the type used for cleaning suede shoes. A considerable amount of scrubbing can take place without fear of harming the mating surfaces. Some difficulty may be encountered when attempting to remove gaskets of the self-vulcanising type, the use of which is becoming widespread, particularly as cylinder head and base gaskets. The gasket should be pared from the mating surface using a scalpel or a small chisel with a finely honed edge. Do not, however, resort to scraping with a sharp instrument unless necessary.
3   Gather together all the necessary tools and have available an oil can filled with clean engine oil. Make sure that all new gaskets and oil seals are to hand, also all replacement parts required. Nothing is more frustrating than having to stop in the middle of a reassembly sequence because a vital gasket or replacement has been overlooked. As a general rule each moving engine component should be lubricated thoroughly as it is fitted into position.
4   Make sure that the reassembly area is clean and that there is adequate working space. Refer to the torque and clearance settings wherever they are given. Many of the smaller bolts are easily sheared if overtightened. Always use the correct size screwdriver bit for the crosshead screws and never an ordinary screwdriver or punch. If the existing screws show evidence of maltreatment in the past, it is advisable to renew them as a complete set.
5   All mating surfaces must be carefully cleaned of all traces of old gaskets or jointing compound and must be absolutely flat and unmarked. Using a clean, lint-free cloth soaked in high flash-point solvent, wipe over all the mating surfaces to remove all traces of oil and grease. Where necessary, apply a thin, continuous bead of sealant to the mating surfaces and assemble the parts immediately.
6   Remember that if the mating surfaces are in a good condition there should be no need for a thick film of sealant. The thinnest smear will usually prove sufficient to seal the joint. If excess sealant is applied it will be pushed out to form a bead on either side of the joint. While the bead on the outside can be peeled off, the bead on the inside is free to break off and block oilways or cause similar problems.

32.4a Use grease to hold the cush drive rubbers in position

32.4b On reassembly position punch marks (arrowed) as described in text

32.5 Ensure shouldered washers are fitted with their shoulders facing the balancer assembly

34 Reassembling the engine/gearbox unit: refitting the lower crankcase components

1 Insert the selector drum into the crankcase half and push it fully into position so that its bearing is flush with the casing. Partially insert the selector fork shaft in the casing and, using the notes made on dismantling, locate the left-hand selector fork in its groove in the selector drum. Push the selector fork shaft in until it engages with the fork then repeat the process on the centre and right-hand forks and push the shaft fully home. Refit the selector drum retaining plate and tighten its retaining bolts securely having first applied a few drops of thread-locking compound to their threads.

2 Fit the washer over the gearchange detent arm stud followed by its return spring. Ensure that the correct return spring is fitted, referring to Section 14 for further information. Locate the detent arm with the return spring and push it onto its stud. Refit the shouldered spacer, ensuring that the shoulder correctly engages with the detent arm, and tighten its retaining nut securely. Check that the detent arm is free to move and

repeat the above sequence for the neutral detent arm. Rotate the selector drum until it is in the neutral position, ie neutral (upper) detent arm engaged with its cutout in the selector drum.

3 Hold the balancer weight assembly in position, ensuring that both the shouldered washers are in place, and insert the balancer shaft from the right-hand side of the casing. Push the balancer shaft fully into position and check that the weight spins freely on the shaft. On ZX1000 B and ZX1100 C models, refit the balancer shaft guide pin and retaining plate. Apply a few drops of thread-locking compound to its retaining bolt and tighten it securely. Also refit the thrust washer over the end of the balancer shaft. On all models apply a small amount of grease to the lips of the oil seal and press it into position so that it is flush with the casing. If necessary the seal can be tapped in using a hammer and suitably sized socket which bears only on the hard outer edge of the seal.

4 Position the shaft so that the line on the shaft is horizontal (with the punch mark at the front) and install its mounting clamp. Tighten both the clamp mounting and pinch bolts securely. Note that the balancer shaft will need adjusting when the engine is first started.

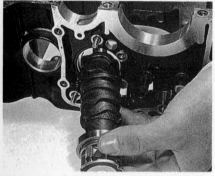

34.1a Refit the selector drum to the casing

34.1b Position the left-hand selector fork and insert the selector fork shaft until it engages with the fork ...

34.1c ... then repeat the process for the centre ...

34.1d ... and right-hand fork and push the selector fork shaft fully in

34.1e Apply thread locking compound to selector drum retaining plate bolts and refit the plate

34.2a Fit plain washer over detent arm stud followed by return spring

34.2b Locate the detent arm with the return spring ...

34.2c ... refit the shouldered spacer as shown and tighten its retaining nut securely

34.3a Position the balancer weight assembly in the casing and refit the shaft

34.3b On ZX1000 B and ZX1100 C models insert the balancer shaft guide pin ...

34.3c ... and secure it with retaining plate and bolt; apply thread-locking compound to the bolt

34.3d Refit the thrust washer (ZX1000 B and ZX1100 C only) ...

34.3e ... and fit a new balancer shaft oil seal

34.4a Position the balancer shaft as described in text ensuring that the punch mark (arrowed) is at the front

34.4b Install the balancer shaft clamp and tighten its mounting and pinch bolts securely

5   Ensuring that each is in its correct position, refit the five main bearing inserts into the casing and main bearing cap. Check that all the insert locating tangs are correctly seated in their recesses and lubricate all inserts with clean engine oil.

35   Reassembling the engine/gearbox unit: refitting the upper crankcase components

Note: *The manufacturer advises that the big-end bolts be renewed on installation due to them having stretched in service.*

1   Fit the big-end bearing inserts to the connecting rods and big-end caps, ensuring that the locating tang of each insert is fitted correctly into its recess. On ZX1000 and ZX1100 C models smear molybdenum-disulfide grease over the outer surface of the connecting rod insert. *Do not apply any grease to the inner surface of the connecting rod insert or to either surface of the big-end cap insert.* On ZX1000 B models measure the length of each big-end cap bolt and make a note of this. On all models, lubricate the crankpins with clean engine oil, refit each rod to its original crankpin and fit the big-end cap. Use the marks made on dismantling or the weight group letter to ensure that the caps are correctly aligned with their respective rods and that the rods are refitted the same way round as before.

2   Fit the cap nuts and tighten them by hand only, then tighten the nuts evenly to their specified torque setting. On ZX1000 and ZX1100 C models the nuts must then be tightened a further 120° more. On ZX1000 models, once the nuts have been fully tightened it is necessary to check that the bolts have not stretched excessively. On ZX1000 A models this is checked by measuring the length of the bolt which protrudes above the top surface of the nut. If more than 0.8 mm (0.03 in) of the bolt is visible, the nut and bolt must be removed and renewed. On ZX1000 B models measure the length of each bolt after it has been tightened and compare this with the measurement taken earlier. If any bolt has stretched by more than 0.31 mm (0.012 in) where an old connecting rod is fitted, or by 0.37 mm (0.014 in) where a new rod is

fitted, it must be removed and a new nut and bolt fitted. This procedure ensures the new nuts and bolts that are fitted are of the required standard and eliminates the possibility of fitting a faulty bolt which could fail in use with disastrous consequences. On all models check that the rods revolve smoothly and easily around their crankpins. Some stiffness is inevitable if new inserts have been fitted, but this must not be excessive.

3   Ensuring that all are in their correct places, refit the five main bearing inserts in the crankcase half. Check that the insert locating tang of each bearing is correctly located in its recess and lubricate all bearing inserts with clean engine oil. Use an oil can to prime the oilways of both crankcase halves and the crankshaft and lower the crankshaft into position in the top half of the casing, ensuring that the connecting rods pass through the crankcase mouth. Refit the main bearing cap, ensuring that the two locating dowels are in position and the arrow on the cap is facing forward, and evenly tighten its retaining bolts to the specified torque setting. Check that the crankshaft revolves smoothly and easily.

4   Position the starter clutch assembly in the crankcase (driven gear facing the right-hand side of the casing) and insert the shaft from the right-hand side of the crankcase half. Locate the starter clutch on the shafts splines and push the shaft fully into position. Refit the alternator cush drive coupling to the left-hand end of the shaft and tighten its retaining bolt to the specified torque setting. Hold the starter clutch idler gear in position and insert its shaft into the casing. Refit the oil spray tube (ZX1100 C models only) and tighten the idler gear shaft retaining bolt securely.

5   Refit the two half ring retainers and the locating pins to the casing. If the clutch drum is being installed with the input shaft, fit the needle roller bearing (ZX1100 C models only) and clutch drum to the clutch centre collar making sure that the dogs on the oil pump drive gear engage with the slots in the back of the drum. Fit the input shaft assembly to the upper crankcase half ensuring that the locating peg on the left-hand side of the casing engages with the hole in the outer needle bearing race of the shaft, and the half ring retainer locates in the groove in the outer race of the ball journal bearing on the opposite end of the shaft. Install the output shaft assembly again ensuring that both the locating peg and half ring retainer engage correctly with their respective

35.1a On ZX1000 B models note the length of big-end cap bolts before installation

35.1b Lubricate the crankpins and refit each connecting rod to its original crankpin

35.2a Tighten big-end cap bolts to their specified torque setting ...

35.2b ... and on ZX1000 A and ZX1100 C models a further 120° more

35.2c On ZX1000 B models measure big-end cap bolt length after tightening to ensure they are not overstretched

35.3a Fit the main bearing inserts to the casing ...

35.3b ... and refit the crankshaft assembly

35.3c Refit the main bearing cap - ensuring arrow cast in top surface points forwards

35.4a Position the starter clutch in the crankcase and insert its shaft

35.4b Refit the alternator coupling and tighten its retaining bolt to the specified torque setting

35.4c Fit the starter clutch idler gear and insert its shaft

35.4d On ZX1100 C models the idler gear retaining bolt also retains an oil spray tube

35.5a Do not omit half ring retainers or locating pins

35.5b Fit large needle roller bearing (ZX1100 C only) and slide clutch drum onto the input shaft

35.5c Ensure recesses in bearing races engage correctly with locating pins

hole or slot on the shaft assembly. Oil all gearbox components, position the gears in neutral and check that each shaft rotates smoothly and easily.

36 Reassembling the engine/gearbox unit: joining the crankcase halves

1 Check that all components are refitted and that they are revolving or sliding smoothly and easily. Use a rag soaked in high flash-point solvent to wipe over the gasket surfaces of both halves to remove all traces of oil. Ensure that the gear selector and gearbox components are in the neutral position and that the crankshaft is positioned with cylinders 1 and 4 at TDC. This can be achieved by temporarily fitting the ignition rotor to the left-hand end of the crankshaft and aligning the T 1.4 mark with the line cast on the casing. Position the balancer weight so that the punch mark on its weighted portion is aligned with the centre of the adjacent oil passage hole in the casing (see accompanying photograph).

Refit the two dowel pins to the upper crankcase half.
2 Apply a thin film of jointing compound to both the upper and lower crankcase faces. Take great care to leave a narrow margin around any oilways and the main bearing inserts so that there is no risk of any surplus compound blocking an oilway. Note: on ZX1100 C models do not apply any compound to the small area of either casing which is between the input and output gearbox shafts on the left-hand side.
3 Ensuring that the main bearing inserts are in position, and all the components are positioned as described in paragraph 1, carefully lower the lower crankcase half onto the upper half. Ensure the selector forks engage with their respective slots in the gearbox and the balancer weight remains in position as the halves are joined. Check that the lower crankcase half is correctly seated and that all components are free to rotate. Refit all the lower crankcase bolts, using the cardboard template to ensure each bolt is refitted in its correct position. Note: do not omit the washers fitted to the three centre main bearing bolts (numbers 1 to 3 on the casing). Tighten all bolts finger-tight.
4 The tightening order for the nine main bearing bolts is indicated by the numbers cast in the casing next to each bolt. Working in this

36.1a Use ignition rotor to position crankshaft as described in text ...

36.1b ... and position balancer shaft so that its punch mark is aligned with centre of adjacent hole

36.1c Do not omit the two crankcase dowels from the upper casing

36.3a Apply jointing compound to the crankcase mating surfaces (see text) and join crankcase halves ...

36.3b ... whilst ensuring the selector forks engage correctly with slots in gear pinions

36.4a Tighten main bearing bolts to their specified torque setting ...

36.4b ... using the numbers stamped on the lower crankcase half

sequence, tighten the main bearing bolts first to their initial torque setting, and then to their final torque setting. Both torque settings are given in the specifications at the start of this Chapter. Then tighten the 7 mm bolt (ZX1100 C and late ZX900 A7-on models only), followed by all the 6 mm bolts, to their specified torque settings. Refit the upper crankcase bolts, again using the cardboard template to ensure each bolt is refitted in its original position. **Note:** *on ZX1100 C and late ZX900 A7-on models do not omit the washer from the front 8 mm bolt. First tighten the 8 mm bolts, then the 6 mm bolts, to their specified torque settings.*

5　Check that the crankshaft rotates smoothly and easily, as should the gearbox shafts. It is impossible to select any gears other than 1st or neutral unless the output shaft can be spun fast enough to disengage

the neutral finding mechanism. If there are any signs of undue stiffness or of any other problem, the fault must be rectified before work can proceed further. Plug the crankcase mouths with clean rag to prevent debris entering the crankcase until the cylinder block has been refitted.

37　Reassembling the engine/gearbox unit: refitting the external gearchange components

1　The neutral and gear position detent arms are refitted as described in Section 34 of this Chapter.
2　Check that the locating post for the gearchange shaft return spring is secure. If it is loose remove the post, apply a thread-locking compound to its threads, refit it and tighten it securely. Ensure that the circlip and washer are fitted to the gearchange shaft and offer up the gearchange to the casing. As the shaft is fitted, ensure that the selector claw engages correctly with the end of the selector drum, and that the return spring engages correctly with its locating post. Check that the gearchange shaft moves easily and centralises quickly with the pressure of the return spring.
3　Refit the two dowels to the crankcase and place a new gasket over them. Apply a small amount of grease to the lips of the output and gearchange shaft oil seals and offer up the cover. Ease it over the ends of the shafts, to prevent damaging the oil seals, and carefully slide it into place. On ZX900 and ZX1000 models apply a thread-locking compound to all the gearchange cover retaining bolts and tighten them securely. On ZX1100 C models apply thread-locking compound to the four bolts arrowed in the accompanying photograph and tighten the bolts to the specified torque setting.

38　Reassembling the engine/gearbox unit: refitting the alternator and starter motor

1　Clean the three alternator mounting points on both the crankcase and the alternator itself. This is most important as the mounting points

37.3a Refit dowels to the crankcase and position a new gasket over them

37.3b Refit the gearchange casing

37.3c On ZX1100 C models apply thread-locking compound to four bolts arrowed

38.2a Refit cush drive rubbers to the alternator coupling

38.2b Refit alternator – apply thread-locking compound to its bolts and tighten to specified torque setting

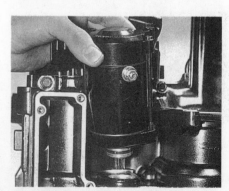

38.3 Apply engine oil to starter motor O-ring and install starter motor, tightening its bolts securely

are used to earth the alternator. Failure to earth the alternator properly will almost certainly lead to it being damaged.

2   Insert the cush drive rubbers into the coupling on the shaft and fit a new O-ring to the alternator. Apply engine oil to the O-ring and cush drive rubbers to aid the refitting procedure. Refit the alternator to its drive coupling ensuring that the rubber segments of the cush drive remain in position and engage correctly with the alternator. Apply a thread-locking compound to the alternator mounting bolts and tighten them to the specified torque setting.

3   Ensure the starter motor mounting points on both the crankcase and the motor itself are clean and free from corrosion. This is most important as the mountings are used to earth the motor. Fit a new O-ring to the starter motor and insert its mounting bolts into their respective holes. Apply a small amount of engine oil to the starter motor O-ring and manoeuvre the assembly into position. Push the motor into the crankcase and tighten its mounting bolts securely. If necessary, refit the external gearchange mechanism cover as described in the previous section.

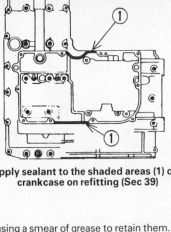

Fig. 1.18 Apply sealant to the shaded areas (1) of sump and crankcase on refitting (Sec 39)

39   Reassembling the engine/gearbox unit: refitting the oil pump and sump

1   If removed, refit the oil nozzle and dowel to the underside of the crankcase, noting that the small hole of the nozzle must be facing the oil pump bracket. Fit a new O-ring over the oil nozzle. Ensure that the slots in the oil pump drive gear and the water pump shaft (as necessary) and the projections on the oil pump shaft are all positioned vertically. Install the oil pump and mounting bracket assembly ensuring that the slots on the oil pump shaft engage with the slots in the drive gear and water pump. Refit the three oil pump bracket mounting bolts and tighten them securely.

2   Fit new O-rings to both of the metal oil pipes and the oil screen. Smear the O-rings with engine oil and refit the metal oil pipes to the bottom of the crankcase, followed by the black plastic pipe and the oil screen.

3   Ensure the dowel is in position and fit the two new O-rings to the oil

pump bracket, using a smear of grease to retain them. Note that the flat surface of the smaller O-ring must face the bracket. On ZX900 A7-on and ZX1100 C models apply silicone sealant to both the crankcase and sump in the area shown in the accompanying illustration. On all models fit a new sump gasket, using a dab of grease to retain it. Place a new O-ring in the groove around the oil filter chamber and refit the sump to the engine unit.

4   Apply thread-locking compound to the threads of the four sump bolts that are fitted next to the triangular marks cast in the sump and refit all sump bolts, along with any oil hose or electrical guides, using the notes made on dismantling. Tighten all sump bolts securely.

5   Refit the oil filter assembly, using a new filter element as described in Routine maintenance and tighten its retaining bolt to the specified torque setting. Also refit both drain plugs, renewing their sealing washers if necessary, and tighten them to the specified torque setting. Offer up the metal oil pipe which links the sump to the crankcase and position a new sealing washer on each side of its unions. Refit the union bolts and tighten them to the specified torque setting.

39.1a Refit the dowel to the underside of the crankcase ...

39.1b ... and install the oil nozzle so that its small hole faces the oil pump bracket and fit a new O-ring

39.1c Ensure the slots in oil pump drive gear and water pump are vertical ...

39.1d ... install the oil pump and bracket assembly ...

39.1e ... and tighten its mounting bolts securely

39.2a Renew all O-rings on the metal oil pipes ...

39.2b ... and refit them to their original positions in the crankcase ...

39.2c ... along with the plastic pipe ...

39.2d ... and oil screen - ZX1100 C shown

39.3a Ensure that dowel is in position and fit two new O-rings to the oil pump bracket

39.3b Fit a new O-ring around the oil filter chamber in the sump ...

39.3c ... fit a new gasket to the crankcase ...

39.3d ... and refit the sump

39.4 Apply thread-locking compound to the four sump bolts fitted next to triangular marks on sump

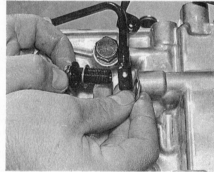

39.5 Fit a new sealing washer on each side of the metal oil pipe union

40   Reassembling the engine/gearbox unit: refitting the clutch

1   If not fitted previously (see Section 31), install the clutch drum as follows. First fit the small thrust washer to the input shaft, followed by the large thrust washer. On early ZX900 and ZX1000 A models where a large chamfered washer is used, ensure this is fitted with its chamfered face pointing inwards. On all models, fit the oil pump drive gear next, so that its dogs are facing outwards. Offer up the clutch drum ensuring that it engages correctly with the oil pump dogs and refit its needle roller bearing (ZX1100 C models only). Hold the clutch drum in position and slide the clutch drum centre collar, with its flat surface facing inwards, along the input shaft and into the clutch drum.

2   Refit the large plain thrust washer, slide the clutch centre into place followed by the large washer. Fit a new clutch nut and tighten it to the specified torque setting whilst holding the clutch centre in the same manner as was used during dismantling.

3   If new clutch plates are to be fitted, apply a coating of oil to their surfaces to prevent seizure. Fit the clutch plates alternately, starting

Fig. 1.19 Where clutch friction plates have diagonal grooves, install as shown (Sec 40)

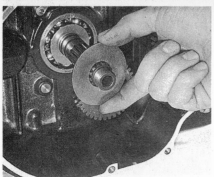

40.1a Fit the small and large thrust washers ...

40.1b ... and the oil pump drive gear

40.1c Locate the clutch drum on the oil pump drive gear dogs ...

40.1d ... refit the needle roller bearing (ZX1100 C models only) ...

40.1e ... and install the clutch drum centre collar

40.2a Fit the large plain washer ...

40.2b ... and refit the clutch centre

40.2c Fit the large washer and a new clutch centre nut and tighten it to the specified torque setting

40.3 Last clutch friction plate must be installed with its tang in the smaller slots in the clutch drum

40.4a On ZX1000 and ZX1100 C models refit the pushrod ...

40.4b ... followed by the needle roller bearing, plain thrust washer ...

40.4c ... and cup

40.4d Refit the pressure plate ...

40.4e ... and the clutch springs and bolts ...

40.4f ... and tighten them evenly and progressively to their specified torque setting

with a friction plate, noting that the last friction plate must be fitted with its tangs in the smaller slots of the clutch drum. Note on models where the grooves in the friction plates are cut diagonally, as opposed to straight, across the friction material, they must be installed as shown in the accompanying illustration.

4   On ZX900 models insert the pushrod into the centre of the input shaft ensuring that its flat end is facing outwards. On ZX1000 and ZX1100 C models apply a small amount of molybdenum-disulfide grease to the inner end of the mushroom headed pushrod and insert it into the input shaft. Refit the needle roller bearing to the pushrod followed by the thrust washer and cup. On all models ensure the pushrod is in the fully retracted position and fit the clutch pressure plate. Refit the clutch springs and bolts, tightening them evenly and progressively to their specified torque setting. If necessary, refit the right-hand crankcase cover as described in Section 41.

41   Reassembling the engine/gearbox unit: refitting the alternator/starter clutch drive components

1   Refit the cush drive rubbers to the outer section of the coupling and insert the inner coupling section whilst ensuring the rubbers remain in position. Fit the cush drive assembly and the sprocket to the drive chain. Offer up the assembly to the engine unit and slide the cush drive and sprocket onto their splined shafts simultaneously. Refit the retaining nut and washer to the cush drive shaft and the bolt and flat washer to the crankshaft. Tighten both to their specified torque settings whilst holding the cush drive coupling with the special tool.

2   Refit the chain guide over its locating stud and insert the collar and washer in the guide. Apply a thread-locking compound to the chain guide retaining bolt and tighten it securely.

41.1a Fit cush drive rubbers and reassemble the coupling

41.1b Fit the drive sprocket and coupling to the chain and install as an assembly

41.1c Refit the nut and washer which retains the coupling ...

41.1d ... and the bolt and washer which retain the sprocket and tighten both to their specified torque settings

41.2a Fit the chain guide over its locating stud ...

41.2b ... refit its collar ...

41.2c ... washer and bolt - apply thread-locking compound to the bolt and tighten it securely

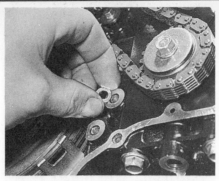

41.3a Use grease to stick the washer to the crankcase

41.3b Lock up the chain tensioner, apply thread-locking compound to its bolts and tighten securely ...

41.3c ... then release the tensioner locking plate

41.4a On ZX1000 B and ZX1100 C apply silicone sealant as described in text before fitting new gasket

41.4b Apply thread-locking compound to the four front casing bolts

3   Compress the tensioner blade and lock up the tensioner by pushing up its locking plate. Stick the flat washer (where fitted) to the upper tensioner bolt hole on the crankcase using a smear of grease. Apply a few drops of thread-locking compound to the tensioner mounting bolts and offer up the tensioner to the crankcase. Refit the mounting bolts, ensuring the top bolt passes through the washer (where fitted), and tighten them securely. Release the tensioner blade by pulling down on the locking plate.

4   Ensure the mating surfaces of the clutch cover and crankcase are clean and dry. On ZX1000 B and ZX1100 C models apply a smear of silicone sealant to the crankcase side of the clutch gasket surface to cover the area which is approximately 3.5 mm each side of the crankcase mating points (see accompanying photograph). On all models fit a new gasket, using a smear of grease to hold it in place if necessary, and offer up the right-hand crankcase cover. Apply thread-locking compound to the four front cover retaining bolts (see accompanying photograph) and refit all the cover bolts along with any relevant hose guides. Tighten all the crankcase cover retaining bolts securely.

42   Reassembling the engine/gearbox unit: refitting the pistons, cylinder block and head

1   Refit the rings to the pistons using the method employed on dismantling and position them as follows. The oil expander ring is fitted first and positioned so that its ends butt together at the back of the piston. The side rails are then fitted on each side of the oil expander ring. Position the side rails so that the end of one rail is approximately 30 – 40° from the front of the piston on one side, and the end gap of the other rail is 30 – 40° from the front of the piston on the opposite side. The second compression ring will have one surface marked 2N, this must be fitted with the 2N mark facing upwards and with its end gap at the back of the piston. On ZX1000 and ZX1100 C models the top compression ring will have an N mark on its upper surface and must be fitted accordingly. On ZX900 models the top ring is not marked and when new can be fitted either way. However, if an old ring is being reused it must be refitted the original way up, this being revealed by the wear marks.

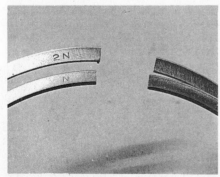

42.1 Compression rings are identified by the mark on their top surface

42.2a Ensure pistons are fitted with the arrow pointing forwards

42.2b Insert the gudgeon pin into the piston ...

42.2c ... and secure it with a new circlip

42.3 Cylinder block refitting can be made easier by supporting the pistons as shown

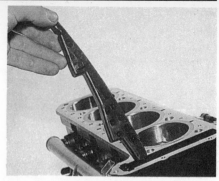
42.5a Refit camchain guide to the block ...

42.5b ... fit a new head gasket ...

42.6a ... and lower the cylinder head assembly onto the block

42.6b Flat-headed cylinder head bolts are fitted to the four outer holes ...

42.6c ... and tapered-headed bolts are fitted to the six inner holes

42.7 Tighten cylinder head bolts to the specified torque setting as described in text

42.10 On ZX1000 B and ZX1100 C models refit the shims to the valves using the notes made on dismantling

On all models position the top compression ring so that its end gap is at the front of the piston.

2   Check that each piston has one new circlip fitted to it and insert the gudgeon pin from the opposite side. If it is a tight fit, the piston should be warmed as described in Section 9. If the original pistons are being refitted, use the marks made on dismantling to ensure that each piston is refitted to its original bore. Lubricate the gudgeon pins, piston bosses and connecting rod small-ends and lower each piston in turn over its respective rod. Push the gudgeon pin through both piston bosses and the connecting rod small-end. If necessary the pins can be tapped carefully into position, using a hammer and suitable drift, whilst supporting the piston and connecting rod. Secure each gudgeon pin with a second new circlip, ensuring that it is correctly seated in its groove. Refit the two dowels to the crankcase mouth and stick the base gasket to the bottom of the block using a smear of grease. Remove any rag used to plug the crankcase mouths.

3   Lubricate the pistons and the surface of the cylinder bores with clean engine oil. It is advisable to enlist the help of an assistant to refit the block. It also helps to support the base of each piston and to position all pistons at the same height. In the absence of the correct Kawasaki service tool, this can be achieved using two long wooden dowels or metal bars. Take great care to avoid damaging the crankcase gasket surface in the process.

4   The cylinder bores have a generous lead-in for the pistons at the bottom, although on a multi-cylinder engine such as this it would be an advantage to use the special Kawasaki piston ring compressors. In the absence of these it is possible to lead the pistons into the bores gently, working across from one side to the other, guiding in one ring at a time whilst gently tapping on the cylinder block. Great care has to be taken not to put too much pressure on the piston rings as they are easily broken. The above process takes time and patience and must not be rushed. Once all the piston rings have entered the bore remove the piston supports and fit the base gasket over both the dowel pins. Push the cylinder block down until it seats firmly on the base gasket and refit the two block retaining bolts to the underside of the block. Tighten the bolts finger-tight only at this stage. Check that the crankshaft can be

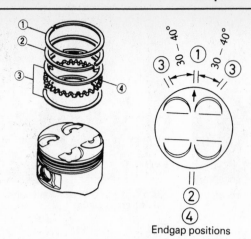

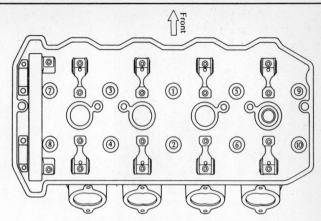

Endgap positions

Fig. 1.20 Piston ring gap positions (Sec 42)

Fig. 1.21 Cylinder head bolt tightening sequence (Sec 42)

1 Top compression ring	*3 Oil expander ring side rails*
2 Second compression ring	*4 Oil expander ring*

rotated smoothly whilst holding the block down and keeping the camchain (if fitted at this stage) taut.

5   Refit the camchain guide to the front of the block ensuring that its lugs are correctly located in the slots in the block. Refit the two dowels to the cylinder block and place a new cylinder head gasket over them. **Note**: *if the work is being carried out with the engine unit in the frame, on ZX900 models it will be necessary to fit the four cylinder head bolts and washers (numbers 3 to 6 in the tightening sequence) to the cylinder head before fitting the head on the barrels. The same applies on ZX1000 B and ZX1100 C models to the left-hand camshaft cap, which along with its dowels and bolts, must also be fitted to the cylinder head prior to installation. The above measures are necessary due to the fact that once the cylinder head is installed there is insufficient clearance between the cylinder head and the frame to insert the bolts. Additionally, on ZX1000 B and ZX1100 C models the inlet cam followers (if removed) must also be refitted before the head is installed.*

6   Lower the cylinder head assembly onto the block and refit all the cylinder head bolts, including the 6 mm bolt which secures the cylinder head to the barrel, and apply molybdenum-disulfide grease (ZX900 and ZX1000 A models) or engine oil (ZX1000 B and ZX1100 C models) to each side of the washers. The four bolts with flat hexagon heads should be fitted to the outer four holes (numbers 7 to 10 in the tightening sequence) and the six tapered head bolts in the inner six holes. **Note**: *On ZX900 A1 and early A2 models all cylinder head bolts are of the flat-head 10 mm thread type – it is not possible to replace the inner bolts with the taper-head 11 mm type fitted to later models.*

7   Using the tightening sequence, shown in the accompanying illustration tighten the cylinder head bolts to their initial specified torque setting, and then to their final specified torque setting. Once all the cylinder head bolts have been tightened, tighten the three cylinder head/block retaining bolts to their specified torque settings.

8   On ZX1000 B and ZX1100 C models refit the flexible oil pipe which runs down the right-hand side of the cylinder block to its union on the

cylinder head. Fit a new sealing washer to the union bolt and position a new collar behind the bottom union of the pipe. Refit the union bolt and tighten it to its specified torque setting.

9   On ZX900 and ZX1000 A models offer up the main oil pipe to the front of the engine unit and fit its retaining bolt finger-tight only. Position a new sealing washer on each side of its three unions and refit the union bolts. Tighten all the union bolts to the specified torque setting and then tighten the oil pipe retaining bolt securely. Using the notes made on dismantling, refit the oil pipe to the inside of the cylinder head. Refit its union bolts, ensuring that they are correctly positioned, and tighten them to their specified torque settings. If the engine unit is in the frame refit the two cylinder head to frame mounting bolts, not forgetting the shim (where fitted) which is fitted between the left-hand side of the cylinder head and the frame, and tighten them to the specified torque setting.

10   Finally, on all models tighten the drain plugs at the front of the block to their specified torque setting, and on ZX1000 B and ZX1100 C models refit the shims to their respective valves using the notes made on dismantling for identification.

43   Reassembling the engine/gearbox unit: refitting the camchain and tensioner blade

1   Stick the camchain tensioner blade rear washer to the crankcase using a smear of grease. Insert the tensioner blade into the top of the cylinder head, lowering it down the camchain tunnel and into position, and refit the sleeve to the tensioner blade bolt hole. Refit the flat washer to the tensioner blade retaining bolt and apply a few drops of thread-locking compound to the threads of the bolt. Refit the bolt to the bottom of the tensioner blade, ensuring that it passes through the washer positioned between the blade and the casing, and tighten it to the specified torque setting.

2   Feed the camchain down through the camchain tunnel and over the end of the crankshaft. Engage the chain on its drive sprocket, refit the metal camchain guide, and tighten its two retaining bolts securely.

43.1a Stick the tensioner rear washer to the crankcase with a smear of grease ...

43.1b ... and lower the tensioner blade into position from top of cylinder head

43.1c Insert the tensioner blade collar ...

43.1d ... and refit the retaining bolt having first applied a thread-locking compound

43.2a Lower the camchain down through the cylinder head ...

43.2b ... fit it to the crankshaft sprocket and refit the chain guide

44.1a Apply thread-locking compound to the pulser coil mounting bolts and install them finger-tight only at this stage

44.1b Fit the ignition rotor to the crankshaft and refit the hexagonal nut and retaining bolt

44.1c Tighten the rotor retaining bolt to the specified torque setting

44   Reassembling the engine/gearbox unit: refitting the ignition rotor components

1   Offer up the pulser coil(s) and refit their mounting bolts finger-tight only, having first applied a few drops of thread-locking compound to their threads. Refit the locating pin (if removed) in the end of the crankshaft and fit the ignition rotor. Ensure the rotor is fitted with its marked surface facing outwards. Refit the rotor retaining bolt along with the large hexagon nut ensuring that the peg in the back of the nut locates with the cutout in the ignition rotor. Tighten the ignition rotor retaining bolt to the specified torque setting whilst holding the large hexagon nut to prevent the crankshaft from rotating.
2   Working as described in Chapter 4, set up the pulser coil/ignition rotor clearance and tighten the pulser coil mounting bolts securely.

45   Reassembling the engine/gearbox unit: refitting the camshafts and setting the valve timing

1   If removed, refit the cam followers as follows. Lubricate the cam follower shaft and followers with clean engine oil and fit new O-rings to the cam follower shaft retaining bolts. Partially insert the cam follower shaft and using the notes made on dismantling, position the left-hand spring and follower in the cylinder head. Push the cam follower shaft in until it locates with the spring and follower and repeat this procedure until all the followers and springs are correctly refitted and the shaft is fully home. If necessary repeat the above procedure for the opposite shaft. On ZX1000 B and ZX1100 C models insert the shaft retaining springs into the cylinder head and stick a new sealing washer to the oil union points using a smear of grease. Offer up the oil pipe union, refit its union bolts and tighten them to the specified torque setting. On ZX900 and ZX1000 A models refit the Allen bolts which secure the cam follower shafts in position and tighten them to the specified torque setting.
2   If removed, refit the camshaft sprockets to the camshafts, using the notes made on dismantling for guidance (see Section 6, paragraph 5 of

this Chapter). Apply a few drops of thread-locking compound to the threads of the sprocket mounting bolts and tighten them to the specified torque setting. Hold the camchain taut and rotate the crankshaft until the T 1.4 mark on the ignition rotor aligns with the line cast in the crankcase casing.

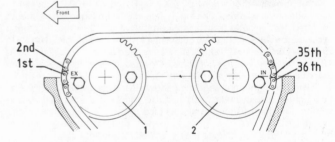

ZX900 and ZX1000 A models

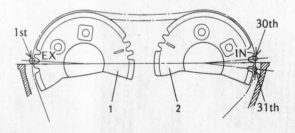

ZX1000 B and ZX1100 C models

Fig. 1.22 Valve timing marks (Sec 45)

1   Exhaust camshaft   2   Inlet camshaft

3   To ensure correct valve timing it is essential that the exhaust camshaft is correctly fitted. With the crankshaft positioned as described above and the front of the camchain held taut, engage the exhaust camshaft sprocket with the camchain and refit the exhaust camshaft to the cylinder head so that the EX mark next to the scribed line on the camshaft sprocket is level with the front surface of the cylinder head.

4   The positioning of the inlet camshaft is determined by counting the number of camchain linkpins between the aforementioned EX mark on the exhaust camshaft sprocket, and the IN mark next to the scribed line on the inlet camshaft sprocket (see accompanying illustration). On ZX900 and ZX1000 A models the IN mark should be between the 35th and 36th pin after the EX mark, and on ZX1000 B and ZX1100 C models it should be between the 30th and 31st pins. Count back the required number of pins from the EX mark and mark the correct position of the IN mark on the camchain with a spirit-based marker. Engage the inlet camshaft sprocket with the camchain, ensuring that the IN mark next to the scribed line is aligned with the mark on the camchain, and refit the camshaft to the cylinder head. The IN and EX marks next to the scribed lines should be in alignment with the cylinder head surface in this position. Note also the position of the sprocket securing bolts as an indication of correct alignment; these should be as shown in the appropriate part of Fig. 1.22. Where two sets of bolt holes are drilled in the sprocket, the bolts on the exhaust camshaft will be in the holes with the circular surround, and those on the inlet camshaft will be in the holes with the square surround.

5   Lubricate the camshaft and bearing caps with clean engine oil and refit all the bearing cap dowels to the cylinder head. Install the bearing caps in their original positions, using the numbers cast on the top surface of each cap, and ensuring the arrow (also cast on the top surface of each cap) is pointing towards the front of the engine unit. Refit the camshaft cap retaining bolts and, working in sequence (see accompanying illustration), tighten them evenly and progressively to their specified torque setting.

6   With both camshafts secured, recheck the valve timing. With the front and top runs of the chain taut, and the crankshaft in the T 1.4 position, check that the scribed lines next to the EX mark on the exhaust camshaft and the IN mark on the inlet camshaft are parallel with the top surface of the cylinder head. If this is not the case there is no need to

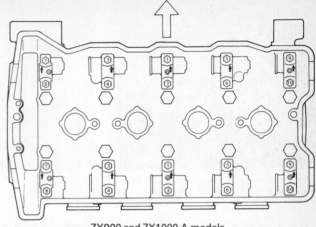

ZX900 and ZX1000 A models

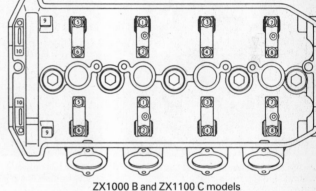

ZX1000 B and ZX1100 C models

Fig. 1.23 Camshaft cap bolt tightening sequence (Sec 45)

45.1a On ZX1000 B and ZX1100 C models do not omit the shaft retaining springs ...

45.1b ... and use a new sealing washer when refitting oil pipe union

45.2 Hold the camchain taut and rotate the crankshaft to the T 1.4 position

45.3a Hold the front of the camchain taut and refit the exhaust camshaft ...

45.3b ... so that the EX mark is level with the cylinder head surface (ZX1000 B and ZX1100 C shown)

45.4a Count back the required number of pins and refit the inlet camshaft (ZX1000 B and ZX1100 C shown) ...

45.4b ... so that the IN mark is level with the cylinder head surface (ZX1000 B and ZX1100 C shown)

45.5a Refit camshaft cap dowels to the cylinder head ...

45.5b ... and install the bearing caps using the arrows and numbers cast into the top surface

45.7 Refit the top camchain guide as described in text

45.8 Ensure tensioner is fitted so that the arrow on the tensioner body points upwards

45.9a Fully retract the tensioner pushrod and refit the tensioner using a new gasket

45.9b Tighten tensioner mounting bolts to the specified torque setting and refit the cap bolt and spring

45.10 Apply silicone sealant to the four semi-circular cutouts in the cylinder head

45.11a On ZX1000 B and ZX1100 C models refit cylinder head cover gaskets to the cylinder head

worry unless the difference is in the order of one or more camchain links, in which case repeat the above procedure to check.

7   Once the camshafts are correctly positioned refit the top camchain guide to the cylinder head. On ZX1000 B and ZX1100 C models apply a thread-locking compound to the threads of its retaining bolts and tighten them securely, whilst on ZX900 and ZX1000 A models refit the bolts and tighten them to the specified torque setting. Install the camchain tensioner as follows.

8   On ZX900 A1 to A6 and ZX1000 A models remove the cap bolt. Fit new O-rings to both the cap bolt and tensioner body. Insert a screwdriver into the back of the tensioner body and turn the screwdriver in a clockwise direction whilst pushing the pushrod back into the tensioner body until the end of the pushrod is approximately 10 mm from the inner surface of the tensioner body. Keeping the screwdriver in position, refit the tensioner assembly to the engine unit, ensuring the arrow cast on the tensioner body is pointing upwards. Push the tensioner hard against the cylinder block, remove the screwdriver, and refit its mounting bolts finger-tight only. **Note:** *at no point should the tensioner body be allowed to come away from the cylinder block. If pressure is released on*

the tensioner and it is pushed away from the block, the tensioner must be removed and the whole installation procedure repeated. Once the tensioner is correctly installed, tighten its mounting bolts to the specified torque setting, refit the cap bolt and tighten it securely.

9   On ZX900 A7-on, ZX1000 B and ZX1100 C models remove the cap bolt from the tensioner body and withdraw the spring. Release the tensioner locking mechanism by pulling the pushrod stopper back towards the tensioner body, and pushing the tensioner pushrod back until it is fully retracted in the tensioner body. Using a new gasket, refit the tensioner to the cylinder block ensuring that the arrow cast on it is facing upwards; tighten its mounting bolts to the specified torque setting. Install the tensioner spring, refit the cap bolt and tighten it securely.

10   On all models rotate the crankshaft a few times, using a ring spanner on the large hexagon ignition rotor nut, to settle all the disturbed components. Check the valve clearances as described in Routine maintenance and adjust if necessary. Lubricate all bearing surfaces with clean engine oil and wipe both the cylinder head and cover gasket surfaces with a rag moistened in a high flash-point solvent. Examine all the cylinder head cover rubber gaskets for signs of damage, renewing

45.11b Do not omit cylinder head cover dowels

45.11c Refit the cylinder head cover ...

45.11d ... and tighten its retaining bolts evenly and progressively to the specified torque setting

them if necessary. Apply silicone sealant to the surfaces of the four semi-circular cutouts in the cylinder head.

11   On ZX900 and ZX1000 A models refit the dowels to the cylinder head cover and refit all the gaskets to the cover. Apply a liquid gasket compound to the gaskets to help hold them in place, and take great care to ensure that the dowels do not drop out of the cover as it is refitted to the cylinder head. On ZX1000 B and ZX1100 C models refit the dowels to the cylinder head and fit the gaskets to the head. On all models refit the cylinder head cover to the engine unit. Fit the six cover retaining bolts and oil seals and tighten them evenly and progressively to their specified torque setting.

12   On all US models refit the air suction (reed) valve assemblies and covers to the cylinder head, using new gaskets, and tighten their retaining screws securely.

46   Refitting the engine/gearbox unit to the frame

1   The assistance of at least one, preferably two, people will be required to lift the engine back into the frame. Remove all traces of corrosion from the engine mounting bolts and apply a smear of grease to their shanks to ease the task of refitting them.

2   Position the unit beneath the frame then lift it up and manoeuvre it in to position. Secure it by inserting both the upper and lower rear mounting bolts. On ZX1000 and ZX1100 C models refit the frame cradle, tighten its retaining bolts to the specified torque setting, then refit the two front engine mounting bolts. On ZX900 models fit the two upper engine mounting bolts not forgetting to refit the shim (where fitted) between the cylinder head and the left-hand frame mounting. On all models tighten all engine mounting bolts to their specified torque settings.

3   Connect the starter motor lead earth strap to the top of the crankcase, and remake the electrical connections to the pulser coil(s), neutral switch, sidestand switch and the oil pressure and temperature switches (as applicable). Refit any cable ties that were removed and refit the wiring to any relevant guide hooks or clamps. On ZX900 models, refit the ignition HT coils and reconnect the low tension leads correctly,

using the marks made on dismantling. On ZX1000 and ZX1100 C models refit the air baffle plate in front of the cylinder head cover. On all models refit the suppressor caps to the spark plugs using the numbers on the HT leads to ensure that they are fitted correctly.

4   Place new exhaust gaskets in the ports, using a dab of grease to stick them in place. Refit the exhaust system as follows, noting that on ZX900 models the exhaust pipes and front fairing bracket must be refitted together.

5   On ZX1000 B models join the left and right sections of the exhaust system (if separated), then on all models offer up the exhaust pipes to the cylinder head. Push the pipes into the ports and hold them there while an assistant lifts up the rear of the exhaust system and inserts the rear exhaust or silencer mounting bolt(s) (as applicable). Tighten the bolt(s) finger-tight only at this stage. Refit the exhaust mounting clamps and the eight mounting nuts. Tighten the front exhaust mounting nuts evenly and securely and then tighten the rear exhaust or silencer mounting bolt(s). On ZX900 and ZX1000 A models refit both the left and right-hand silencers and tighten their mounting bolts and clamps securely. On ZX1100 C models refit the right-hand silencer, positioning the exhaust clamp as shown in the accompanying photograph, and then tighten both the mounting bolts and clamp securely. On ZX1000 B models tighten the exhaust clamp which secures the left and right-hand sections of the exhaust system together. On ZX900 models refit the lower fairing bracket, using the marks made on dismantling for guidance, and tighten both the lower and front fairing bracket mounting bolts securely.

6   On all models, engage the sprocket on the drive chain and refit it to the splines on the output shaft. Inspect the tab washer, if it is weakened due to repeated bending of its tab renew it (see the note below concerning the ZX1100 C model). Refit the sprocket retaining nut and tighten it to the specified torque setting whilst applying the rear brake hard to prevent the sprocket from rotating (transmission in gear and rear wheel touching the ground). Using slip-joint pliers flatten a section of the tab washer against one of the flats of the nut. Adjust the drive chain tension as described in Routine Maintenance. **Note:** *A modified tab washer was introduced for all ZX1100 C models in late 1993. It can be identified by its shaped periphery and convex cross-section; refer to a Kawasaki dealer for details. Kawasaki advise that when fitting the new*

46.4 Use grease to hold new exhaust gaskets in position

46.5a Refit the exhaust pipes to the ports ...

46.5b ... and fit the exhaust system rear mounting bolt

46.5c Refit the exhaust pipe front clamps and nuts and tighten as described in text

46.5d On ZX1100 C models the exhaust clamp must be positioned as shown, approximately 45° to the rear

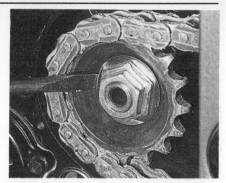

46.6 Tighten the drive sprocket nut to the specified torque setting and secure it with the locking tab

46.7a Insert the clutch pushrod as described in text

46.7b Refit the dowels to the crankcase ...

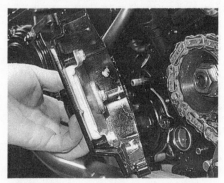

46.7c ... and refit the sprocket casing to the engine unit

46.7d Using the marks made on dismantling refit the gearchange linkage to the shaft tightening its pinch bolt securely

46.8 On ZX1100 C models do not omit shouldered spacer from behind front air filter housing mounting bolt

46.9 Fit a new sealing washer on each side of all oil cooler hose unions

washer, the nut also be renewed, and that a light coating of oil is applied to the shaft threads and both sides of the washer. A section of the washer should be flattened fully against one of the nut flats to form a 90° angle.

7   Lubricate the clutch pushrod and insert it into the engine ensuring that its rounded end is facing outwards. Fit the two sprocket casing locating dowels in the crankcase (if removed) and refit the casing itself. Fit a new insulating gasket to the slave cylinder, push its piston in as far as possible with hand pressure and install the slave cylinder in the sprocket casing. Refit the three retaining bolts and tighten these and the sprocket casing mounting bolts securely. Ensure that the clutch hydraulic hose and metal pipe are secured by the clamps provided. Operate the clutch lever to bring the piston into contact with the pushrod; if there is evidence of air in the system it must be bled as described in Chapter 6, Section 13. Using the marks made on dismantling, refit the gearchange linkage on to its shaft and tighten its pinch bolt securely.

8   On ZX900 and ZX1000 A models, install the air filter housing and fit its mounting bolt(s) finger-tight only. On all models refit the carburettors

as described in Chapter 3. Once refitted, check the throttle and choke cable freeplay as described in Routine maintenance and adjust if necessary. On US models refit all clean air and emission control system components, referring to Chapter 3 for further information. On all ZX1100 C models fit the front section of the air filter housing not forgetting to connect the vent hose to the carburettors and to fit the shouldered spacer behind the front housing mounting bolt. On all models tighten all disturbed components securely.

9   Refit the radiator and cooling fan assembly, and the water pump. Fill the cooling system as described in Chapter 2. Offer up the oil cooler assembly and tighten its mounting bolts securely. Route the oil hoses correctly, using the notes made on dismantling, and position a new sealing washer on both sides of each hose union. Refit the union bolts and tighten them to their specified torque settings.

10   Reconnect the battery, remembering to connect the negative terminal last. Refit the fuel tank as described in Chapter 3. Working as described in Routine maintenance, fit a new oil filter element and add the required amount of oil to the engine. Be prepared to top up the oil

47.4 Adjusting the balancer shaft

once the engine has been run as the level will drop as soon as the oil begins to circulate. Do not refit the fairing until the engine has been run and the balancer shaft adjusted as described in the following Section.

47 Starting and running the rebuilt engine

1   Attempt to start the engine using the usual procedure adopted for a cold engine. Do not be disillusioned if there is no sign of life initially, especially on ZX1000 B and ZX1100 C models where due to the nature of the fuel system it can take anything up to 30 seconds of turning the engine over just to refill the carburettors with fuel. A certain amount of perseverance may prove necessary to coax the engine into activity even if new parts have not been fitted. Should the engine persist in not starting, check that the spark plugs have not become fouled by the oil used during reassembly. Failing this go through the fault diagnosis section and work out what the fault is methodically.
2   When the engine does start, keep it running as slowly as possible to allow the oil to circulate. The oil pressure warning light should go out almost immediately the engine has started, although in certain instances a very short delay can occur whilst the oilways fill and the pressure builds up. If the light does not go out the engine should be stopped before damage can occur, and the cause determined. Open the choke as soon as the engine will run without it. During the initial running, a certain amount of smoke may be in evidence due to the oil used in the reassembly sequence being burnt away. The resulting smoke should gradually subside.
3   Check the engine for blowing gaskets and oil leaks. Before using the machine on the road, check that all the gears select properly, and that the controls function correctly.
4   Before the engine warms the balancer shaft must be adjusted. Start the engine and allow it to idle. Slacken the balancer shaft pinch bolt and using a flat-bladed screwdriver turn the balancer shaft anticlockwise until the balancer gear starts to make a noise. Then turn the shaft back slowly in a clockwise direction until the noise stops. Tighten the pinch bolt securely whilst holding the balancer shaft in position.
5   Warm the engine up to normal operating temperature and thoroughly check for any oil or coolant leaks. If no leaks are present check both the oil and coolant levels as described in Routine maintenance and top up as necessary. Do not forget to check these both before and after the machine has been for a run. Refit the fairing as described in Chapter 5 and make a final check that all disturbed components have been securely tightened before taking the machine on the road.

48 Taking the rebuilt machine on the road

1   Any rebuilt machine will need time to settle down, even if parts have been refitted in their original order. For this reason it is highly advisable to treat the machine gently for the first few miles to ensure oil has circulated throughout the lubrication system and that new parts fitted have begun to bed down.
2   Even greater care is necessary if the engine has been rebored or if a new crankshaft has been fitted. In the case of a rebore, the engine will have to be run in again, as if the machine were new. This means greater use of the gearbox and a restraining hand on the throttle until at least 500 miles have been covered. There is no point in keeping to any set speed limit; the main requirement is to keep a light loading on the engine and to gradually work up performance until the 500 mile mark is reached. These recommendations can be lessened to an extent when only a new crankshaft is fitted. Experience is the best guide since it is easy to tell when an engine is running freely.
3   If at any time a lubrication failure is suspected, stop the engine immediately and investigate the cause. If an engine is run without oil, even for a short period, irreparable engine damage is inevitable.
4   When the engine has cooled down completely after the initial run, recheck the various settings, especially the valve clearances. During the run most of the engine components will have settled into their normal working locations. Check the various oil levels, particularly that of the engine as it may have dropped slightly now that the various passages and recesses have filled.

49 Engine: compression test

1   A good indication of the engine's condition can be gained by carrying out a compression test. A compression gauge will be required, together with a suitable adaptor. Note that a gauge, adaptor and sealing gasket can be obtained for this purpose from Kawasaki dealers.
2   Check the valve clearances as described in Routine maintenance.
3   Run the engine until it reaches normal operating temperature, then stop it and remove all four spark plugs. Refit the plugs in the plug caps and arrange the plug electrodes so that their metal bodies are earthed (grounded) to the cylinder head; this will prevent damage to the ignition system as the engine is spun over. On ZX900 models, it will be necessary to remove the ignition HT coils; reconnect the earth (ground) wire to the rearmost of the coil mountings on the frame, using a suitable nut and bolt. Install the compression gauge in one of the spark plug holes and as a precaution against the risk of fire, plug the other three holes with a small wad of rag.
4   Open the throttle fully and spin the engine over on the starter motor until the highest gauge reading is recorded. After one or two revolutions the pressure should build up to a maximum figure and then stabilise. Take a note of the reading and then repeat the test on the three remaining cylinders.
5   The correct pressures are given in the Specifications. If the results fall within this range and all are relatively equal, the engine is in good condition. If there is a marked discrepancy between the readings, or if the readings are lower than specified, examination of the top end components should be made.
6   Low compression pressure may be due to worn cylinder bores, pistons or rings, failure of the cylinder head gasket, worn valve seals, or poor valve seating. To distinguish between cylinder/piston wear and valve leakage, pour a small quantity of oil into the bore to temporarily seal the piston rings, then carry out the above compression tests. If the readings show a noticeable increase this confirms that the cylinder bore, piston or rings are worn. If, however, no change is indicated, the cylinder head gasket or valves should be examined.
7   Readings in excess of those specified indicate excessive carbon build-up in the combustion chamber and on the piston crown.

Chapter 2 Cooling system

Refer to Chapter 8 for information on the ZX1100 D model

Contents

Specifications

Coolant

Mixture type...	Distilled water, and corrosion-inhibited ethylene-glycol antifreeze suitable for use in aluminium engines
Standard recommended mixture ratio – down to –35°C (–31°F)	50% antifreeze/50% distilled water

Total capacity of system:

ZX900 models..	2.9 lit (5.1 Imp pt, 3.0 US qt)
ZX1000 models	3.1 lit (5.5 Imp pt, 3.2 US qt)
ZX1100 C models...	2.5 lit (4.4 Imp pt, 2.6 US qt)

Thermostat

Valve opening temperature:

ZX1000 B UK models..	69 – 73°C (156 – 163°F)
All other models	80 – 84°C (176 – 183°F)
Valve lift @ 95°C (203°F)	More than 8 mm (0.31 in)

Radiator

Cap valve opening pressure:

ZX900 and ZX1000 A models....................................	0.75 – 1.05 kg/cm² (11 – 15 psi)
ZX1000 B and ZX1100 C models...............................	0.95 – 1.25 kg/cm² (14 – 18 psi)

Torque settings

Component	kgf m	lbf ft
Coolant drain plug	0.8	6.0
Cooling fan switch unit:		
ZX900 and ZX1000 A models....................	0.75	5.5
ZX1000 B and ZX1100 C models	1.8	13.0
Temperature sender unit:		
ZX900 and ZX1000 A models....................	0.8	6.0
ZX1000 B and ZX1100 C models	1.5	11.0
Thermostat housing bleed valve	0.8	6.0
Water pump mounting bolts:		
ZX1100 C models....................................	1.0	7.0
Other models	Not available	

1 General description

The cooling system uses a water/antifreeze mixture to carry away excess energy in the form of heat. The cylinders are surrounded by a water jacket from which the heated coolant is circulated by thermo-syphonic action in conjunction with a water pump which is driven off the oil pump shaft. The hot coolant passes upwards to the thermostat and through to the radiator, mounted on the frame front downtubes to take maximum advantage of the passing airflow. The coolant then flows across the radiator core, down to the water pump and back up to the engine where the cycle is repeated.

A thermostat is fitted in the system to prevent the coolant flowing through the radiator when the engine is cold, therefore accelerating the speed at which the engine reaches normal operating temperature. A thermostatically controlled cooling fan is also fitted to aid cooling in extreme conditions.

On most UK models the coolant is also used to warm the carburettor bodies via an arrangement of small hoses. The coolant travels from the rear of the cylinder block, through a filter, through the carburettor castings and then rejoins the main cooling system at the water pump. A check valve is fitted above the water pump to ensure the correct flow of coolant.

The complete cooling system is partially sealed and pressurised, the pressure being controlled by a valve contained in the spring-loaded radiator cap. The overflow pipe from the radiator is connected to an expansion tank into which excess coolant is expelled under pressure. The discharged coolant automatically returns to the radiator when the engine cools.

2 Cooling system: draining

Note: *to avoid the risk of personal injury such as scalding, the cooling system should only be drained when the engine and cooling system are cold. Coolant will attack painted surfaces; wash away any spilt coolant immediately with fresh water.*

1   Place the machine on its centre stand on a level surface. To gain access to the radiator cap on ZX900 models, remove the seat, side-panels and the fuel tank mounting bolts. Move the fuel tank backwards, noting that it is not necessary to disconnect or remove it. On ZX1000 A models remove the inner fairing section, as described in Chapter 5. On ZX1000 B and ZX1100 C models, remove the two bolts which retain the small cover to the right-hand inner fairing section and lift the cover away from the machine.

2   If the engine is cold remove the cap by turning it in an anticlockwise direction. If the engine is still warm place a thick rag over the cap and turn it slightly until all the pressure in the system has been allowed to escape. A rag must be used to prevent escaping steam from scalding the hands. If the cap is removed suddenly, the drop in pressure could allow the coolant to boil violently and be expelled from the filler neck, scalding the skin and damaging paintwork. Where time and circumstances permit it is therefore strongly recommended that a hot engine is allowed to cool before the cap is removed.

3   Remove the lower fairing section as described in Chapter 5 and place a suitably sized container underneath the drain plug, located at the bottom of the left-hand engine coolant pipe. If the coolant is to be reused, ensure that it is drained into a clean non-metallic container. Unscrew the drain plug and allow the coolant to drain fully into the container. Once drained, refit the drain plug and tighten it to the specified torque setting. If damaged, the drain plug sealing washer must be renewed.

4   Complete draining of the system will require that the cylinder block drain plugs be removed to allow the escape of residual coolant from the engine castings. These drain plugs are situated on the front edge of the block, although note that access to them may be rather limited. Have ready a suitable container to catch the escaping coolant as the plugs are unscrewed. If damaged, renew the drain plug sealing washers and tighten the plugs securely.

5   If necessary the expansion tank can also be drained. On ZX900 and

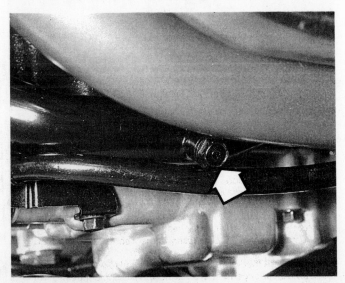

2.3 Location of cooling system drain plug

ZX1000 A models this can be achieved by simply removing the tank mounting bolts and tipping its contents out. On ZX1000 B and ZX1100 C disconnect the pipe from the union at the base of the tank and allow the contents to drain into a suitable container. On ZX1000 B models to do this it is necessary to remove the right-hand middle fairing section, as described in Chapter 5.

6   The manufacturer recommends that the coolant is changed at regular intervals (see Routine maintenance).

3 Cooling system: flushing

1   After extended service the cooling system will slowly lose efficiency, due to the build-up of scale, deposits from the water and other foreign matter which will adhere to the internal surfaces of the radiator and coolant passages. This condition will worsen if distilled water has not been used at all times. Removal of the deposits can be carried out easily using a suitable flushing agent in the following manner.

2   Drain the system as described in the previous Section. Refit the drain plug and refill the system with clean water and the specified amount of flushing agent. Any proprietary flushing agent can be used in either liquid or dry form, providing it is recommended for use in aluminium engines. *Never use a compound suitable for iron engines as it will react violently with the aluminium alloy.* The manufacturer of the flushing agent will give instructions on the quantity of flushing agent to be used.

3   Run the engine for ten minutes at normal operating and then drain the system. Repeat the procedure twice and then again using only clean cold water. Finally refill the system as described in the following Section.

4 Cooling system: filling

Note: *to avoid the risk of personal injury such as scalding, the cooling system should only be drained when the engine and cooling system are cold. Coolant will attack painted surfaces; wash away any spilt coolant immediately with fresh water.*

1   Before filling the system first check that the drain plugs have been fitted and tightened to the specified torque setting (where given). Check that all coolant pipes and hoses are correctly fitted and held securely by their hose clips.

2   The recommended mixture of coolant given in the Specifications will give protection against the coolant freezing in temperatures of down to -35°C (-31°F). To give adequate protection against wind chill factors and other variables, the coolant should always be prepared for temperatures 5°C (9°F) lower than the lowest anticipated temperature.

3   Use only good quality antifreeze of the type specified, never use an alcohol based antifreeze. In view of the small quantities used, always use distilled water and never tap water. Against its extra cost can be set the fact that it will keep the system cleaner and save the time and effort spent flushing the system that would otherwise be necessary with tap water. However, tap water that is known to be soft, or rainwater caught in a non-metallic container and filtered before use, may be used in an emergency. Never use hard tap water as the risk of scale building up is too great.

4   So that a reserve is left for subsequent topping up, prepare approximately 3.5 litres (6.2 Imp pint/3.7 US qt) of coolant in a clean non-metallic container. At the standard recommended mixture strength this will mean mixing equal quantities of both antifreeze and distilled water, although adjustments can be made if lower temperatures are expected.

5   Add the coolant via the radiator filler neck, pouring it in slowly to reduce the amount of air which will be trapped in the system. When the level is up to the base of the filler neck, slacken the bleed bolt situated at the top of the water pump housing until coolant starts to trickle slowly out of the bolt hole. Once the coolant starts to flow from the hole tighten the bolt securely, and mop up any spilt coolant. This procedure bleeds the water pump of air. Top up the radiator if necessary, to the base of the filler neck. A further bleed bolt is situated on the thermostat housing, in the form of a bleed valve. Slacken the bleed valve and allow coolant to flow from the valve whilst adding coolant via the filler neck. When the flow of coolant is free of air bubbles, tighten the bleed valve to the specified torque setting. Check that the coolant level is topped up to the base of the filler neck and refit the radiator cap. Fill the expansion tank to

its upper level line and refit the expansion tank cap.

6   Start the engine and allow it to idle until it reaches normal operating temperature and the cooling fan comes on. Stop the engine at this point and allow it to cool. When the engine is cool check the level in the expansion tank as described in Routine maintenance and top up if necessary.

7   When the machine has been ridden for the first time after refilling, allow the engine to cool down and check the level at the radiator filler cap to ensure that no further pockets of air have been expelled, topping up if necessary. All subsequent checks of the level at the recommended maintenance intervals should be checked at the expansion tank, as described in Routine maintenance.

5   Radiator: removal, cleaning, examination and refitting

1   Remove the fairing as described in Chapter 5. On ZX1000 B and ZX1100 C models it is also necessary to remove the fuel tank as described in Chapter 3. **Note:** *on all models the cooling fan and switch are connected directly to the battery, enabling the fan to operate with the ignition switched off. For this reason ensure that the engine is cold before attempting to remove the radiator and disconnect the battery negative lead. Failure to do so could lead to injury from the fan blades should the fan come on unexpectedly.*

2   Drain the coolant as described in Section 2 of this Chapter.

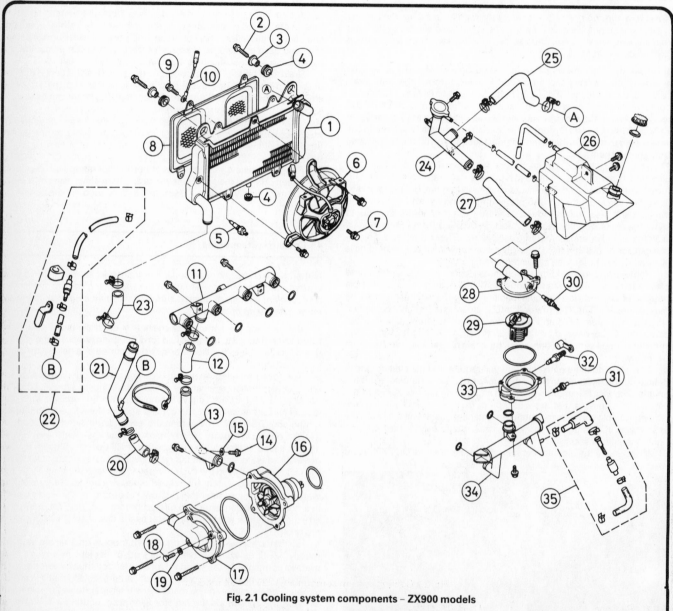

Fig. 2.1 Cooling system components – ZX900 models

1 Radiator	11 Front coolant pipe	19 Sealing washer	28 Thermostat cover
2 Bolt – 2 off	12 Water pump to cylinder	20 Lower hose	29 Thermostat
3 Spacer – 2 off	hose	21 Lower metal pipe	30 Temperature sensor switch
4 Mounting rubber – 2 off	13 Water pump to cylinder	22 Carburettor warmer pipe	31 Fan switch
5 Fan switch	metal pipe	check valve assembly △	32 Bleed valve
6 Fan	14 Drain plug	23 Lower hose	33 Thermostat housing
7 Bolt – 3 off	15 Sealing washer	24 Radiator cap assembly	34 Rear coolant pipe
8 Radiator guard	16 Water pump	25 Filler cap to radiator hose	35 Carburettor warmer pipe
9 Bolt – 4 off	17 Water pump cover	26 Expansion tank	filter assembly △
10 Earth wire	18 Bleed bolt	27 Upper hose	
			△ UK models only

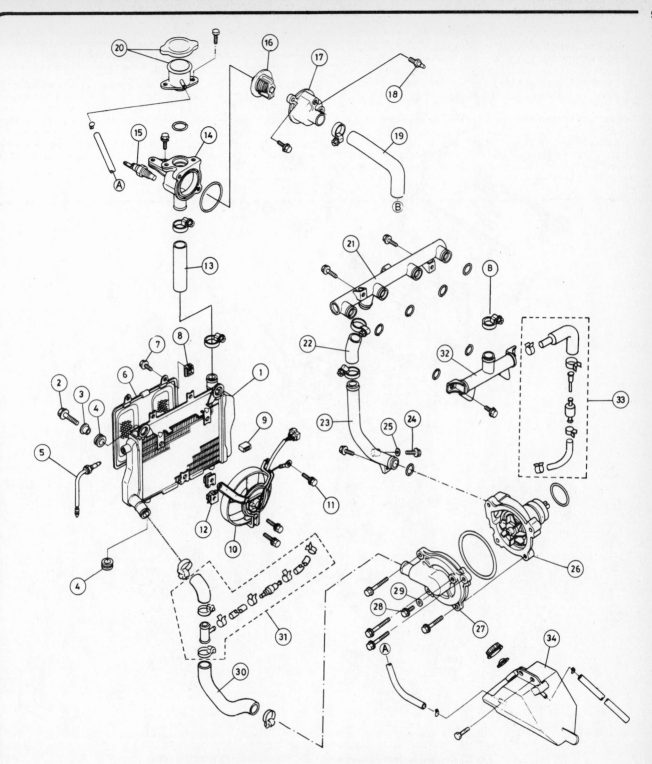

Fig. 2.2 Cooling system components – ZX1000 A models

1	Radiator	11	Bolt – 3 off
2	Bolt – 2 off	12	Nut – 3 off
3	Spacer – 2 off	13	Radiator to thermostat hose
4	Mounting rubber – 4 off	14	Thermostat housing
5	Fan switch	15	Temperature sensor switch
6	Radiator guard	16	Thermostat
7	Bolt – 4 off	17	Thermostat cover
8	Nut – 4 off	18	Bleed valve
9	Mounting rubber – 2 off	19	Upper hose
10	Fan	20	Radiator cap assembly

21	Front coolant pipe	30	Lower hose
22	Water pump to cylinder hose	31	Carburettor warmer pipe check valve assembly △
23	Water pump to cylinder metal pipe	32	Rear coolant pipe
24	Drain plug	33	Carburettor warmer pipe filter assembly △
25	Sealing washer	34	Expansion tank
26	Water pump		
27	Water pump cover	△ UK models only
28	Bleed bolt		
29	Sealing washer		

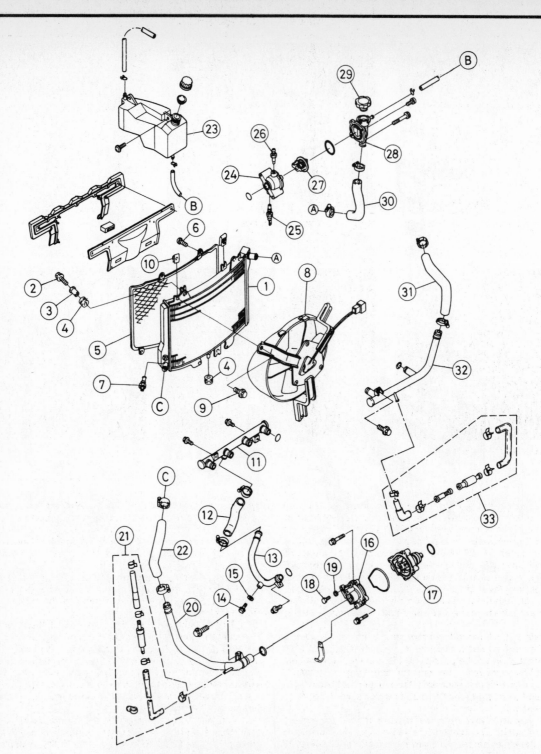

Fig. 2.3 Cooling system components – ZX1100 models (ZX1000 B similar)

1 Radiator	11 Front coolant pipe	20 Lower metal pipe	29 Radiator cap
2 Bolt – 2 off	12 Water pump to cylinder hose	21 Carburettor warmer pipe	30 Radiator to thermostat hose
3 Spacer – 2 off	13 Water pump to cylinder metal	check valve assembly △	31 Upper hose
4 Mounting rubber – 3 off	pipe	22 Lower hose	32 Upper metal pipe
5 Radiator guard	14 Drain plug	23 Expansion tank	33 Carburettor warmer pipe
6 Screw – 4 off	15 Sealing washer	24 Thermostat housing	filter assembly △
7 Fan switch	16 Water pump cover	25 Temperature sensor switch	
8 Fan	17 Water pump	26 Bleed valve	△ UK models only
9 Bolt – 3 off	18 Bleed bolt	27 Thermostat	
10 Nut – 3 off	19 Sealing washer	28 Thermostat cover/filler neck	

Note: carburettor warmer pipe assembly differed slightly on UK ZX1000 B1 model. The filter assembly (item 33) was taken off the thermostat housing (item 24), and the check valve shown in item 21 was omitted.

5.3a Slacken the clamps and remove both the upper ...

5.3b ... and lower radiator hoses

5.4a Remove the radiator mounting bolts ...

5.4b ... and disconnect the cooling fan switch ...

5.4c ... and cooling fan wiring – ZX1100 C shown

6.2 Radiator cap can be tested if necessary equipment is available

3   Slacken the hose clamps on both the lower and upper radiator hoses and disconnect the hoses from the radiator. On ZX900 models remove the mounting bolts from the lower fairing mounting bracket and push the bracket downwards to disengage it from the peg on the bottom of the radiator. On ZX1000·A models remove the mounting bolts from both the oil cooler and its mounting bracket, and push the oil cooler mounting bracket clear of the radiator. Tie the oil cooler to the frame to avoid placing any strain on its hoses. On ZX1000 and ZX1100 C models disconnect both the horns and remove them along with their mounting brackets. Each horn bracket is retained by a single mounting bolt.

4   On all models, remove the radiator mounting bolts and disconnect the cooling fan and switch electrical connectors. On ZX900 and ZX1000 A models note that it will not be possible to disconnect these until the radiator is partially removed. The radiator can then be carefully manoeuvred out of position. If necessary the radiator and cooling fan can be separated by removing the three bolts which secure the fan to the back of the radiator.

5   Remove any obstructions from the radiator matrix using compressed air from behind. To prevent the radiator vanes from being damaged keep the air jet perpendicular to the radiator and at least 20 inches away from the radiator core. The conglomeration of moths, flies and road dust which usually builds up in the radiator matrix restricts the air flow and severely reduces the efficiency of the cooling system.

6   The interior of the radiator is easily cleaned whilst the radiator is in position on the machine, using the flushing procedure described in Section 3. Additional flushing can be carried out by placing a hose in the radiator filler neck and allowing water to flow through for about ten minutes. Under no circumstances should the hose be connected to the filler neck mechanically as a sudden blockage in the radiator outlet would subject the radiator to the full pressure of the mains supply (about 50 psi). The radiator should never be pressurised to more than 15 psi.

7   Bent fins can be straightened, if care is exercised, by using a flat-bladed screwdriver. Badly damaged fins cannot be repaired. As a rule a new radiator should be fitted if bent fins obstruct more than 20% of the air flow.

8   If the radiator is found to be leaking repairs are usually impractical and a new component will have to be fitted. Very small leaks may sometimes be stopped by the addition of a special sealing agent in the coolant. If an agent of this type is used follow the manufacturer's instructions very carefully. Soldering, using soft solder, may be effective for caulking large leaks but this is a specialist repair which is best left to the experts.

9   Inspect the radiator mounting rubbers for perishing or compaction. Renew the rubbers if there is any doubt as to their condition. The radiator could be damaged by vibration if the isolating effect of the rubbers is lost.

10   The radiator is refitted by a reversal of the removal sequence. Remount the cooling fan on the radiator and tighten its mounting bolts securely. On ZX1000 A models do not forget to refit the cooling fan switch earth lead to one of the fan bolts. Refit the radiator to the machine and connect both the cooling fan and switch leads. Refit the radiator mounting bolts and tighten them securely. On ZX900 models do not forget to refit the cooling fan switch earth lead to the top left-hand radiator mounting bolt.

11   On ZX900 models reposition the fairing bracket, ensuring that it locates correctly with the peg on the bottom of the radiator, and refit its mounting bolts. On ZX1000 A models refit the oil cooler and bracket ensuring that the bracket locates correctly with the pegs on the bottom of the radiator and those on the oil cooler. On ZX1000 B and ZX1100 C models refit the radiator cover. On ZX1000 and ZX1100 C models refit the horns and connect their electrical leads. On all models tighten all disturbed nuts and bolts securely.

12   Refit the coolant hoses to the radiator and secure them with the hose clips. Fill the cooling system as described in Section 4 and refit the fairing.

6 Radiator cap: testing

1   If the valve or valve spring in the radiator cap is faulty the pressure in the cooling system will be reduced, causing the coolant to boil over.

2   The only satisfactory way of testing the radiator cap is to pressure test it. This requires special equipment not normally found in the home

workshop. The cap should therefore be taken to an authorized Kawasaki dealer who will have the necessary equipment available to test it. The only other means of testing the cap is by substitution.

3   If the correct equipment is available, wet the sealing surfaces of the cap and fit it to the pressure tester. Apply a pressure of 11 – 15 psi (0.79 – 1.1 kg/cm²) on ZX900 and ZX1000 A models and 14 – 18 psi (1 – 1.25 kg/cm²) on ZX1000 B and ZX1100 C models, usually by means of a hand-operated plunger. *Never exceed the upper limit of the specified pressures when testing the cap.* The pressure must be held for a period of 6 seconds, during which time it should remain within the specified limits with no measurable loss. If the cap is found to be faulty it must be renewed.

4   In addition to pressure testing the cap the same equipment can be used to pressurise the cooling system and check for leakage of coolant. Remove the radiator cap, check that the coolant level is topped up, and connect the equipment to the filler neck. Apply a pressure of no more than 15 psi (1.1 kg/cm²) on ZX900 and ZX1000 A models, and 18 psi (1.25 kg/cm²) on ZX1000 B and ZX1100 C models, by means of the hand-operated plunger. Any leaks should soon become apparent. Most leaks will however be readily apparent due to the tell-tale traces of antifreeze left on the components in the immediate area of the leak.

7   Coolant hoses and pipes: removal, refitting and checking for leaks

1   The cooling system can be regarded as a semi-sealed system, the only normal coolant loss being minute amounts through evaporation in the expansion tank. If, however, significant coolant loss is experienced, the source of the leak should be promptly investigated before engine damage results.

2   The radiator is connected to the engine by various flexible hoses and metal pipes, best illustrated by reference to the accompanying figure. The hoses should be periodically inspected and renewed if any sign of cracking or perishing is discovered. The most likely problem area is around the clips which secure each hose to its unions. Another area which should be regularly checked is the unions between the metal coolant pipes and the engine. All these unions are sealed by O-rings which will in time perish and allow coolant to leak. On UK models do not forget to include the carburettor warmer hoses when checking the cooling system for leaks.

3   Before removing any of the hoses or coolant pipes drain the coolant as described in Section 2. To disconnect the hoses, use a screwdriver to slacken the clamps then slide them back along the hose and clear of the union spigot, noting that it may be necessary to remove the radiator mounting bolts, or alternately the coolant pipe retaining bolts, to allow the hose to be removed. The hoses can be worked off with relative ease when new or slightly warm, using a twisting action. Do not, however, attempt to disconnect any part of the system whilst it is still hot due to the risk of personal injury. Note that the radiator unions and the metal coolant pipes are fragile. *Do not use excessive force when attempting to remove the hoses.* If a hose proves stubborn, try to release it by rotating it on its union before working it off. If all else fails, cut the hose with a sharp knife then slit it at each union so that it can be peeled off in two pieces. Whilst this is expensive it is preferable to buying a new radiator.

4   Serious leakage will be self-evident, though slight leakage can be difficult to spot. It is likely that the leak will only be apparent when the machine is running and the system is under pressure, and even then the rate of escape may be such that the hot coolant evaporates as soon as it reaches the atmosphere, although traces of antifreeze should reveal the source of the leak. If not it will be necessary to use the test equipment described in the previous Section of this Chapter to pressurise the system when cold and trace the leak. This operation is best entrusted to an authorized Kawasaki dealer who will have access to the necessary equipment.

5   Other possible sources of leakage are the O-rings on the water pump casing and thermostat housing and the water pump's mechanical seal. The latter can easily be checked by examining the drainage hole on the bottom of the water pump housing as described in Section 9.

6   In very rare cases the leak may be due to a broken head gasket, in which case the coolant will be drawn into the engine and expelled as vapour in the exhaust gases. If this proves to be the case it will be necessary to remove the cylinder head for further investigation.

7   When refitting the hoses, first slide the clips onto the hose and then work the hose onto its spigots. *Do not use a lubricant of any kind, if necessary the hose can be softened up by soaking it in boiling water before refitting, although care is obviously necessary to prevent scalding the hands in the process.* When the hose is refitted rotate it on its spigots to settle it and check that the two components it joins are securely fastened so that the hose is correctly positioned before sliding its clips into place and tightening them securely. Note that on some hoses there is a small white dot or arrow which must be aligned with the mark, usually in the form of a line cast into the surface of the pipe, on the relevant union.

8   Thermostat: removal and testing

1   The thermostat remains in the closed position when the engine is cold, restricting the flow of the coolant, and opens only when the engine reaches its normal operating temperature. This enables the engine to warm up quickly when it is cold. If the thermostat malfunctions it will probably remain closed even when the engine has reached its normal operating temperature. The flow of the coolant will be impeded and will not be able to pass through the radiator and consequently the engine temperature will rise abnormally, causing the coolant to boil over. Alternately the thermostat could remain open which would mean the engine would take an abnormally long time to warm up from cold. If the performance of the thermostat is suspect, it should be removed from the machine and tested as follows.

2   Drain the coolant as described in Section 2 of this Chapter.

ZX900 models

3   The thermostat is situated between the cylinder head and the carburettors. Remove the fuel tank as described in Chapter 3, noting that on US models it is also necessary to remove the air suction valves and hoses. Remove the cylinder head cover as described in Chapter 1.

4   Slacken the hose clips on each end of the upper radiator hose which connects the thermostat and radiator, and remove the hose. Slacken the choke cable adjuster locknut and rotate the adjuster to obtain the

7.2a Cooling system hoses are secured with clamps ...

7.2b ... whilst pipes are retained by bolts (note bleed bolt – A) ...

7.2c ... and sealed with O-rings

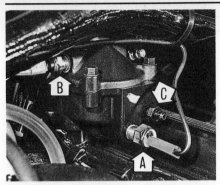

8.3 Thermostat housing – ZX900 models (note fan switch A, temperature sensor B, bleed valve C)

8.10a On ZX1000 B and ZX1100 C models ensure thermostat bypass hole (arrowed) is positioned at the top

8.10b Fit a new O-ring to thermostat housing cover ...

8.10c ... tighten its retaining screws securely

8.10d Fit a new O-ring to the back of the housing ...

8.10e ... before securing to frame with long Allen-headed bolts

maximum amount of free play possible. Disconnect the cable from the carburettors and remove the choke cable mounting clamp screw. Disconnect the wires from the fan switch and temperature sensor on the thermostat body. Remove the mounting bolt from the underside of the thermostat housing and withdraw the thermostat.

ZX1000 and ZX1100 C models
5   The thermostat is located just beneath the radiator pressure cap assembly. To gain access to the thermostat housing it is first necessary to remove the fairing as described in Chapter 5.
6   Disconnect the wire from the temperature sender unit and disconnect the expansion tank hose from the filler neck. Slacken the hose clip which secures the short radiator hose to the bottom of the thermostat housing and remove the two Allen-headed housing mounting bolts.

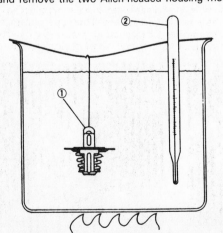

Fig. 2.4 Thermostat operation test (Sec 8)
Ensure thermostat (1) is completely submerged and that it and the thermometer (2) do not touch sides or bottom of container

Free the thermostat housing from the coolant hose and manoeuvre it out of the frame.

All models
7   Slacken the two screws which retain the thermostat housing cover, lift off the cover and remove the thermostat. Examine it visually before carrying out tests. If it remains open at room temperature it should be discarded. If however it appears to be serviceable it should be tested as follows.
8   Suspend the thermostat by a piece of wire in a glass heat-proof vessel of cold water. Place a thermometer in the water so that its bulb is close to the thermostat. Heat the water up, noting the temperature at which the thermostat begins to open and approximately how much lift the valve has when it is fully open. Compare the results obtained with those given in the Specifications. If the results obtained differ from those specified, the thermostat must be renewed.
9   If the thermostat is faulty it can be removed and the machine used without it as an emergency measure. Take care when starting the machine from cold as the warm-up will take much longer than usual, and ensure that a new unit is fitted as soon as possible.
10   The thermostat is refitted by a reversal of the removal procedure, noting that on ZX1000 B and ZX1100 C models where the thermostat is mounted vertically, ensure that the small bypass hole in the thermostat is positioned at the top. Renew both the O-rings on the thermostat housing cover regardless of their apparent condition. Fill the cooling system as described in Section 4 of this Chapter and refit all disturbed components.

9   Water pump: removal, examination and refitting

1   To prevent the leakage of water or oil from the cooling system to the lubrication system and vice versa, two seals are fitted on the pump shaft. On ZX1000 B and ZX1100 C models there is also a drainage hole situated on the underside of the pump body. If either seal fails this hole

9.1 Examine drainage hole for signs of coolant leakage

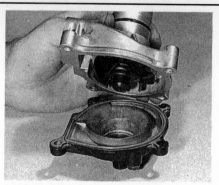

9.6a On refitting, renew the water pump cover O-ring ...

9.6b ... and housing O-ring and ensure that slot in the pump shaft engages with the oil pump shaft projection

should allow the coolant or oil to escape and prevent the oil and coolant mixing.

2   On all models, the seal on the water pump side is of the mechanical type which bears on the rear face of the impeller. The second seal, mounted behind the mechanical seal, is of the normal 'feathered' lip type. However, neither seal is available as a separate item and should either one fail the only solution is to renew the complete pump assembly as follows.

3   Drain the coolant as described in Section 2 of this Chapter.

4   On ZX1000 and ZX1100 C models remove the left-hand side fairing section. Marking its shaft so that it can be refitted in the same position, slacken and remove the gearchange linkage pinch bolt and pull the linkage off the gearchange shaft splines. Release the retaining bolts from the clutch slave cylinder and remove it from the engine sprocket casing. Push the piston as far back as possible by hand and then slowly bring the clutch operating lever back to the handlebars and hold it there with a stout elastic band. This will prevent the slave cylinder piston from being expelled. Slacken and remove the sprocket casing retaining bolts and remove the casing from the engine. Withdraw the clutch pushrod and store it with the casing for safekeeping.

5   On ZX900 and ZX1000 A models, slacken the hose clip which secures the flexible coolant hose to the water pump cover and work the hose off its union. On ZX1000 B and ZX1100 C models, remove the bolt which retains the metal coolant pipe to the pump cover and pull the pipe clear. On all models release the bolt which retains the inner metal coolant pipe and disengage it from the pump housing. Before removing the water pump, place a suitable container beneath the engine to catch any oil which may be released when the pump is removed, then release the pump mounting bolts, withdraw the pump assembly from the machine and lift off the pump cover.

6   The pump assembly is a sealed unit and cannot be repaired. If either seal fails or the impeller is damaged or corroded it must be renewed. Renew all O-rings as a matter of course.

7   The water pump is fitted by a reversal of the removal procedure. When fitting the pump to the engine unit ensure the slot on the impeller shaft aligns with the projection on the oil pump shaft and that the two components engage correctly. Tighten the pump mounting screws securely (to the specified torque setting where given) and refit the coolant pipes and hoses (as applicable) to the pump. Fill the cooling system as described in Section 4 of this Chapter and top up the oil level as necessary. Refit the clutch pushrod, ensuring that its rounded end is facing outwards, and refit the sprocket casing and clutch slave cylinder. Refit the gearchange shaft, using the marks made on dismantling and tighten the engine casing, slave cylinder and gearchange pinch bolts securely. Finally refit the lower fairing section and thoroughly check for leaks before taking the machine on the road.

10   Cooling system electrical components: general

The cooling system electrical components can be removed and refitted, and if necessary tested, as described in the relevant Sections of Chapter 7.

Chapter 3 Fuel system and lubrication

Refer to Chapter 8 for information on the ZX1100 D model

Contents

Specifications

Fuel tank capacity

	Litre	Imp gal	US gal
ZX900 models:			
Overall	22.0	4.85	5.8
Reserve	4.4	0.97	1.2
ZX1000 A models:			
Overall	21.0	4.63	5.5
Reserve	3.0	0.66	0.8
ZX1000 B models:			
Overall	22.0	4.85	5.8
Reserve	4.0	0.88	1.1
ZX1100 C models – overall	21.0	4.63	5.5

Fuel grade ..... Unleaded or leaded, minimum octane rating 91 (Research method/RON)

Carburettors

	ZX900	ZX1000 B	ZX1100 C
Make	Keihin	Keihin	Keihin
Type	CVK34	CVKD36	CVKD40
Main jet:			
UK models	132 (100 – A7-on)	130	155 – C1 140 – C2-on
US models	135	130 (128*)	155 (152*) – C1 140 (152*) – C2-on
Main air jet	100	100	70
Jet needle:			
UK models	N27B (N67I – A7-on)	N54D	N60U
US models	N27A	N14C	N60U
Pilot jet:			
UK models	35	38	38
US models	35	38 (35*)	38 (35*)
Pilot air jet	160	130	130
Starter jet:			
UK models	42	55	55
US 49-state models	42	52	55
California models	38	52	55
Pilot screw – turns out:			
UK models	2½ (1½ – A7-on)	2	2
US models	Preset	Preset	Preset
Fuel level – below mark	0.5 mm (0.02 in)	5.0 mm (0.20 in)	4.5 mm ± 1 mm (0.18 ± 0.04 in)
Float height	17 mm (0.67 in)	13 mm (0.51 in)	13 mm ± 2 mm (0.51 ± 0.08 in)
Idle speed – rpm	950 – 1050	950 – 1050	950 – 1050

Carburettors

	ZX1000 A
Make	Keihin
Type	CVK36
Main jet:	
UK models	132
US 49-state models	132 (130*)
California models	138 (135*)
Main air jet	100
Jet needle:	
Cylinders 1 and 4	N36D
Cylinders 2 and 3	N36E
Pilot jet:	
UK models	35
US models	35 (32*)
Pilot air jet	140
Starter jet:	
UK models	50
US 49-state models	50
California models	45
Pilot screw – turns out:	
UK models	1¾
US models	Preset
Fuel level – below mark	2.0 mm (0.08 in)
Float height	17 mm (0.67 in)
Idle speed – rpm:	
UK and US 49-state models	950 – 1050
California models	1150 – 1250

Note: specifications denoted by the asterisk (*) apply when the machine is used above 4000 ft (1216 m).

Cylinder identification
Left to right, 1-2-3-4

Lubrication system

Recommended oil grade	SAE 10W/40, 10W/50, 20W/40 or 20W/50 SE or SF class
Capacity:	
Oil change only:	
ZX1100 C models	3.2 lit (5.7 Imp pt/3.4 US qt)
All other models	2.7 lit (4.8 Imp pt/2.9 US qt)
Oil and filter change:	
ZX1100 C models	3.5 lit (6.2 Imp pt/3.7 US qt)
All other models	3.0 lit (5.3 Imp pt/3.2 US qt)
After engine rebuild:	
ZX1000 B models	4.0 lit (7.1 Imp pt/4.3 US qt)
All other models	Not available
Oil pressure – oil temperature 90°C (194°F):	
ZX900 and ZX1000 A models	2.7 – 3.3 kg/cm^2 (38 – 47 psi) @ 4000 rpm
ZX1000 B and ZX1100 C models	2.0 – 3.0 kg/cm^2 (24 – 43 psi) @ 4000 rpm
Relief valve opening pressure	4.4 – 6.0 kg/cm^2 (63 – 85 psi)

Torque settings

Component	kgf m	lbf ft
Oil pump mounting bolts	1.2	8.5
Oil filter retaining bolt	2.0	14.5
Oil drain plug(s)	3.0	22.0
Oil pressure switch	1.5	11.0
Oil temperature switch – ZX900 only	0.8	5.8
Oil pressure passage blanking plug	1.8	13.0
Oil cooler hose to matrix union bolts	2.5	18.0
Oil cooler hose to sump union bolts (14 mm)	3.5	25.0
Oil cooler hose to sump union bolt (8 mm) – ZX1100 C only	1.5	11.0

1 General description

The fuel system comprises a tank from which fuel is fed to the carburettor float chambers. The ZX900 and ZX1000 A models use an automatic vacuum-operated tap to control the flow of the fuel, whereas ZX1000 B and ZX1100 C models are fitted with an electrically-operated fuel pump and fuel filter, together with a simplified fuel tap.

All models are fitted with four Keihen carburettors which are of the constant vacuum type. For cold starting a mixture-richening circuit is brought into operation via the handlebar mounted choke lever and cable.

Engine lubrication is of the wet sump type, the oil being contained in a sump at the bottom of the crankcase. The gearbox is also lubricated from the same source, the whole engine unit being pressure fed by a mechanical oil pump, driven off the clutch. Oil temperature is controlled by an oil cooler which is mounted on the frame front downtubes.

2 Precautions to be observed when working on the fuel system

Warning: petrol (gasoline) is extremely flammable, particularly when in the form of vapour. Precautions must be taken, as described below, to prevent the risk of fire or explosion when working on any part of the fuel system. Note that petrol (gasoline) vapour is heavier than air and will collect in poorly ventilated corners of buildings. Avoid getting petrol (gasoline) in the eyes or mouth and try to avoid skin contact. In case of accidents flush the affected area immediately with copious quantities of water and seek prompt medical advice.

1   Always perform service procedures in a well-ventilated area to prevent a build-up of fumes.
2   Never work in a building containing a gas appliance with a pilot light, or any other form of naked flame. Ensure that there are no naked light bulbs or any sources of flame or sparks nearby.
3   Do not smoke (or allow anyone else to smoke) while in the vicinity of petrol (gasoline) or of components containing petrol. Remember the possible presence of petrol (gasoline) vapour from these sources and move well clear before smoking.

4   Check all electrical equipment belonging to the house, garage or workshop where work is being undertaken (see the Safety first! section of this manual). Remember that certain electrical appliances such as drills, cutters etc create sparks in the normal course of operation and must not be used near petrol (gasoline) or any component containing it. Again, remember the possible presence of petrol (gasoline) fumes before using electrical equipment.
5   Always mop up any spilt fuel and safely dispose of the shop towel or rag used.
6   Any stored fuel, or fuel that has been drained off during servicing work, must be kept in sealed containers that are suitable for holding petrol (gasoline), and clearly marked as such; the containers themselves should be kept in a safe place. Note that this last point applies equally to the fuel tank, if it is removed from the machine; also remember to keep its cap closed at all times.
7   Read the Safety first! section of this manual carefully before starting work.
8   Owners of machines used in the US, particularly California, should note that their machines must comply at all times with Federal or State legislation governing the permissible levels of noise and of pollutants such as unburnt hydrocarbons, carbon monoxide etc that can be emitted by those machines. All vehicles offered for sale must comply with legislation in force at the date of manufacture and must not subsequently be altered in any way which will affect their emission of noise or of pollutants. In practice, this means that adjustments may not be made to any part of the fuel, ignition or exhaust systems by anyone who is not authorized or mechanically qualified to do so, or who does not have the tools, equipment and data necessary to carry out the task properly. Also if any part of these systems is to be renewed it must be replaced only by the genuine Kawasaki components or by components which are approved under the relevant legislation, and the machine must never be used with any part of these systems removed, modified or damaged.

3 Fuel tank: removal, renovation and refitting

1   To remove the fuel tank it is first necessary to remove the seat and sidepanels. On ZX1100 C models it will also be necessary to remove both the left and right-hand inner fairing sections.

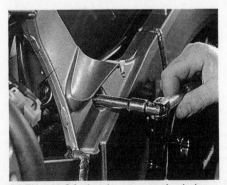

3.2 ZX1100 C fuel tank rear mounting bolts can be reached through access holes in frame

3.3a On ZX1100 C models do not disconnect the lower fuel tap hose

3.3b Disconnect fuel level sender unit wiring at block connector

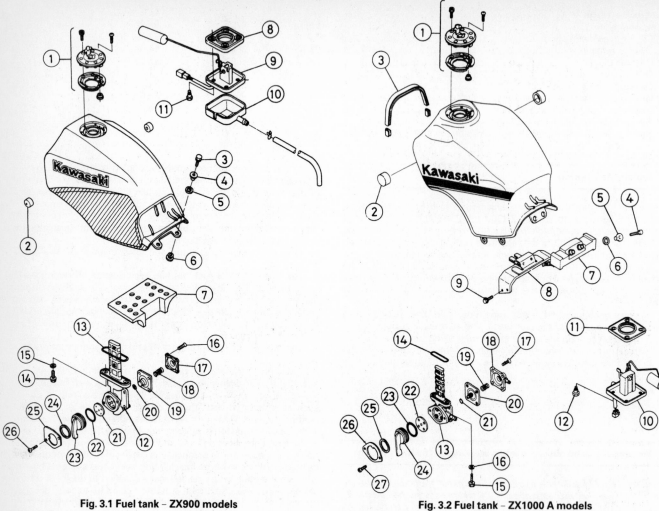

Fig. 3.1 Fuel tank – ZX900 models

1	Filler cap	13	O-ring
2	Front mounting rubber – 2 off	14	Bolt – 2 off
3	Bolt – 2 off	15	Washer – 2 off
4	Spacer – 2 off	16	Screw – 4 off
5	Upper damping rubber – 2 off	17	Diaphragm cover
6	Lower damping rubber – 2 off	18	Return spring
7	Rear mounting rubber	19	Diaphragm
8	Seal	20	O-ring
9	Fuel lever sender unit	21	Seal
10	Lower cover	22	O-ring
11	Bolt – 4 off	23	Tap lever
12	Fuel tap	24	Wave washer
		25	Retainer plate
		26	Screw – 2 off

Fig. 3.2 Fuel tank – ZX1000 A models

1	Filler cap	15	Bolt – 2 off
2	Front mounting rubber – 2 off	16	Washer – 2 off
3	Trim	16	Washer – 2 off
4	Bolt – 2 off	17	Screw – 4 off
5	Spacer – 2 off	18	Diaphragm cover
6	Damping rubber – 2 off	19	Return spring
7	Damping block	20	Diaphragm
8	Rear mounting bracket	21	O-ring
9	Bolt – 4 off	22	Seal
10	Fuel level sender unit	23	O-ring
11	Seal	24	Tap lever
12	Bolt – 4 off	25	Wave washer
13	Fuel tap	26	Retainer plate
14	O-ring	27	Screw – 2 off

2   Remove all fuel tank mounting bolts and turn the fuel tap to the OFF position. Note that on ZX900 and ZX1000 A models the tap should be positioned in the ON position. On all California models, disconnect the fuel return and breather pipes from the fuel tank and block the end of the fuel return pipe with a suitable plug; this will prevent any fuel from entering the charcoal canister.

3   Lift the fuel tank and disconnect all the pipes and the fuel level sender unit block connector. On ZX1100 C models *do not* remove the lower pipe from the fuel tap. All pipes are disconnected by squeezing together the ears of their retaining clips and sliding the clips down the pipe, which can then be worked off its stub with the aid of a small

screwdriver. Once the relevant pipes and wiring connectors have been disconnected the tank can be lifted away from the machine.

4   Fuel tank repairs are a task for the expert only. Any welding or brazing must be preceded by careful flushing out, once the fuel tank has been stripped of all its ancillary components. A resin-based tank sealing compound is a much more satisfactory and easier way of curing leaks. Accident damage repairs will inevitably involve re-painting the tank. Matching of modern paint finishes, especially metallic ones, is a very difficult task. It is therefore recommended that the tank be removed and taken to a motorcycle dealer or similar expert for professional attention.

5   Repeated contamination of the fuel tap filter and carburettor by

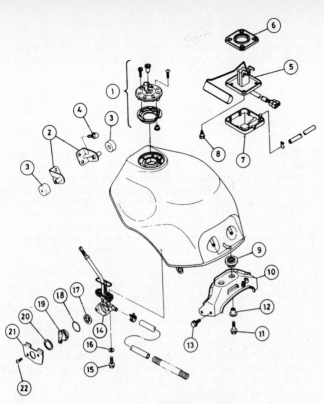

Fig. 3.3 Fuel tank – ZX1000 B models

1 Filler cap	12 Spacer – 2 off
2 Front mounting brackets	13 Bolt – 4 off
3 Front mounting rubber – 2 off	14 Fuel tap
4 Bolt – 4 off	15 Bolt – 2 off
5 Fuel level sender unit	16 Washer – 2 off
6 Seal	17 Seal
7 Lower cover	18 O-ring
8 Bolt – 4 off	19 Tap lever
9 Rear damping rubber – 2 off	20 Wave washer
10 Rear mounting bracket	21 Retainer plate
11 Bolt – 2 off	22 Screw – 2 off

Fig. 3.4 Fuel tank – ZX1100 C models

1 Filler cap	14 Fuel level sender unit
2 Bolt – 2 off	15 Screw – 2 off
3 Spacer – 2 off	16 Washer – 2 off
4 Upper mounting rubber – 2 off	17 Fuel tap
5 Lower mounting rubber – 2 off	18 Screw – 2 off
6 Trim	19 Seal
7 Rear mounting rubber – 2 off	20 O-ring
8 Bolt – 2 off	21 Tap lever
9 Rear mounting bracket	22 Wave washer
10 Bolt – 2 off	23 Retainer plate
11 Spacer – 2 off	24 Screw – 2 off
12 Upper mounting rubber – 2 off	25 Connecting pipe
13 Lower mounting rubber – 2 off	26 Fuel filter
	27 O-ring

water or rust and paint flakes indicate that the tank should be removed for flushing with clean fuel and internal inspection. Rust problems can be cured by using a resin tank sealant.

6 The fuel tank is refitted by a reversal of the removal procedure. Examine the rubber mounting dampers which are positioned underneath the tank for signs of deterioration and damage and renew if necessary. Smear a small amount of lubricant on the rubbers to allow the tank to slide easily into position. Connect the pipes, noting that on California models the blue marked (breather) pipe is fitted to the right-hand tank stub and the red marked (fuel return) pipe is fitted to the centre stub, except on ZX900 models where it is fitted to the left-hand stub.

7 Secure all the pipes with their retaining clips and reconnect the fuel level sender wiring connector. Turn the fuel tap to the ON position (PRI position on ZX900 and ZX1000 A models) and check for any fuel leaks. Refit the mounting bolts, tightening them securely, followed by the sidepanels, seat and inner fairing sections (where applicable).

4 Fuel tap: removal, examination and refitting

ZX900 and ZX1000 A models

1 The fuel tap is of the vacuum type and is automatic in operation. The tap lever has three positions marked ON, RES (reserve) and PRI (prime).

In the first two of these settings, fuel flow is controlled by a diaphragm and plunger held closed by a light coil spring. When the engine is started, the low pressure in the intake tract opens the plunger allowing fuel to flow through the tap to the carburettors. When the tap is set to the Pri position, the diaphragm and plunger are bypassed.

2   In the event of failure, the most likely culprits are the vacuum pipe or diaphragm. If a leak develops in either of these the tap will not operate in anything other than the Pri position. Check the vacuum pipe for obvious splits or cracks, and renew if necessary. If the diaphragm itself is suspect set the tap lever to ON or RES and disconnect the fuel and vacuum pipes at the carburettor. Suck gently on the vacuum pipe. If fuel does not flow, remove the tap for inspection as follows:

3   Remove the fuel tank as described in Section 3. If the tank is full or nearly full, drain it into a clean container suitable for holding petrol (gasoline), taking great care to prevent the risk of fire. Place the tank on its side on some soft cloth, arranging it so that the tap is near the top. Slacken and remove the two tap mounting bolts and lift the tap away, taking care not to damage the O-ring which seals it.

4   From the front of the tap remove the two small cross-head screws which secure the tap lever assembly. Withdraw the retainer plate, wave washer, tap lever, O-ring and the tap seal. Examine the tap seal and tap lever O-ring, especially if there has been evidence of leakage. Check that the tap seal has not become damaged and caused a blockage of the outlet hole. Fit a new O-ring and tap seal if required, and reassemble the tap lever assembly by reversing the above sequence.

5   Working from the rear of the tap, remove the four countersunk screws which retain the diaphragm cover, noting the direction in which the vacuum stub faces, and lift it away taking care not to damage the rather delicate diaphragm. Remove the small return spring. Very carefully dislodge the diaphragm assembly and remove it from the tap body. The diaphragm assembly contains a plastic diaphragm plate sandwiched between two thin diaphragm membranes. Carried through the centre of the assembly is the fuel plunger which supports a sealing O-ring.

6   Examine the diaphragm closely for signs of splitting or other damage. Carefully remove any dust or grit which may have found its way into the assembly. Check the condition of the O-ring on the end of the plunger. If wear or damage of the above components is discovered, it will be necessary to renew the diaphragm assembly complete. Note that one side of the diaphragm plate has a groove in it, and this must face towards the O-ring on the plunger. When fitting the diaphragm assembly and cover, check that the diaphragm lies absolutely flat, with no creases or folds. Fit the cover with the vacuum stub facing in the correct direction (this varies according to the model). Tighten the securing screws evenly and securely.

ZX1000 B and ZX1100 C models

7   The fuel tap is much simpler in design to that which is described above. Fuel should flow when the tap is in the ON or RES (ZX1000 B only) positions and not in the OFF position. During normal operation the tap can be left in the ON position, only needing to be turned OFF when the fuel tank is to be removed, as the flow of the fuel is controlled by an electrically operated pump.

8   To remove the fuel tap, remove the fuel tank as described in Section 3 and drain the fuel into a clean metal container. Place the tank on its side on some soft cloth so that the fuel tap is positioned at the top. Slacken and remove the two screws that retain the tap assembly and lift the tap away, taking care not to damage the sealing O-ring.

9   The fuel tap can then be overhauled as described in paragraph 4 of this Section.

All models

10   Examine the fuel tap sealing O-ring for sign of damage or deterioration and renew it if necessary. Refit the tap to the fuel tank and tighten its retaining screws securely. Refit the fuel tank to the machine as described in Section 3 and thoroughly check the tap assembly for fuel leaks before taking the machine on the road.

5   Fuel system pipes: general

1   Thin-walled synthetic rubber tubing is used for many purposes, whether in the fuel system, emission control system or as drain or breather pipes. All pipes are of the push-on type, being secured by small wire clips. Normally it is necessary to renew pipes only if they become hard or split; it is unlikely that the clips will need frequent renewal as the main seal between hose and union is effected by the interference fit.

2   Check carefully at periodic intervals that the pipes are correctly fitted, undamaged, and secured to the frame by any clamps or ties provided. Check that they are correctly routed and that no drain or breather pipes are long enough to interfere with the final drive chain and gearbox sprocket or with the rear brake or suspension. If the pipes split, it is normally at the end, on or close to the union. In such cases the damaged length can be cut off and the pipe refitted.

3   If any pipe has to be renewed, use only the genuine Kawasaki replacement parts, particularly on emission control systems. Where pipes are moulded to a particular shape or where they are of an unusual size, this will be necessary anyway. The only exception to this is that it is permissible to use proprietary synthetic rubber or neoprene tubing for vacuum, breather and drain pipes and, in an emergency, for fuel pipes. Never use natural rubber tubing or clear plastic petrol pipe; neither of these is suitable for such use.

6   Fuel pump and filter: removal and refitting – ZX1000 B and ZX1100 C models

1   Remove the fuel tank and the carburettors as described in Sections 3 and 7 of this Chapter. The fuel pump and filter are located on the frame cross member, situated just below the carburettors.

2   Disconnect the fuel pipes from the inlet side of the filter and the outlet side of the pump. Separate the fuel pump wiring block connector and remove the pump and filter assembly from the machine. Before separating the pump and filter, mark the pump inlet stub (filter side of the pump) to avoid connecting the fuel hoses wrongly on refitting.

3   If necessary, the fuel pump can be tested as described in Chapter 7.

4   The pump is refitted by a reversal of the removal procedure. Fit the fuel filter to the pump inlet stub, using the mark made on removal to align it correctly. Ensure that the arrow on the filter body is pointing towards the fuel pump. Refit the pump and filter assembly to the machine and connect the relevant fuel pipes and the fuel pump block connector. Check that all fuel pipes are correctly routed and securely held by their retaining clips. Refit the carburettors and fuel tank as

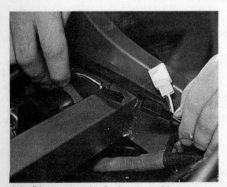

6.2a Disconnect the fuel pump wiring at block connector ...

6.2b ... and remove the fuel pump and filter assembly

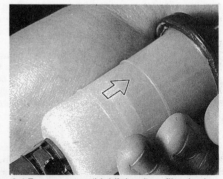

6.4 Ensure arrow (highlighted) on filter body is pointing towards the pump

described in Sections 7 and 3 of this Chapter, and thoroughly check for any fuel leaks before taking the machine on the road.

7 Carburettors: removal and refitting

1 Remove the fuel tank as described in Section 3 of this Chapter. Disconnect the carburettor warmer (coolant) pipes from both the left and right-hand side of the carburettors (where fitted) and block the ends of the pipes with a suitably-sized plug, such as a wooden bung or clean screw or bolt, to prevent excess coolant escaping. Mop up any spilt coolant and follow the procedure given under the relevant sub-heading. On California models note that it will also be necessary to disconnect the relevant emission control pipes from the carburettors before removal.

ZX900 models
2 Slacken fully all the inlet stub clamp screws and roll the spring clips on the air filter hoses towards the housing. Slacken both the throttle and choke cable adjuster locknuts and fully screw in the adjusters so that the maximum freeplay possible is obtained on both cables. Remove the two air filter housing mounting bolts and position the air filter housing as far rearwards as possible.
3 Pull the carburettor assembly to the rear to clear it from the inlet rubbers and twist it carefully to disengage the air filter hoses. Manoeuvre the carburettors out to the right-hand side of the machine until both the throttle and choke cables can be disconnected and the carburettors freed from the machine.
4 The above procedure describes the bare essentials of what is a very awkward and difficult procedure. When removing the carburettors, great care and patience must be exercised at all times to ensure they are not damaged in any way.

ZX1000 and ZX1100 C models
5 Remove the air filter element as described in Routine maintenance.

6 On ZX1000 models roll the spring clips on the air filter hoses towards the filter housing and remove the casing from the machine. Note that on ZX1000 A models it will be necessary to remove the fuel tank mounting bracket to allow the air filter casing to be removed from the machine.
7 On ZX1100 C models the rear section of the air filter housing is mounted onto the carburettors by eight bolts, seven of which are covered by plugs. To remove the filter housing, prise out the rubber blanking plugs and remove all the housing mounting bolts. The housing can then be lifted off the carburettors.
8 On all models, slacken the inlet stub clamp screws and the throttle and choke cable adjuster locknuts. Screw the adjusters in fully to obtain the maximum freeplay possible on both cables. On ZX1000 B and ZX1100 C models also disconnect the fuel line, which joins the carburettors to the fuel pump, from the underside of the carburettors. Pull the carburettors to the rear to disengage them from the inlet rubbers and disconnect the throttle and choke cables. If it proves difficult to disconnect the throttle cables from the carburettors the task can be made easier by first removing the two screws from the right-hand handlebar switch and disconnecting the cables from the twistgrip. Once the cables have been disconnected the carburettors can then be lifted away from the machine.

All models
9 The carburettors are refitted by a reversal of the removal procedure. A small amount of light grease may be smeared over the insides of the inlet stubs and air filter hoses to ease the task. Position the carburettors and connect both the throttle and choke cables. Carefully manoeuvre the carburettors into position and insert them into the inlet stubs. Ensure the carburettors are pushed fully home at both ends and tighten the inlet stub clamps securely. Adjust the throttle and choke cable freeplay as described in Routine maintenance.
10 Install the air filter housing (if removed) and refit the hoses to the carburettors. Ensure the pipes are correctly located on the carburettors and secure them with the spring clips. On ZX900 and ZX1100 C models refit the housing mounting bolts and tighten them securely. On ZX1100 C models do not forget to refit the rubber plugs which fit into the air filter housing.

7.7a On ZX1100 C models remove rubber plugs from air filter housing and slacken the mounting bolts

7.7b Disconnect air filter housing from the breather cover ...

7.7c ... and lift the housing clear

7.8a On ZX1000 B and ZX1100 C models disconnect the fuel pipe from underside of carburettors

7.8b If necessary, disconnect throttle cables from twistgrip

7.9 Ensure inlet stub clamps are correctly positioned before fitting carburettors

7.10 On ZX1100 C models do not omit O-rings from the carburettors

11   On ZX1000 and ZX1100 C models refit the air filter element as described in Routine maintenance.
12   Reconnect the carburettor warmer (coolant) pipes, mopping up any spilt coolant. Check the level of coolant in the expansion tank as described in Routine maintenance and top up if necessary. Reconnect the emission control pipes on California models. Refit the fuel tank as described in Section 3 of this Chapter. Check that the throttle cables operate freely and that there are no fuel leaks before taking the machine on the road.
13   On ZX1000 B and ZX1100 C models do not be alarmed if the engine fails to start immediately. Due to the nature of the fuel supply system (fuel pump only operates when the starter button is pressed) it may take anything up to 30 seconds to refill the carburettors with fuel and the engine to start. *Do not operate the starter motor continuously for more than 5 seconds at a time, and wait 15 seconds before operating the starter again, otherwise the starter motor may overheat and be damaged as a result.*

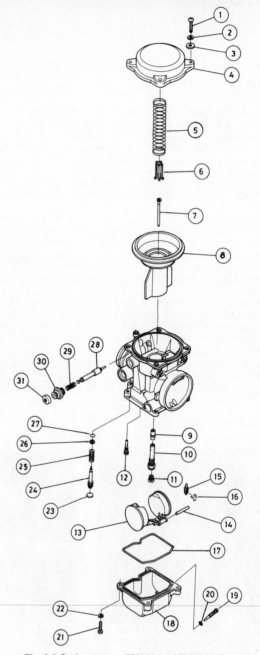

Fig. 3.5 Carburettor – ZX900 and ZX1000 A models

8 Carburettors: dismantling, examination and reassembly

1   Remove the carburettors from the machine as described in Section 7. Never remove the carburettors from their mounting brackets unless absolutely necessary; each carburettor can be dismantled sufficiently for all normal cleaning or adjustment procedures whilst in position on the brackets. If necessary, however, the carburettors can be separated as described in Section 9. Note that it is necessary to separate the carburettors to dismantle the choke mechanism.
2   Working on one carburettor at a time to avoid the accidental interchange of components, slacken and remove the four screws which retain the top cover. Lift off the cover and remove the spring from inside the piston. Carefully peel the diaphragm away from its sealing groove in the carburettor and withdraw the diaphragm and piston assembly; do not use a sharp instrument to displace the diaphragm as it is easily damaged. Remove the needle retaining clip from inside the piston and separate the needle and piston. On ZX1000 B and ZX1100 C models take care not to lose the small air jet situated in the top surface of the carburettor body. If possible it should be removed for safekeeping but do not risk damaging the valve on removal if it is stuck in the carburettor body.

1 Screw – 4 off	17 O-ring
2 Spring washer – 4 off	18 Float chamber
3 Washer – 4 off	19 Drain screw
4 Carburettor top cover	20 O-ring
5 Spring	21 Screw – 4 off
6 Needle retainer	22 Spring washer – 4 off
7 Jet needle	23 Blanking plug – US only
8 Diaphragm/piston	24 Pilot screw
assembly	25 Spring
9 Needle jet	26 Washer
10 Needle jet holder	27 O-ring
11 Main jet	28 Choke plunger
12 Pilot jet	29 Spring
13 Floats	30 Nut
14 Pivot pin	31 Cap
15 Needle valve	
16 Clip	

8.2a Remove four screws and lift off top cover. Withdraw return spring ...

8.2b ... followed by piston assembly

8.2c Remove needle retaining clip ...

8.2d ... and tip out the jet needle

8.2e On ZX1000 B and ZX1100 C models note air jet set in diaphragm or carburettor casting

8.3a Remove float bowl to gain access to jets

8.3b On ZX1000 B and ZX1100 C models remove float pin retaining screw ...

8.3c ... and lift out the float and needle assembly

8.3d Needle valve seat is also retained by a screw

8.3e Clean needle valve seat filter and renew the O-ring

8.4a Main jet is a screw fit into the needle jet ...

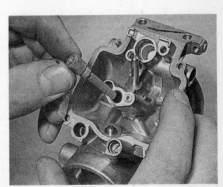

8.4b ... and needle jet is a screw fit into the carburettor body

8.4c Pilot jet is situated beside main jet

3   Remove the four screws which retain the float chamber to the bottom of the carburettor and lift off the chamber to gain access to the various jets. On ZX900 and ZX1000 A models press out the float pivot pin and remove the float and needle valve assembly. On ZX1000 B and ZX1100 C models the float pivot pin is retained by a crosshead screw which must be removed before the float and needle valve assembly can be removed. On these models the needle valve seat can also be removed. Slacken and remove the valve seat retaining screw and pull out the seat, followed by the O-ring and fuel filter which is situated behind it. Clean the fuel filter in some fresh fuel and examine it for any cracks, renewing it if necessary. On all models separate the needle valve and float.

4   The main jet is a screw fit into the bottom of the needle jet and can be removed with a flat-bladed screwdriver. The needle jet is also a screw fit into the carburettor body and can be unscrewed using a suitably sized spanner. On ZX900 and ZX1000 A models the needle jet comprises two components, a holder and the needle jet itself. The holder can be removed as described above and the needle jet can be pushed out of position from the top of the carburettor with a wooden dowel. The pilot jet is located next to the main jet and can be unscrewed using a small flat-bladed screwdriver.

5   The pilot air (mixture) screw is situated in the bottom of the carburettor body. On all US models the pilot screw drilling will be sealed with a blanking plug which must be removed to allow the pilot screw to be withdrawn. The plug should be deformed, using a punch or scriber, then levered out of position. On all models screw the pilot screw in until it seats lightly, counting the number of turns necessary to do so, then remove the screw along with its flat washer and O-ring. The screw should be renewed if bent or damaged.

6   The choke assembly can be removed, providing the carburettors have been separated (see Section 9), by unscrewing the nut which retains it in the carburettor body. If the plunger does not operate smoothly and easily or is damaged, it must be renewed. The return spring should also be renewed if at all suspect.

7   Carefully check the carburettor body, float chamber and carburettor top for damage such as cracks, splits or distorted sealing faces. Whilst it may be possible to repair small defects it will usually be necessary to renew the damaged component.

8   Check that the diaphragm is not split, perished or damaged. Holding it up to a strong light will usually reveal even the smallest hole. The diaphragm must be renewed even if only slight damage is found; it is not repairable. Check that the needle is straight by rolling it on a flat surface such as a sheet of glass. If it is bent it must be renewed as a set along with the needle jet and holder (as applicable).

9   Check that the floats are in good order and are not punctured. If either float is punctured it will produce the wrong fuel level in the float chamber, leading to an over-rich mixture and flooding. If the floats are damaged they must be renewed as a satisfactory repair is not possible.

10   The needle valve and seat will wear after lengthy service and should be closely examined, with a magnifying glass if necessary. Wear usually takes the form of a groove or ridge, which will cause the needle

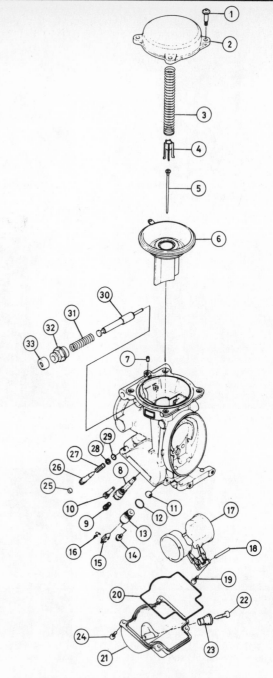

Fig. 3.6 Carburettor – ZX1000 B and ZX1100 C models

1	Screw – 4 off	18	Pivot pin
2	Carburettor top cover	19	Screw
3	Spring	20	O-ring
4	Needle retainer	21	Float chamber
5	Jet needle	22	Drain screw
6	Diaphragm/piston assembly	23	Shield
7	Air jet	24	Screw – 4 off
8	Needle jet	25	Blanking plug – US only
9	Main jet	26	Pilot screw
10	Pilot jet	27	Spring
11	Filter	28	Washer
12	O-ring	29	O-ring
13	Needle valve seat	30	Plunger
14	Screw	31	Spring
15	Needle valve	32	Nut
16	Clip	33	Cap
17	Floats		

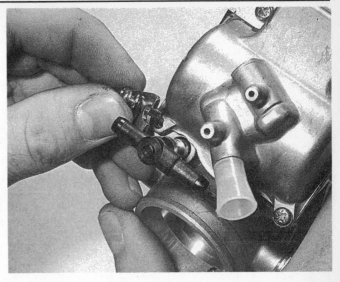

8.11a Renew O-rings on carburettor warmer hose fittings (where fitted) ...

8.11b ... and secure them with their retaining plates

to seat imperfectly. Test the spring-loaded tip on the bottom of the needle valve by pushing it into the body of the needle. The tip should return quickly and easily with the spring pressure. If the needle valve or seat are damaged both should be renewed as a set. On ZX900 and ZX1000 A models the needle valve seat is an integral part of the carburettor body and is not available separately.

11 The carburettors are reassembled by a reversal of the removal procedure, renewing all sealing O-rings as a matter of course. Use only close-fitting spanners and screwdrivers to tighten the jets and tighten each one by just enough to secure it. Avoid overtightening as the jets are easily sheared. On ZX1000 B and ZX1100 C models do not omit the filter which is fitted behind the needle valve seat. Insert the piston into the carburettor body and lightly push it down, ensuring the needle is correctly aligned with the needle jet, then press the diaphragm outer edge into its groove. On ZX1000 B and ZX1100 C models ensure the small tongue is correctly seated around the small air valve situated in the top of the carburettor body. On all models check the diaphragm is not creased, and the piston moves smoothly up and down the bore before refitting the spring and top cover.

9 Carburettors: separation

1 Remove the carburettors as described in Section 7 of this Chapter. Mark each carburettor body with its respective cylinder number to ensure they are positioned correctly on reassembly.

2 Disengage the choke bracket return spring and release the three screws which secure the bracket to the carburettors. Remove the

bracket together with the six plastic washers which are fitted on each side of the bracket. On ZX900 and ZX1000 A models remove the sixteen screws which secure the carburettors to the mounting brackets and lift the brackets away from the carburettors. On ZX1000 B and ZX1100 C models release the eight screws from the bottom mounting bracket, then slacken and remove the long 5 mm nut and bolt which holds all the carburettor bodies together.

3 On all models, very carefully disengage each carburettor from its neighbour, freeing the fuel, vent and warmer pipes (as applicable) and noting exactly how the throttle linkages engage with each other. Catch the two coil springs that will be released from each throttle linkage when the carburettors are separated. Note that it may be necessary to slacken the throttle linkage screws to gain sufficient space to disengage the linkages.

4 On reassembly line up the carburettors on a flat surface ensuring that the throttle linkages are correctly engaged and the larger coil springs are positioned in between each carburettor. Very carefully push the carburettors together ensuring that all the fuel, vent and warmer pipes are correctly aligned. On ZX900 and ZX1000 A models position both mounting brackets and fit all the mounting screws finger-tight only. On ZX1000 B and ZX1100 C models refit the long 5 mm bolt which passes through the carburettor bodies, followed by the mounting bracket and screws, again tighten them only finger-tight at this stage.

5 On all models, use a sheet of glass or a straightedge to ensure the carburettors are correctly aligned both horizontally and vertically, then tighten all mounting screws and bolts securely. Position a plastic washer on each side of the choke bracket and tighten the three retaining screws securely. Refit the choke bracket return spring and check that the choke mechanism operates smoothly and returns quickly. Finally refit the throttle linkage springs and check that the throttle operates smoothly and closes quickly.

9.4a Ensure all connecting pipes, springs and linkages are aligned before joining carburettor bodies

9.4b On ZX1000 B and ZX1100 C models refit the long 5 mm bolt ...

9.4c ... then the bottom mounting bracket and screws

Fig. 3.7 Carburettor linkage – ZX900 and ZX1000 A models

1 Choke bracket
2 Screw – 6 off
3 Plastic washer – 6 off
4 Return spring
5 Front mounting bracket
6 Screw – 8 off
7 Spring washer – 8 off
8 Rear mounting bracket
9 Screw – 8 off
10 Spring washer – 8 off
11 Throttle linkage spring – 2 off
12 Throttle cable bracket
13 Screw
14 Spring washer
15 Choke cable plate
16 Screw
17 Spring washer
18 Synchronising screw – 3 off
19 Spring – 3 off
20 Spring – 3 off
21 Pipe unions
22 Pipe unions
23 Idle speed knob – ZX900 shown
24 Washer
25 Spring

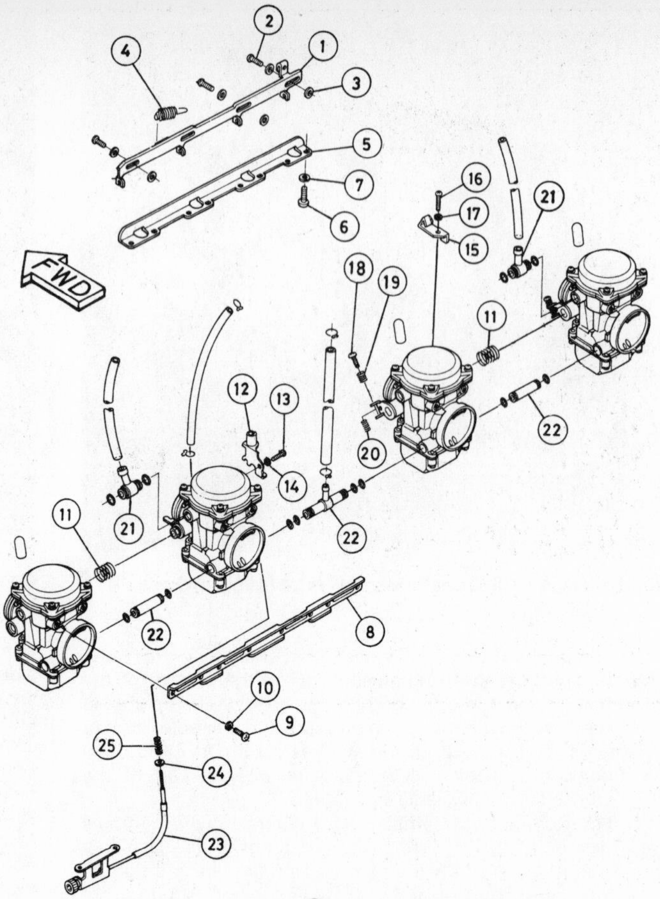

Fig. 3.8 Carburettor linkage – ZX1000 B and ZX1100 C models

1 Choke bracket
2 Screw – 6 off
3 Plastic washer – 6 off
4 Return spring
5 Bolt
6 Nut
7 Bottom mounting bracket
8 Screw – 8 off
9 Throttle linkage spring – 2 off
10 Throttle cable bracket
11 Screw
12 Choke cable plate
13 Screw
14 Spacer
15 Synchronising screw – 3 off
16 Spring – 3 off
17 Spring – 3 off
18 Pipe unions
19 Pipe unions
20 Idle speed knob
21 Washer
22 Spring

A – warmer hose connection points (UK models)

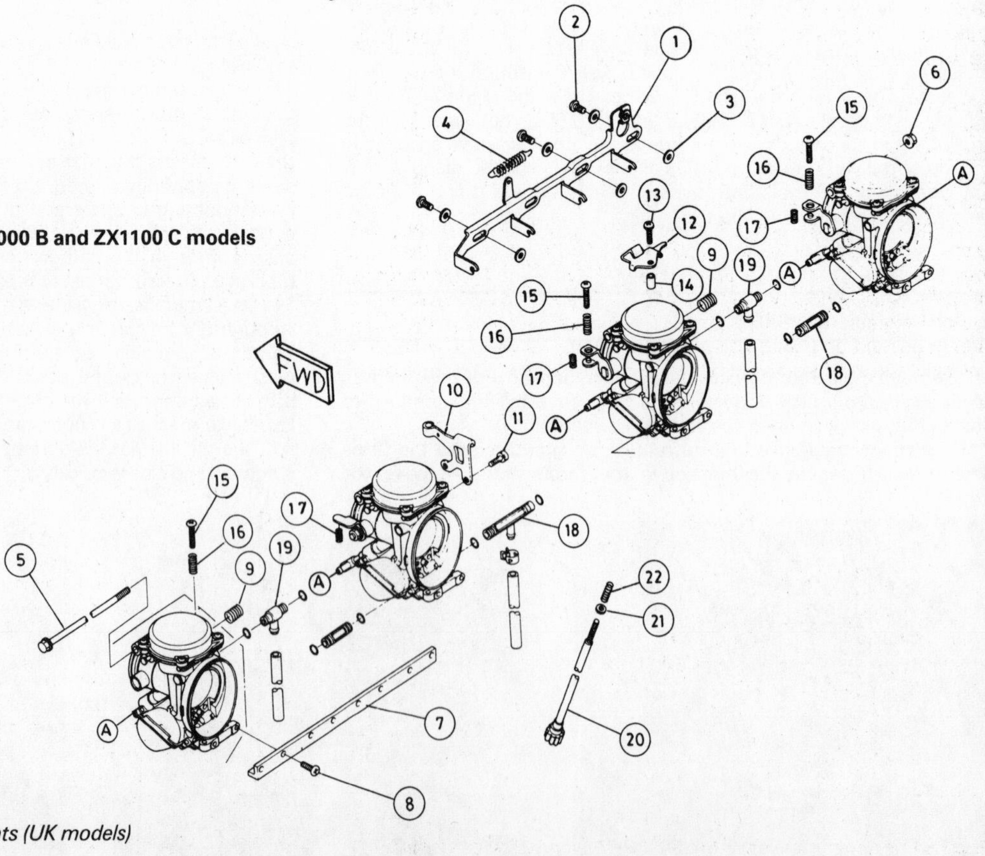

9.5a Position a plastic washer each side of the choke bracket mounting points ...

9.5b ... and refit throttle linkage springs

10 Carburettors: checking the settings

1   The various jet sizes are predetermined by the manufacturer and should not require modification. Check with the Specifications at the beginning of this Chapter if there is any doubt about the types fitted. If a change appears necessary it can often be attributed to a developing engine fault unconnected with the carburettors. Although carburettors wear in service, this process occurs slowly over an extended length of time and hence wear of the carburettors is unlikely to cause sudden or extreme malfunction. If a fault does occur, check first other main systems, in which a fault may give similar symptoms, before proceeding with carburettor examination or modification.

2   Where non-standard items, such as exhaust systems, air filters or camshafts have been fitted to a machine, some alterations to carburation may be required. Arriving at the correct settings often requires trial and error, a method which demands skill born of previous experience. In many cases the manufacturer of the non-standard equipment will be able to advise on correct carburation changes.

3   As a rough guide, up to $\frac{1}{8}$ throttle is controlled by the pilot jet, $\frac{1}{8}$ to $\frac{1}{4}$ by the throttle valve cutaway, $\frac{1}{4}$ to $\frac{3}{4}$ throttle by the needle position and from $\frac{3}{4}$ to full by the size of the main jet. These are only approximate divisions, which are by no means clear cut. There is a certain amount of overlap between the various stages. The above remarks apply only in part to constant depression carburettors which utilise a butterfly valve in place of the throttle valve. The first and fourth stages are controlled in

a similar manner. The second stage is controlled by the by-pass valve which is uncovered as soon as the throttle valve (piston) is opened. During the third stage the fuel passing through the main jet is metered by the needle jet working in conjunction with the piston needle (jet needle).

4   If alterations to the carburation must be made, always err on the side of a slightly rich mixture. A weak mixture will cause the engine to overheat which may cause engine seizure. Reference to Routine maintenance will show how, after some experience has been gained, the condition of the spark plug electrodes can be interpreted as a reliable guide to mixture strength.

Fuel level measurement

5   If the mixture is persistently too weak or too rich the fuel level should be checked. Position the machine on its centre stand on a level surface and attach the Kawasaki service tool, Part No 57001-1017. This is a clear plastic tube graduated in millimetres; an alternative is to use a length of clear plastic tubing and an accurate ruler. Connect one end of the tube to the float chamber drain outlet (use the drain tube if the Kawasaki tool is being used) and place the tube upper end against the carburettor body as shown in the accompanying illustration. Mark the tube at a point several millimetres above the bottom edge of the carburettor body (use the O mark on the service tool), then unscrew the float chamber drain plug by one or two full turns and switch on the fuel supply. Wait for the fuel level to stabilise then very slowly bring the tube down the carburettor body until the mark is level with its bottom edge. On ZX1000 B and ZX1100 C models, as the carburettors are mounted at an angle, the mark on the tube should be aligned with the mark situated just above the float chamber on the right-hand side of the carburettor body. On all models, do not lower the tube beyond the specified mark and raise it again or the level will be inaccurate. Measure the distance between the mark and the top of the fuel level in the tube or gauge. This distance is the fuel level.

6   The fuel level should be noted and the process repeated on the remaining carburettors. If any level is outside the tolerances given in the Specifications the carburettors must be removed from the machine and the setting altered by adjusting the float height as follows:

Float height measurement

7   Remove the float chambers and hold the carburettor assembly vertical with the air filter side upwards, then slowly invert it until each float is just resting on its needle, yet not compressing it. (See the accompanying illustration.) Measure the distance between the bottom gasket surface of the carburettor body and the bottom of each float. If there is any discrepancy it can be corrected by bending the bridge piece carefully. Note the float heights of all carburettors to be adjusted, then remove the float and bend as necessary the tang which bears on the float needle. Bending the tang up increases the float height and lowers the fuel level, therefore bending it down decreases the float height and raises the fuel level. Be very careful when bending the tang; only the smallest movement is necessary to effect a major change in float height.

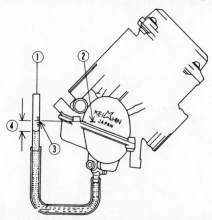

Fig. 3.9 Fuel level measurement – ZX1000 B and ZX1100 C models (Sec 10)

1   Level tube   3   O mark on level tube
2   Carburettor casting mark   4   Fuel level

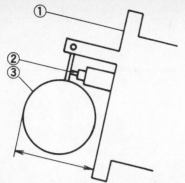

Fig. 3.10 Float height measurement (Sec 10)

1 Gasket surface   *3 Float*
2 Float needle valve

8   When adjustment is complete, reassemble the carburettors and recheck the fuel level. Make the adjustments again, if necessary, but note that if serious difficulties are encountered, the float assembly, float needle and seat must be removed and checked very carefully for wear. Refit the carburettors to the machine when all carburettor fuel levels are at the correct setting, or at least within tolerances.

Pilot screw adjustment

9   Where these are given as 'Preset' in the Specifications, the pilot screw settings should be regarded as fixed and should not be altered except by an experienced and qualified mechanic using the necessary diagnostic equipment. This is beyond the scope of most private owners. It is recommended that the same attitude be applied to all other models, the factory setting is usually best for all normal use and while badly-adjusted pilot screws will have a serious effect on engine performance, setting them accurately is by no means easy for the inexperienced. The object is to find the setting at which the engine runs fastest and smoothest when warmed up to normal operating temperature.

---

11   Carburettors: adjustment and exhaust emissions – general

---

1   In some countries legal provision is made for describing and controlling the types and levels of toxic emissions from motor vehicles.
2   In the US exhaust emission legislation is administered by the Environmental Protection Agency (EPA) which has introduced stringent regulations relating to motor vehicles. The Federal law entitled The Clean Air Act, specifically prohibits the removal (other than temporary) or modification of any component incorporated by the vehicle manufacturer to comply with the requirements of the law. The law extends the prohibition to any tampering which includes the addition of components, use of unsuitable replacement parts or maladjustment of components which allows the exhaust emissions to exceed the prescribed levels. Violations of the provisions of this law may result in penalties of up to $10 000 for each violation. It is strongly recommended that appropriate requirements are determined and understood prior to making any change to or adjustments of components in the fuel, ignition, crankcase breather or exhaust systems.
3   To help ensure compliance with the emission standards some manufacturers have fitted to the relevant systems fixed or pre-set adjustment screws as anti-tamper devices. In most cases this is restricted to plastic or metal limiter caps fitted to the carburettor pilot adjustment screws, which allow normal adjustment only within narrow limits. Occasionally the pilot screw may be recessed and sealed behind a small metal blanking plug, or locked in position with a thread-locking compound, which prevents normal adjustment.
4   It should be understood that none of the various methods of discouraging tampering actually prevents adjustment, nor in itself, is adjustment an infringement of the current regulations. Maladjustment, however, which results in the emission levels exceeding those laid down, is a violation. It follows that no adjustments should be made unless the owner feels confident that he can make those adjustments in such a way that the resulting emissions comply with the limits. For all practical purposes a gas analyzer will be required to monitor the exhaust

gases during adjustment, together with EPA data of the permissible Hydrocarbon and CO levels. Obviously, the home mechanic is unlikely to have access to this type of equipment or the expertise required for its use, and therefore, it will be necessary to place the machine in the hands of a competent motorcycle dealer who has the equipment and skill to check the exhaust gas content.

---

12   Carburettors: synchronisation

---

1   Carburettor synchronisation must be checked at the interval specified in Routine maintenance, and whenever the carburettors have been disturbed or if the engine is running roughly. Always check the valve clearances before starting work. A set of accurate vacuum gauges is essential for the synchronisation, and if these are not available the job should be entrusted to an authorized Kawasaki dealer. On no account attempt to adjust synchronisation by 'feel'. It will almost certainly make things worse.
2   Remove the fuel tank and arrange a temporary fuel supply, either by using a small temporary tank or by using extra long fuel pipes to the now remote fuel tank on a nearby workbench. **Note:** if the vacuum pipe is bypassed (where applicable) it is important to plug its open end before attempting the check. Connect the vacuum gauge hoses to the four vacuum take-off points, having first disconnected the relevant hoses(s) and cap(s); the vacuum take-off points are to be found on the top or bottom of the intake stubs, or on the top of each carburettor body, where it enters the intake stub. Start the engine and allow it to warm up to normal operating temperature. If the gauges are fitted with damping adjustment, set this so that needle flutter is just eliminated but so that they can still respond to small changes in pressure.
3   Running the engine at idle speed, check that all needles produce the same reading. A tolerance of up to 2 cm Hg between cylinders is permissible but it is better to have all cylinders adjusted to the same reading; this is by no means as difficult as it would appear, requiring only a little care and patience. Note that it does not matter what the reading is; only that it is the same for all cylinders. Stop the engine and allow it to cool down if it overheats.
4   The carburettors are adjusted by the three screws which are situated in between the carburettors in the throttle linkage. First check that the two left-hand carburettors are the same, then check that the two right-hand carburettors are equal. Adjust them if necessary, using the outer adjusting screws, then balance both pairs against each other using the centre screw. Do not press down on the screw whilst adjusting it, otherwise a false reading will be obtained. When all the carburettors are synchronised, open and close the throttle quickly to settle the linkage, and recheck the gauge readings, readjusting if necessary.
5   When the carburettors are correctly synchronised, stop the engine, disconnect the gauges and refit all disturbed components.

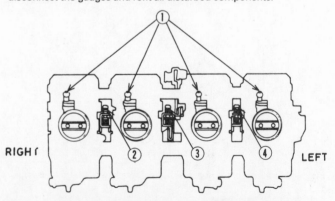

Fig. 3.11 Synchronisation screw locations (Sec 12)

1 Vacuum gauge take-off points
2 Adjusting screw for cylinders 3 and 4
3 Adjusting screw for left and right-hand pairs
4 Adjusting screw for cylinders 1 and 2

12.2 Vacuum take off points – ZX900 models

13 Evaporative Emission Control System: description and examination – California models

1   To comply with legislation in force in California and applying to all machines sold from 1984 onwards, these machines are fitted with equipment which prevents the escape into the atmosphere of any vapours produced by evaporation in any part of the fuel system. The equipment consists of a modified fuel tank, a canister of activated charcoal and a separator/pump unit, in addition to the connecting pipes and fittings.

2   Whilst the engine is stopped, vapour emitted by the evaporation of fuel in the tank passes through a blue-marked vent pipe to the top of the separator, where some of it condenses and passes through the separator into the pump unit, but the majority passes into the canister. Vapour emitted from the carburettor float chambers passes through a yellow-marked pipe directly to the canister. From there it can only escape to the atmosphere by passing through the activated charcoal which traps the vapour completely. This works equally well in reverse when the engine is running, air passing via the air filter and the green-marked purge pipe to the canister and backwards through the system into the fuel tank and carburettors to compensate for the fuel consumed.

3   As soon as the engine is started, the system is purged using the partial vacuum created at various points as the engine is running. All vapour remaining in the canister is drawn via the green-marked pipe into the air filter casing where it passes into the engine in the usual way. At the same time a simple pump, operated by the vacuum transmitted from number 3 carburettor inlet tract by the white-marked pipe, returns all liquid fuel in the separator to the fuel tank; both these purging operations being completed within moments of starting the engine. Since the pump runs automatically whenever the engine is running, it maintains the system at a pressure below that in the air filter casing, allowing air to enter the system so that the fuel system components can 'breathe' as described above.

Fuel tank

4   This is fitted with a sealed cap in addition to the vent and fuel return pipes, and requires no maintenance other than to ensure that the cap seal, gasket and mounting screw O-rings are in good condition at all times. Renew the seals immediately if there is any doubt about their condition. On a general note, always plug the left-hand (fuel return) pipe

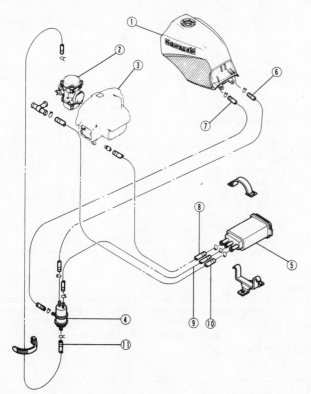

Fig. 3.12 Evaporative Emission Control System – ZX900 California models

1 Fuel tank	7 Red-marked fuel return pipe
2 Carburettor	8 Green-marked purge pipe
3 Air filter casing	9 Blue-marked vent pipe
4 Separator unit	10 Yellow-marked vent pipe
5 Canister	11 White-marked vacuum pipe
6 Blue-marked vent pipe	

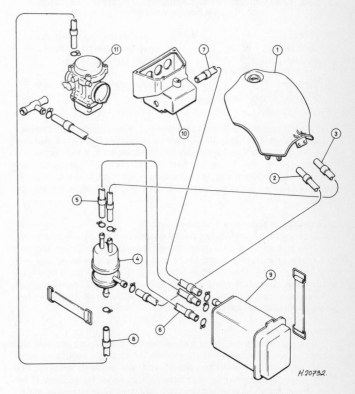

Fig. 3.13 Evaporative Emission Control System – ZX1000 A California models

1 Fuel tank	7 Green-marked purge pipe
2 Red-marked fuel return pipe	8 White-marked vacuum pipe
3 Blue-marked vent pipe	9 Canister
4 Separator	10 Air filter casing
5 Blue-marked vent pipe	11 Carburettor
6 Yellow-marked vent pipe	

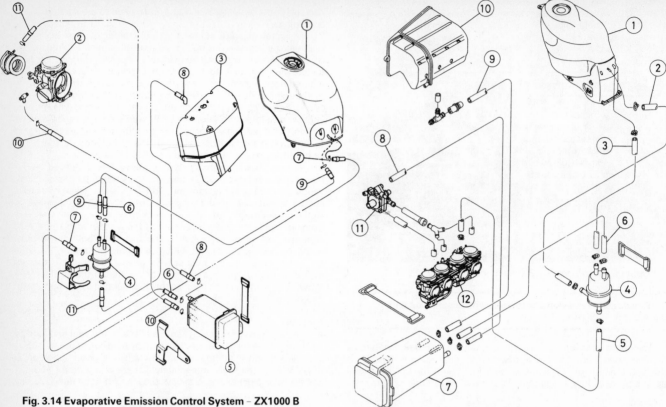

Fig. 3.14 Evaporative Emission Control System – ZX1000 B California models

1 Fuel tank	7 Red-marked fuel return pipe
2 Carburettor	8 Green-marked purge pipe
3 Air filter casing	9 Blue-marked vent pipe
4 Separator	10 Yellow-marked vent pipe
5 Canister	11 White-marked vacuum pipe
6 Blue-marked vent pipe	

Fig. 3.15 Evaporative Emission Control System – ZX1100 C California models

1 Fuel tank	7 Canister
2 Red-marked fuel return pipe	8 Yellow-marked vent pipe
3 Blue-marked vent pipe	9 Green-marked purge pipe
4 Separator	10 Air filter casing
5 White-marked vacuum pipe	11 Vacuum valve
6 Blue-marked vent pipe	12 Carburettor

union whenever the tank is removed with fuel still inside it, to prevent the loss of fuel, and never fill the tank to above the bottom of the filler neck. If fuel rises under expansion into the filler neck, it may enter the system via the vent hose and flood it, which would produce hard starting and indifferent engine performance due to an over-rich mixture. Use compressed air to clear the cap vent and tank pipes if they are blocked.

Liquid/vapour separator and pump unit
5   Test the unit by removing the blue-marked vent pipe from its top, and then add about 20 cc of gasoline via the hose fitting. Disconnect the fuel return pipe from the tank union and place the pipe open end in a container, level with the tank top. Start the engine and allow it to idle; all the gasoline should be ejected into the container almost immediately. If not, the unit must be renewed. Keep it upright at all times to prevent surplus fuel from escaping.

Charcoal canister
6   This should last the life of the machine in normal use and will not require attention of any sort other than to check its mountings and connections, but it should be noted that if fuel, solvent, water or any other liquid is allowed into the canister, its absorbing ability will be reduced to the point where it must be renewed. Check closely, therefore, for cracks or other damage.

Pipes
7   These should be examined and renewed if necessary as described in Section 5. Use only genuine Kawasaki replacement parts and ensure that the pipes are connected following the instructions given in the accompanying illustration whenever they are disturbed.
8   Check that the pipes are not pinched or trapped, or unusual symptoms may arise. If the engine performs erratically at high speeds or if it

stops with apparent signs of fuel starvation, or if the tank sides bulge out because of excessive internal pressure, check the blue-marked vent pipe. If the engine is difficult to start and hesitates due to an over-rich mixture (ie produces clouds of black smoke), this is due to the canister being flooded because liquid fuel cannot return to the tank; check the red-marked fuel return pipe and the white-marked vacuum pipe, but note that similar symptoms may be caused by the presence of excess fuel vapour due to a blocked or pinched green-marked purge pipe. If the engine is difficult to start and hesitates due to a weak mixture, or stops with apparent signs of fuel starvation, check the yellow-marked vent pipe.

General
9   The system is subject to the anti-tampering legislation currently in force in the US which means that the machine must never be used with any part of the system disconnected, missing, rendered inoperative or altered in any way. Use only genuine Kawasaki parts if renewal of any component is necessary.

14   Air filter: general

1   The air filter element can be removed and cleaned as described in Routine maintenance. Never run the machine with the air filter disconnected or the element removed. Apart from the risk of increased engine wear due to unfiltered air being allowed to enter, the carburettors are jetted to compensate for the presence of the filter and a dangerously weak mixture will result if the filter is omitted which could lead to engine damage.
2   US owners should note that the air filter is subject to the anti-

tampering legislation currently in force, which means the machine must never be run with the filter element removed or rendered inoperative, or with the assembly altered in any way. Furthermore, only genuine Kawasaki replacement parts may be used if the renewal of any component is necessary.

15   Exhaust system: general

1   All models except ZX1100 C models are fitted with an exhaust system consisting of two exhaust pipe/silencer assemblies that are joined by a connector pipe underneath the engine. The ZX1100 C models are fitted with a 4 into 1 exhaust system which branches out into two silencers that are joined underneath the engine.

2   The exhaust system can be removed as described in Section 4 of Chapter 1 and refitted as described in Section 46 of Chapter 1. Apply liberal amounts of penetrating fluid to the mounting bolts and allow time for it to work before trying to remove them. Renew all gaskets whenever the exhaust system is removed. No maintenance is required except to ensure all the mounting bolts and nuts are secure.

3   Corrosion from inside and out is the most serious problem. Take care to keep the system as clean as possible and to protect it using a non-abrasive wax polish or by applying a light film of WD40.

4   Owners of US machines should note that if any part of the system is to be renewed only genuine Kawasaki parts should be used to ensure that the machine complies with all noise and pollution regulations in force. Under US federal law it is an offence to replace any part of the exhaust system with a component that is not EPA-approved, or to modify the system in any way if the modification results in an increase in noise levels.

16   Clean air system: description and renovation – US models

1   The US models incorporate an air injection system designed to enhance the burning of hydrocarbons in the exhaust gases, thus reducing toxic emissions. The system employs a modified cylinder head and cover, in which air is drawn in through a reed valve arrangement into the exhaust pipes.

2   The clean air system is automatic in operation and should not normally require attention. The most likely fault is that unfiltered air may be drawn into the system through a damaged air filter element or leaking hose, making the tickover unstable and reducing engine power. Backfiring or other unusual noises may be apparent.

Air suction valve (reed valve)
3   The reed valves may be removed for examination after releasing their covers from the cylinder head cover. Check each valve for signs of deterioration, specifically examining the reeds for signs of delamination, cracking or scoring. Wash off any contaminants with a suitable solvent, and guard against scraping or scoring the sealing faces. The reeds and stopper plates may be removed if necessary, noting that Loctite or a similar thread-locking compound must be applied to the screw threads prior to reassembly.

Vacuum switch valve
4   Regular inspection of the vacuum switch valve is unnecessary, and should be avoided unless a fault has been indicated. A vacuum gauge and a syringe-type vacuum pump are required to check that the valve opens and closes at the specified pressures. Since few owners will have access to this type of equipment, it is suggested that the check is made by an authorized Kawasaki dealer, or by the temporary substitution of a sound valve. Note that Kawasaki state that a faulty valve **must** be renewed and that adjustment is not permitted, despite the adjuster screw and locknut fitted to the valve.

Pipes
5   Damaged or perished pipes are probably the most likely cause of trouble in the system, and are fortunately the cheapest problem to remedy. Remember that air leaks will cause erratic running, and if located between the vacuum switch valve and reed valves, will allow unfiltered air to enter the reed valves.

General
6   The removal and refitting of the system components is described in Sections 4 and 46 of Chapter 1, and that of the air suction valves in

Sections 6 and 45 of the same Chapter. The system is subject to the anti-tampering legislation currently in force in the US which means that the machine must never be used with any part of the system disconnected, missing, rendered inoperative or altered in any way. Use only genuine Kawasaki replacement parts if renewal of any component is necessary.

17   Oil pump: examination and renovation

1   The oil pump and bracket assembly is removed as described in Section 12 of Chapter 1.

2   Remove the three bolts that secure the oil pump to the bracket and separate the pump and bracket, taking care not to lose the dowels which are fitted between the two components. Slacken and remove the three screws from one end of the pump, lift off the cover, remove both the inner and outer pump rotors and withdraw the pin from the oil pump shaft. Turn the pump around and repeat the above procedure on the opposite end of the pump and withdraw the oil pump shaft.

3   Wash all the pump components and the oil screen in a high flash-point solvent and allow them to dry. Examine the pump casing and internal components for any signs of wear or scoring. Damage will occur if metal particles find their way into the pump. Renewal of the affected parts is the only remedy, bearing in mind that either set of rotors (inner and outer) should be renewed as a matching pair. The oil screen must be renewed if split or damaged and all sealing O-rings must be renewed as a matter of course.

4   Reassemble the oil pump by reversing the dismantling procedure. Ensure that all pump components are absolutely clean and lubricate all

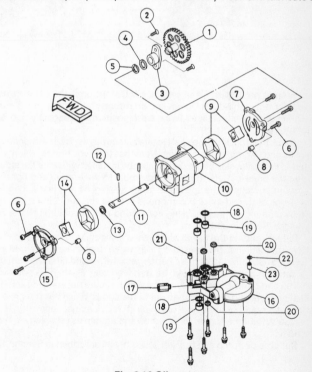

Fig. 3.16 Oil pump

1	Drive gear	13	Thrust washer
2	Screw – 2 off	14	Thinner rotor set
3	Gear holder	15	End cover
4	Washer	16	Pump bracket
5	Circlip	17	Pressure relief valve
6	Screw – 6 off	18	O-ring – 3 off
7	End cover	19	Dowel – 3 off
8	Dowel – 2 off	20	Seal – 3 off
9	Thicker rotor set	21	Dowel
10	Pump body	22	O-ring
11	Pump shaft	23	Oil feed quill
12	Pin – 2 off		

17.3 Examine pump rotors for signs of scoring

17.4a Refit pin to the oil pump shaft ...

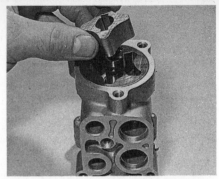

17.4b ... and install both the inner and outer pump rotors

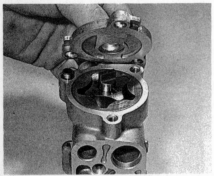

17.4c Ensure dowel is in position before refitting end cover

17.5a Renew all O-rings and refit pump to the bracket

17.5b Apply thread-locking compound to oil pump mounting bolts and tighten to the specified torque setting

the internal parts with clean engine oil. Do not omit the plain thrust washer from behind the inner set of rotors. Refit the end covers, ensuring the cover locating dowels are in position, and securely tighten all the screws.

5   Check that the oil pump shaft rotates smoothly and refit the locating dowels and O-rings to the bracket. Note that the two O-rings which are fitted to the outlet side of the pump must be installed with their flat sides facing the bracket. Refit the pump assembly to the bracket and tighten its mounting bolts to the specified torque setting, having first applied a few drops of thread-locking compound to their threads. Do not use an excess amount of thread-locking compound as this could block the oil passages. Refit the oil screen.

6   Before refitting the pump and bracket assembly to the engine it is recommended that the pressure relief valve should be examined as described in Section 19 of this Chapter, and the second oil screen which is located in the sump should be removed and cleaned as follows. Slacken and remove the three screws which secure the sump oil screen retaining plate and lift the screen out of the sump. Wash the screen in a high flash-point solvent and examine it for damage, renewing it if necessary. Refit the screen to the sump and tighten its retaining screws securely.

7   Refit the oil pump and bracket assembly as described in Section 39 of Chapter 1.

pose. The best course of action is to obtain the correct Kawasaki pressure gauge and adaptor, Part Nos 57001-164 and 57001-1188 respectively.

2   Start by checking the pressure with the engine cold. Remove the end plug and fit the adaptor and gauge into position. Start the engine and note the pressure reading at various engine speeds. If the system is working normally, the reading should comply with that given in the Specifications. If it exceeds the higher figure by a significant amount it is likely that the relief valve is stuck closed. Conversely, an abnormally low reading indicates that either the valve is stuck open or the engine is very badly worn. This test should now be repeated after the engine has been warmed up. Take the pressure reading at 4000 rpm. If the oil pressure is significantly below the figure given in the Specifications, and no obvious oil leakage is apparent, the oil pump should be removed for examination. On no account should the machine be used with low oil pressure, as plain bearing engines in particular rely on oil pressure as much as volume for effective lubrication.

3   It is likely that the normal oil pressure will be slightly above the specified pressure, but if it proves to be abnormally high, it is likely to be due to the oil pressure relief valve being jammed or damaged. This component is fitted to the inside of the sump. Refer to Section 19 for details.

19 Oil pressure relief valve: removal and testing

1   The pressure relief valve is located on the oil pump mounting bracket. To remove the relief valve, remove the oil pump assembly as described in Section 12 of Chapter 1, and then unscrew the valve from the mounting bracket. Kawasaki caution against dismantling the valve, because it is felt that such action would cause inaccuracy in the assembly. It can, however, be tested as follows:

2   Using a wooden dowel or plastic rod, push the ball off its seat

18 Lubrication system: checking the oil pressure

1   The efficiency of the lubrication system is dependent on the oil pump delivering oil at the correct pressure. This can be checked by fitting an oil pressure gauge to the right-hand oil passage plug, which is located immediately below the ignition pick-up housing. Note that the correct threaded adaptor must be obtained or fabricated for this pur-

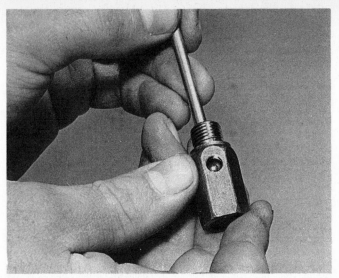

19.2 Check that relief valve ball is free to move smoothly

19.3 On refitting apply thread-locking compound to its threads

against spring pressure, noting that the ball should move smoothly and with no rough spots. If any hesitation is felt, wash the valve in a high flash-point solvent and blow it dry with compressed air. Check the valve again. If no improvement is noted, renew the relief valve assembly. Note that this test is by no means conclusive, if any doubt remains about the condition of the valve it should be renewed.

3   On reassembly, apply thread-locking compound to the threads of the relief valve and tighten it securely. Refit the oil pump and bracket assembly as described in Section 39 of Chapter 1.

20   Oil filter bypass valve: examination and renovation

1   The filter bypass valve is situated in the centre bolt of the oil filter assembly and is therefore removed and refitted with the oil filter as described in Routine maintenance. Note that if the engine oil and filter are renewed at the specified intervals, it is unlikely that the bypass valve will ever come into operation or give trouble of any sort.

2   Its function is to ensure that the engine always receives a supply of oil (even if it is unfiltered) if the filter itself is too clogged to pass oil in sufficient quantities. In this event, the oil is diverted underneath it and into the centre bolt via the bottom pair of holes which are kept open by the presence of the coil spring and flat washer. The bypass valve ball is forced off its seat when subjected to this extra pressure so that the oil can pass on into the engine.

3   It will be evident that diagnosis of a bypass valve fault is very difficult, but as the valve is so simple and so rarely used it is not likely to give trouble. It should be washed in a high flash-point solvent whenever it is removed, and care should be taken when refitting the filter to ensure that the valve can operate correctly if the need arises. If dismantling is necessary, place a wad of rag over the centre bolt open end, press out the retaining pin and tip out the spring and ball. All components should be examined for signs of wear, which should be evident, except for the spring which can only be compared with a new component, and renewed if necessary. Check that dirt is not present in the centre bolt, then refit the ball and spring. Compress the spring while inserting the retaining pin.

21   Oil pressure and oil temperature switches: removal and refitting

Oil pressure switch

1   The oil pressure switch is located on the left-hand side of the sump, opposite the oil filter housing. To remove the switch, drain the engine oil as described in Routine maintenance and disconnect its electrical lead. The switch can then be unscrewed from the sump.

2   If the oil warning lamp lights and the oil pressure is known to be correct, the switch should be tested as described in Chapter 7.

3   On refitting, wipe the threads of the switch and the surrounding area of the sump clean. Apply a silicone sealant to the threads of the switch and then tighten it to the specified torque setting.

Oil temperature switch – ZX900 models only

4   The oil temperature switch is located on the front right-hand corner of the sump. To remove, drain the oil as described in Routine maintenance and disconnect its electrical lead. Unscrew the switch from the sump.

5   On refitting, apply a thread-locking compound to the threads of the switch and tighten to the specified torque setting.

22   Oil cooler: removal, examination and refitting

1   An oil cooler is fitted to limit the oil temperature during hard riding. The oil cooler matrix is positioned across the frame front downtubes to gain the best possible benefit from the airflow.

2   To remove the oil cooler matrix it will first be necessary to remove the lower and side fairing sections as described in Chapter 5. Drain the engine oil as described in Routine maintenance.

21.1 Oil pressure switch location

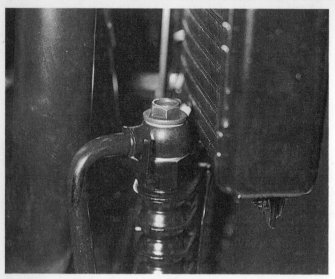

22.5 Ensure oil cooler hoses are positioned correctly on refitting

3   Disconnect the oil hose union bolts from the oil cooler and remove the sealing washers. Release all the matrix mounting bolts and lift it clear of the machine. If necessary the hoses can also be removed by releasing the union bolts which secure them to the sump and freeing any clamps or ties which secure them to the frame.

4   To maintain peak efficiency the matrix should be kept clear of any debris, preferably by using an air jet directed from behind the matrix to blow out the air channels. Avoid using sharp instruments to dislodge any foreign matter as this could easily damage the vanes. Should the matrix become damaged and leakage occur, renewal of the component will probably be the only satisfactory solution as repair is unlikely to be successful. Hoses should be checked for cracks and splits or signs of leakage, renewing them if necessary. Renew all sealing washers as a matter of course.

5   The oil cooler assembly is refitted by reversing the removal process. Examine the rubber dampers that are fitted to the matrix mounting bolts and renew any that are worn or perished. Install the matrix and tighten its mounting bolts securely. Refit the hoses ensuring that a new sealing washer is positioned on each side of the unions, and tighten the union bolts to their specified torque settings. Do not forget to refit any clamps or ties that secure the hoses to the frame.

6   Refill the engine with the correct amount of oil as described in Routine maintenance, and thoroughly check for oil leaks before taking the machine on the road.

Chapter 4 Ignition system

Refer to Chapter 8 for information on the ZX1100 D model

Contents

Specifications

Ignition timing
ZX900 and ZX1000 A models	10° BTDC @ 1000 rpm – 35° BTDC @ 3500 rpm
ZX1000 B models	10° BTDC @ 1000 rpm – 35° BTDC @ 7500 rpm
ZX1100 C models:	
UK models..	10° BTDC @ 1000 rpm – 40° BTDC @ 6000 rpm
US 49-state models	7.5° BTDC @ 1000 rpm – 40° BTDC @ 6000 rpm
US California models	7.5° BTDC @ 1200 rpm – 40° BTDC @ 6000 rpm

Pulser coil
Resistance:	
ZX900 models..	390 – 590 ohms
ZX1000 models	400 – 490 ohms
ZX1100 C models	380 – 570 ohms
Air gap:	
ZX900 and ZX1000 A models	0.5 – 0.9 mm (0.020 – 0.036 in)
ZX1000 B and ZX1100 C models	0.7 mm (0.028 in)

Ignition HT coil
Primary windings resistance:	
ZX900 and ZX1000 A models	1.8 – 2.8 ohms
ZX1000 B models	2.6 – 3.2 ohms
ZX1100 C models...................................	2.3 – 3.5 ohms
Secondary windings resistance:	
ZX900 and ZX1000 A models	10 – 16 K ohms
ZX1000 B models	13 – 17 K ohms
ZX1100 C models	12 – 18 K ohms
Minimum sparking distance:	
ZX900 and ZX1000 A models	7 mm (0.28 in)
ZX1000 B and ZX1100 C models	6 mm (0.24 in)

Cylinder identification
Left to right 1-2-3-4

Firing order
1-2-4-3

Spark plugs
	NGK	Nippon-denso
Recommended grade:		
ZX900 and ZX1000 A models:		
UK models	DR8ES	X27ESR-U
US models	D8EA	X24ES-U
ZX1000 B and ZX1100 C models:		
UK models	CR9E	U27ESR-N
US models	C9E	U27ES-N

Electrode gap:	
ZX900 and ZX1000 A models	0.6 – 0.7 mm (0.024 – 0.028 in)
ZX1000 B and ZX1100 C models	0.7 – 0.8 mm (0.028 – 0.032 in)

Torque settings

Component	kgf m	lbf ft
Spark plugs..	1.4	10
Ignition rotor retaining bolt..	2.5	18

1 General description

Due to the lack of mechanical parts in the magnetically-triggered electronic ignition system it is totally maintenance free. The system comprises a rotor, pulser coil(s), IC ignitor unit and two ignition HT coils.

The raised trigger on the rotor, fitted to the left-hand end of the crankshaft, magnetically operates the pulser coil(s) as the crankshaft rotates. The pulser coil(s) send a signal to the ignitor unit which in turn supplies the ignition HT coils with the power necessary to produce the spark at the plugs. Each coil supplies two spark plugs. Cylinders 1 and 4 operate off one coil and cylinders 2 and 3 off the other. For any given cylinder, the plug is fired twice for every engine cycle, but one of the sparks occurs during the exhaust stroke and therefore performs no useful function. This arrangement is commonly known as a 'spare spark' or 'wasted spark' system.

2 Precautions to be observed when working on the ignition system

Warning: the very high output of the ignition system means that it can be very dangerous or even fatal to touch live components or terminals of any part of the ignition system while it is still in operation. Therefore take great care to avoid personal contact with any part of the system while the engine is running, or even when the engine is stopped but the ignition is switched on.

1   When working on any part of the ignition system, always cut off the power supply either by switching off the ignition key or by disconnecting the battery (negative terminal first). If test procedures require the system to be in operation, take great care to prevent personal contact with any part of the system.

2   Do not attempt to run the engine with the battery disconnected or with its connections made to the wrong terminals; this will destroy the ignition trigger assembly and may damage the alternator and other electrical components.

3   Never disconnect or attempt to disconnect the ignition HT leads at the coils or spark plugs while the engine is running; apart from the personal risk described above, the coils and control unit would almost certainly be damaged.

4   Never use a meter or megger with a large capacity battery to test the IC ignitor unit as this will almost certainly damage the ignitor unit. It is recommended that only the Kawasaki tester (Part No 57001-983) is used to ensure the readings obtained are correct.

5   If the resistance of any other part of the system is to be tested, ensure that the power supply is cut off (see above) and that the wires leading to the pulser coils or ignitor unit are disconnected. This is to prevent the risk not only of personal injury but also of damage, either to the tester or to any of the system's components.

6   Note: owners of machines used in the US, particularly in California, should note the possible legal implications of attempting to service any part of the ignition system before undertaking such work. Refer to Chapter 3, Section 11.

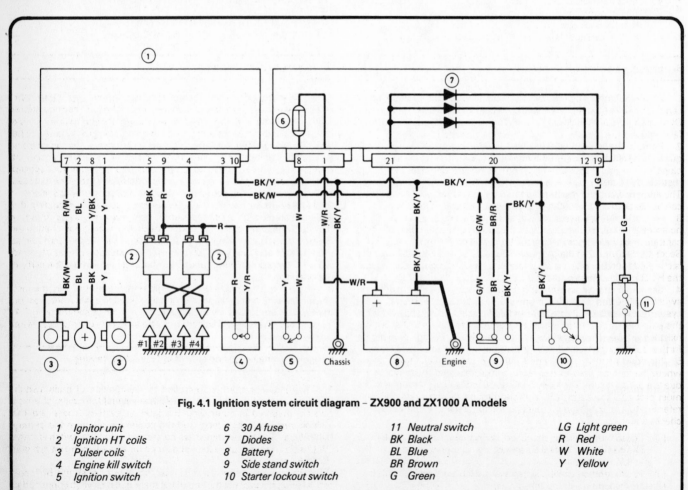

Fig. 4.1 Ignition system circuit diagram – ZX900 and ZX1000 A models

1	Ignitor unit	6	30 A fuse
2	Ignition HT coils	7	Diodes
3	Pulser coils	8	Battery
4	Engine kill switch	9	Side stand switch
5	Ignition switch	10	Starter lockout switch

11	Neutral switch	LG	Light green
BK	Black	R	Red
BL	Blue	W	White
BR	Brown	Y	Yellow
G	Green		

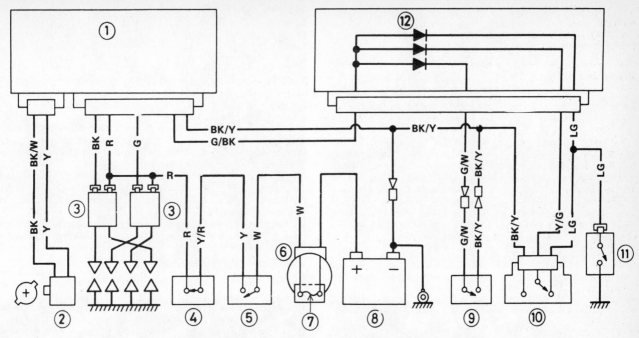

Fig. 4.2 Ignition system circuit diagram – ZX1000 B and ZX1100 C models

1	Ignitor unit	5	Ignition switch	9	Side stand switch
2	Pulser coil	6	Starter relay	10	Starter lockout switch
3	Ignition HT coils	7	30 A fuse	11	Neutral switch
4	Engine kill switch	8	Battery	12	Diodes

BK	Black
G	Green
LG	Light green
R	Red
W	White
Y	Yellow

3 Ignition system: fault diagnosis

1   As no means of adjustment is available, any failure of the system can be traced to failure of a system component or a simple wiring fault. Of the two possibilities, the latter is by far the most likely. In the event of failure, check the system in a logical fashion, as described below.

2   Remove the spark plugs from No 3 and No 4 cylinders, giving them a quick visual check noting any obvious signs of flooding or oiling. Fit the plugs into their plug caps and rest them on the cylinder head so that the metal body of each plug is in good contact with the cylinder head metal. The electrode ends of the plugs should be positioned so that sparking can be checked as the engine is spun over using the starter motor.

3   **Note:** the energy levels in electronic systems can be very high. On no account should the ignition be switched on whilst the plugs or plug caps are being held. Shocks from the HT circuit can be most unpleasant. Secondly, it is vital that the plugs are soundly earthed when the system is checked for sparking. The IC ignitor unit can be seriously damaged if the HT circuit becomes isolated.

4   Check that the kill switch is in the RUN position, turn the ignition switch to ON and turn the engine over on the starter motor. If the system is in good condition a regular, fat blue spark should be evident at the plug electrodes. If the spark appears thin or yellowish, or is non-existent, further investigation will be necessary. Before proceeding further, turn the ignition off and remove the key as a safety measure.

5   Ignition faults can be divided into two categories, namely those where the ignition system has failed completely, and those which are due to a partial failure. The likely faults are listed below, starting with the most probable source of failure. Work through the list systematically, referring to the subsequent sections for full details of the necessary checks and tests.

(a)   Loose, corroded or damaged wiring connections, broken or shorted wiring between any of the component parts of the ignition system

(b)   Faulty ignition switch, side stand switch or engine kill switch

(c)   Faulty ignition HT coil(s)

(d)   Faulty pulser coil(s)

(e)   Faulty IC ignitor unit

4 Ignition system: checking the wiring

1   The wiring should be checked visually, noting any signs of corrosion around the various terminals and connectors. If the fault has developed in wet conditions it follows that water may have entered any of the connectors or switches, causing a short circuit. A temporary cure can be effected by spraying the relevant area with one of the proprietary de-watering aerosols such as WD40 or similar. A more permanent solution is to dismantle the switch or connector and coat the exposed parts with silicone grease to prevent the ingress of water. The exposed backs of connectors can be sealed off using a silicone rubber sealant.

2   Light corrosion can normally be cured by scraping or sanding the affected area, though in serious cases it may prove necessary to renew the switch or connector affected. Check the wiring for chafing or breakage, particularly where it passes close to part of the frame or its fittings. As a temporary measure damaged insulation can be repaired with PVC tape, but the wire concerned should be renewed at the earliest opportunity.

3   Using the appropriate wiring diagram at the end of this manual, check each wire for breakage or short circuits using a multimeter set on the resistance scale or a dry battery and bulb, wired as shown in Fig. 7.1. In each case, there should be continuity between the ends of each wire.

5 Ignition, engine kill and side stand switches: testing

1   The ignition system is controlled by the ignition or main switch, mounted on the top yoke. The switch has several terminals, of which two are involved in controlling the ignition system. These are the ignition terminal (yellow lead) and the power supply from the battery (white lead). The two terminals are connected when the switch is in the ON position and the connection should be broken when the switch is in the OFF position.

2   If the operation of the switch is suspect, reference should be made to the wiring diagrams at the end of the manual. The switch connections are shown in diagrammatic form and indicate which are connected in the various switch positions. Trace the wiring back from the switch,

5.3 Engine kill switch is located in the right-hand handlebar switch

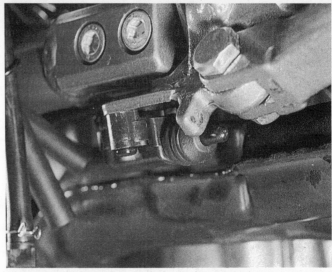

5.5 Sidestand switch is mounted on frame, below footrest

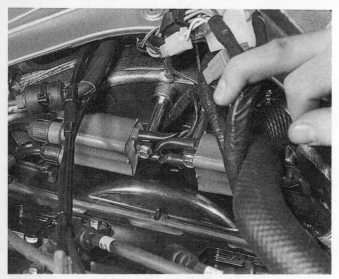

6.1a HT coil location – ZX1000 B and ZX1100 C models

6.1b HT coil location – ZX900 models

disconnect it from the main wiring loom, and check the operation of the switch using a multimeter set to the resistance scale.

3   The engine kill switch is incorporated in the right-hand handlebar switch and can be tested in a similar manner. Trace the wiring back from the switch to its block connector and disconnect it from the main wiring loom. Using the multimeter, continuity should be present between the yellow/red and red terminals when the switch is in the RUN position and an open circuit when the switch is in the OFF position.

4   If either switch is found to be faulty it must be renewed. While each is a sealed unit and can only be repaired by renewal, note that there is nothing to be lost by attempting a repair. Depending on the owner's skill, worn contacts may be reclaimed by building them up with solder or in some cases, simply by cleaning them with WD40 or a similar water dispersant spray.

5   The side stand switch is also linked into the ignition system and is designed to kill the ignition if the clutch is engaged with the transmission in gear whilst the side stand is down. Trace the wiring back from the switch, disconnect it and carry out the following test on the switch side of the wiring.

6   On ZX900 and ZX1000 A models when the side stand is up there should be continuity between the brown and black/yellow terminals, and when the stand is down there should be continuity between the black/yellow and green/white terminals. If not, the switch is at fault and must be renewed.

7   On ZX1000 B and ZX1100 C models there should be continuity between the two switch terminals when the stand is down and an open

circuit when the stand is up. If not, the switch is faulty and must be renewed.

6   Ignition HT coils: testing

1   The ignition coils are situated underneath the fuel tank where they are mounted on the frame, except on ZX1000 A models where they are mounted on the bottom of the fairing bracket. By far the most accurate method of testing the ignition coils is to use the Kawasaki spark gap tester, but some idea of the condition of the coil can be gained by measuring the resistances of its primary and secondary windings as follows. These tests can be performed with the coils fitted to the machine.

2   To check the condition of the primary windings, disconnect the low tension leads from the terminals on the ignition coil and, using a multimeter set to the ohms x 1 scale, measure the resistance between the two terminals. To check the secondary winding, unscrew the suppressor caps from the HT leads and set the meter to the K ohms x 1 scale. Connect a meter probe to each HT lead, ensuring a good contact is made, and note the reading obtained. Compare both the primary and secondary resistance readings to those given in the Specifications. If either of the results obtained are not within the specified limits the coil should be taken to an authorized Kawasaki dealer for confirmation of your findings by testing the coils on a spark gap tester. If either coil is

proved faulty it should be renewed; a satisfactory repair will not be possible.

7 Pulser coils: testing

1   The pulser coil(s) are located on the left-hand side of the crankshaft. Note that a small amount of oil will be expelled as the pickup cover is removed so place a container beneath the cover in which to drain the oil and then remove the cover. On ZX1000 and ZX1100 C models it will be necessary to remove the side fairing section, as described in Chapter 5. Trace the pulser coil wiring back to its block connector and disconnect it from the main loom; make the following test on the engine side of the wiring.

2   Using a multimeter set to the ohms x 100 scale, measure the resistance between the black and yellow wire terminals and compare the reading obtained with that given in the Specifications. On ZX900 and ZX1000 A models, carry out the same test using the black/white and blue wire terminals. If the actual reading is significantly different to that specified, the unit(s) are faulty and should be renewed. Note that on ZX900 and ZX1000 A models the pulser coils are not available separately and can only be purchased as a set.

3   If very little resistance is measured, indicating a short circuit, or if a very high resistance is measured, indicating an open circuit, note that this may be due to the wires being trapped or damaged at some point along their length. Such faults may be traced and easily repaired in the home workshop.

4   The pulser coil(s) can be removed from the machine once their mounting bolts have been removed. On refitting apply thread-locking compound to the threads of the mounting bolts and set up the pulser coil air gap as follows:

5   Using a large ring spanner on the engine turning hexagon, rotate the crankshaft anticlockwise until the raised trigger on the rotor is in line with the pulser coil and tighten the pulser coil mounting bolts finger-tight only. Using feeler gauges adjust the gap between the pulser coil and ignition trigger until the correct air gap (see Specifications) is obtained. Tighten the pulser coil mounting bolts securely. On ZX900 and ZX1000 A models repeat the above sequence for the second coil noting that it is important that the air gap on both coils is identical.

6   On ZX1100 C models ensure the tube situated between the pulser coil and rubber grommet is positioned at the coil end of the wiring and apply a small amount of silicone sealant around the crankcase mating surfaces to ensure the cover seals correctly.

7   On all models refit the cover, using a new gasket, and tighten its retaining bolts securely. Note that the top two cover retaining bolts, situated directly under the cylinder barrel, should have a thread-locking compound applied to their threads prior to installation. Remove the oil filler plug from the top of the left-hand engine casing and top up the oil

7.7 Apply thread-locking compound to the top two pulser coil cover bolts (arrowed)

level as described in Routine maintenance. On ZX1000 and ZX1100 C models refit the fairing section as described in Chapter 5.

8 IC ignitor unit: testing

1   The location of the IC ignitor unit varies depending on the model. On ZX900 models it is situated below the rear of the fuel tank, which must be removed to gain access to the unit. On ZX1000 A models the unit is mounted on the right-hand side of the rear mudguard and it will be

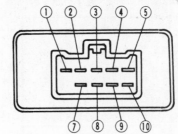

	Value (kΩ)
∞	Infinity
A	2 – 6
B	5 – 11
C	9 – 20
D	15 – 28
E	25 – 55

	Tester (+) Lead Connection								
Terminal Number	1	2	3	4	5	7	8	9	10
1		A	D	B	B	A	A	B	A
2	A		D	B	B	A	A	B	A
3	D	D		E	E	D	D	B	D
4	∞	∞	∞		∞	∞	∞	∞	∞
5	∞	∞	∞	∞		∞	∞	∞	∞
7	A	A	D	B	B		A	B	A
8	A	A	D	B	B	A		B	A
9	B	B	B	C	C	B	B		A
10	A	A	C	A	A	A	A	A	

(Left column label: Tester (−) Lead Connection)

Fig. 4.4 Ignitor unit test table – ZX900 models (Sec 8)

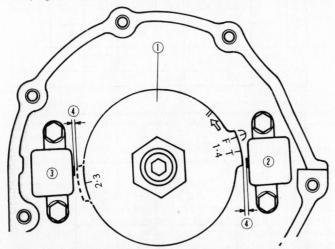

Fig. 4.3 Pulser coil air gap measurement – ZX900 and ZX1000 A models shown (Sec 7)

1   Ignition trigger
2   Pulser coil for cyl 1 and 4
3   Pulser coil for cyl 2 and 3
4   Air gap

8.1a IC ignitor unit location – ZX900 models

8.1b IC ignitor unit location – ZX1100 C models

necessary to remove the tail section of the bodywork to gain access to it. On ZX1000 B models the ignitor is situated behind the left-hand sidepanel, where it is mounted next to the battery, and on ZX1100 C models the unit can be found behind the right-hand sidepanel.

2   To test the unit it is best to remove it from the machine. Kawasaki recommend that only their multimeter, Part no. 57001-983, should be used to test the ignitor unit as any other meter could produce different readings. However, it should be possible to gain an indication of the unit's condition with another type of meter, and then to have your findings confirmed by a Kawasaki dealer if a fault is indicated. *Do not use a meter with a large battery capacity as this will almost certainly damage*

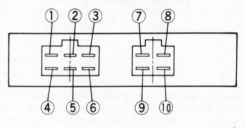

(kΩ)

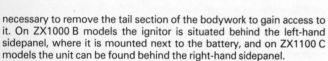

Value (kΩ)	
0	Zero
A	0.3 – 4.2
B	6.6 – 21.4
C	25 – 75
D	125 – 375
∞	Infinity

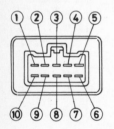

	Tester Positive (+) Lead Connection									
Termi- nal No.	1	2	3	4	5	6	7	8	9	10
1		D	D	D	D	D	D	D	D	∞
2	D		D	D	D	D	D	D	D	∞
3	C	C		B	B	B	B	B	B	∞
4	∞	∞	∞		∞	∞	∞	∞	∞	∞
5	∞	∞	∞	∞		∞	∞	∞	∞	∞
6	C	C	B	A	A		A	0	0	∞
7	C	C	B	A	A	A		A	A	∞
8	C	C	B	A	A	0	A		0	∞
9	C	C	B	A	A	0	A	0		∞
10	∞	∞	∞	∞	∞	∞	∞	∞	∞	

(Tester Negative (−) Lead Connection)

Fig. 4.5 Ignitor unit test table – ZX1000 A models (Sec 8)

	Tester (+) Lead Connection					
Termi- nal No.	1	2	3	4	5	6
1		∞	∞	∞	∞	∞
2	30 – 70		30 – 70	30 – 70	40 – 100	18 – 30
3	13 – 45	15 – 70		13 – 45	8.5 – 13	5 – 9.5
4	∞	∞	∞		∞	∞
5	35 – 150	40 – 150	8.5 – 13	35 – 150		18 – 35
6	2 – 3.8	2.6 – 5	4 – 6.5	2 – 3.8	12 – 24	

(Tester (−) Lead Connection)

(kΩ)

	Tester (+) Lead Connection			
Terminal Number	7	8	9	10
7		∞	∞	∞
8	∞		∞	35 – 70
9	∞	∞		∞
10	∞	28 – 60	∞	

(Tester (−) Lead Connection)

Fig. 4.6 Ignitor unit test table – ZX1000 B models (Sec 8)

(x 1 kΩ)

Tester (−) Lead Connection	Tester (+) Lead Connection							
	R	BK/Y	Y	BK/W	G	BK	G/BK	BK/R
R	−	2.4 ~ 9.8	4.3 ~ 17	2.4 ~ 10	6.1 ~ 24	6.1 ~ 24	5.9 ~ 24	16 ~ 66
BK/Y	∞	−	1.4 ~ 5.8	0	2 ~ 8	2 ~ 8	2.6 ~ 10	9.2 ~ 37
Y	∞	1.4 ~ 5.8	−	1.4 ~ 5.8	4 ~ 16	4 ~ 16	4 ~ 17	11 ~ 44
BK/W	∞	0	1.4 ~ 5.8	−	2 ~ 8	2 ~ 8	2.6 ~ 10	9.1 ~ 37
G	∞	∞	∞	∞	−	∞	∞	∞
BK	∞	∞	∞	∞	∞	−	∞	∞
G/BK	∞	2.7 ~ 11	4.2 ~ 17	2.7 ~ 11	5.8 ~ 23	5.8 ~ 23	−	13 ~ 52
BK/R	∞	13 ~ 54	16 ~ 62	13 ~ 54	25 ~ 100	25 ~ 100	18 ~ 70	−

Fig. 4.7 Ignitor unit test table – ZX1100 C models (Sec 8)

the unit. If in any doubt the unit should be taken to an authorized Kawasaki dealer for testing.

3   Make various tests between the wires from the ignitor block connector as shown in the accompanying table. If the results obtained do not closely resemble those in the table the ignitor unit must be renewed.

9 HT leads and suppressor caps: examination

1   Erratic running faults and problems with the engine suddenly cutting out in wet weather can often be attributed to leakage from the high tension leads and suppressor caps. If this fault is present, it will often be possible to see tiny sparks around the leads at night. One cause of this problem is the accumulation of mud and road grime around the leads, and the first thing to check is that the leads and caps are all clean. It is possible to cure the problem by cleaning the components and sealing them with an aerosol ignition sealer, which will leave an insulating coating on all components.

2   Water dispersant sprays are also highly recommended where the system has become swamped with water. Both these products are easily obtainable at most garages and accessory shops. Occasionally, a suppressor cap or lead may break down internally. If this is suspected, the components should be renewed.

3   Where the HT leads are permanently attached to the ignition coils it is recommended that the renewal of the lead is entrusted to an auto-electrician who will have the expertise to solder on a new lead without damaging the coil windings.

10 Spark plugs: general

Information relating to spark plug cleaning, adjusting and renewal will be found in Routine maintenance, together with a colour condition guide which can be used to determine mixture strength and running conditions.

Chapter 5 Frame and forks

Refer to Chapter 8 for information on the ZX1100 D model

Contents

Specifications

Front forks

Wheel travel:

ZX900 models	140 mm (5.51 in)
ZX1000 models	135 mm (5.31 in)
ZX1100 C models	125 mm (4.92 in)

Air pressure – ZX900 A1 to A6 and ZX1000 A models :

Standard	0.5 kg/cm² (7.1 psi)
Usable range	0.4 – 0.6 kg/cm² (5.7 – 8.6 psi)

Fork spring free length:

	Standard	Service limit
ZX900 A1 to A6 models	522 mm (20.6 in)	511 mm (20.1 in)
ZX900 A7-on models	430.5 mm (16.9 in)	421 mm (16.6 in)
ZX1000 A models	504.5 mm (19.9 in)	494 mm (19.4 in)
ZX1000 B models	488 mm (19.2 in)	478 mm (18.8 in)
ZX1100 C models	438 mm (17.2 in)	429 mm (16.9 in)

Fork oil capacity per leg – after reassembly:

	cc	Imp fl oz	US fl oz
ZX900 A1 to A6 models	318 ± 4	11.2 ± 0.14	10.7 ± 0.13
ZX900 A7-on models	496 ± 4	17.5 ± 0.14	16.8 ± 0.13
ZX1000 A models	348 ± 4	12.2 ± 0.14	11.7 ± 0.13
ZX1000 B models	418 ± 4	14.7 ± 0.14	14.1 ± 0.13
ZX1100 C models	458 ± 4	16.1 ± 0.14	15.5 ± 0.13

Fork oil capacity (approx) per leg – at oil change:

ZX900 A1 to A6 models	270	9.5	9.1
ZX900 A7-on models	420	14.8	14.2
ZX1000 A models	295	10.4	10.0
ZX1000 B models	360	12.7	12.2
ZX1100 C models	390	13.7	13.2

Fork oil level:*

ZX900 A1 to A6 models	357 ± 2 mm (14.1 ± 0.08 in) fork fully extended
ZX900 A7-on models	110 ± 2 mm (4.3 ± 0.08 in) fork fully compressed
ZX1000 A models	348 ± 4 mm (13.7 ± 0.16 in) fork fully extended
ZX1000 B models	130 ± 2 mm (5.1 ± 0.08 in) fork fully compressed
ZX1100 C models	149 ± 2 mm (5.9 ± 0.08 in) fork fully compressed

Oil level is measured from the top of the stanchion with fork spring removed.

Recommended fork oil:

ZX900 A1 to A6 and ZX1000 A models	SAE 10W fork oil
ZX900 A7-on, ZX1000 B and ZX1100 C models	SAE 10W/20 fork oil

Rear suspension

Wheel travel:

ZX900 models	115 mm (4.53 in)	
ZX1000 A models	130 mm (5.12 in)	
ZX1000 B and ZX1100 C models	120 mm (4.72 in)	
Air pressure:	**Standard**	**Usable range**
ZX900 models	0.5 kg/cm^2 (7 psi)	0.5 – 1.5 kg/cm^2 (7 – 21 psi)
ZX1000 A models	0.5 kg/cm^2 (7 psi)	0 – 1.5 kg/cm^2 (0 – 21 psi)
ZX1000 B models	Atmospheric pressure	0 – 1 kg/cm^2 (0 – 14 psi)
ZX1100 C models	10 kg/cm^2 (142 psi)	Non adjustable

Torque settings

Component	kgf m	lbf ft
Handlebar to top yoke mounting bolts:		
ZX900 A7-on models	1.9	13.5
All other models	2.0	14.5
Top yoke retaining nut	4.0	29.0
Yoke pinch bolts:		
ZX900 and ZX1000 A models – top and bottom	2.1	15.0
ZX1000 B models – top and bottom	2.9	21.0
ZX1100 C models:		
Top	2.9	21.0
Bottom	2.1	15.0
Front fork top bolts	2.3	16.5
Front fork damper rod retaining bolt:		
ZX900 A1 to A6 models	3.0	22.0
ZX1000 models	4.0	29.0
ZX900 A7-on and ZX1100 C models	6.2	45.0
Swinging arm pivot shaft nut(s)	9.0	65.0
Suspension unit and linkage pivot bolts:		
All suspension unit and linkage bolts except ZX900 upper suspension unit mounting bolt	6.0	43.0
ZX900 upper suspension unit mounting bolt:		
ZX900 A2 on models	3.0	22.0
ZX900 A1 model	4.0	29.0

1 General description

All models are fitted with forks of the conventional coil-spring hydraulically damped telescopic type. Those fitted to the ZX900 A1 to A6 and ZX1000 A models are air assisted and feature an adjustable anti-dive unit. The ZX1100 C forks feature an 8 position preload and a 4 position damping adjuster.

Frame design varies from model to model. The ZX900 models employ a diamond type frame, constructed of tubular steel and using the engine unit as a stressed member. The frame on ZX1000 A models is of a full cradle design and is constructed of square-section steel. Both the ZX1000 B and ZX1100 C models use a full cradle type frame constructed totally in an aluminium alloy and braced to increase rigidity.

All models employ Kawasaki's Uni-trak rear suspension system where a square-section aluminium swinging arm acts on a single suspension unit via a linkage. The rear suspension unit has a 4 position damping adjuster and all units except that fitted to ZX1100 C models are air assisted.

2 Front forks: removal

1 Place the machine on its centre stand and remove the fuel tank and complete fairing. Place some blocks underneath the crankcases and remove the front wheel as described in Section 2 of Chapter 6.

2 Slacken the top yoke cover retaining screws (where fitted) and remove the cover. Remove the Allen bolts which secure the handlebar castings to the top yoke and lift them clear. Support the handlebars to avoid placing any strain on the hydraulic hoses and also to prevent the possible leakage of fluid from the master cylinders. On ZX900 A1 to A6 and ZX1000 A models remove the two Allen bolts which secure each anti-dive plunger assembly to the top of its valve and also remove the junction box retaining bolts. On all models remove the mudguard retaining bolts and lift it clear of the machine.

3 Remove the valve cap(s) and depress the valve core(s) (where fitted) to release the air pressure from the forks. Remove the fork top bolts on ZX900 A2 to A6 models. Note if the forks are to be dismantled slacken the top plugs before removing them from the yokes. On ZX900 A1 to A5 and early ZX1000 A1 models it will also be necessary to slacken the clamps which retain the air pressure balance union in position.

4 The fork legs can then be removed by twisting each stanchion whilst pulling the leg downwards. If the stanchions are stuck in the yokes, apply penetrating fluid, allow time for it to work, and try again. In extreme cases it is permissible to fully remove the pinch bolts and lever

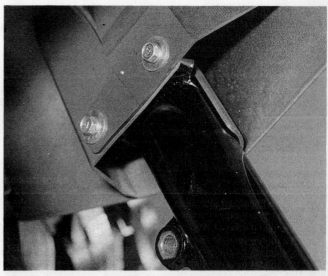

2.2a Mudguard retaining bolts are on the inside of the mudguard

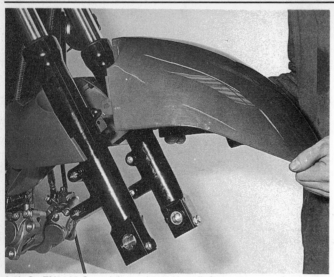

2.2b On ZX1100 C models mudguard is split for easy removal

the yoke clamps apart by wedging a screwdriver blade between them, but great care must be taken when doing this or the clamps may be broken, necessitating the renewal of the yoke.

5   When both legs are removed the air pressure balance union (where fitted) can be removed. If the fork legs are not to be dismantled, tape over the air holes in the stanchions to prevent the oil from escaping.

---

3 Front forks: dismantling and reassembly

1   Remove the fork legs from the machine as described in the previous

Section. Dismantle each leg separately to avoid interchanging parts.

2   Remove the top bolt, followed by the spacer and spring seat (as applicable) and withdraw the fork spring; take a note of whether the closer-pitched coils are at the top or bottom of the spring as a guide to reassembly. Invert the fork assembly over a suitable container and pour out the fork oil. Note that on ZX900 A1 to A6 and ZX1000 A models care must be taken to tip the fork up slowly as the TCV (Travel Control valve) valve will also fall out. Catch the valve as it emerges to prevent it being damaged. If the valve does not come out, gently tap the side of the lower leg until it is released from the stanchion end.

3   Carefully lever out the dust seal from the top of the lower leg and prise out the fork oil seal retaining circlip and washer (where fitted). Using a vice equipped with soft jaws, firmly clamp the lower leg by the brake caliper mounting lugs so that it is horizontal.

4   Remove the wheel spindle pinch bolt(s) and unscrew the Allen bolt situated at the bottom of the fork leg to release the damper rod assembly. If one is lucky this will unscrew easily. If, however, the bolt turns without unscrewing it will be necessary to hold the damper rod whilst it is slackened. The Kawasaki service tool for holding the damper rod consists of an adaptor which is fitted to a long T-handle and passed down through the stanchion to engage with the damper rod head. A suitable alternative can be made by grinding a coarse taper on a wooden rod of sufficient length; the tapered end can then be passed down the stanchion to engage in the damper rod head. With an assistant holding the protruding end of the wooden rod with a self-locking wrench and applying pressure to the damper rod head, the Allen bolt can be removed. The stanchion and lower leg can now be separated by pulling the two components apart.

5   Push the stanchion fully into the lower leg and pull it out as sharply as possible. Repeat the operation several times, using the slide-hammer action of the bottom bush against the top bush to dislodge the oil seal, until the stanchion is freed from the lower leg. Invert the stanchion and tip out the damper rod and rebound spring. The oil seal, washer and top bush can then be slid off the stanchion. Removal of the lower bush should only be attempted if renewal is required; it can be removed by inserting a screwdriver into the vertical split and levering the two ends

3.5 If necessary, the bottom bush can be removed using a flat-bladed screwdriver

3.7 Refit the rebound spring to the damper rod and insert the rod fully into the stanchion

3.8a Fit the damper rod seat to end of rod, lubricate guide bush and insert stanchion assembly into lower leg

3.8b Apply thread-locking compound to damper rod Allen bolt and tighten to specified torque setting

3.9a Slide a new seal down the stanchion and press it into position as described in text

3.9b Secure the seal with the circlip ...

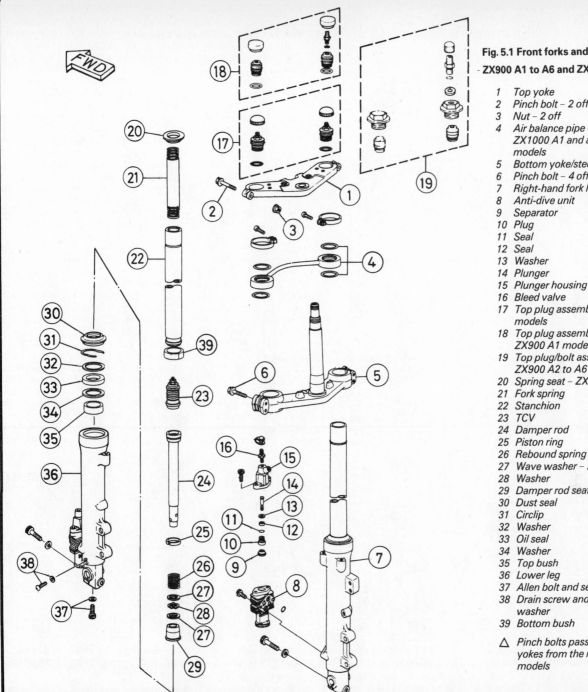

FWD

Fig. 5.1 Front forks and steering yokes – ZX900 A1 to A6 and ZX1000 A models

1 Top yoke
2 Pinch bolt – 2 off △
3 Nut – 2 off
4 Air balance pipe – early ZX1000 A1 and all ZX900 models
5 Bottom yoke/steering stem
6 Pinch bolt – 4 off △
7 Right-hand fork leg
8 Anti-dive unit
9 Separator
10 Plug
11 Seal
12 Seal
13 Washer
14 Plunger
15 Plunger housing
16 Bleed valve
17 Top plug assembly – ZX1000 models
18 Top plug assembly – ZX900 A1 model
19 Top plug/bolt assembly – ZX900 A2 to A6 models
20 Spring seat – ZX1000 models
21 Fork spring
22 Stanchion
23 TCV
24 Damper rod
25 Piston ring
26 Rebound spring
27 Wave washer – 2 off
28 Washer
29 Damper rod seat
30 Dust seal
31 Circlip
32 Washer
33 Oil seal
34 Washer
35 Top bush
36 Lower leg
37 Allen bolt and sealing washer
38 Drain screw and sealing washer
39 Bottom bush

△ Pinch bolts pass through yokes from the rear on ZX900 models

3.9c ... and refit the dust seal

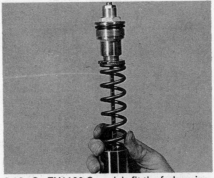

3.10a On ZX1100 C models fit the fork spring, spring seat and top plug as an assembly ...

3.10b ... and ensure the damping adjuster rod engages correctly with damper rod

Fig. 5.2 Front forks and steering yokes – ZX900 A7-on, ZX1000 B and ZX1100 C models

1   Top plug ○ △
2   O-ring
3   Top yoke ○
4   Pinch bolt – 2 off
5   Top plug/damping adjuster
    rod □
6   Top yoke □ △
7   Bottom yoke/steering stem
8   Pinch bolt – 4 off
9   Nut – 4 off
10 Spacer ○
11 Spring seat ○
12 Fork spring
13 Stanchion
14 Bottom bush
15 Damper rod
16 Piston ring
17 Rebound spring
18 Damper rod seat
19 Dust seal
20 Circlip
21 Oil seal
22 Washer
23 Top bush
24 Lower leg
25 Allen bolt and sealing washer
26 Drain screw and sealing
    washer ○

△   ZX900 A7-on models
○   ZX1000 B models
□   ZX1100 C models

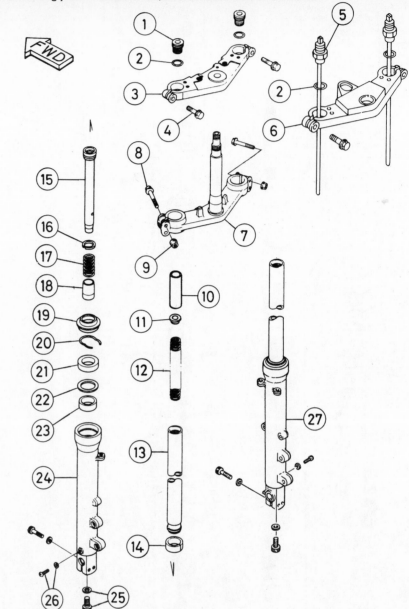

apart by just enough to allow the bush to be slid off the bottom of the stanchion. Invert the lower leg and tip out the damper rod seat. Note that on ZX900 A1 to A6 and ZX1000 A models there will also be three washers to remove from the lower leg.

6   When all components have been cleaned and examined or renewed as described in the following section, they should be reassembled in the reverse of the removal sequence.

7   Refit the rebound spring to the damper rod and insert into the upper end of the stanchion, pushing it down using either the fork spring or wooden rod until it projects fully from the lower end of the stanchion. On ZX900 A1 to A6 and ZX1000 A models refit the three washers over the damper rod end. The flat washer should have a wave washer positioned on each side of it. On all models refit the damper rod seat to the end of the rod and carefully refit the bottom bush (if removed) to the lower end of the stanchion, ensuring that it is correctly positioned in its locating groove.

8   Smear the bottom bush and stanchion with oil and insert the assembly into the lower leg. Press the stanchion fully into the lower leg to centralise the damper rod seat. Check the condition of the sealing washer on the Allen bolt and renew if necessary. Apply a few drops of thread-locking compound to the threads of the Allen bolt and install in the stanchion. Hold the damper rod using the method employed when

dismantling, and tighten the bolt to the specified torque setting. Refit the spindle pinch bolt(s).

9   Lubricate the top bush and slide it down over the stanchion, fit the large plain washer on top of it and press the bush into position noting that the slit of the bush must be positioned on either the left or right-hand side of the stanchion. On no account should the slit be placed facing the front or rear of the stanchion. If necessary the bush can be tapped into position using a hammer and drift, such as a socket spanner, placed on top of the washer. Smear the oil seal lip with fork oil and slide it down the stanchion. Press the seal squarely into the lower leg as far as possible by hand only and refit the second plain washer (where fitted). The seal can be tapped fully into place using a length of tubing, which bears only on the seal's hard outer edge; check first that there are no burrs or sharp raised edges which could damage the seal. As soon as the circlip groove is exposed withdraw the tube and refit the seal retaining circlip, ensuring that it is correctly seated. Pack a small amount of grease above the oil seal and refit the dust seal.

10 Fill each leg with the specified amount of fork oil and slowly pump the stanchion up and down to distribute the oil. When the level has settled measure the oil level as described in Routine maintenance, correcting it if necessary. When the oil level is correct, refit the TCV valve (where fitted), ensuring that the two nuts are at the top. Fit the fork

spring, ensuring that it is installed with its closer-pitched coils as noted on dismantling. Install the spring seat, spacer and top plug (as applicable). On ZX1100 C models refit the spring, seat and top plug as an assembly, ensuring that the spring seat is located on the stepped portion of the top plug and that the damping adjuster rod correctly engages with the hole in the damper rod upper end. Tighten the top plug by hand only at this stage as it is much easier and safer to tighten it once the fork is clamped in the yokes.

4 Front forks: examination and renovation

1 Wash all fork components thoroughly to remove all traces of old oil. Check particularly carefully that all dirt has been removed from the bottom of the fork lower leg and from the passageways in the damping mechanism. On ZX900 A1 to A6 models and ZX1000 A models, it is advisable to remove the anti-dive valve unit so that one can be certain of cleaning it thoroughly and drying it completely. Refer to Section 6.

2 Discard the fork oil seal; this should be renewed whenever it is disturbed. Similarly check the dust seals for splits, cracks or other damage, and check all sealing O-rings and washers. Renew any component that is found to be worn or damaged. On models so equipped, do not forget the seals around the air valves and, where applicable, in the air union. Also check the piston ring around the head of the damper rod. This ring must fit closely and seal tightly in its bore if the damping mechanism is to function efficiently.

3 On ZX900 A1 to A6 and ZX1000 models check the TCV (Travel Control Valve), especially if damping problems have been experienced. The valve assembly should not be dismantled and no replacement parts are available; if found to be faulty, it must be renewed. If a fault is suspected first inspect the piston ring of the damper rod before turning attention to the TCV, then go on to check that the oil holes of the TCV are clear. If no damage is found the TCV must be renewed. Note that the valve depends on an accurate fork oil level for correct operation.

4 Apart from the above, the only other components likely to wear are the bearing surfaces of the stanchion and lower leg. Insert the stanchion into the lower leg, complete with bushes, and feel for free play between the two at all points, from full compression to full extension. No specifications are given, therefore if free play appears to be excessive, the worn components should be renewed. Excessive wear is normally revealed by score marks on one or both surfaces; if such signs are found the component concerned must be renewed. Take the components to an authorized Kawasaki dealer for an expert opinion if in doubt. Note that both the top and bottom bushes are available separately.

5 The stanchions can be checked for straightness by rolling them on a flat surface such as a sheet of plate glass; any bending or distortion should immediately be evident. It is usually possible to straighten slightly bent stanchions provided that the work is undertaken only by an expert; any local motorcycle dealer should be able to recommend such a person. However if the stanchion is bent so much that the tubing has creased or even split, it must be renewed; straightening, even if possible, would induce severe stresses resulting in a fatigue failure at a later date.

6 Check that the stanchions' upper surfaces are clean and free from chips, dents or corrosion which might weaken the tubing or cause oil seal failure. Use fine emery paper to polish off any corrosion; but chips or dents, if minor, can be filled with Araldite or similar and rubbed down to restore the original shape when the filling compound has set. UK owners should note that such damage will cause the machine to fail its DOT test certificate. If in doubt about the stanchion's strength, renew it in the interests of safety.

7 The fork springs will take a permanent set after considerable usage and will require renewal if the fork action becomes spongy. The service limit for the total spring free length is given in the Specifications.

8 Make a careful check of all other fork leg components, checking for cracks in castings, damaged threads, defective air valves, and any other signs of wear or damage, renewing any faulty components.

5 Front forks: refitting

1 Apply a small amount of grease to the stanchion upper end and the air union sealing O-rings (where fitted). Insert the stanchion into the bottom yoke and slide the air union and its retaining clamp (where fitted) into position. Slide the stanchion through the top yoke, whilst holding the air union against the bottom yoke, and lightly tighten the top and bottom pinch bolts.

ZX900 A1 to A6 and ZX1000 A models

2 Slide the handlebars over the fork stanchions and refit their mounting bolts. Position each stanchion so that its top edge is level with that of the handlebar casting and tighten both the top and bottom yoke pinch bolts and the handlebar retaining bolts to their specified torque settings. Ensure that the air union (where fitted) is positioned hard against the top surface of the bottom yoke and tighten its retaining clamps securely. Refit the anti-dive plunger assembly (where fitted), tightening the mounting bolts to the specified torque settings, and remount the junction box on each fork leg.

ZX900 A7-on, ZX1000 B and ZX1100 C models

3 On ZX900 A7-on and ZX1000 B models, position the stanchion so that its top edge protrudes 15 mm (0.60 in) above the surface of the top yoke. On ZX1100 C models the stanchion should be 11.5 mm (0.45 in) above the top yoke. Once the stanchion is correctly positioned, tighten both the top and bottom yoke pinch bolts to their specified torque settings. Refit the handlebar castings and tighten their mounting bolts to the specified torque setting.

All models

4 Refit the mudguard and tighten its retaining bolts to the specified torque setting. If the fork legs were dismantled, also tighten their top plugs to their specified torque setting. On ZX900 A2 to A6 models, refit the fork top bolts and tighten them to the specified torque setting. Refit the wheel as described in Section 3 of Chapter 6, followed by the fairing and fuel tank. Charge the forks with the specified amount of air (as applicable) and refit the valve caps. Thoroughly check the operation of the front forks and brake before taking the machine on the road.

5.3a Position the fork legs in the yokes as described in text ...

5.3b ... then tighten all yoke pinch bolts to the specified torque setting

5.3c Refit the handlebars and tighten their mounting bolts to the specified torque setting

6   Anti-dive valve assembly: testing and renewal – ZX900 A1 to A6 and ZX1000 A models

1   The valve assembly is mounted on the front of each fork lower leg, being retained by four Allen screws. The oil passages are each sealed by O-rings. Note that no replacement parts are available with which the assembly can be reconditioned. If it becomes worn out or is damaged in an accident, each assembly can only be renewed as a single unit. Note that actual wear is unlikely; the unit is most likely to fail due to dirt jamming a valve.
2   Note that the anti-dive is hydraulically activated; refer to the relevant Sections of Chapter 6 for information on the plunger assembly and hydraulic system. To test the valve assembly, remove the fork legs from the machine as described in Section 2, then remove the fork top plug and the fork spring and tape over the air union hole (models with air balance pipe) drilled in the stanchion. Clamp the fork leg vertically in a vice, ensuring that the vice has soft alloy or wooden jaw covers that bear only on the wheel spindle lug, then set the anti-dive to the softest (Number 1) setting, ie fully anticlockwise.
3   Ensuring that no oil is spilled, pump the stanchion gently and smoothly up and down through its full travel, feeling the amount of damping present on both compression and rebound strokes when the anti-dive is not operating. Insert a rod such as an Allen key into the hole in the top of the valve assembly and press firmly downwards; do not apply heavy pressure as it is not necessary; this may damage the valves. The hydraulic plunger should extend by only 2 mm. Repeat the pumping action and compare the difference when the rod is released with when it is depressed, then repeat the test with the anti-dive on each of the stronger settings.
4   The amount of effort required to compress the fork should increase noticeably as soon as the rod is depressed and should return to normal as soon as the rod is released. As the setting is increased to its stiffest position the effort required to compress the fork should increase in proportion, yet should still return to normal when the rod is released. If compression damping is heavy when no pressure is applied to the rod, or if it does not return to normal when the rod is released, also if there is no difference in damping with pressure applied to the rod, the anti-dive unit is faulty and must be renewed. As a safety measure the manufacturer recommends that the assembly should not be dismantled with a view to repair and does not supply replacement parts as a result.

7   Steering head: removal

1   Remove the seat and fuel tank as described in Chapter 3. Remove the front forks as described in Section 2. On ZX900 models it may also be necessary to remove the fairing mounting bracket.
2   Remove the two bolts which secure the front brake union joint to the bottom yoke and position the brake hose clear of the steering head assembly. Tie the hoses and calipers to the frame to avoid placing any strain on them. On ZX900 A7-on and ZX1100 C models, prise out the large circular cap to gain access to the nut which secures the top yoke to the steering stem. On all other models it will be necessary to release the two screws which retain the top yoke cover and remove the cover to gain access to the nut.
3   Slacken and remove the nut and washer and lift the top yoke assembly off the steering stem. Position the yoke behind the steering head and secure it to the frame to avoid straining the hydraulic hoses or electrical leads. Remove the lock washer and slacken the steering head bearing adjusting nut with a suitable C-spanner whilst supporting the bottom yoke. Lift off the dust seal and O-ring and lower the bottom yoke and steering stem assembly out of the headstock. The top bearing inner race can then be removed.

8   Steering head bearings: examination and renovation

1   The inner races are easily checked after all traces of old grease have been removed by washing in a suitable solvent. Turn each race slowly, checking for marks or discoloration of the roller faces.
2   Clean the outer races and examine the bearing surface for wear or

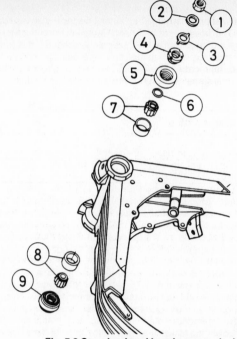

Fig. 5.3 Steering head bearings – typical

1	Nut	6	O-ring
2	Washer	7	Top bearing
3	Lock washer	8	Bottom bearing
4	Adjusting nut	9	Dust seal – where fitted
5	Dust seal		

damage. If any wear is discovered, Kawasaki recommend that both bearings, including their outer races, should be renewed.
3   If renewal is necessary, removal of the old bearing outer races and installation of the new outer races may be accomplished using the correct Kawasaki service tools. If these tools are not available proceed as follows:
4   The outer races are a fairly tight fit in the headstock. Most universal slide-hammer type bearing extractors will work here, and these can often be hired from tool shops. Alternatively, a long drift can be passed through one race and used to drive out the opposite item. Tap firmly and evenly around the race to ensure that it drives out squarely. It may prove advantageous to curve the end of the drift slightly to improve access. Note that with this method there is a real risk of damage unless care is taken. If the race refuses to move, stop; leave the job until a proper extractor can be obtained.
5   The lower inner race can be levered off the steering stem, using

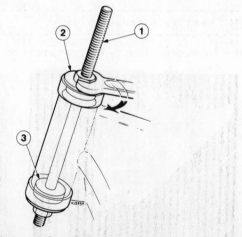

Fig. 5.4 Drawbolt tools for refitting bearing outer races (Sec 8)

1	Drawbolt	3	Guide
2	Thick washer		

screwdrivers on opposite sides to work it free. To fit the new item, find a length of tubing slightly larger in its internal diameter than the steering stem. This will suffice as a tubular drift. Grease the bearing thoroughly and wipe a trace of grease around the steering stem. Drive the bearing home evenly and fully.

6   The new outer races can be installed using a home-made version of the drawbolt arrangement shown in the accompanying illustration.

9   Steering head: refitting

1   On refitting coat both bearings and the steering stem with grease. Offer up the bottom yoke and stem to the frame and fit the top bearing, followed by the O-ring and dust seal, and refit the slotted adjuster nut finger-tight. It is important to bed the bearings in on assembly, before final adjustment – proceed as follows:

2   To preload the bearings, a C-spanner, preferably the correct Kawasaki item (Part No 57001-1100), will be required. If using any other spanner, note that it will be necessary to make some provision for a spring balance to be attached to a point 180 mm (7.1 in) from the centre of the steering stem. To this end, extend the spanner as required and drill a hole in the handle at the correct distance. A spring balance capable of reading above 22.2 kg (48.94 lb) will also be required.

3   Fit the C-spanner and apply 4.0 kgf m (29 lbf ft) to the adjuster nut. This is achieved by hooking the spring balance to the hole in the C-spanner and pulling on it until a reading of 22.2 kg (48.94 lb) is shown. Check that the steering head assembly turns smoothly with no evidence of play or tightness.

4   Slacken the nut slightly until pressure is just released, then turn it slowly clockwise until pressure is just evident. Take great care not to apply excessive pressure because this will cause premature failure of the bearings. The object is to set the adjuster so that the bearings are under a very light loading, just enough to remove any free play. Once set correctly refit the lock washer, ensuring that its tangs engage correctly with the slots of the nut. Refit the top yoke, washer and nut, securing the nut only finger-tight at this stage. Tighten the nut to the recommended torque setting after the forks have been refitted in the yokes as described in Section 5. Continue reassembly in the reverse of the dismantling sequence, noting that all fasteners should be tightened to the specified torque settings on completion.

5   Referring to the relevant section of Routine maintenance, check that the steering head bearings are correctly adjusted as soon as the forks, handlebars and front wheel are refitted.

6   Continue assembly by reversing the dismantling sequence. Check that all electrical cables and control cables are routed so that they do not impede steering movement. When refitting the wiring connectors, if disconnected, check that the wiring colour codes match up. When assembly has been completed check the operation of the front brake, throttle and clutch and adjust the headlamp alignment and rear view mirror setting.

10   Frame: examination and renovation

1   The frame is unlikely to require attention unless accident damage

has occurred. In some cases, renewal of the frame is the only satisfactory remedy if it is badly out of alignment. Only a few frame specialists have the jigs and mandrels necessary for resetting the frame to the required standard of accuracy, and even then there is no easy means of assessing to what extent the frame may have been overstressed.

2   After the machine has covered a considerable mileage, it is advisable to examine the frame closely for signs of cracking or splitting at the welded joints. Rust corrosion can also cause weakness at these joints. Minor damage can be repaired by welding or brazing, depending on the extent and nature of the damage.

3   Remember that a frame which is out of alignment will cause handling problems and may even promote 'speed wobbles'. If misalignment is suspected, as a result of an accident, it will be necessary to strip the machine completely so that the frame can be checked, and if necessary, renewed.

11   Rear suspension unit: removal

1   Place the machine on its centre stand, then remove the seat and sidepanels. Place a suitably sized block underneath the rear wheel to prevent the wheel dropping when the suspension unit bolts are removed.

ZX900 models

2   Firstly, disconnect the battery as a safety precaution (negative terminal first). Remove the two bolts which secure the coolant expansion tank to the frame, remove the filler cap and drain its contents into a suitable container. Have ready a wooden bung or clean screw of suitable diameter with which to plug the tank pipe when disconnected, then swiftly pull the pipe off the tank union and plug its open end. Wipe up any spilt coolant immediately. Free the starter relay mounting bracket from the left-hand side of the frame. Release the rear suspension unit air valve from the frame by removing its mounting nut. Slacken the rear damping adjuster rod locknut situated at the top of the suspension unit, unscrew the damping adjuster rod and remove it along with the adjuster knob.

3   Slacken the suspension unit upper mounting bolt and nut but do not remove it at this stage. Slacken and remove the lower suspension unit mounting bolt and the tie-rod lower mounting bolt, allowing the relay bracket to pivot downwards. Now remove the suspension unit upper bolt and lower the suspension unit out of the swinging arm and away from the machine.

ZX1000 A models

4   Remove the four bolts which secure the fuel tank mounting bracket to the frame and remove the fuel tank along with its mounting bracket. Disconnect the battery (negative lead first) and remove it from the machine. Remove the air filter element as described in Routine maintenance and displace the four spring clips which retain the air filter hoses on the carburettors. The air filter housing can then be lifted out of the frame. Release both silencer mounting clamps and bolts and detach the silencers from the main exhaust pipes.

5   Slacken both the starter and fan relay mounting bolts and remove them from the battery bracket. Free the suspension unit air valve from

11.2a ZX900 models – remove expansion tank mounting bolts (arrowed) and drain its contents

11.2b Slacken the damping adjuster locknut and unscrew the adjuster from the unit

11.2c Remove the air valve mounting nut

11.3a Remove tie-rod to relay arm bolt and
suspension unit lower ...

11.3b ... and upper mounting bolts ...

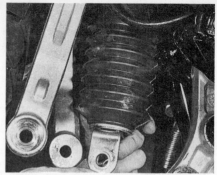

11.3c ... then lower the unit out of the frame

the frame by releasing its mounting nut. Release the bolt which secures
the rear damping adjuster mounting bracket to the battery bracket, then
slacken the battery bracket retaining bolts and remove it from the
machine.
6   Remove the upper suspension unit mounting bolt and unscrew the
damping adjuster cable from the unit. Remove the cable and adjuster
assembly, taking care not to displace the pinion gear from the suspension unit. Remove the lower suspension unit mounting bolt and lower
the unit out of the frame.

ZX1000 B models
7   Disconnect the battery (negative lead first) and remove it from the
machine. Remove all the mounting screws from the tail section of the
bodywork, noting that two are located inside the small compartment on
the left-hand side of the tail section, and disconnect the turn signal and
rear lamp wiring block connectors. Pull the tail section to the rear and
remove it from the machine. Slacken the four bolts which secure the
rear section of the rear mudguard to the frame and remove it. Release
the IC ignitor mounting bolts, disconnect it from the wiring harness, and
remove it from the machine. Remove the rear brake reservoir and
starter relay mounting bolts. Tie the brake reservoir to the frame to
avoid placing any strain on its connecting hose or the possible spillage
of brake fluid. Disconnect the junction box block connectors and remove the box. Release the rear mudguard mounting bolt and remove it
from the machine.
8   Remove the rear suspension unit air valve mounting nut and the
damping adjuster mounting bolts. Disconnect the adjuster from the
cable and remove it from the machine. Slacken and remove the suspension unit upper and lower mounting bolts and the lower tie-rod bolt,
then withdraw the unit from the frame.

ZX1100 C models
9   Remove the fuel tank as described in Chapter 3 and release the fuel
tank mounting bracket retaining bolts and lift it clear of the frame.
Remove all the electrical components which are mounted on the rear
mudguard, releasing their wiring and the rear suspension unit reservoir
hose from any clamps or guides. Withdraw the mudguard rear section
after removing its four mounting bolts, followed by the front (main)
section which has a single mounting bolt.
10   To gain access to the rear suspension unit upper mounting bolt it
will be necessary to remove the mudguard mounting bracket, retained
by two bolts. Free the rear suspension unit oil reservoir from the frame
by removing its mounting bolt. *On no account attempt to separate the
reservoir from the suspension unit. If the hose connections are loosened
pressure will be lost and the complete assembly will have to be renewed.*
Remove the upper and lower suspension unit mounting bolts and the
tie-rod to relay arm bolt, and manoeuvre the suspension unit and
reservoir out from below the swinging arm.

---

12   Rear suspension unit: examination and renovation

1   The most likely defect in the unit is poor damping, a failing which is
ultimately inevitable. Typical symptoms are bouncing on undulating
roads and wheel patter on broken surfaces. If handling problems do
occur the unit should be renewed promptly.
2   The suspension unit is of a sealed construction and is not repairable
in any way; if defective, it must be renewed. The only serviceable items
are the bearings or mounting bushes which can be examined as follows.

ZX1000 A models
3   Needle roller bearings are fitted at the mounting points. Lever out
the oil seals from both sides of the unit and remove all traces of old
grease and road dirt. Examine the pivot bolts for signs of wear or
corrosion and the needle roller bearings for wear or discoloration. If
either bearing is damaged in any way both must be renewed together.
The old bearings can be drifted out of place and the new items fitted
using a drawbolt arrangement as shown in the accompanying illustration. Renew the oil seals as a matter of course. On installation pack the

11.10 On ZX1100 C models do not attempt to separate the suspension
unit and oil reservoir

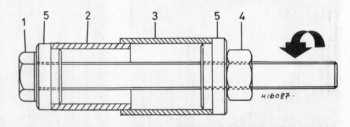

**Fig. 5.5 Drawbolt tool for installing bearings or bushes in rear
suspension components (Sec 12)**

1 Drawbolt   4 Nut
2 Bearing or bush   5 Thick washers
3 Housing

bearings and lubricate the pivot bolt with molybdenum disulphide grease.

All other models

4   A single rubber bush is fitted at the upper mounting point. If there is excessive movement in the bush when the mounting bolt is inserted, it should be renewed. The bush can be removed and fitted using a drawbolt arrangement as shown in the accompanying illustration.

13   Rear suspension unit: refitting

1   Lubricate the suspension unit and tie-rod mounting bolts with molybdenum disulphide grease prior to assembly and proceed as described below.

ZX900 models

2   Offer up the suspension unit and refit its upper mounting bolt. Fit the lower suspension unit and tie-rod mounting bolts and tighten both suspension unit and tie-rod mounting bolts to their specified torque settings. Refit the damping adjuster rod assembly, tightening its locknut securely, and secure the suspension unit air valve with its retaining nut. Remount the relay bracket on the left-hand side of the frame and install

Fig. 5.6 Rear suspension unit pinion gear position – ZX1000 A models (Sec 13)

the coolant expansion tank. Swiftly unplug the expansion tank pipe and reconnect to the tank stub. Top up the expansion tank with the specified coolant as described in Routine maintenance. Re-connect the battery.

ZX1000 A models

3   Before installing the suspension unit remove the dust cover from the top of the unit and set the damping adjuster gear to the number 1 position. This should be marked with a red painted line on the side of the gear and should be positioned in the centre of the cutaway. Refit the small pinion gear so that the square hole at its centre is as shown in the accompanying figure. Also, set the remote damping adjuster to the number 1 position.

4   Offer up the suspension unit and refit both mounting bolts. Reconnect the damping adjuster cable and tighten the suspension unit mounting bolts to the specified torque setting. Refit the battery bracket and mount the damping adjuster and the suspension unit air valve on the frame. Refit the starter and fan relay to the battery bracket and tighten all the above mentioned mounting bolts and nuts securely.

5   Install the air filter housing and refit the element as described in Routine maintenance. Ensure that the air filter hoses are correctly fitted to the carburettors and secure them with the spring clips. Refit the battery and fuel tank, together with its mounting bracket.

ZX1000 B models

6   Before refitting the suspension unit it will be necessary to set up the damping adjuster gear as described in paragraph 3, noting that there is no small pinion to be fitted to the unit.

7   Position the unit in the frame and fit both the suspension unit mounting bolts. Reconnect the damping adjuster cable and tighten the suspension unit mounting bolts to the specified torque setting. Refit the suspension unit air valve to the frame and tighten its retaining nut securely.

8   Refit the rear mudguard to the machine, tighten all its mounting bolts securely, and refit the rear brake reservoir and starter relay retaining bolts. Connect the IC ignitor and junction box to the main loom and remount them on the machine. Refit the tail section, tightening all its mounting screws securely, and connect the rear lamp and turn signal block connectors. Refit the battery.

13.9a On ZX1100 C models offer up the suspension unit and refit its upper mounting bolt

13.9b Refit the tie-rod to relay arm bolt ...

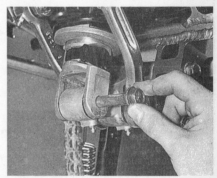

13.9c ... and the lower suspension unit bolt; tighten all to their specified torque settings

13.9d Refit the oil reservoir to the frame, tightening its mounting bolt securely

13.10a Install the mudguard mounting bracket ...

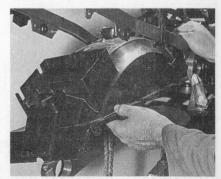

13.10b ... followed by the mudguard front and rear sections

ZX1100 C models

9   Install the rear suspension unit with the oil reservoir hose union bolt facing the rear and refit both its mounting bolts. Refit the tie-rod to relay arm pivot bolt. Tighten the suspension unit and relay arm pivot bolts to the specified torque setting and refit the oil reservoir mounting bolt.

10   Refit the mudguard mounting bracket and install the mudguard sections. Tighten the mudguard retaining bolts and refit all the electrical components which were removed. Ensure that the electrical wires and the reservoir hose are correctly routed and retained by the clamps. Refit the fuel tank mounting bracket and fuel tank.

All models

11   Set the required suspension unit damping setting and air pressure and refit the seat and sidepanels. Thoroughly check the operation of the rear suspension before taking the machine on the road.

14   Swinging arm: removal

ZX900 models

1   Remove the rear wheel as described in Chapter 6 and the rear suspension unit as described in Section 11.

2   Release both silencer mounting clamps and bolts and remove them

from the exhaust pipes. Remove the Allen-headed outer swinging arm pivot nuts and the rear brake caliper mounting bolts. Disconnect the rear brake stop lamp switch wires and release the brake fluid reservoir retaining bolt. Slacken all the Allen bolts which secure the right-hand footrest bracket to the frame and release the rear brake hose from clamps. The footrest and complete rear brake assembly can then be manoeuvred out of the frame. Take care to keep the brake fluid reservoir upright to prevent the spillage of fluid.

3   Remove all the left-hand footrest bracket retaining bolts and partially withdraw the bracket. Remove the circlip and washer which retain the gearchange pedal to the bracket and lift the bracket clear. Slacken the left-hand pivot shaft nut and withdraw the pivot shaft from the right-hand side whilst supporting the swinging arm. If necessary, due to a build-up of corrosion, the shaft can be tapped out using a hammer and a suitable drift. The swinging arm and tie-rod assembly can then be manoeuvred out of the frame. Remove a circlip from either end of the shaft which secures the tie-rods to the swinging arm, and withdraw the shaft to separate the tie-rods from the swinging arm.

ZX1000 A models

4   Remove the rear wheel as described in Section 4 of Chapter 6.

5   Release both silencer mounting clamps and bolts and remove them from the exhaust pipes. Slacken all the left-hand footrest bracket

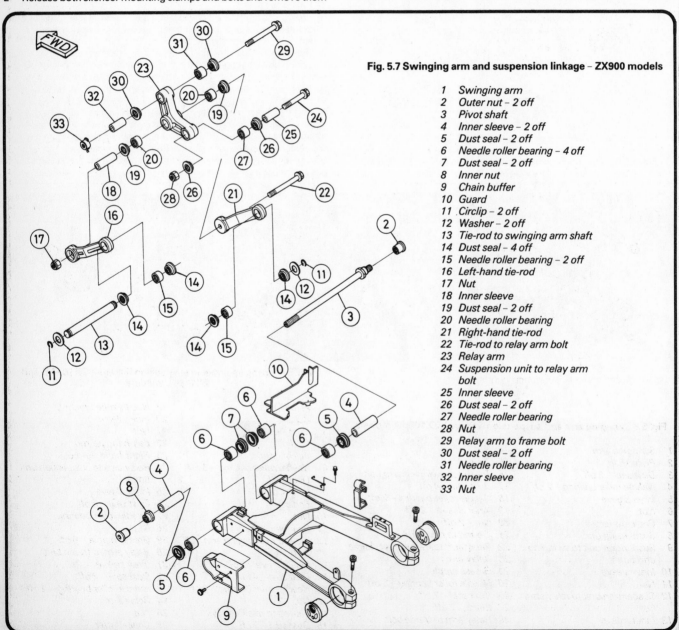

Fig. 5.7 Swinging arm and suspension linkage – ZX900 models

1	Swinging arm
2	Outer nut – 2 off
3	Pivot shaft
4	Inner sleeve – 2 off
5	Dust seal – 2 off
6	Needle roller bearing – 4 off
7	Dust seal – 2 off
8	Inner nut
9	Chain buffer
10	Guard
11	Circlip – 2 off
12	Washer – 2 off
13	Tie-rod to swinging arm shaft
14	Dust seal – 4 off
15	Needle roller bearing – 2 off
16	Left-hand tie-rod
17	Nut
18	Inner sleeve
19	Dust seal – 2 off
20	Needle roller bearing
21	Right-hand tie-rod
22	Tie-rod to relay arm bolt
23	Relay arm
24	Suspension unit to relay arm bolt
25	Inner sleeve
26	Dust seal – 2 off
27	Needle roller bearing
28	Nut
29	Relay arm to frame bolt
30	Dust seal – 2 off
31	Needle roller bearing
32	Inner sleeve
33	Nut

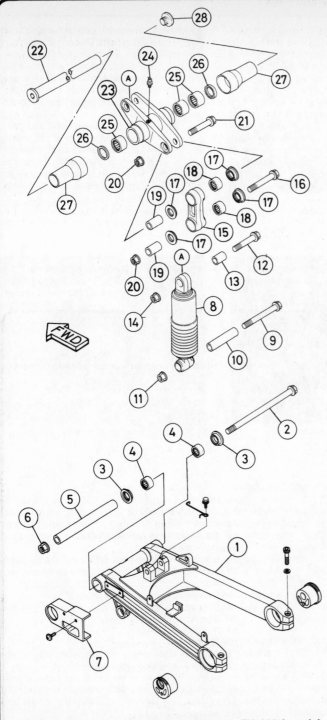
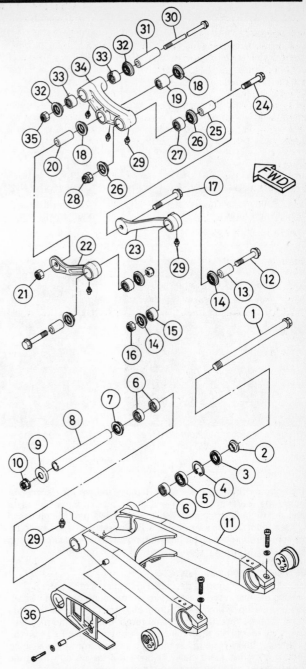

Fig. 5.8 Swinging arm and suspension linkage – ZX1000 A models

1	Swinging arm	14	Nut
2	Pivot shaft	15	Tie-rod
3	Dust seal – 2 off	16	Tie-rod to swinging arm bolt
4	Needle roller bearing – 2 off	17	Dust seal – 4 off
5	Inner sleeve	18	Needle roller bearing – 2 off
6	Nut	19	Inner sleeve – 2 off
7	Chain buffer	20	Nut – 2 off
8	Suspension unit	21	Tie-rod to relay arm bolt
9	Suspension unit to swinging arm bolt	22	Relay arm to frame pivot sleeve
10	Inner sleeve	23	Relay arm
11	Nut	24	Grease nipple
12	Suspension unit to relay arm bolt	25	Needle roller bearing – 3 off
13	Inner sleeve	26	Dust seal – 2 off
		27	Collar – 2 off
		28	Relay arm to frame bolt

Fig. 5.9 Swinging arm and suspension linkage – ZX1000 B and ZX1100 C models

1	Pivot shaft	19	Needle roller bearing
2	Collar	20	Inner sleeve
3	Dust seal	21	Nut
4	Circlip	22	Left-hand tie-rod
5	Ball bearing	23	Right-hand tie-rod
6	Needle roller bearing – 3 off	24	Relay arm to suspension unit bolt
7	Dust seal	25	Inner sleeve
8	Inner sleeve	26	Dust seal – 2 off
9	End cap	27	Needle roller bearing
10	Nut	28	Nut
11	Swinging arm	29	Grease nipple – 6 off
12	Tie-rod to swinging arm bolt – 2 off	30	Relay arm to frame bolt
13	Inner sleeve – 2 off	31	Inner sleeve
14	Dust seal – 4 off	32	Dust seal – 2 off
15	Needle roller bearing – 2 off	33	Needle roller bearing – 2 off
16	Nut – 2 off	34	Relay arm
17	Tie-rod to relay arm bolt	35	Nut
18	Dust seal – 2 off	36	Chain buffer

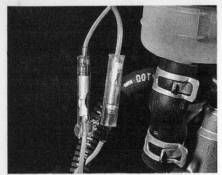
14.2a On ZX900 models disconnect the stoplamp switch wires ...

14.2b ... and remove right-hand footrest together with rear brake assembly

14.3a Note bracket which front two left-hand footrest bracket bolts screw into

14.3b Free the gearchange pedal from the left-hand footrest bracket and remove the bracket

14.3c Support the swinging arm and withdraw the pivot shaft

14.3d Tie-rod pivot shaft is retained by circlips

retaining bolts and lift the bracket clear. Remove the swinging arm pivot shaft nuts, the lower suspension unit pivot bolt and the tie-rod to swinging arm mounting bolt and withdraw them all from the right-hand side whilst supporting the swinging arm. If necessary, due to a build-up of corrosion, the shaft can be tapped from position using a hammer and drift. The swinging arm can then be lowered out of the frame.

ZX1000 B and ZX1100 C models

6   Remove the rear wheel as described in Section 4 of Chapter 6.
7   Remove the rear brake master cylinder mounting bolt and disconnect the stop lamp switch wiring from the main loom. Slacken the right-hand footrest mounting bolts and remove it from the machine, along with the rear brake reservoir and caliper assembly. Remove the chainguard and brake hose guide retaining screws from the swinging arm and lift the chainguard clear. Remove the torque arm to frame mounting bolt and lower the arm away from the machine.
8   Slacken and remove the suspension unit lower pivot bolt and the tie-rod to relay arm mounting bolt. Remove the swinging arm pivot shaft nut and withdraw the shaft whilst supporting the swinging arm. If necessary, due to a build-up of corrosion, the pivot shaft can be tapped out of position using a hammer and drift. The swinging arm can then be manoeuvred out of the frame and the tie-rods separated from it if necessary.

15   Suspension linkage: removal

ZX900 models

1   Remove the swinging arm as described in Section 14 of this Chapter.
2   To remove the relay arm it is necessary to retract the centre stand. A suitable support must therefore be placed under the crankcases and the machine safely and securely mounted on the support before retracting the stand. Once the machine is safely positioned, retract the stand and remove the relay arm to frame pivot bolt. The relay arm can then be removed from the machine.

ZX1000 A models

3   To remove the suspension linkage components it is necessary to remove the fuel tank and mounting bracket, air filter and battery bracket as described in paragraphs 4 and 5 of Section 11. Place a suitably sized block underneath the rear wheel to prevent the wheel dropping when the suspension linkage bolts are removed.
4   Remove the upper suspension unit mounting bolt and the tie-rod to relay arm pivot bolt. Slacken and remove the relay arm to frame pivot bolt and withdraw the pivot sleeve from the left-hand side of the frame. The relay arm can then be manoeuvred out of the frame. The tie-rod can then be removed after releasing the bolt which secures it to the swinging arm.

ZX1000 B and ZX1100 C models

5   Place a suitably sized block underneath the rear wheel to prevent the wheel dropping when the suspension bolts are removed.
6   Release both silencer mounting clamps and bolts and remove them from the exhaust pipes. Remove the bolt which secures the rear brake torque arm to the caliper mounting bracket and swing the torque arm clear of the suspension linkage.
7   Slacken and remove the two tie-rod upper mounting bolts and the tie-rod lower mounting bolt, then remove the tie-rods. Release the suspension unit lower mounting bolt and the relay arm to frame pivot bolt. The relay arm can then be manoeuvred out of the frame.

16   Swinging arm and suspension linkage: examination and renovation

1   Press or tap the inner sleeves out of position, noting that on ZX1000 B and ZX1100 C models the swinging arm pivot sleeve must be withdrawn from the left-hand side, and carefully lever out the dust seals. Clean off all the old grease and road dirt so that the components can be checked for wear. Do not remove the needle roller bearings unless renewal is necessary.
2   Examine the pivot sleeves for wear or corrosion and the needle

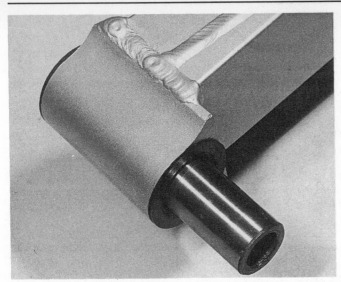

16.2a Examine pivot inner sleeves ...

16.2b ... and needle roller bearings for wear or damage

roller bearings for signs of damage or discoloration. If either component is damaged in any way both the bearing(s) and sleeve should be renewed as a set. The needle roller bearings can be drifted out of position and the new ones fitted using a drawbolt arrangement as shown in the accompanying illustration. The pivot shaft should also be examined for wear or damage. Check for trueness by rolling the shaft across a flat surface, renewing it if bent. The dust seals should be renewed regardless of their apparent condition.

3   On ZX1000 B and ZX1100 C models the outer right-hand needle roller bearing is of the ball journal type and is retained by a circlip. This can be checked for wear by spinning the inner race of the bearing. If there is any sign of roughness the bearing should be renewed. It can be drifted out once the circlip has been removed and the bearing tapped into position using a suitably sized socket, which bears only on the outer race of the bearing. Refit the circlip ensuring that it is correctly seated in its groove.

4   Press the dust seals into place and pack the bearings with molybdenum disulphide grease. Grease the inner sleeves and insert them in the bearings.

17 Suspension linkage: refitting

1   Lubricate all suspension unit and linkage mounting bolts with

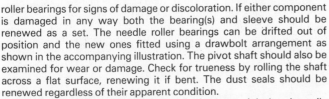

molybdenum disulphide grease, having first checked them for wear as described in the previous section.

ZX900 models
2   Offer up the relay arm, ensuring that the arrow cast on one side of the arm is pointing forwards, and refit the relay arm to frame mounting bolt. Tighten the bolt to the specified torque setting and manoeuvre the machine off its temporary stand and place it on the centre stand. Refit the swinging arm as described in Section 18 of this Chapter.

ZX1000 A models
3   Refit the tie-rod to the swinging arm and tighten its mounting bolt to the specified torque setting. Offer up the relay arm, ensuring that the arrow cast on one side of the arm is pointing forwards. Refit the pivot sleeve from the left-hand side of the frame having first applied molybdenum disulphide grease to its outer surface. Fit the suspension unit upper bolt, the relay arm to frame pivot bolt and the tie-rod to relay arm pivot bolt, tightening them all to the specified torque setting. Refit the battery bracket, air filter assembly and fuel tank with mounting bracket as described in paragraphs 4 and 5 of Section 13.

ZX1000 B and ZX1100 C models
4   Offer up the relay arm and install the relay arm to frame pivot bolt and the lower suspension unit mounting bolt, tightening both to the specified torque settings. Position the tie-rods and refit both of their upper mounting bolts, followed by the lower mounting bolt; tighten them to the specified torque setting. Refit the rear brake torque arm to caliper bracket retaining bolt, tightening it to its specified torque setting, and refit the silencers.

All models
5   Thoroughly check the operation of the rear suspension before taking the machine on the road.

18 Swinging arm: refitting

1   Lubricate the pivot bolts of all the disconnected suspension linkage components and also the swinging arm pivot shaft with molybdenum disulphide grease.

ZX900 models
2   Refit the tie-rods to the swinging arm and tighten the mounting bolt to the specified torque setting. Offer up the swinging arm assembly and fit the pivot shaft from the right-hand side. Refit the pivot shaft nut and tighten it to the specified torque setting.
3   Remount the gearchange linkage on the left-hand footrest bracket, securing it with the circlip, and fit the bracket to the machine. Install the

17.2 Ensure relay arm is fitted with arrow pointing forwards (ZX900)

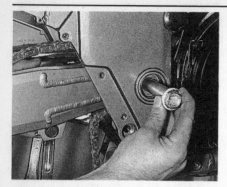

18.5a Offer up the swinging arm, refit the pivot shaft and tighten it to the specified torque setting

18.5b Refit the rear brake torque arm, tightening its retaining bolt to the specified torque ...

18.5c ... and fit the chainguard to the swinging arm

right-hand footrest bracket and rear brake assembly and tighten the bracket retaining bolts securely. Refit the brake reservoir mounting bolt and connect the rear brake stop lamp switch wires. Fit the outer swinging arm pivot shaft nuts and tighten them to the specified torque setting. Refit the exhaust silencers.

ZX1000 A models
4   Offer up the swinging arm and refit the pivot shaft from the right-hand side. Refit the suspension unit lower mounting bolt and the swinging arm to tie-rod mounting bolt from the right-hand side. Tighten all the above bolts to their specified torque settings. Refit the left-hand footrest bracket, securely tightening its retaining bolts, and refit the silencers.

ZX1000 B and ZX1100 C models
5   Position the swinging arm and refit its pivot shaft, followed by the suspension unit lower bolt and the tie-rod to relay arm bolt, tightening them all to the specified torque setting. Refit the rear brake torque arm, tightening its mounting bolts to the specified torque setting, and secure the brake hose guides and chainguard to the swinging arm. **Note:** *Make sure that the brake hose is held well clear of the brake disc by the clamps on the swinging arm.* Fit the right-hand footrest bracket and rear brake assembly to the machine and tighten the reservoir and footrest bracket mounting bolts securely. Reconnect the stop lamp switch wiring.

All models
6   Refit the rear wheel as described in Section 5 of Chapter 6 and thoroughly check the operation of the rear suspension and brake before taking the machine on the road.

19   Footrests, stands and controls: examination and renovation

1   At regular intervals all footrests, the stand, the brake pedal and the gearchange lever should be checked and lubricated at the intervals specified in Routine maintenance. Check that all mounting nuts and bolts are securely fastened, using the torque settings where these are given. Check that any securing split pins are correctly fitted.
2   Check that the bearing surfaces at all pivot points are well greased and unworn, renewing any component that is excessively worn. If lubrication is required, dismantle the assembly to ensure that grease can be packed fully into the bearing surface. Return springs, where fitted, must be in good condition with no traces of fatigue and must be securely mounted.
3   If accident damage is to be repaired, check that the damaged component is not cracked or broken. Such damage may be repaired by welding, but note that welding of aluminium components should only be entrusted to an expert in this field. Note, however, that such a repair will destroy the finish of the component, and renewal may therefore be the most satisfactory course of action. If a steel component is merely bent it can be straightened after the affected area has been heated to a dull cherry red colour, using a blowlamp or welding torch. Again the finish will be destroyed, but the surface can be refinished at relatively low cost.

20   Speedometer and tachometer heads: removal, examination and refitting

1   The instrument assembly is secured to the fairing mounting bracket by two bolts. On ZX900 and ZX1000 A models these bolts are readily accessible, although on ZX1100 C models it will first be necessary to remove the upper fairing, and on ZX1000 B models the upper fairing inner sections and screen.
2   Remove the instrument panel mounting bolts and partially withdraw the assembly. Unscrew the speedometer drive cable retaining ring from the underside of the panel and separate the instrument panel wiring from the main loom. The assembly can then be lifted clear of the machine.
3   Slacken all the screws which retain the bottom cover and remove it from the assembly. Release the two nuts which secure the instruments to the mounting bracket and separate the two components. The top cover can be removed once its retaining screws have been withdrawn.
4   Each instrument head is mounted onto the housing by two small crosshead screws. Before removing the speedometer on ZX900 and ZX1000 models it is first necessary to remove the upper speedometer drive gearbox. This is also retained by two small crosshead screws. On all models disconnect the tachometer wiring before attempting to remove the instrument head.
5   Note that these instruments are delicate and should be handled carefully at all times. Do not drop them or hold them upside down as this will damage the heads. Also do not allow them to come into contact with any dirt, grease, oil or water.
6   The speedometer and tachometer heads are sealed units and cannot be dismantled any further. Apart from defects in the drive or drive cable (speedometer) or relevant wiring (tachometer) an instru-

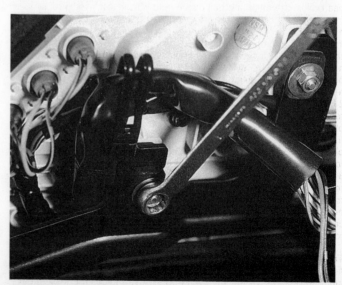

20.3 Instrument are retained to mounting bracket by two nuts

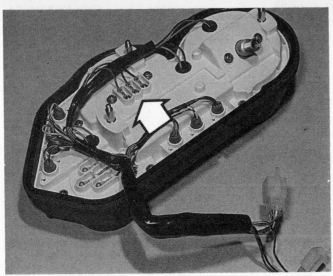

20.4 Disconnect the tachometer wiring connectors (arrowed) before attempting to remove it from the panel

22.2 Unscrew knurled retaining ring to remove speedometer cable (ZX1100 shown)

ment is difficult to repair and must be renewed. Alternatively, it may be possible to have the instrument repaired by a suitable specialist or to obtain a second-hand item from a breaker.

7   The electronic tachometer can be tested as described in Chapter 7.

8   Remember that a speedometer in correct working order is a statutory requirement in the UK. Apart from this legal necessity, reference to the odometer readings is the most satisfactory means of keeping track with the maintenance schedules.

9   The instrument heads are refitted by a reversal of the removal procedure, taking care not to overtighten the instrument panel screws. Examine the damping rubbers fitted to the mounting bracket, renewing them if necessary.

21   Speedometer and tachometer drives: examination and renovation

Speedometer

1   On ZX900 and ZX1000 models the speedometer has two drive gearboxes, the main one being mounted on the left-hand side of the front wheel and the other just under the instrument. The ZX1100 C models use only the wheel mounted gearbox. The gearbox in the instrument assembly (where fitted) serves only to transmit the drive through 90° and is maintenance free; if a fault develops in this component, it should be renewed. The main wheel-mounted gearbox should be lubricated with a high melting-point grease whenever the wheel is removed, and if failure occurs it can be overhauled as follows:

2   Remove the front wheel as described in Section 2 of Chapter 6 and remove the gearbox assembly from the wheel. The speedometer drive plate is retained in the hub by a circlip. Lever out the oil seal and tip out the larger drive gear. If it proves necessary to renew the small driven pinion or bush, the roll pin must be removed from the housing as follows.

3   Pass a 1 mm drill up through the centre of the pin and drill through the gearbox housing. Using the 1 mm hole as a pilot hole, drill a 3.0 - 3.5 mm hole in the underside of the gearbox housing. The roll pin can then be tapped out of place with a drift. The bush, pinion and thrust washers can then be removed from the housing. On reassembly always fit a new roll pin and stake it in place to prevent it dropping out.

Tachometer

4   The tachometer is electrically operated and is controlled by the ignition system. Should the tachometer malfunction the instrument head and relevant wiring should be examined as described in Chapter 7.

22   Speedometer drive cable: examination and maintenance

1   The cable is secured at each end by knurled rings which should be slackened and tightened with a pair of pliers. If the cable is thought to be at fault, remove it from the machine, and spin the inner cable at one end. If the other end of the cable fails to turn, the cable is broken and should be renewed.

2   If the operation of the speedometer has become jerky and excessive force is needed to turn the cable manually as described above, the cable should be renewed. Lubrication is difficult with this type of cable, but an aerosol chain lubricant or a silicone-based lubricant can often be introduced using the aerosol's thin extension nozzle. Do not apply excess lubricant to the upper end of the cable otherwise there is a risk of it working up into the instrument head. On refitting ensure the cable is correctly routed, secured by any ties or guides and is not trapped or kinked anywhere.

23   Fairing: removal and refitting

ZX900 models

1   Slacken and remove the eight screws which secure the lower fairing to the middle fairing and the screws which retain the lower fairing inner covers. Release both the lower fairing mounting bolts and nuts and lower the fairing away from the machine.

2   Remove the six middle fairing mounting bolts, all of which are situated below the radiator, and carefully lower the middle fairing away from the machine noting the tangs that locate with the upper fairing. If necessary, the cowlings fitted to each side of the radiator can then be removed once their retaining screws have been released.

3   Slacken and remove the top yoke cover retaining screws and lift the cover clear. Release the knurled ring which retains the upper end of the speedometer cable and free the cable from the instrument panel. Remove the two bolts which mount the instrument assembly to the fairing bracket and pull the assembly upwards. Cover the fuel tank with a clean thick cloth and rest the instruments on the fuel tank. Ensure the instruments are left in an upright position to prevent them being damaged in any way.

4   Release the screws which retain each of the upper fairing inner covers and manoeuvre them out of the fairing, taking care not to scratch the windscreen. Remove the rear view mirror mounting screws and remove both mirrors from the fairing. Slacken and remove the two headlamp cover retaining bolts situated on the underside of the upper

Fig. 5.10 Fairing – ZX900 models

1   Windscreen
2   Upper fairing inner covers
3   Rear view mirrors
4   Upper fairing
5   Upper fairing mounting
    bracket
6   Headlamp inspection cover
7   Middle fairing
8   Damping rubbers
9   Lower fairing
10 Lower fairing inner covers
11 Bracket
12 Lower fairing bracket

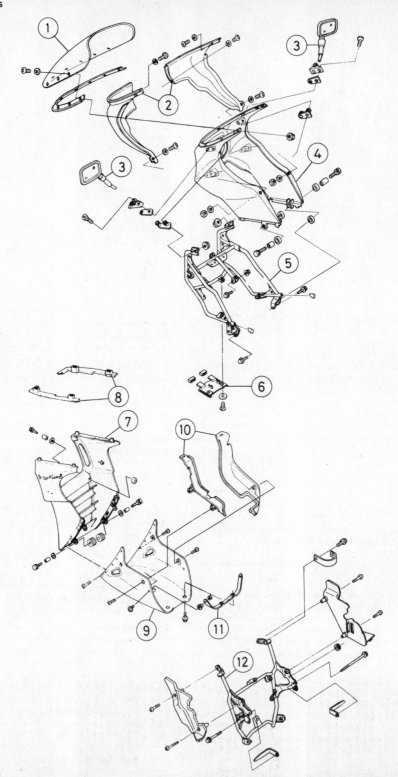

fairing and lower the cover away from the machine. Disconnect the turn signal and headlamp wiring connectors and remove the fairing mounting bolts. The upper fairing can then be manoeuvred clear of its mounting bracket.

5   If the fairing mounting bracket is also to be removed it will first be necessary to remove the fuel tank as described in Chapter 3. Disconnect all the wiring connectors situated on the left-hand side of the bracket and remove all the bracket mounting bolts. Lift the bracket away from the machine taking care not to damage the radiator.

6   On refitting tighten all the fairing mounting bracket bolts securely (if

removed) and connect the relevant wiring. Install the upper fairing and refit the mounting bolts and rear view mirrors. Do not omit the rubber dampers which are fitted behind both the rear view mirrors and on all the mounting bolt holes, or the collars which are fitted to the mounting bolts. Refit the inner covers, again taking care not to scratch the windscreen, and tighten their retaining screws securely. Remount the instrument assembly on the fairing bracket and reconnect the speedometer cable to its drive gearbox, ensuring that the speedometer cable is correctly routed and the left-hand instrument assembly retaining bolt is positioned in the left-hand hole in the fairing bracket. Connect

23.1 ZX900 – note the nuts fitted to the two lower fairing mounting bolts

23.2a Middle fairing section is retained by two bolts on each side ...

23.2b ... and two bolts at the front

23.2c Radiator cowlings are retained by two screws

23.3 Cover the fuel tank with a clean rag and rest the instrument panel on the tank

23.4a Slacken the upper inner fairing retaining screws and carefully remove the inner fairing sections

23.4b Remove the rear view mirror mounting screws ...

23.4c ... and disconnect the turn signal wiring connectors

23.4d Remove the upper fairing mounting screws ...

23.4e ... and bolts to permit its removal

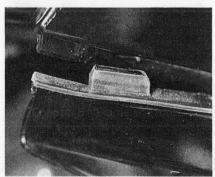

23.7a On refitting do not omit rubber dampers which are fitted to the tangs on the middle fairing section ...

23.7b ... or the spacers that are fitted to its mounting bolts

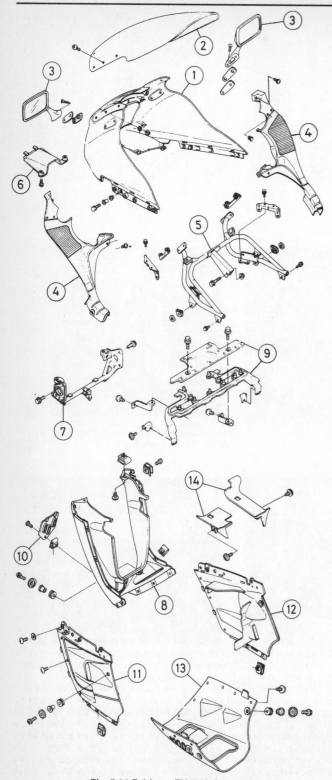

Fig. 5.11 Fairing – ZX1000 A models

1	Upper fairing	8	Centre fairing
2	Windscreen	9	Centre fairing bracket
3	Rear view mirrors	10	Coolant expansion tank
4	Upper fairing inner covers		inspection cover
5	Upper fairing mounting	11	Left-hand side fairing
	bracket	12	Right-hand side fairing
6	Headlamp inspection	13	Lower fairing
	cover	14	Side fairing inner covers
7	Oil cooler bracket		

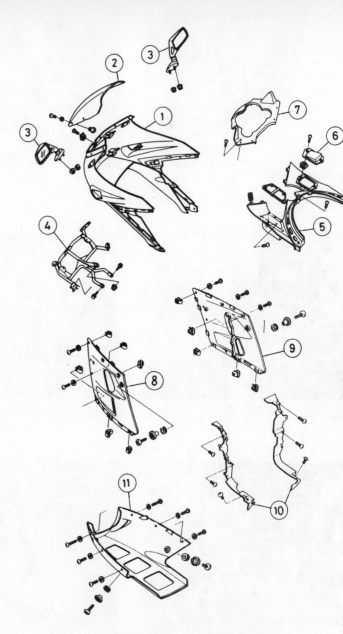

Fig. 5.12 Fairing – ZX1000 B models

1	Upper fairing	7	Front inner cover
2	Windscreen	8	Left-hand side fairing
3	Rear view mirrors	9	Right-hand side fairing
4	Upper fairing bracket	10	Side fairing inner covers
5	Upper fairing inner cover	11	Lower fairing
6	Reservoir access cover		

the turn signal and headlamp wiring connectors and refit the headlamp cover.

7   Before installing the middle fairing ensure the rubber dampers are fitted correctly to the tangs at the top of the section and the bolt holes at the bottom, and refit the radiator cowlings (if removed). Fit the middle fairing, ensuring that the tangs locate correctly in the upper fairing, and tighten its mounting bolts securely. Position the lower fairing and install the bottom mounting bolts finger-tight only. Refit the inner covers to the lower fairing and again tighten their retaining screws finger-tight only. Finally fit the screws that join the lower fairing to the middle fairing and tighten all the lower fairing screws securely.

Fig. 5.13 Fairing – ZX1100 C models

1   *Windscreen*
2   *Upper fairing*
3   *Rear view mirrors*
4   *Front inner cover*
5   *Reservoir access cover*
6   *Upper fairing inner covers*
7   *Upper fairing mounting
    bracket*
8   *Left-hand side fairing*
9   *Side fairing inner covers*
10 *Right-hand side fairing*
11 *Inner cover bracket*

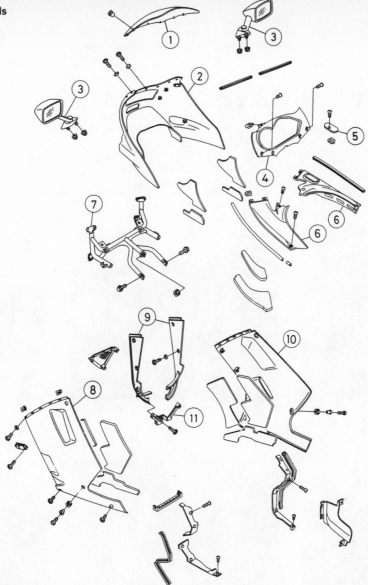

ZX1000 A models

8   Slacken and remove all screws which secure the lower fairing to the front and side fairings followed by the two main mounting screws and lower the fairing away from the machine. Prise out the caps which cover the front turn signal retaining screws and release the screws. Remove the turn signals from the fairing and disconnect their wiring connectors. Remove all the screws which secure each side fairing section to the upper and front fairings followed by the main mounting screw, and lift each one clear of the machine. Release the screws which secure the front fairing to the upper fairing and the front fairing mounting screws and remove the front fairing section.

9   Release the upper fairing inner cover retaining screws and manoeuvre them out of the fairing, taking care not to damage the windscreen. Disconnect the headlamp bulb wiring connector. Prise out the caps which cover the rear view mirror mounting screws, slacken the screws and remove both mirrors. Release the two upper fairing mounting bolts and remove it from the machine.

10   On refitting, do not omit the rubber dampers which are fitted to all the mounting bolt holes and behind the rear view mirrors, or the collars fitted to all the mounting bolts. Install the upper fairing and refit the rear view mirrors and both mounting bolts. Before tightening the mounting bolts ensure the turn signal wiring connectors are positioned in the cutaways on the lower edge of the fairing. Connect the headlamp wiring and refit the inner covers, taking care not to scratch the windscreen, and

tighten its retaining screws securely. Align the upper edge of the front fairing with the flange on the lower edge of the upper fairing and fit all its mounting bolts finger-tight. Once all the bolts are in place and the fairing is correctly positioned tighten the bolts securely.

11   Ensure the rubber dampers are in position on the inside of each side fairing section and fit the side fairings to the machine. Locate the tabs on the front edge of the side fairings with the slots in the front section of the fairing and refit all the mounting bolts. Ensure the dampers are in position on the lower fairing inner covers and install the lower fairing. Align the lower fairing with the flanges on the front and side sections and fit all the mounting screws. Once all the screws are in place and the lower fairing is correctly positioned, tighten all the screws securely.

ZX1000 B models

12   Slacken and remove the six screws which secure the lower fairing to the side fairings and the two main mounting bolts. The lower fairing can then be lowered away from the machine. Remove all the screws which retain the side fairings and lift both side fairings clear .

13   Release the windscreen from the fairing by slackening its mounting screws. Remove all the upper fairing front inner cover retaining screws and lift the cover away from the instrument assembly. Slacken the nuts which retain the rear view mirrors and remove them from the machine. Disconnect the turn signal and headlamp wiring block connec-

tor and remove the upper fairing from the machine. If necessary, the inner fairing covers can be removed by releasing the relevant screws.

14   The fairing is fitted by a reversal of the removal sequence. Do not omit the rubber dampers and collars that are fitted to the side and lower fairing mounting bolts and avoid overtightening the windscreen mounting screws.

ZX1100 C models

15   Slacken and remove all the screws which retain the lower fairing side sections to the upper fairing and the frame and lift them clear of the machine.

16   Remove the seven screws that secure the windscreen to the fairing and remove the screen. Release all the screws which retain the upper fairing front inner cover and lift it away from the instrument assembly. Then remove both the left and right-hand side inner covers, each one being retained by two screws. Disconnect the turn signal and headlamp wiring block connector. Release the nuts which retain the rear view mirrors and remove them both. The upper fairing can then be removed from the machine.

17   The fairing is fitted by a reversal of the removal procedure. Do not omit the rubber dampers and collars from the lower fairing mounting bolts (where fitted) and avoid overtightening the windscreen mounting screws. Also ensure that the insulating rubbers that are fitted to the inside of the lower fairing sections are correctly fitted.

23.16a ZX1100 C – on refitting do not omit insulating rubbers from lower fairing sections

23.16b Offer up the upper fairing section ...

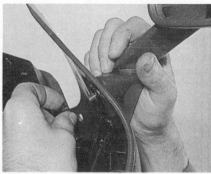
23.16c ... and refit the rear view mirrors

23.16d Refit the front inner cover ...

23.16e ... and screen; tighten screen retaining screws securely

23.16f Refit both right and left side inner fairing sections

23.16g Offer up the lower fairing sections ...

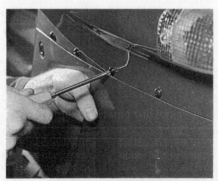
23.16h ... fit all its retaining screws ...

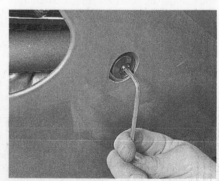
23.16i ... and bolts tightening them securely

Chapter 6 Wheels, brakes and tyres

Refer to Chapter 8 for information on the ZX1100 D model

Contents

Specifications

Wheels

Type	Cast alloy
Rim maximum runout:	
Radial	0.8 mm (0.032 in)
Axial	0.5 mm (0.020 in)

Brakes

Minimum disc thickness:	
Front:	
ZX900 A7-on models...	4.0 mm (0.16 in)
All other models...	4.5 mm (0.18 in)
Rear:	
ZX900 A1 to A6 models...	6.0 mm (0.24 in)
All other models...	5.0 mm (0.20 in)
Disc maximum warpage	0.3 mm (0.0118 in)
Recommended brake fluid	DOT 4 specification

Tyres

	Front	Rear
Type	Tubeless	
Size:		
ZX900 A1 to A6 models	120/80V16-V250	130/80V18-V250
ZX900 A7-on models	120/70V17-V250	150/70V18-V250
ZX1000 A models	120/80V16-V270	150/80V16-V270
ZX1000 B models	120/70VR17-V280	160/60VR18-V280
ZX1100 C models	120/70VR17-V290	170/60VR17-V290

Tyre pressures

	Front	Rear
UK ZX900 A1 to A6 models:		
Up to 97.5 kg (215 lb) load, below 130 mph (210 kmh)	2.25 kg/cm²(32 psi)	2.50 kg/cm²(36 psi)
97.5 – 181 kg (215 – 399 lb) load, below 130 mph (210 kmh)	2.50 kg/cm²(36 psi)	2.50 kg/cm²(36 psi)
Above 130 mph (210 kmh)..	2.50 kg/cm²(36 psi)	2.90 kg/cm²(41 psi)
UK ZX900 A7-on models..	2.50 kg/cm²(36 psi)	2.90 kg/cm²(41 psi)
US ZX900 A1 to A3 models:		
Up to 97.5 kg (215 lb) load...	2.25 kg/cm²(32 psi)	2.50 kg/cm²(36 psi)
97.5 – 180 kg (215 – 397 lb) load	2.50 kg/cm²(36 psi)	2.50 kg/cm²(36 psi)
UK ZX1000 A models:		
Below 130 mph (210 kmh)..	2.50 kg/cm²(36 psi)	2.50 kg/cm²(36 psi)
Above 130 mph (210 kmh)..	2.50 kg/cm²(36 psi)	2.90 kg/cm²(41 psi)
UK ZX1000 B models:		
Up to 97.5 kg (215 lb) load, below 130 mph (210 kmh).................	2.50 kg/cm²(36 psi)	2.50 kg/cm²(36 psi)
97.5 – 181 kg (215 – 399 lb) load, below 130 mph (210 kmh)	2.50 kg/cm²(36 psi)	2.90 kg/cm²(41 psi)
Above 130 mph (210 kmh)..	2.50 kg/cm²(36 psi)	2.90 kg/cm²(41 psi)
US ZX1000 A and ZX1000 B models.................................	2.50 kg/cm²(36 psi)	2.90 kg/cm²(41 psi)
ZX1100 C models	2.90 kg/cm²(41 psi)	2.90 kg/cm²(41 psi)

Torque settings

Component	kgf m	lbf ft
Wheel spindles:		
ZX900 models – front and rear	9.0	65.0
ZX1000 A models:		
Front..	6.5	47.0
Rear...	9.0	65.0
ZX1000 B models:		
Front..	9.0	65.0
Rear...	11.0	80.0

Torque settings (continued)

Component	kgf m	lbf ft
ZX1100 C models – front and rear..	11.0	80.0
Front spindle pinch bolts:		
ZX900 and ZX1000 A models..	2.1	15.0
All other models	2.0	14.5
Rear wheel chain adjuster pinch bolts..	4.0	29.0
Rear sprocket retaining nuts:		
ZX900 A1 to A6 models:		
Before Frame No. ZX900A-016130	7.0	51.0
After Frame No. ZX900A-016131	8.8	64.0
ZX1000 A models	11.0	80.0
ZX900 A7-on, ZX1000 B and ZX1100 C models....................	7.5	54.0
Brake disc bolts:		
ZX900, ZX1000 A and ZX1100 C models	2.3	17.0
ZX1000 B models:		
Front disc	3.5	25.0
Rear disc	2.3	17.0
Brake caliper mounting bolts:		
ZX900 A1 to A6 and ZX1000 A models	3.4	24.0
ZX900 A7-on, ZX1000 B and ZX1100 C models....................	3.5	25.0
Front brake caliper joining bolts – ZX900 A7 and 1100 C models.......	2.1	15.0
Front master cylinder clamp bolts:		
ZX900 A1 to A6 and ZX1000 A models	0.9	6.5
ZX900 A7-on, ZX1000 B and ZX1100 C models....................	1.1	8.0
Brake hose union bolts	2.5	18.0
Torque arm nuts/bolts..	2.5	18.0
Metal brake pipe gland nuts – anti-dive models only............................	1.5	11.0
Anti-dive plunger housing bolts...	0.45	3.3
Bleed nipples	0.8	5.8

1 General description

All models use cast alloy wheels which are designed to run with tubeless tyres. Although the wheels vary in size and style, all are very similar in construction. Both front and rear brakes are hydraulically operated discs, a twin disc set up at the front and a single at the rear.

On ZX900 A1 to A6 models and ZX1000 A models, the front braking system is also used to actuate the anti-dive units fitted to the front forks. These are hydraulically operated from a junction box situated on each lower fork leg.

2 Front wheel: removal

1   Place the machine on its centre stand, leaving adequate space around the wheel area. Slacken the knurled ring which retains the speedometer cable to its drive gearbox and pull the cable clear of the wheel.
2   On all models except the ZX900 A1 to A6, remove the brake caliper mounting bolts and lift both calipers clear of the discs. Place a wooden wedge between the brake pads to prevent their expulsion if the brake lever is accidentally operated, and tie both calipers to the frame to avoid straining the hydraulic hoses.
3   On ZX900 A1 to A6 models it is necessary to remove only one of the calipers. Remove the caliper mounting bolts and wait until the wheel has been lowered out of the forks as described below before removing the caliper.
4   On all models, release the wheel spindle pinch bolt(s) situated on the right-hand lower fork leg and slacken the wheel spindle from the right-hand side.
5   Remove the lower fairing, as described in Chapter 5, and place some blocks or a suitable stand underneath the engine so that the front wheel is raised clear of the ground. Support the wheel and withdraw the spindle from the right-hand side. The wheel can then be lowered to the ground and removed from the machine. On ZX900 A1 to A6 models slide the caliper off the disc, placing a wedge between the pads and tying the caliper to the machine as described above.
6   Note that the wheel should not be placed on its side with the weight resting on one of the brake discs as this could distort the disc. Place a wooden block beneath the wheel rim or rest the wheel against a wall.
7   Refer to Routine maintenance for details of wheel examination.

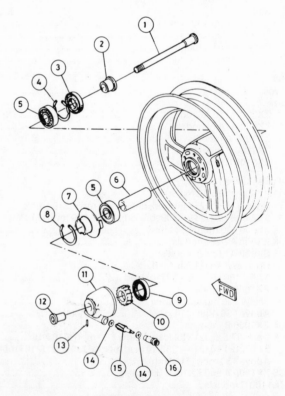

Fig. 6.1 Front wheel - typical

1	Wheel spindle	9	Oil seal
2	Right-hand spacer	10	Speedometer drive gear
3	Oil seal	11	Drive gear housing
4	Circlip	12	Nut
5	Bearing – 2 off	13	Pin
6	Central spacer	14	Washer – 2 off
7	Speedometer drive ring	15	Speedometer driven gear
8	Circlip	16	Bush

3 Front wheel: refitting

1   On reassembly, grease the speedometer gearbox and the lips of the oil seal fitted to the right-hand side of the hub. Refit the speedometer gearbox to the left-hand side of the wheel, ensuring that the tangs on its drive plate engage correctly with the slots in the hub. Insert the spacer into the right-hand side of the hub. Check that the spindle is straight and free from corrosion and smear a small amount of high melting-point grease along its shank.

2   Remove the wooden wedge from the brake caliper and refit it to the relevant disc on the wheel (ZX900 A1 to A6 models only). Offer up the wheel and insert the spindle from the right-hand side. Position the speedometer gearbox so that the projection on the gearbox is in contact with the lug on the lower fork leg and then tighten the wheel spindle and pinch bolts to their specified torque settings.

3   On all other models except the ZX900 A1 to A6, remove the wooden wedges from the brake calipers and refit the calipers to the discs. On all models, refit the caliper mounting bolts, tightening them to the specified torque setting, and refit the speedometer cable.

4   Remove the blocks or stand from underneath the engine and refit the lower fairing section. Push the machine off the centre stand and apply the front brake, pumping the lever until normal operation of the brake returns. Thoroughly check the operation of the front brake and forks before taking the machine on the road.

4 Rear wheel: removal

1   Place the machine on its centre stand on level ground. On ZX900 and ZX1000 A models, release the right-hand silencer mounting clamp and bolt and remove the silencer from the exhaust pipe. On all models remove the rear caliper mounting bolts and remove the caliper from the disc. Place a wooden wedge between the brake pads to prevent their expulsion if the brake pedal is accidentally operated, and support the caliper in such a way as to avoid placing any strain on the brake hose.

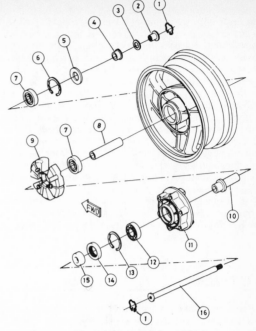

Fig. 6.2 Rear wheel – typical

1   Circlip – 2 off
2   Nut
3   Washer
4   Right-hand spacer
5   Oil seal
6   Circlip
7   Wheel bearing – 2 off
8   Central spacer
9   Cush drive rubbers
10 Cush drive hub spacer
11 Cush drive hub/sprocket carrier
12 Bearing
13 Circlip
14 Oil seal
15 Left-hand spacer
16 Wheel spindle

3.1a Refit speedometer gearbox ensuring that it is correctly located ...

3.1b ... and refit spacer to right-hand side of the wheel

3.2a Manoeuvre the wheel into position and refit the spindle

3.2b Ensure lugs on speedometer gearbox are correctly positioned ...

3.2c ... then tighten the wheel spindle ...

3.2d ... and pinch bolts to their specified torque settings

2   ZX900 models release the locknut on the caliper bracket fixing bolt and then remove both the fixing bolt and the caliper bracket collar retaining bolt. Remove the caliper bracket collar from the swinging arm lug and store it with the bolts for safekeeping. On all other models, slacken and remove the caliper bracket to torque arm retaining bolt.

3   Slacken both chain adjuster pinch bolts situated in the ends of the swinging arm, and rotate one of the adjusters to obtain the maximum drive chain free play possible. Using a small flat-bladed screwdriver, prise out the right-hand wheel spindle retaining circlip and remove the spindle nut and washer. Remove the left-hand spindle circlip and withdraw the wheel spindle whilst supporting the wheel. The spindle can be tapped out of position if necessary using a hammer and a suitable drift. Remove the caliper mounting bracket from the right-hand side of the wheel and lower the wheel to the ground. Disengage the drive chain from its sprocket and loop the chain over the swinging arm end. Remove the wheel from the machine.

4   Note that the wheel should not be placed on its side with the weight resting on the brake disc as this could distort the disc.

5   Refer to Routine maintenance for details of wheel examination.

5   Rear wheel: refitting

1   Apply a small amount of grease to the lips of the rear wheel oil seals and refit the spacers. Check that the wheel spindle is straight and free from corrosion and smear a small amount of high melting-point grease along its shank to assist refitting.

2   Loop the final drive chain over the sprocket, offer up the wheel and partially insert the spindle from the left-hand side. Slide the caliper mounting bracket into position and push the spindle fully in. Refit the left-hand spindle retaining circlip, ensuring that it is correctly seated in the groove provided, and fit the spindle nut and washer. Tighten it by hand only at this stage.

3   On ZX900 models refit the caliper collar, collar retaining bolt and caliper bracket fixing bolt. Do not tighten either bolt at this stage, until the wheel alignment and chain tension have been set. On all other

models refit the caliper bracket to torque arm bolt, tightening it finger-tight only.

4   Remove the wooden wedge from between the brake pads, install the caliper on the disc and refit its mounting bolts, tightening them to the specified torque setting.

5   Adjust the wheel alignment and chain tension as described in Routine maintenance. Tighten the wheel spindle, chain adjuster pinch bolts and the caliper bracket to torque arm bolt to their specified torque settings and ensure that the right-hand spindle retaining circlip is correctly seated in its groove. On ZX900 and ZX1000 A models refit the right-hand silencer and tighten its mounting bolt and clamp securely.

6   Finally, on all models pump the rear brake pedal until the pads are pushed back into contact with the disc and thoroughly check the operation of the rear brake before taking the machine on the road.

6   Wheel bearings: removal, examination and refitting

Front wheel

1   Remove the front wheel from the machine as described in Section 2. Although it is not strictly necessary to remove the brake discs for this task, it is strongly advised due to the fact that this will make the task easier and prevent the discs being damaged.

2   Remove the circlip from the left-hand side of the hub and withdraw the speedometer drive plate. Working from the right-hand side of the hub carefully lever out the oil seal, using a large flat-bladed screwdriver, and remove the circlip behind it.

3   Support the wheel so that the hub is clear of the work surface. Pass a long drift through the hub, push the internal spacer to one side and drive out the right-hand bearing, tapping evenly all around its inner race. The spacer will drop out. Invert the wheel and drive out the remaining bearing.

4   Removing the bearings in this way will almost certainly damage them if they are a tight fit, but there is no alternative. Wash each bearing thoroughly removing all old grease, then spin each one. If any signs of roughness can be heard or felt, if any free play can be felt or if any pitting

5.1a Do not omit the right-hand ...

5.1b ... and left-hand wheel spacers

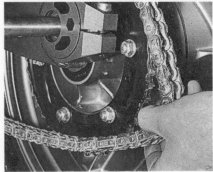

5.2a Engage the final drive chain on the sprocket ...

5.2b ... then lift up the wheel and partially insert spindle

5.2c Slide the rear brake caliper assembly into position ...

5.2d ... push the spindle fully in and fit the washer and spindle nut

6.5a Drive first wheel bearing into position ...

6.5b ... then invert the wheel and insert central spacer

6.5c Grease the cavity and fit the second bearing

6.5d On the front wheel locate speedometer drive plate with slots in hub ...

6.5e ... and secure with the circlip

can be seen on the balls or their tracks, the bearings must be renewed. The oil seal should be renewed as a matter of course.

5   On reassembly, pack the bearings with high melting-point grease and refit the bearings with their sealed surface facing outwards. Drive the bearing into place using a tubular drift such as a socket spanner which bears only on the bearing's outer race. Turn the wheel over and refit the spacer, then pack the central recess no more than 2/3 full with high melting-point grease and refit the right-hand bearing, sealed surface outwards, as described above. Refit the circlip and oil seal to the right-hand side of the hub. Refit the speedometer drive plate to the left-hand side of the hub, ensuring that the tangs on the plate are correctly engaged in the slots in the hub, followed by the circlip. Refit the brake discs, if removed, and tighten their mounting bolts to the specified torque setting.

Rear wheel

6   Remove the rear wheel from the machine as described in Section 4 and remove the sprocket carrier assembly. Lever out the oil seal from the right-hand side of the hub and remove the circlip behind it.

7   Remove, examine and install the bearings as described above for the front wheel.

---

7 Rear wheel cush drive: examination and renovation

---

1   Remove the rear wheel as described in Section 4. The sprocket is retained by six nuts, these being easier to slacken whilst the assembly is still fitted to the wheel.

2   Remove the carrier assembly from the wheel then remove the

sprocket retaining nuts and lift off the sprocket. Pull out the spacers from each side of the assembly, noting which way round the shouldered inner spacer is fitted, then carefully lever out the oil seal and remove the circlip to allow the bearing to be driven out from the inside.

3   Remove the bearing, clean and examine it as described in Section 6,

7.5a Renew cush drive rubbers if perished

7.5b Do not omit spacer from sprocket carrier on reassembly

8.3 Where discs show a stamped arrow ensure this faces in normal direction of wheel rotation

renewing it if necessary. Pack the bearing with high melting-point grease and fit it to the carrier, securing it with the circlip. The oil seal should be renewed regardless of its condition.

4   If the rear sprocket teeth are hooked, chipped, missing or worn the sprocket must be renewed, but this should be done only in conjunction with a new gearbox sprocket and final drive chain. Refit the sprocket on the carrier and tighten all retaining nuts to the specified torque setting. Insert the spacers into both sides of the carrier assembly, ensuring that they are refitted in their original positions.

5   Examine the cush drive rubber block; if perished, split, damaged or compressed to the extent that there is excessive movement between the sprocket carrier and wheel, it must be renewed. It can be pulled out of the hub by hand. The new rubber block will be a tight fit; lubricate it with a very small amount of soapy water, not oil, to aid installation. Note that on some ZX1000B1 models instances have occurred of the cush drive rubbers distorting, leading to excessive backlash at the rear wheel. In such cases a modification is available from the manufacturer, consisting of three plastic inserts which are glued to the rubbers to strengthen them.

8   Brake discs: examination and renovation

1   Examine the brake discs for scoring, particularly the rear unit which is more vulnerable to accumulations of road dirt. Damaged discs will cause poor braking and will wear pads quickly, and should therefore be renewed. The disc thickness can be measured with a micrometer and should not be less than the service limit specified.

2   Check for warpage with the relevant wheel raised clear of the ground, using a dial gauge probe running near the edge of the disc. Warpage must not exceed the maximum figure when the disc is rotated. Note that a warped disc will cause judder during braking.

3   The discs can be removed after the appropriate wheel has been removed from the machine. Each disc is retained by a number of bolts. When refitting the disc, ensure that the mating surfaces are clean and that the chamfered hole side of the disc faces inwards or the marked surface outwards, as appropriate. Tighten the retaining bolts to the specified torque setting. On some models the brake discs are marked with an arrow; if this is the case the disc must be fitted with the arrow pointing in the normal direction of wheel rotation.

9   Brake calipers: removal, overhaul and refitting

Note: *brake fluid will discolour or remove paint if contact is allowed. Avoid this where possible and remove accidental splashes immediately. Similarly, avoid contact between the fluid and plastic parts such as the instrument lenses and fairing.*

1   When working on the front brake dismantle the calipers separately to avoid interchanging components.

2   To remove the caliper, slacken and remove the union bolt which secures the hose to the caliper having first placed a suitable container underneath it in which to drain the fluid. Stop the flow of fluid from the reservoir by holding the front brake lever in against the handlebars; this is easily done by using a stout elastic band. On the rear caliper the flow of fluid can be stopped simply by attaching the hose union to the highest possible point of the frame. It may be necessary to remove the hose clamps to enable this.

3   When the fluid stops flowing from the hose union, clean the connections carefully and secure the hose end and fittings inside a clean polythene bag, to await reassembly. It is most important to keep each component scrupulously clean, and to prevent the ingress of any foreign matter. For this reason, it is as well to prepare a clean area in which to work, before further dismantling. Ensure that the outside of the caliper is thoroughly cleaned down.

4   Remove the caliper from the machine and the brake pads from the caliper as described in Routine maintenance.

ZX900 A1 to A6 and ZX1000 A models

5   Separate the mounting bracket from the caliper by pushing it away from the piston, then displace the two rubber dust covers and the anti-rattle spring. The piston may be expelled from the caliper body by an air jet – a foot pump if necessary. Remove the piston seal and dust seal from the caliper body. Under no circumstances should any attempt be made to lever or prise the piston out of the caliper. If the compressed air method fails, temporarily reconnect the caliper to the flexible hose, and use the handlebar lever to displace the piston hydraulically. Wrap some rag around the caliper to catch the inevitable shower of brake fluid. Whichever method is used take great care to avoid getting your fingers trapped by the emerging piston. Once the piston is out, remove both the dust and fluid seals, taking great care not to damage the piston bore.

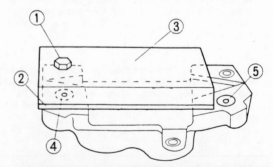

Fig. 6.3 Method of blocking brake fluid passages during piston removal – ZX900 A7-on and ZX1100 C models (Sec 9)

1   Bolt and nut
2   Rubber facing
3   Wooden block
4   Sealed fluid passage
5   Open fluid passage

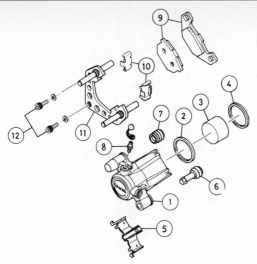

Fig. 6.4 Front brake caliper – ZX900 A1 to A6 and ZX1000 A models

1 Caliper body	7 Dust cover
2 Fluid seal	8 Bleed nipple
3 Piston	9 Brake pads
4 Dust seal	10 Anti-rattle springs
5 Pad spring	11 Mounting bracket
6 Dust cover	12 Bolt – 2 off

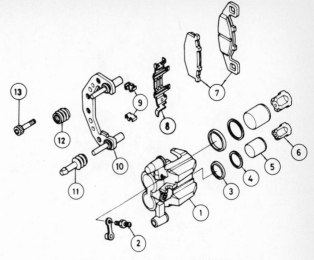

Fig. 6.5 Front brake caliper – ZX1000 B models

1 Caliper body	8 Pad spring
2 Bleed nipple	9 Anti-rattle springs
3 Fluid seal – 2 off	10 Mounting bracket
4 Dust seal – 2 off	11 Dust cover
5 Piston – 2 off	12 Dust cover
6 Piston insulator – 2 off	13 Bolt – 2 off
7 Brake pads	

6   Clean all components carefully, removing all traces of road dirt, friction material and corrosion. Note that only clean hydraulic fluid (or ethyl or isopropyl alcohol) should be used to clean hydraulic components; all normal cleaning solvents will attack the rubber seals. It is permissible to use a wire brush gently to remove dirt and corrosion except in the caliper bores and on the piston surfaces.

7   Renew both fluid and dust seals as a matter or course. Never reuse a hydraulic seal after it has been disturbed and note that the piston seal must be in excellent condition as its secondary role is to return the piston when lever or pedal pressure is released, thus preventing brake drag. Carefully examine the mounting bracket dust covers, renewing them if they are perished, split or otherwise damaged. Similarly discard the sealing washers fitted each side of the brake hose union; these should be renewed as a matter of course.

8   Examine the piston surface and caliper bore for signs of wear or scoring, normally caused by the presence of road dirt or corrosion. If wear is found, or deep scoring or scratches which might cause fluid leaks, the component concerned must be renewed.

9   Check that there is no free play between the caliper body and its mounting bracket. Renew any components that are found to be worn. It is essential that single-piston brake calipers can slide smoothly on their mountings. Make a final check that there are no signs of damage on any other part of the caliper assembly.

10   On reassembly, soak the new fluid and dust seals in clean hydraulic fluid and carefully fit them into the caliper bore, ensuring that each is correctly seated in its groove. Smear hydraulic fluid over the caliper bore and piston surface and refit the piston, rotating it slightly while keeping it square to the caliper bore so that it does not stick or displace either seal.

11   Apply PBC (Poly Butyl Cuprysil) grease to all sliding surfaces on the caliper body and mounting bracket and refit the bracket to the caliper, ensuring that the rubber dust covers are correctly fitted and refit the anti-rattle spring. Check that the caliper body moves smoothly from side to side and refit the pads as described in Routine maintenance.

ZX1000 B models

12   The brake calipers fitted to these models are basically a dual piston version of that which is fitted to the ZX900 A1 to A6 and ZX1000 A models. Therefore the caliper can be overhauled as described above noting the following points.

13   When removing the pistons from the caliper ensure that both pistons leave the bores at the same time. If one sticks at any point the other piston must be restrained by firm hand pressure so that the full pressure can overcome the resistance. It would be very difficult to

extract one piston alone from this type of caliper without risking damage. Note that the insulators fitted to the brake pad side of each piston are a push fit in the piston body.

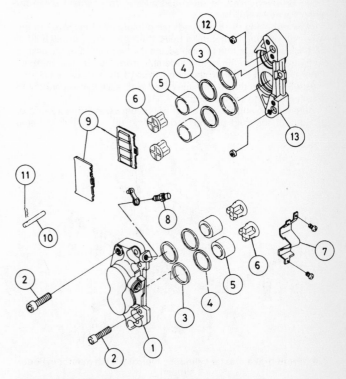

Fig. 6.6 Front brake caliper – ZX900 A7-on and ZX1100 C models

1 Caliper half	8 Bleed nipple
2 Bolt – 6 off	9 Brake pads
3 Fluid seal – 4 off	10 Pad retaining pin
4 Dust seal – 4 off	11 R-pin
5 Piston – 4 off	12 Seal – 2 off
6 Piston insulator – 4 off	13 Caliper half
7 Pad spring	

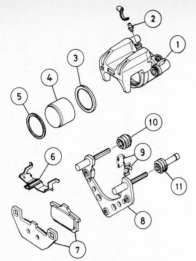

Fig. 6.7 Rear brake caliper – ZX900 A1 to A6 and ZX1000 A models

1	Caliper body	7	Brake pads
2	Bleed nipple	8	Mounting bracket
3	Fluid seal	9	Anti-rattle springs
4	Piston	10	Dust cover
5	Dust seal	11	Dust cover
6	Pad spring		

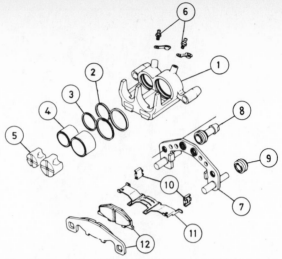

Fig. 6.8 Rear brake caliper – ZX1000 B and ZX1100 C models (ZX900 A7-on similar)

1	Caliper body	7	Mounting bracket
2	Fluid seal – 2 off	8	Dust cover
3	Dust seal – 2 off	9	Dust cover
4	Piston – 2 off	10	Anti-rattle springs
5	Piston insulator – 2 off	11	Pad spring
6	Bleed nipples	12	Brake pads

ZX900 A7-on and ZX1100 C models

14   These models employ two different types of caliper. The front brake uses two four-piston opposed calipers while the rear brake uses a dual piston caliper which is similar to that fitted to the ZX1000 B models, and can be overhauled as described above. To overhaul the front calipers proceed as follows.

15   After removing the brake pads temporarily refit the caliper to the fork leg and tighten its mounting bolts. With the caliper firmly held in place slacken the four bolts which secure the two halves of the caliper together and remove the caliper assembly from the fork leg. Remove the four bolts and separate the two halves of the caliper, noting the O-rings which fit in the oil passages. Deal with each half separately to avoid interchanging components.

16   Before removing the pistons it will be necessary to block one or both sides of the fluid passages, depending on which half is being

worked on. This can be achieved using a block of wood one side having a rubber surface which is bolted to the caliper half as shown in the accompanying illustration. When working on the inner half of the caliper, block one oil passage and apply compressed air into the opposite passage, and when working on the outer half of the caliper, block both oil passages and apply the air into the union bolt hole. Remove both pistons as described in paragraph 13. The caliper components can be checked and refitted as described above. Note that the insulators fitted to the brake pad side of each piston are a push fit in the piston body.

17   Fit new O-rings to both oil passages and join the two halves together. Refit the four caliper bolts, tightening them to the specified torque setting, and refit the brake pads as described in Routine maintenance.

All models

18   Refit the caliper to the machine and tighten its mounting bolts to the specified torque setting. Position a new sealing washer on each side of the hose union and tighten the union bolt to the specified torque setting. Bleed the system as described in Section 13 after filling the reservoir with new hydraulic fluid, then check for leakage of fluid whilst applying the brake lever. Push the machine forward and bring it to a halt by applying the brake. Do this several times to ensure that the brake is operating correctly before taking the machine for a test run. During the run, use the brakes as often as possible and on completion, recheck for signs of fluid loss.

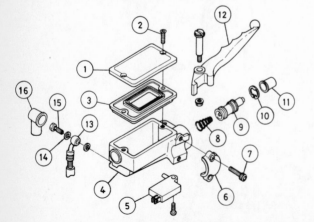

Fig. 6.9 Front brake master cylinder – typical (clutch master cylinder similar)

1	Cover	9	Primary piston assembly
2	Screw – 2 off	10	Circlip
3	Diaphragm	11	Dust boot
4	Reservoir	12	Brake lever
5	Brake stop lamp switch	13	Hose union
6	Handlebar clamp	14	Sealing washer – 2 off
7	Bolt – 2 off	15	Union bolt
8	Spring	16	Rubber cover

10   Front brake master cylinder: removal and refitting

Note: *brake fluid will discolour or remove paint if contact is allowed. Avoid this where possible and remove accidental splashes immediately. Similarly, avoid contact between the fluid and plastic parts such as the instrument lenses and fairing.*

1   Disconnect the stop lamp switch wires at the switch. The switch need not be disturbed unless the master cylinder is to be renewed. Place a clean container below one of the brake calipers and run a clear plastic tube from the caliper bleed nipple to the container. Unscrew the bleed nipple by one full turn and drain the system by operating the brake lever repeatedly until all fluid has drained from the reservoir.

2   Position a wad of clean rag beneath the point where the brake hose

joins the master cylinder to prevent drops of brake fluid contacting the components below. Pull back the rubber cover from the head of the union bolt and remove the bolt. Once any excess fluid has drained from the union connection, wrap the end of the hose in rag or polythene and then attach it to a point on the handlebars. Remove the brake lever by unscrewing its locknut and shouldered bolt. Remove the reservoir cover and lift out the diaphragm. Release the two master cylinder clamp bolts and remove the master cylinder from the machine.

3   Use the flat of a small screwdriver to prise out the rubber dust seal boot from the end of the piston assembly. This will expose a retaining circlip which must be removed using a pair of circlip pliers which have long, straight jaws. With the circlip removed, the piston and cup assembly can be pulled out. Be very careful to note the exact order in which these components are fitted.

4   Note that if a vice is used to hold the master cylinder at any time during dismantling and reassembly, its jaws must be padded with soft alloy or wooden covers and the master cylinder must be wrapped in soft cloth to prevent it being marked or distorted.

5   Place all the master cylinder components in a clean container and clean each part thoroughly. Lay the parts out on a sheet of clean paper and examine each one as follows.

6   Examine the piston surface and master cylinder bore for signs of wear or corrosion. Renew both components if damaged in any way; new seals will not compensate for scoring and will wear out quickly. Check the primary and secondary seals for damage or swelling, renewing them unless in perfect condition. The cups are sold as a kit together with the piston and spring. Renew the dust seal at the same time to preclude road dirt entering the assembly. Ensure that the supply port and the smaller relief port between the cylinder and reservoir are clear, especially where swollen or damaged cups have been noted. Inspect the threads of the brake hose union bolt for signs of failure and renew the bolt if in the slightest doubt. Renew the sealing washers located on each side of the union as a matter of course.

7   Check before reassembly that any traces of contamination remaining in the reservoir body have been removed. Inspect the diaphragm to see that it is not perished or split. It must be noted at this point that any reassembly work must be undertaken in ultra-clean conditions. Particles of dirt entering the components will serve only to score the working points of the cylinder and thereby cause early failure of the system.

8   When reassembling and fitting the master cylinder, follow the removal and dismantling procedures in reverse, whilst paying attention to the following points. Make sure that the piston components are fitted the correct way round and in the correct order. Immerse the piston components in new brake fluid prior to reassembly and refer to the figure accompanying this text when in doubt as to their correct positions.

9   When refitting the master cylinder assembly to the handlebar, position it so that the reservoir will be exactly horizontal when the machine is in use. Tighten the clamp top bolt first, and then the bottom bolt to the specified torque setting. Connect the brake hose to the master cylinder, ensuring that a new sealing washer is placed on each side of the hose union, and tighten the hose union bolt to the specified torque setting. Finally, refit the rubber union cover and reconnect the brake lamp switch wiring.

10   Fill the reservoir with new brake fluid and bleed the system as described in Section 13. Check for fluid leakage with the brake lever applied, before taking the machine out on the road. During the run, use the brakes as often as possible and on completion, recheck for signs of fluid loss.

11   Rear brake master cylinder: removal, overhaul and refitting

Note: *brake fluid will discolour or remove paint if contact is allowed. Avoid this where possible and remove accidental splashes immediately. Similarly, avoid contact between the fluid and plastic parts.*

1   Remove the right-hand sidepanel and drain the hydraulic system as described in paragraph 1 of Section 10. Drain the system fully to ensure that all fluid has also drained from the reservoir to master cylinder hose. Release the reservoir mounting bolt and disconnect the hose which joins it to the master cylinder. Remove the reservoir from the machine and wipe up any spilt fluid. Disconnect the brake hose from the master cylinder and place the hose union and bolt inside a polythene bag,

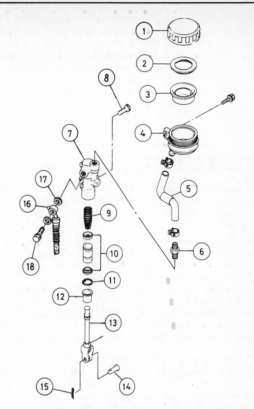

Fig. 6.10 Rear brake master cylinder – ZX1000 B and ZX1100 C models (other models similar)

1	Cap	10	Primary piston assembly
2	Diaphragm plate	11	Circlip
3	Diaphragm	12	Dust boot
4	Reservoir	13	Operating rod
5	Connecting hose	14	Clevis pin
6	Union	15	Split pin
7	Master cylinder	16	Hose union
8	Bolt – 2 off	17	Sealing washer – 2 off
9	Spring	18	Union bolt

securing the bag with an elastic band. This will prevent dirt entering the system whilst the hose is disconnected.

ZX900

2   Disconnect the rear stop lamp switch wires from the main wiring loom and remove the bolt which secures the right-hand silencer to the footrest bracket. Slacken and remove the swinging arm pivot shaft nut and the five bolts which retain the footrest bracket to the frame, then remove the bracket assembly from the machine.

All models

3   Remove the split pin and clevis pin which retain the forked end of the master cylinder pushrod to the brake pedal. Release the two master cylinder mounting bolts and lift the cylinder away from the footrest bracket.

4   Pull off the dust seal and remove it together with the pushrod. Displace the retaining clip and continue dismantling and overhaul of the piston assembly as described in Section 10.

5   The master cylinder is refitted by reversing the removal sequence. Refit the master cylinder to the footrest bracket and tighten its mounting bolts to the specified torque setting. Insert the clevis pin into the pushrod end and secure it with a new split pin. On ZX900 models, refit the bracket assembly, tightening all mounting bolts and the swinging arm pivot shaft nut to their specified torque settings, and reconnect the stop lamp switch wires.

6   Position a new sealing washer on each side of the hose union and tighten the union bolt to the specified torque setting. Connect the reservoir hose to the master cylinder and refit the reservoir mounting bolt.

7   Bleed the brake system after refilling the reservoir with new hydraulic fluid, then check for leakage of fluid whilst applying the brake pedal. With the machine on its centre stand, spin the rear wheel and apply the rear brake. Do this several times to ensure that the brake is operating correctly, then check the brake pedal height and the operation of the rear brake lamp switch as described in Routine maintenance, before taking the machine on a test run. During the test run, use the brakes as often as possible and on completion, recheck for any sign of fluid loss.

12   Brake hoses and pipes: general

Note: *brake fluid will discolour or remove paint if contact is allowed. Avoid this where possible and remove accidental splashes immediately. Similarly, avoid contact between the fluid and plastic parts such as the instrument lenses and fairing.*

1   Brake hoses will deteriorate through age and must be renewed at the specified interval for safety reasons (see Routine maintenance). If any splits, kinks, leaks or any other damage is found on a hose at any time, it must be renewed immediately.
2   Drain the hydraulic system completely as described in Section 10. Slacken the union bolts, noting the exact route of the hose and in particular the notches in the calipers and three-way union mounted on the bottom yoke. These notches should locate with the hose unions when the hose is correctly fitted. Remove the faulty hose and clean the union.
3   Fit the new hose, ensuring that it is correctly routed, and position a new sealing washer on each side of its unions. Refit the union bolts and tighten them to the specified torque setting. Refill and bleed the system as described in the following section, and check for leaks. Thoroughly check the operation of the braking system before taking the machine out on the road.

13   Bleeding the braking system

Note: *brake fluid will discolour or remove paint if contact is allowed. Avoid this where possible and remove accidental splashes immediately. Similarly, avoid contact between the fluid and plastic parts such as the instrument lenses and fairing.*

1   If the brake action becomes spongy, or if any part of the hydraulic system is dismantled (such as when a hose is renewed) it is necessary to bleed the system in order to remove all traces of air. The procedure for bleeding the hydraulic system is best carried out by two people.
2   Check the fluid level in the reservoir and top up with new fluid of the specified type if required. Keep the reservoir at least half full during the bleeding procedure; if the level is allowed to fall too far air will enter the system requiring that the procedure be started again from scratch. Refit the reservoir cap to prevent the ingress of dust or the ejection of a spout of fluid.
3   Remove the dust cap from the caliper bleed nipple and clean the area with a rag. Place a clean glass jar below the caliper and connect a pipe from the bleed nipple to the jar. A clear plastic pipe should be used so that air bubbles can be more easily seen. Pour enough clean hydraulic fluid in the glass jar so that the pipe end is immersed below the fluid surface; ensure that the pipe end remains submerged (to prevent air returning to the system whenever the pressure is released) throughout the operation.
4   If parts of the system have been renewed, and thus the system must be filled, open the bleed nipple about one turn and pump the brake lever until fluid starts to issue from the clear pipe. Tighten the bleed nipple and then continue the normal bleeding operation as described in the following paragraphs. Keep a close check on the reservoir level whilst the system is being filled.

Front brake
5   Remove the reservoir cap and starting from the brake caliper and working back to the master cylinder, lightly tap the brake hose. Slowly pump the brake lever or pedal several times until no air bubbles can be seen rising up through the fluid in the reservoir. This operation bleeds the air from the master cylinder and brake hose.

13.3 Bleed the brakes as described in text

6   Operate the brake lever as far as it will go and hold it in this position against the fluid pressure. If spongy brake operation has occurred it may be necessary to pump the brake lever rapidly a number of times until pressure is built up. With pressure applied, loosen the bleed nipple about half a turn. Tighten the nipple as soon as the lever has reached its full travel and then release the lever. Repeat this operation until no more air bubbles are expelled with the fluid into the glass jar.
7   On ZX900 A1 to A6 and ZX1000 A models it will be necessary to repeat the operation using first the bleed nipple on the anti-dive unit and then the nipple on the union block which is situated on the lower fork leg, directly above the caliper.
8   On all models complete the bleeding process by repeating the above on the opposite caliper and associated components (as applicable). When no more air bubbles are expelled, the air bleeding operation should be complete, resulting in a firm feel to the brake lever. If sponginess is still evident repeat the bleeding operation; it may be that an air bubble trapped at the top of the system has yet to work down through the caliper.

Rear brake
9   The rear brake system can be bled as described above for the front brake, noting that on ZX900 A7-on, ZX1000 B and ZX1100 C models, it will be necessary to repeat the process using the second bleed nipple fitted to the caliper.

Front and rear brakes – all models
10   When all traces of air have been removed from the system, top up the reservoir and refit the diaphragm and cap. Check the entire system for leaks, and check also that the brake system in general is functioning efficiently before using the machine on the road.
11   Brake fluid drained from the system will almost certainly be contaminated, either by foreign matter or more commonly by the absorption of water from the air. All hydraulic fluids are to some degree hygroscopic, that is, they are capable of drawing water from the atmosphere, and thereby degrading their specifications. In view of this, and the relative cheapness of the fluid, old fluid should always be discarded.

14   Anti-dive system: testing and renewal – ZX900 A1 to A6 and ZX1000 A models

Note: *brake fluid will discolour or remove paint if contact is allowed. Avoid this where possible and remove accidental splashes immediately. Similarly, avoid contact between the fluid and plastic parts such as the instrument lenses and fairing.*

1   The anti-dive system is activated by hydraulic pressure whenever the front brake is applied, pressure being transmitted via metal brake pipes from the union block at the top of each fork leg to the anti-dive units.

2   To test the system, place the machine on its centre stand, unbolt the union block from each fork lower leg and remove the two Allen screws securing the plunger assembly to the top of the anti-dive valve unit, then withdraw the plunger assemblies, taking care not to distort the brake pipe.

3   Lightly apply the front brake with a finger over each plunger in turn. The plunger should move out by 2 mm when pressure is applied at the lever and should return easily under finger pressure when the lever is released.

4   If this is not the case, or if any signs of hydraulic fluid leakage are discovered, the plunger assembly should be dismantled for examination. Drain the brake fluid as described in Section 10 and disconnect the brake pipe from the top of the plunger housing. Remove the large hexagon-headed top plug and withdraw the plunger and seal assembly. Examine the components for wear or damage and renew as necessary. Note that the seals should be renewed once disturbed in the interests of safety. On reassembly, tighten the top plug securely. Tighten the two Allen headed plunger housing screws and the metal brake pipe gland nuts to the specified torque setting.

5   Note that the plunger assemblies must be renewed at fixed intervals for safety reasons alone, regardless of their apparent condition. Refer to Routine maintenance.

15 Tyres: removal and refitting

1   It is strongly recommended that should a repair to a tubeless tyre be necessary, the wheel is removed from the machine and taken to a tyre fitting specialist or an authorized dealer. This is because the force required to break the seal between the wheel rim and tyre bead is considerable and is considered to be beyond the capabilities of an individual working with normal tyre removing tools. Any abortive attempt to break the rim to bead seal may also cause damage to the wheel rim, resulting in expensive wheel renewal. If, however, a suitable bead releasing tool is available, and experience has already been gained in its use, tyre removal and refitting can be accomplished as follows.

2   Remove the wheel from the machine. Deflate the tyre by removing the valve core and when it is fully deflated, push the bead of the tyre away from the wheel rim on both sides so that the bead enters the well of the rim. As noted, this operation will almost certainly require the use of a bead releasing tool.

3   Insert a tyre lever close to the valve and lever the edge of the tyre over the outside of the wheel rim. Very little force should be necessary; if resistance is encountered it is probably due to the fact that the tyre beads have not entered the well of the wheel rim all the way round the tyre. Should the initial problem persist, lubrication of the tyre bead and the inside edge and lip of the rim will facilitate removal. Use a recommended lubricant, a diluted solution of washing-up liquid or french chalk. Lubrication is usually recommended as an aid to tyre fitting but its use is equally desirable during removal. The risk of lever damage to wheel rims can be minimised by the use of proprietary plastic rim protectors placed over the rim flange at the point where the tyre levers

are inserted. Suitable rim protectors can be fabricated very easily from short lengths (4 – 6 inches) of thick-walled nylon petrol pipe which have been split down one side using a sharp knife. The use of rim protectors should be adopted whenever levers are used and, therefore, when the risk of damage is likely.

4   Once the tyre has been edged over the wheel rim, it is easy to work around the wheel rim so that the tyre is completely free on one side.

5   Working from the other side of the wheel, ease the other edge of the tyre over the outside of the wheel rim, which is furthest away. Continue to work around the rim until the tyre is freed completely from the rim.

6   Refer to the following sections for details of puncture repair, tyre renewal and valves.

7   Tyre refitting is virtually a reversal of the removal procedure. If the tyre has a balance mark (usually a spot of coloured paint), this must be positioned alongside the tyre valve. Similarly, any arrow indicating direction of rotation must face the right way.

8   Starting at the point furthest from the valve, push the tyre bead over the edge of the wheel rim until it is located in the well. Continue to work around the tyre in this fashion until the whole of one side of the tyre is on the rim. It may be necessary to use a tyre lever during the final stages. Here again, the use of a lubricant will aid fitting. It is strongly recommended that when fitting the tyre only a recommended lubricant is used because such lubricants also have sealing properties. Do not be over generous in the application of lubricant or tyre creep may occur.

9   Fitting the other bead is similar to fitting the first bead. Start by pushing the bead over the rim and into the well at a point diametrically opposite the tyre valve. Continue working around the tyre, each side of the starting point, ensuring that the bead opposite the working area is always in the well. Apply lubricant as necessary. Avoid using tyre levers unless absolutely essential, to help reduce damage to the soft wheel rim. Use of the levers should be required only when the final portion of bead is to be pushed over the rim.

10   Lubricate the tyre beads again prior to inflating the tyre, and check that the wheel rim is evenly positioned in relation to the tyre beads. Inflation of the tyre may well prove impossible without the use of a high pressure air hose. The tyre will retain air completely only when the beads are pressed firmly against the rim edges at all points and it may be found when using a foot pump that air escapes at the same rate as it is pumped in. This problem may also be encountered when using an air hose on new tyres which have been compressed in storage and by virtue of their profile hold the beads away from the rim edges. To overcome this difficulty, a tourniquet may be placed around the circumference of the tyre, over the central area of the tread. The compression of the tread in this area will cause the beads to be pushed outwards in the desired direction. The type of tourniquet most widely used consists of a length of hose closed at both ends, with a suitable clamp fitted to enable both ends to be connected. An ordinary tyre valve is fitted at one end of the tube so that after the hose has been secured around the tyre it may be inflated, giving a constricting effect. Another possible method of seating beads to obtain initial inflation is to press the tyre into the angle between a wall and the floor. With the airline attached to the valve additional pressure is then applied to the tyre by the hand and shin, as shown in the accompanying illustration. The application of pressure at four points around the tyre's circumference whilst simultaneously applying the airline will often effect an initial seal between the tyre beads and wheel rim, thus allowing inflation to occur.

11   Having successfully accomplished inflation, increase the pressure to 40 psi and check that the tyre is evenly disposed on the wheel rim. This may be judged by checking that the thin positioning line found on each tyre wall is equidistant from the wheel rim around the total circumference of the tyre. If this is not the case, deflate the tyre, apply additional lubrication and reinflate. Minor adjustments to the tyre position may be made by bouncing the wheel on the ground.

12   Always run the tyres at the recommended pressures and never under- or over-inflate. The correct pressures are given in the Specifications at the start of this chapter. Note that if non-standard tyres are fitted check with the tyre manufacturer or supplier for recommended pressures. Finally refit the valve dust cap.

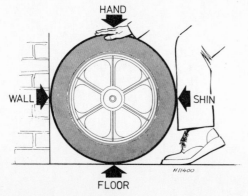

HAND

WALL

SHIN

FLOOR

H11400

Fig. 6.11 Method of seating the beads on tubeless tyres (Sec 15)

16 Tyres: puncture repair and tyre renewal

1   If a puncture occurs, the tyre should be removed for inspection for damage before any attempt is made at remedial action. *The temporary*

repair of a punctured tyre by inserting a plug from the outside should not be attempted. The manufacturers strongly recommend that no such repair is carried out on a motorcycle tyre. Not only does the tyre have a thin carcass, which does not give sufficient support to the plug, but the consequences of a sudden deflation are often sufficiently serious that the risk of such an occurrence should be avoided at all costs.

2   The tyre should be inspected both inside and out for damage to the carcass. Unfortunately the inner lining of the tyre – which takes the place of the inner tube – may easily obscure any damage and some experience is required in making a correct assessment of the tyre condition.

3   There are two main types of repair which are considered safe for adoption in repairing tubeless motorcycle tyres. The first type of repair consists of inserting a mushroom-headed plug into the hole from the inside of the tyre. The hole is prepared for insertion of the plug by reaming and the application of an adhesive. The second repair is carried out by buffing the inner lining in the damaged area and applying a cold or vulcanised patch. Because both inspection and repair, if they are to be carried out safely, require experience in this type of work, it is recommended that the tyre be placed in the hands of a repairer with the necessary skills, rather than repaired in the home workshop. The manufacturer recommends that a repaired tyre must not be run at speeds in excess of 60 mph (100 kmh) for the first 4 hours after the repair, and must thereafter not exceed 110 mph (180 kmh) for reasons of safety.

4   Note that the manufacturer specifically advises against the fitting of a tubed type tyre or an inner tube to these machines. Additionally, both tyres must be of the same manufacture and more importantly, must conform to the size and construction given in the Specifications. *Fitting tyres of the wrong construction and speed rating may lead to impaired or dangerous handling, or a tyre regulation prosecution.* If for any reason it is wished to change from the standard recommendation advice must first be sought from the motorcycle manufacturer as to the suitability of such a change.

17   Tyre valves: description and renewal

1   To renew the valve the tyre must first be removed from the wheel. In the case of a 'car type' rubber valve, cut off the valve's inner retaining shoulder and pull the remains out of the rim. Lubricate the new valve thoroughly and push it through the rim from the outside towards the centre (having first removed its dust cap). It must then be drawn into place by screwing the correct valve puller tool onto its threaded end to provide purchase. This tool should be available at any tyre-fitting establishment, although if great care is taken to avoid crushing the valve end, it is possible to screw a suitably-sized nut onto the valve threads and to grip this with a large pair of pliers. Check that the rubber locating shoulders lock securely into place on each side of the rim. Where a clamp-in type metal valve is used, the sealing components must be fitted in the correct sequence. The locknut must not be overtightened to avoid damage to the sealing washer(s).

2   The valve dust caps are a significant part of the tyre valve assembly. Not only do they prevent the ingress of road dirt in the valve, but also act as a secondary seal which will reduce the risk of sudden deflation if a valve should fail.

18   Wheel balancing

1   It is customary on all high performance machines to balance the wheels complete with the tyre, and if fitted, the tube. The out of balance forces which exist are eliminated and the handling of the machine is improved in consequence. A wheel which is badly out of balance produces through the steering a most unpleasant hammering effect at high speeds.

2   Some tyres have a balance mark on the sidewall, usually in the form of a coloured spot. This mark must be in line with the tyre valve when the tyre is fitted to the rim. Even then the wheel may require the addition of balance weights to offset the weight of the tyre valve itself.

3   If the wheel is raised clear of the ground and is spun, it will probably come to rest with the tyre valve or the heaviest part downward and will always come to rest in the same position. Balance weights must be added to a point diametrically opposite this heavy spot until the wheel comes to rest in *any* position after it has been spun.

4   Balance weights are available from Kawasaki dealers in 10, 20 and 30 gram sizes. These are recommended since they are designed to fit Kawasaki rims and will not cause deflation problems when used with tubeless tyres.

5   To fit the weights clip the hooked end over the bead and tap the weight home, deflating the tyre slightly to allow this, if necessary.

6   While the rear wheel is much more tolerant of out-of-balance forces, it should be balanced also when a new tyre is fitted or whenever any serious vibration problems are encountered. Remove the wheel from the machine and place it on a stand to test it; the drag of the chain would make any check ineffective.

Tyre changing sequence — tubeless tyres

Deflate tyre. After releasing beads, push tyre bead into well of rim at point opposite valve. Insert lever adjacent to valve and work bead over edge or rim.

Use two levers to work bead over edge of rim. Note use of rim protectors.

When first bead is clear, remove tyre as shown.

Before fitting, ensure that tyre is suitable for wheel. Take note of any sidewall markings such as direction of rotation arrows.

Work first bead over the rim flange.

Use a tyre lever to work the second bead over rim flange.

Chapter 7 Electrical system

Refer to Chapter 8 for information on the ZX1100 D model

Contents

Specifications

Electrical system
Voltage	12
Earth (ground)...	Negative

Battery
Capacity	14 Ah
Electrolyte specific gravity	1.280 @ 20°C (68°F)

Alternator
Type..	Three-phase AC
Rated output:	
ZX900 and ZX1000 A models...	25A @ 6000 rpm, 14 volts
ZX1000 B models..	24A @ 6000 rpm, 14 volts
ZX1100 C models..	28.6A @ 6000 rpm, 14 volts
Charging voltage – headlight on:	
ZX900 and ZX1000 A models...	13.5 volts @ 4000 rpm
ZX1000 B and ZX1100 C models	14.5 volts @ 4000 rpm
Stator coil resistance...	Less than 1 ohm
Rotor coil resistance:	
ZX1000 B2 and B3 models	Approximately 6 ohms
All other models	Approximately 4 ohms
Slip ring diameter..	14.4 mm (0.57 in)
Service limit..	14.0 mm (0.55 in)
Carbon brush projection length	10.5 mm (0.41 in)
Service limit..	4.5 mm (0.18 in)

Starter motor
Carbon brush length:	
ZX900 and ZX1000 B models...	12 mm (0.47 in)
Service limit...	8.5 mm (0.33 in)
ZX1000 A and ZX1100 C models...	12 – 12.5 mm (0.47 – 0.49 in)
Service limit...	6 mm (0.24 in)
Commutator diameter..	28 mm (1.10 in)
Service limit..	27 mm (1.06 in)
Commutator groove depth:	
ZX900 models and ZX1000 A models...................................	0.45 – 0.75 mm (0.018 – 0.030 in)
Service limit...	0.2 mm (0.008 in)
ZX1000 B and ZX1100 C models	0.7 mm (0.028 in)
Service limit...	0.2 mm (0.008 in)

Fuel level sender unit resistances
ZX900 models:

    Empty .... 70 – 120 ohms

    Full .... 3 – 12 ohms

ZX1000 models:

    Empty .... 90 – 100 ohms

    Full .... 4 – 10 ohms

ZX1100 C model .... see text

Fuses
ZX900 and ZX1000 A models:

    Main 30A

    Horn 10A

    Tail 10A

    Lights 10A

    Turn signals 10A

    Fan 10A

    Accessory – ZX900 only .... 10A x 2

ZX1000 B and ZX1100 C models:

    Main 30A

    Headlamp 10A

    Fan 10A

    Accessory 10A

Bulbs
Headlamp 12V 60/55W

Parking lamp – UK models only 12V 4W

Stop/tail lamp:

    UK models 12V 5/21W

    US models 12V 8/27W

Turn signal lamps:

    UK models 12V 21W

    US models 12V 23W

Instrument illuminating lamps 12V 3W

Warning lamps 12V 3.4W

Torque settings

Component	kgf m	lbf ft
Alternator coupling bolt	1.0	7.0
Radiator mounted fan switch:		
ZX900 and ZX1000 A models	0.75	5.5
ZX1000 B and ZX1100 C models	1.8	13.0
Coolant temperature sender unit:		
ZX900 and ZX1000 A models	0.8	6.0
ZX1000 B and ZX1100 C models	1.5	11.0
Thermostat housing fan switch – ZX900 models	0.8	6.0
Oil pressure switch	1.5	11.0
Oil temperature switch – ZX900 models	0.8	6.0

1 General description

The electrical system is powered by a three-phase alternator driven from the crankshaft via the starter clutch shaft by a chain on the right-hand end of the crankshaft. The shaft is fitted with two cush drive assemblies to damp out shock loads. The alternator is a self-contained unit which includes the regulator and rectifier.

The starter motor drives the crankshaft, through a series of reduction gears and the starter clutch, via the same chain which drives the alternator.

2 Electrical system: general information and preliminary checks

1   In the event of an electrical system fault, always check the physical condition of the wiring and connectors before attempting any of the test procedures described here and in subsequent sections. Look for chafed, trapped or broken electrical leads and repair or renew as necessary. Leads which have broken internally are not easily spotted, but may be checked using a multimeter or a simple battery and bulb circuit as a continuity tester. This arrangement is shown in the accompanying illustration. The various multi-pin connectors are generally trouble-free but may corrode if exposed to water. Clean them carefully, scraping off any surface deposits, and pack with silicone grease during assembly to

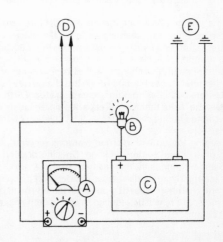

Fig. 7.1 Simple testing equipment for checking the wiring (Sec 2)

A   Multimeter or ohmeter   D   Positive probe

B   12V bulb   E   Negative probe

C   Battery

avoid recurrent problems. The same technique can be applied to the handlebar switches.

2   The wiring harness is colour-coded and will correspond with the wiring diagrams at the end of this manual. Where socket connections are used, they are designed so that reconnection can be made only in the correct position.

3   Visual inspection will usually show whether there are any breaks or frayed outer coverings which will give rise to short circuits. Occasionally a wire may become trapped between two components, breaking the inner core but leaving the more resilient outer cover intact. This can give rise to mysterious intermittent or total circuit failure. Another source of trouble may be the snap connectors or sockets, where the connector has not been pushed fully home in the outer housing, or where corrosion has occurred.

4   Intermittent short circuits can often be traced to a chafed wire that passes through or is close to a metal component such as a frame member. Avoid tight bends in the lead or situations where a lead can become trapped between casings.

5   A sound, fully charged battery, is essential to the normal operation of the system. There is no point in attempting to locate a fault if the battery is partly discharged or worn out. Check battery condition and recharge or renew the battery before proceeding further.

6   Many of the test procedures described in this chapter require voltages or resistances to be checked. This necessitates the use of some form of test equipment such as a simple and inexpensive multimeter of the type sold by electronics or motor accessory shops.

7   If you doubt your ability to check the electrical system, entrust the work to an authorized Kawasaki dealer. In any event have your findings double-checked before consigning expensive components to the scrap bin.

3   Battery: examination and maintenance

1   Details of the regular checks needed to maintain the battery in good condition are given in Routine maintenance, together with instructions on removal and refitting and general battery care. Batteries can be dangerous if mishandled; read the Safety first! section at the front of this manual before starting work, and always wear overalls or old clothing in case of accidental acid spillage. If acid is ever allowed to splash into your eyes or onto your skin, flush it away with copious quantities of fresh water and seek medical advice immediately.

2   When new, the battery is filled with an electrolyte of dilute sulphuric acid having a specific gravity of 1.280 at 20°C (68°F). Subsequent evaporation, which occurs in normal use, can be compensated for by topping up with distilled or demineralised water only. Never use tap water as a substitute and do not add fresh electrolyte unless spillage has occurred.

3   The state of charge of a battery can be checked using an hydrometer.

4   The normal charge rate for a battery is $\frac{1}{10}$ of its rated capacity, thus for a 14 ampere hour unit charging should take place at 1.4 amp. Exceeding this figure can cause the battery to overheat, buckling the plates and rendering it useless. Few owners will have access to an expensive current controlled charger, so if a normal domestic charger is used check that after a possible initial peak, the charge rate falls to a safe level. If the battery becomes hot during charging **stop.** Further charging will cause damage. Note that the cell caps should be loosened and the vents unobstructed during charging to avoid a build-up of pressure and risk of explosion.

5   After charging top up with distilled water as required, then check the specific gravity and battery voltage. Specific gravity should be above 1.270 and a sound, fully charged battery should produce 15 – 16 volts. If the recharged battery discharges rapidly if left disconnected it is likely that an internal short caused by physical damage or sulphation has occurred. A new battery will be required. A sound item will tend to lose its charge at about 1% per day.

4   Alternator: general

To avoid damage to the alternator, and indeed many other components, the following precautions must be observed:

(a)   Do not disconnect the battery or alternator whilst the engine is running

(b)   Do not allow the engine to turn the alternator when the latter is not connected

(c)   Do not test for output from the alternator by 'flashing' the output lead to earth

(d)   Do not use a battery charger of more than 12 volts output, even as a starting aid

(e)   Disconnect the battery and the alternator before carrying out any electric arc welding on the machine

(f)   Always observe correct battery polarity

(g)   When disconnecting the battery always remove the negative lead first and when reconnecting connect it last

5   Alternator: checking the output

1   If the battery is known to be in a good condition yet fails to hold its charge when fitted to the machine, the alternator should be tested as follows.

2   Remove the three nuts which retain the alternator cover and lift the cover away from the alternator. Visually examine the alternator leads and connections for signs of corrosion or damage and repair as necessary. If all appears to be in order it will be necessary to check the alternator output. Note: for the following check to be accurate the battery must be fully charged.

3   Connect a dc voltmeter across the battery terminals and start the engine taking note of the voltage reading. If the alternator is in good condition the measured voltage should be higher than 13.5 volts, although not excessively high (see following paragraph). If the measured voltage is lower than 13.5 volts, stop the engine and repeat the above test having first grounded the F terminal of the regulator (see accompanying photograph) to earth using an insulated auxiliary wire. If the voltage reading obtained is now higher than 13.5 volts the regulator is at fault and should be tested further, if the reading is still below 13.5 volts the fault must lie in either the carbon brushes and slip rings, rectifier, stator coil or rotor coil.

4   Occasionally the condition may arise where the alternator output is excessive. Clues to this condition are constantly blowing bulbs with the brightness of the lights varying considerably with engine speed, and the battery overheating, needing the electrolyte level to be frequently topped up. This condition is almost certainly due to a faulty regulator which should be tested individually.

5   If the alternator has become noisy whilst the engine is running it is most likely that its bearings are worn. To check the bearings the alternator will have to overhauled.

5.3 Ground the alternator F terminal (arrowed) to test regulator

6 Alternator: overhaul

1 Note, it is not necessary to remove the alternator assembly from the machine to remove the regulator, rectifier or carbon brushes. However, if work on these components is to be carried out with the assembly fitted to the engine unit, first disconnect the alternator block connector from the main wiring loom. Overhaul the relevant alternator components using the information given under the relevant sub-heading. If necessary, the alternator can be removed and refitted as described in Chapter 1.

Carbon brushes

2 Release the three nuts which retain the alternator end cover and remove the cover from the alternator. Remove the two screws which retain the carbon brush holder and lift it off the slip rings. Measure the length of the projected portion of each of the carbon brushes fitted to the holder. If they are worn down to or below the service limit, the old brushes will have to be unsoldered and removed and new ones soldered into place. Some skill with a soldering iron will be required to do this, ensuring that the solder does not run down the brush leads. The brush springs should also be renewed if at all suspect. When fitted, the new brushes must move freely in the holder and be firmly in contact with the slip rings. If the original brushes are still serviceable, check that they are free to move easily in the holder and that their ends bear fully on the slip rings.

3 Whilst the brush holder is removed, take the opportunity to clean the slip rings with a cloth moistened with high flash-point solvent. If badly marked, tidy up the slip rings with a piece of 400 grade emery cloth. Using a vernier caliper, measure the slip ring diameter; this should not exceed the service limit at any point.

Regulator

4 Remove the brush holder as described above then release the regulator mounting screws and remove it from the assembly. The regulator can then be checked using either, or both, of the methods described in the following paragraph.

5 To conduct the first test two fully charged 12 volt batteries, a 12 volt 3.4 watt bulb and three auxiliary insulated wires will be needed. Connect one battery and the bulb to the regulator unit as shown in part A of Fig. 7.2, taking great care not to allow either wire to contact the regulator's metal case. With the circuit connected as described the bulb should be illuminated. Replace the one battery with both the batteries joined together in series as shown in part B of Fig. 7.2 and repeat the test. In this case, the bulb should not light up. If either circuit fails to produce the required results, the regulator is defective and must be renewed. Alternately the condition of the regulator can be determined by making various resistance checks across its terminals with an ohmmeter or multimeter. If the readings obtained differ greatly from those in Fig. 7.2 the regulator is faulty and must be renewed.

Rectifier

6 Remove the brush holder and regulator as described above, then release the rectifier mounting screws. The electrical wires must then be unsoldered from the rectifier and the rectifier removed from the assembly. Note, the wires must be unsoldered quickly from the rectifier terminals. If the high temperatures of the soldering iron are applied for more than a few seconds the rectifier's diodes could be damaged by excessive heat.

7 The condition of the rectifier can then be determined by measuring the resistance of each of its six diodes in both directions, as shown in the accompanying illustration. Never use a multimeter with a large capacity battery to test the rectifier; severe damage could result.

8 With the meter set to the ohms x 1 scale connect the positive probe to the P1 terminal and the negative probe to the B terminal and note the reading obtained. Swap the meter probes around, again noting the reading. Repeat this test between the P2 terminal and B terminal, and the P3 terminal and B terminal. Then carry out the same tests as described above but instead of using the B terminal, use the E (earth) point, making six further tests. Compare the two readings obtained for each diode. One value should be considerably higher than the other. Note that the actual values obtained will vary depending on the type of test meter used, but if the unit is functioning correctly, there should be continuity (very low resistance) in one direction and no continuity (infinite resistance) with the meter probes reversed. If either condition exists in both directions for any diode, the rectifier is faulty and must be renewed.

9 On refitting, the wires must be soldered quickly and cleanly to the rectifier terminals to prevent excess heat building up and damaging the rectifier unit.

Rotor coil, stator coil and alternator bearings

10 To remove these components the alternator must first be removed from the machine and the carbon brush holder, regulator and rectifier units removed as described above.

11 Slacken and remove the alternator cush drive coupling retaining bolt whilst holding the blades of the coupling with a self-locking wrench. Lift off the coupling and remove the three screws situated behind the coupling which retain the right-hand side of the alternator housing to the bearing plate. Tape over the splined end of the rotor shaft to protect the oil seal and lift off the right-hand side of the alternator housing along with the stator coil.

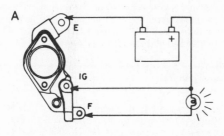

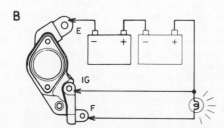

Meter Range	Connections		Reading
	Meter (+) to	Meter (−) to	
x 100 Ω	F	E	170 Ω
x 1 kΩ	E	F	4 kΩ
x 100 Ω	IG	E	800 Ω
x 1 kΩ	E	IG	2 kΩ
x 1 kΩ	F	IG	2 kΩ
x 100 Ω	IG	F	150 Ω

Fig. 7.2 Regulator test connections and table – see text (Sec 6)

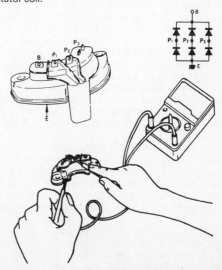

Fig. 7.3 Rectifier test (Sec 6)

6.2a Remove the rubber brush holder cover ...

6.2b ... and measure projected length of each brush

6.4 Regulator is retained by two screws

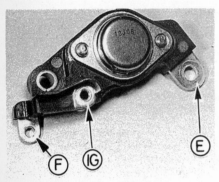

6.5 Regulator terminal identification

6.6 Unsolder terminal wires quickly to avoid damaging the rectifier

6.11 Stator coil is retained by three screws situated behind drive coupling

12   Using a multimeter set to the ohms x 1 scale measure the resistance between the three stator coil wires (3 tests). If the resistance between any two of the wires greatly exceeds 1 ohm the stator coil windings can be considered faulty and must be renewed. Set the meter to the highest resistance scale possible and check for continuity between each stator coil winding and the core of the coil. If there is any reading at all, the stator coil windings have short circuited and must be renewed. Examine the oil seal fitted to the right-hand alternator for signs of wear or damage, renewing as necessary.

13   To check the rotor coil windings set the meter to the ohms x 1 scale and measure the resistance between the two slip rings. If the reading obtained does not resemble that given in the specifications the rotor coil windings can be considered defective and must be renewed. Set the meter to the highest ohms scale possible and check for continuity between the rotor shaft and each of the slip rings. If any reading is obtained, the slip rings have short circuited on the shaft and the rotor coil must also be renewed. Note that if the slip rings are contaminated in any way clean them prior to this test as described in paragraph 3 above.

14   Examine the bearing on the right-hand end of the rotor coil shaft for any signs of freeplay and check that it spins freely without any trace of notchiness. The left-hand bearing can be checked by holding the rotor coil and spinning the alternator housing. The housing should spin easily and smoothly on the shaft without binding. If either bearing is faulty, renew them both as a pair.

15   To remove the rotor coil from the alternator housing access to an hydraulic press will be needed. Therefore it is recommended that if the alternator rotor coil and (or) bearings require renewal the work should be entrusted to an authorized Kawasaki dealer who will have the necessary equipment. On no account attempt to tap the rotor coil out of the housing using a hammer. This will almost certainly damage the slip rings.

16   On reassembly, tape over the splined end of the rotor shaft and carefully fit the right-hand alternator housing to the rotor shaft. Ease the housing into position, aligning the bolt holes in the housing with the bearing plate. Fit the three bearing plate screws and tighten them securely. Remove the tape from the end of the rotor shaft and locate the alternator cush drive coupling on the splines of the shaft. Tighten the coupling retaining bolt to its specified torque setting whilst holding the coupling with a self-locking wrench. Refit the rectifier, regulator and brush holder and refit the cover. Tighten all screws and nuts securely.

7   Fuses: general

1   Most circuits are protected by fuses of different ratings. On ZX900 and ZX1000 A models all fuses can be found in the junction box, located behind the left-hand sidepanel. On ZX1000 B and ZX1100 C models all fuses except the main fuse are located in the junction box which is directly under the seat. The main fuse is fitted to the starter relay which is under the right-hand sidepanel on ZX1000 B models, and under the left-hand sidepanel on ZX1100 C models. On all models the junction box fuses are labelled for ease of identification.

2   Blown fuses can be easily recognised by the melted metal strip. Each is clearly marked with its rating and must be replaced only by a fuse of the correct rating. Never put in a fuse of a higher rating or bridge the terminals with any other substitute, however temporary it may be. Serious damage may be done to the circuit, or a fire might start. Always carry a spare supply of spare fuses of each rating (10 and 30 Amps) on the machine.

3   While an isolated fault may occasionally blow a fuse and never occur again, such cases are rare and generally due to faulty connections, although fuses do sometimes blow due to old age or similar factors. However, if the fuse for any circuit blows repeatedly, a more serious fault is indicated which must be traced and remedied as soon as possible.

8   Starter system: checks

1   In the event of a starter malfunction, always check first that the battery is fully charged. A partially discharged battery may be able to

7.1a Junction box components – ZX900 (UK) models

7.1b On ZX1000 B and ZX1100 C models main fuse is fitted to starter relay – ZX1100 C shown

8.3 Starter relay location – ZX900 models

provide enough power for the lighting circuit, but not the heavy current required for starting the engine. Look also for broken, chafed or corroded wiring before proceeding further.

Starter motor power supply

2   Disconnect the starter motor lead from its terminal on the motor. Set the test meter to the x 20 volts dc scale and connect its positive probe to the starter lead and its negative probe to earth. Ensure the transmission is in neutral, the side stand is up and the engine kill switch is in the RUN position. Turn the ignition switch on, pull in the clutch lever and operate the starter button. As the button is pressed a reading of approximately 12 volts (battery voltage) should be obtained, if not the fault lies in either the starter relay or the starter switch circuit. If the correct voltage reading is obtained the starter motor itself is at fault, and the unit should be overhauled as described in the following section. Reconnect the machine's battery.

Starter relay (solenoid)

3   On ZX1000 B models the starter relay is situated behind the right-hand sidepanel, and on all other models it is behind the left-hand sidepanel. Disconnect the battery terminals prior to this test to prevent the risk of short circuits. Remove the sidepanel and disconnect the starter motor lead and the positive power supply lead from the starter motor relay. Disconnect the block connector from the relay and remove it from the machine.
4   Set a test meter to the ohms x 1 scale and connect it across the relay terminals. Using a fully charged 12 volt battery and two insulated auxiliary wires, connect the positive terminal of the battery to the yellow/red terminal of the relay, and the negative terminal to the black/yellow terminal of the relay. At this point the relay should click and the multimeter read 0 ohms. If this is the case the relay is serviceable and the fault lies in the starter switch circuit, if not, the relay is faulty and must be renewed.

Starter switch circuit

5   Disconnect the block connector from the starter relay. Make the test on the wiring harness side of the block connector. Set the test meter to the dc volts x 20 scale and connect its positive probe to the yellow/red terminal of the block connector, and its negative probe to the black/yellow terminal. Ensure that the transmission is in neutral, the side stand is up and the engine kill switch is in the RUN position. Turn the ignition switch on, pull in the clutch lever and operate the starter button. As the button is pressed a reading of approximately 12 volts (battery voltage) should be shown on the multimeter. If not, one or more of the components in the starter circuit are faulty and should be checked as follows.

Starter switch circuit relay – ZX900 and ZX1000 A models

6   Remove the starter circuit relay (bottom relay) from the junction box. To test the relay an ohmmeter or multimeter, a 12 volt battery and two insulated auxiliary wires will be needed. Set the meter to the ohms x 1 scale and connect the battery and meter to the relay as shown in Fig. 7.4. When the battery is connected to the relay a reading of 0 ohms should be shown on the meter, and when the battery is disconnected there should be an open circuit indicated (infinite resistance). If this is not the case, the relay must be renewed.

Starter switch circuit relay – ZX1000 B and ZX1100 C models

7   Disconnect the junction box from its block connectors and remove it from the machine. To test the relay an ohmmeter or multimeter, a 12 volt battery and two insulated auxiliary wires are needed. Refer to Fig. 7.5 to identify the junction box terminals, set the meter to the ohms x 1 scale, and connect its probes first to terminals 11 and 13, and then to terminals 12 and 13. If the relay is functioning correctly, there should be an open circuit (infinite resistance) indicated in each test. Connect a wire from the battery positive terminal to the terminal 11 on the junction box, and another wire from its negative terminal to terminal 12 on the junction box. With the battery connected in this way, connect the test meter across terminals 11 and 13 of the junction box; continuity (low resistance) should be indicated on the meter. If the results are not as shown, the junction box should be renewed.

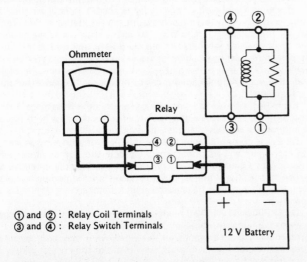

① and ② : Relay Coil Terminals
③ and ④ : Relay Switch Terminals

Fig. 7.4 Starter switch circuit relay test connections (Sec 8)

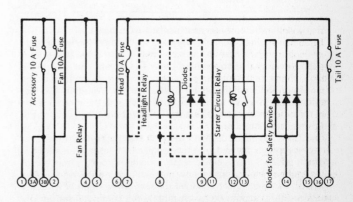

Fig. 7.5 Junction box circuit diagram – ZX1000 B and ZX1100 C models

Starter switch circuit diode – ZX900 and ZX1000 A models
8   The diode is situated in the junction box, just to the right of the starter switch circuit relay. Remove the diode from the junction box and using a test meter set to the ohms scale, measure the resistance between its terminals in both directions. A low resistance reading should be obtained in one direction, and a significantly higher reading in the other (approximately ten times higher), if the diode is functioning correctly. If not, the diode should be renewed.

Starter circuit diodes – ZX1000 B and ZX1100 C models
9   The diodes are an integral part of the junction box. Disconnect its wiring block connectors and remove the junction box from the machine for testing. Refer to Fig. 7.5 to identify the terminals, and using a test meter set to the resistance range, measure the resistance between terminals 12 and 14, 15 and 14, and 16 and 14. Make these tests in both directions so that a total of six readings are obtained. In each case there should be low resistance in one direction and high resistance in the other (approximately ten times higher) if the diodes are functioning correctly. If the results are not as shown the junction box must be renewed.

Starter button
10   Trace the wiring from the right-hand handlebar switch back to its block connectors, disconnect them and make the following test on the switch side of the wiring. Using a multimeter set to the ohms x 1 scale check for continuity between the two black terminals on ZX900 and ZX1000 A models, and the two black/red terminals on ZX1000 B and ZX1100 C models. When the button is pressed there should be continuity between the two, and when the button is released there should be an open circuit. If not the starter button is faulty and must either be repaired or the right-hand handlebar switch renewed.

Ignition and engine kill switches
11   The test procedure for these is described in Section 5 of Chapter 4.

Neutral switch
12   Pull off the neutral switch lead from the switch itself and connect one probe of the multimeter set to the resistance function to the switch terminal and the other to earth. There should be continuity between the switch and earth when the transmission is in neutral and an open circuit when the transmission is put into gear. If not the neutral switch is defective and must be renewed.

Clutch lever switch
13   Trace the wiring back from the left-hand handlebar switch and disconnect its block connectors from the wiring harness. Check for continuity between the three terminals on the switch side of the wiring with the clutch lever pulled into the handlebar, and then with the lever released. With the lever pulled in there should be continuity (low resistance) between the black/yellow and yellow/green terminals only. Whereas with the lever released there should be continuity (low resistance) between the yellow/green and light green terminals only. If the results are other than expected the switch should be renewed, although note that nothing is lost by attempting a repair.

---

9   Starter motor: overhaul

1   Remove the starter motor as described in Chapter 1.
2   On ZX900 models, mark the front and rear ends of the motor body and the end covers so that all can be refitted in their original positions. Also tape over the starter pinion teeth to prevent the seal being damaged. Remove the two long retaining screws from the front of the starter motor and carefully lift off the front cover. Withdraw the rear cover, until the brushes slide off the commutator end, and remove the cover and brush holder plate as a single unit. Withdraw the commutator from the starter motor body.
3   On ZX1000 and ZX1100 C models, tape over the teeth of the starter pinion and remove the two long retaining screws from the rear of the motor. Lift off the front cover and remove all shims from the front end of the commutator. Make a note of how these shims are arranged to use as a reference for reassembly. Remove the rear cover together with any shims fitted to the commutator. Withdraw the commutator from the front end of the motor body.
4   On all models, disengage the carbon brushes from the brush holder

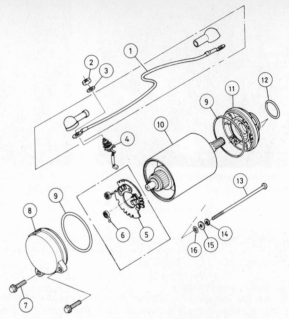

Fig. 7.6 Starter motor – ZX900 models

1 Motor lead	9 O-ring – 2 off
2 Nut	10 Motor body/armature
3 Spring washer	11 Right-hand end cover
4 Positive brush lead	12 O-ring
5 Brush holder plate	13 Screw – 2 off
6 Brush spring – 2 off	14 Spring washer – 2 off
7 Bolt – 2 off	15 Washer – 2 off
8 Left-hand end cover	16 O-ring – 2 off

plate and measure the length of each brush. If any brush has worn to or beyond the service limit given in the Specifications, renew the brushes as a set. As the brushes are soldered to either the brush holder plate (negative brushes) or the terminal bolt (positive brushes), they cannot be renewed separately; both the brush plate and terminal bolt assemblies will be required.
5   If the brush lengths are within the service limits check the brush wiring as follows. Using an ohmmeter or multimeter set to the ohms x 1 scale, check for continuity between the terminal bolt and positive brush(es). Continuity should be shown; if no continuity (high resistance) is shown, renewal is required. Repeat the test between the brush plate and negative brush tips; renew if no continuity (high resistance) is indicated. Set the meter to the K ohm scale and measure the resistance between the brush plate and brush holders and then between the terminal bolt and brush plate; in each case no continuity (high resistance) should be shown. If continuity is shown, it is likely that the insulation has broken down at some point. If this is the case, remove the terminal bolt retaining nut, followed by all the washers. Make a careful note of how these washers are arranged as a guide to reassembly. Examine the insulating washers for cracks or other damage and renew if necessary. Note that although they are not listed as being available separately, suitable replacements can be purchased from most automotive suppliers.
6   Examine the brush retaining springs for any signs of damage. Spring tension can only be ascertained by comparison with a new item. Renew the springs if in any doubt about their condition.
7   Clean the commutator segments and grooves with a rag soaked in high flash-point solvent. If necessary, smooth the surface of the commutator with a piece of fine emery cloth. Measure its diameter using a vernier caliper; if worn beyond the service limit the complete starter motor must be renewed because the commutator cannot be purchased separately.
8   On ZX900 and ZX1000 B models, measure the depth of the grooves between the commutator segments. If less than the service limit, the starter motor should be renewed. Alternatively, it may be possible to undercut the grooves using a hacksaw blade of the correct width. Be very careful not to cut into the segment material if this is done, and ensure that the groove is left square-sided. Also do not cut beyond the

9.4 Measure the length of all starter motor brushes

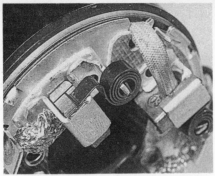

9.11a Hook springs over the brush holders to allow commutator to be refitted ...

9.11b ... then locate springs in brush grooves – ZX1100 C shown

9.11c Refit any shims in original positions using notes made on dismantling

9.11d Fit a new O-ring ...

9.11e ... and install the rear cover ensuring peg in the body locates with the groove in the cover

9.12a On ZX1000 and ZX1100 C models refit front commutator shims in their original positions ...

9.12b ... and fit toothed washer to the front cover

9.13 Fit a new O-ring and install front cover as described in text

standard groove depth specification.

9   On all models, check the condition of the commutator windings. Using a multimeter set to the ohms x 1 scale, check the resistance between various pairs of commutator segments. If a high resistance is shown between any two segments, one of the windings is open and the starter motor should be renewed. Set the meter to the K ohms scale and measure the resistance between each commutator segment and the armature core. No continuity (high resistance) should be shown. Continuity will indicate a short between the commutator and shaft and will necessitate starter motor renewal.

10 If oil is found in the starter motor assembly, the seal pressed into the front cover is faulty and must be renewed. However, this seal is not listed as a separate part and is only available as part of the complete starter motor assembly. The same applies to the commutator bearings (where fitted). To avoid unnecessary expense, it is worth contacting an automotive parts supplier, who may be able to supply a suitable substitute. Ensure that all the relevant seal or bearing markings are quoted so that the correct item is selected. If necessary take the complete motor or old components along as a pattern.

11 Hook the brush retaining springs over the end of the holder and refit the brushes in their original positions. Insert the commutator into the brush plate and push the brush springs into place, ensuring that the end of each spring is correctly seated in the groove in each brush. Check that the brushes are seated fully against the commutator and are also free to move in their holders. On ZX900 models, refit the commutator and brush plate assembly to the rear starter motor cover. On ZX1000 and ZX1100 C models refit the shims (where fitted) to the rear of the armature. Ensure that the brush plate is correctly located in the rear cover or body (as applicable). Fit a new O-ring to the rear cover and assemble the rear cover and starter motor body, ensuring that the locating peg on the motor body engages with the groove in the rear cover. Note that on ZX900 models the peg is on the rear cover and the groove is in the body.

12 On ZX1000 and ZX1100 C models, use the notes taken on dis-

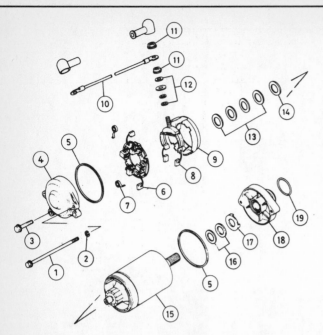

Fig. 7.7 Starter motor – ZX1000 and ZX1100 C models

1 Screw – 2 off	11 Nut – 2 off
2 Spring washer – 2 off	12 Terminal washer
3 Bolt – 2 off	assembly
4 Left-hand end cover	13 Shims – as required
5 O-ring – 2 off	14 Washer
6 Negative brush assembly	15 Motor body/armature
7 Brush spring – 4 off	16 Shims – as required
8 Positive brush assembly	17 Toothed washer
9 Brush holder	18 Right-hand end cover
10 Motor lead	19 O-ring

mantling to return the shims on the front end of the commutator to their original positions. Refit the toothed washer to the front cover so that its teeth locate with the ribs on the cover.

13   Grease the lips of the front cover oil seal and ensure that the teeth of the starter motor pinion are covered with tape to protect the seal on installation. Fit a new O-ring to the front of the motor body and carefully refit the front cover to the motor body. On ZX900 models, ensure that the projection in the motor body engages with the slot in the front cover and that the marks made prior to dismantling align. On ZX1000 A models, all lines cast on the motor body and end covers should align. On ZX1000 B and ZX1100 C models, position the cover by aligning the line cast on its edge with the motor terminal bolt.

14   Refit the two long retaining screws and tighten them securely. Remove the tape from the teeth of the starter motor pinion and refit the motor as described in Chapter 1.

10   Oil pressure warning lamp circuit: testing

1   This circuit consists of a simple pressure switch mounted on the sump, which lights a warning lamp in the instrument panel whenever the ignition is switched on. As soon as the engine is started, and the oil pressure rises above a certain point, the lamp should go out.

2   If the lamp fails to light, first check the bulb and renew it if blown. If this fails to cure the fault, disconnect the switch lead and earth it briefly on the sump. If the lamp comes on when the lead is earthed, the switch is defective and must be renewed. If the lamp still fails to come on the wiring between the switch and warning lamp is at fault, and this should be checked with a continuity tester as described in Section 2 to trace the wire breakage.

3   If the lamp lights while the engine is running, pull over and stop the engine immediately; serious engine damage is likely if the engine is run with low oil pressure. Check first the level of the engine oil and top up if

necessary. If this does not cure the problem check the oil pressure, as described in Chapter 3, at the earliest possible opportunity. If the oil pressure is correct the oil pressure switch is likely to be faulty. The switch can be tested only by the substitution of a new component.

11   Switches: general

1   While the switches should give little trouble, they can be tested using a multimeter set to the resistance function or a battery and bulb test circuit. (See Section 2.) Using the information given in the wiring diagrams at the end of this Manual, check that full continuity exists in all switch positions and between the relevant pairs of wires. When checking a particular circuit follow a logical sequence to eliminate the switch concerned.

2   As a simple precaution always disconnect the battery (negative lead first) before removing any of the switches, to prevent the possibility of a short circuit. Most troubles are caused by dirty contacts, which can be cleaned, but in the event of the breakage of some internal part, it will be necessary to renew the complete switch.

3   If a switch is tested and found to be faulty, there is nothing to be lost by attempting a repair. It may be that worn contacts can be built up with solder, or that a broken wire terminal can be repaired, again using a soldering iron. The handlebar switches may be dismantled to a certain extent. It is however up to the owner to decide if he has the skill to carry out this sort of work.

4   While none of the switches require routine maintenance, some regular attention will prolong their life. The regular and constant application of WD40 or a similar water-dispersant spray not only prevents problems occurring due to water-logged switches and the resulting corrosion, but also makes the switches much easier and more positive to use. Alternatively, the switch may be packed with a silicone based grease to achieve the same result.

12   Cooling fan system: testing

1   In the event of a malfunction in the cooling fan system, check first that the fan fuse is intact. Refer to the accompanying circuit diagrams and examine all the relevant wiring and connectors for signs of broken or chafed wires or corroded connections. If the fault cannot be traced to the wiring, test the circuit components as described below.

ZX900 models
2   Disconnect the 6-pin block connector from the fan switch relay

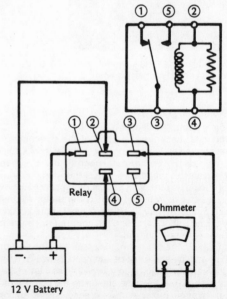

Fig. 7.8 Cooling system fan switch relay test connections – ZX900 models (Sec 12)

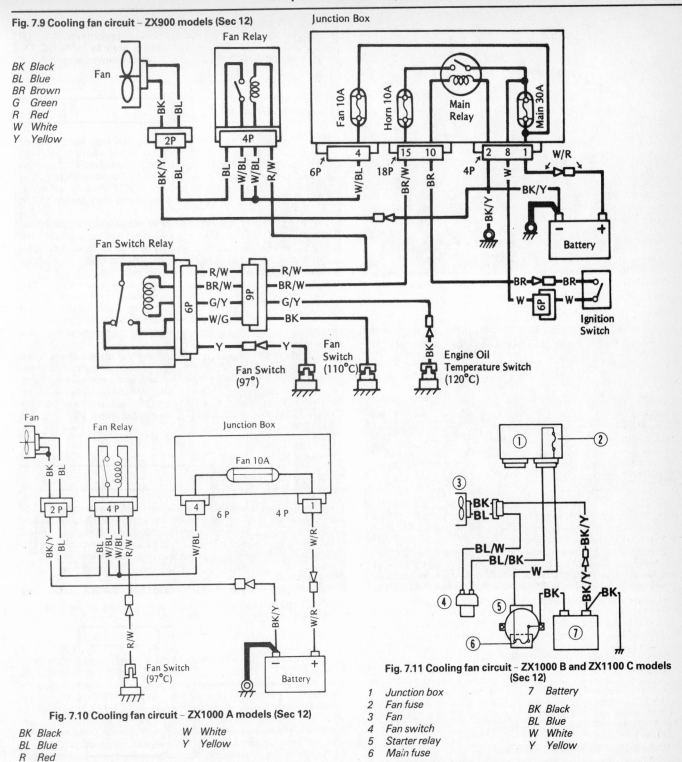

Fig. 7.9 Cooling fan circuit – ZX900 models (Sec 12)

BK Black
BL Blue
BR Brown
G Green
R Red
W White
Y Yellow

Fig. 7.10 Cooling fan circuit – ZX1000 A models (Sec 12)

BK Black
BL Blue
R Red

W White
Y Yellow

Fig. 7.11 Cooling fan circuit – ZX1000 B and ZX1100 C models (Sec 12)

1 Junction box
2 Fan fuse
3 Fan
4 Fan switch
5 Starter relay
6 Main fuse

7 Battery

BK Black
BL Blue
W White
Y Yellow

situated below the headlamp unit in the upper fairing section. Using an auxiliary wire connect the red/white wire from the wiring side of the connector to earth. If the fan operates, the fault lies in either the fan switch relay or the fan and oil temperature switches. If not, either the fan relay or the cooling fan itself is at fault.

ZX1000 A models

3 Disconnect the red/white lead from the fan switch on the radiator and ground it to earth. If the fan comes on the switch is at fault, and if not either the fan relay or the cooling fan is defective.

ZX1000 B and ZX1100 C models

4 Disconnect the two wires from the fan switch on the radiator and

using an auxiliary wire connect them together. If when the wires are joined the fan comes on then the fan switch is at fault, if the fan fails to come on the cooling fan is defective.

Fan switch relay – ZX900 models only

5 Remove the relay from the machine. Connect a 12 volt battery to the terminals of the relay, as shown in the accompanying figure, and check for continuity between the three other terminals using a multimeter set to the ohms x 1 scale. When the battery is connected there should be continuity between terminals 3 and 5 only (red/white and white/green), and when the battery is disconnected there should be continuity between numbers 1 and 3 only (yellow and red/white). If this is not the case the relay is defective and must be renewed.

12.5 Fan switch relay is mounted on the upper fairing bracket - ZX900

12.6 Fan relay is situated beside the junction box – ZX900

12.7 Fan switch is situated on the left-hand side of the radiator

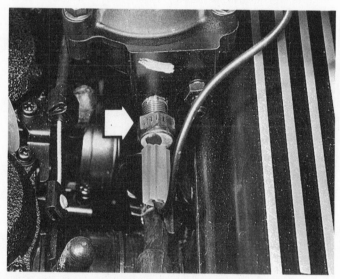

12.10 On ZX900 models do not confuse the thermostat fan switch (arrowed) with the temperature sender unit

Fan relay – ZX900 and ZX1000 A models only

6   On ZX900 models the fan relay is situated just in front of the junction box, and on ZX1000 A models it can be found behind the right-hand sidepanel where it is mounted in front of the rear suspension unit damping adjuster. The fan relay is identical to the starter circuit relay and can be tested as described in paragraph 6 of Section 8 of this Chapter. If faulty, the relay must be renewed.

Radiator mounted fan switch – all models

7   Disconnect the wire(s) from the switch and slacken it using a suitable spanner. Unscrew the switch as fast as possible, withdraw it from the radiator and plug the opening to stop the coolant escaping. To test the switch a heatproof container, a small gas-powered camping stove, a thermometer capable of reading up to 100°C (212°F) and an ohmmeter or multimeter will be required.

8   Fill the container with water and suspend the switch on some wire so that just the sensing portion and the threads are submerged. On ZX900 and ZX1000 A models connect one probe of the meter to the switch terminal and the other to the body of the switch, and on ZX1000 B and ZX1100 C models connect the meter probes to both switch terminals. Suspend the thermometer so that its bulb is close to the switch. Note that no component should be allowed to touch the container.

9   Start to heat the water up, stirring it gently, until the water is between 95 – 100°C (203 – 212°F). This must be done very carefully to avoid the risk of personal injury. With the water at this temperature the resistance of the fan switch should be less than 0.5 ohms (switch on). Carry on heating the water until it reaches 100°C (212°F) then turn the stove off. Note the resistance reading of the fan switch as the water temperature falls. As the water temperature falls the resistance of the switch should rise so that by the time the water temperature is down to 91°C (196°F) the resistance of the switch should be greater than 1 M ohm (switch off). If this is not the case the switch is defective and must be renewed. On refitting, tighten the switch to its specified torque setting and replace any lost coolant.

Thermostat housing fan switch and oil temperature switch – ZX900 models only

10   Remove the fuel tank as described in Section 3 of Chapter 3, and disconnect the wire from the thermostat housing fan switch which is situated in the bottom half of the housing. Do not confuse this with the temperature sender unit which is in the top half of the thermostat housing. Unscrew the switch as fast as possible, withdraw it from the housing and plug the opening to stop the coolant escaping. The oil temperature switch is removed as described in Section 21 of Chapter 3.

11   Both these switches are tested using the equipment described

previously. Set up the equipment as described in paragraph 8 noting the container should be filled with oil instead of water. Great care must be taken to avoid the risk of personal injury.

12   When testing the fan switch, heat the oil up gently until it is between 107 – 113°C (225 – 235°F). With the oil at this temperature the switch should have a resistance of less than 0.5 ohms (switch on) . Carry on heating the oil until it reaches 115°C (239°F), then switch off the stove and allow the oil to cool. As the oil cools, the resistance of the fan switch should increase so that by the time the oil temperature falls to 104°C (219°F) the resistance of the switch should be greater than 1 M ohm. If not, the switch is faulty and must be renewed. Allow the oil to cool sufficiently then test the oil temperature switch as follows.

13   Gently heat the oil until it is between 117 – 123°C (243 – 253°F), with the oil at this temperature the switch should have a resistance reading greater than 1 M ohm (switch off). Carry on heating the oil until it reaches 125°C (257°F), then turn off the stove and allow the oil to cool. As the oil cools, the resistance of the oil temperature switch should decrease so that by the time the oil has cooled to 113°C (235°F) the switch should have a reading of less than 0.5 ohms. If this is not the case, the oil temperature switch is faulty and must be renewed.

14   On refitting, apply a silicone sealant to the threads of the thermostat fan switch, and thread-locking compound to the threads of the oil temperature switch. Tighten both to their specified torque settings.

Cooling fan – all models

15   Remove the fuel tank as described in Section 3 of Chapter 3, and disconnect the 2-pin block connector from the cooling fan, which is mounted on the back of the radiator. Using a 12 volt battery and two insulated auxiliary wires, connect the battery across the two terminals on the fan side of the connector. Once connected the fan should operate. If not, the fan motor is defective and must be renewed. The radiator and cooling fan assembly can be removed and refitted as described in Chapter 2.

13   Coolant temperature gauge circuit: testing

1   The circuit consists of the sender unit mounted in the thermostat housing and the gauge assembly mounted in the instrument panel. If the system malfunctions check first that the battery is fully charged and that the horn and main fuses (ZX900 and ZX1000 A) or main fuse (ZX1000 B and ZX1100 C) are intact. Then, referring to either Fig. 7.12 or 7.13, as applicable, examine the wiring for broken or chafed wires or corroded connections.

2   To test the circuit, turn the ignition switch ON and disconnect the wire from the temperature sender unit. The temperature needle should point to C on the temperature gauge. Ground the sender unit wire to earth. When the wire is earthed the needle should swing immediately over to H on the gauge. Do not earth the lead any longer than is necessary to take the reading, or the gauge may be damaged. If the needle moves as described above, the sender unit is defective and must be renewed, although a more comprehensive test is described in

13.1 Temperature sender unit (arrowed) is situated in thermostat housing – ZX900 shown

paragraph 3 below. If the needle's movement is still faulty, or if it does not move at all, the fault lies in the main relay (ZX900 and ZX1000 A models only), ignition switch or the gauge itself which should be tested as described in paragraph 4 onwards.

3   Unscrew the temperature sender unit as quickly as possible, remove it from the thermostat housing and plug the opening to prevent the coolant escaping. The sender unit is tested in the same way as the fan switch, referring to paragraph 8 of Section 12. Heat the water gently, stirring it slowly to keep a uniform temperature throughout, and note the resistance readings obtained. A serviceable sender should have a resistance of about 52 ohms at 80°C (176°F), and about 27 ohms at 100°C (212°F). If not, the sender must be renewed. On refitting, apply a silicone sealant to the threads of the sender unit and tighten it to its specified torque setting.

4   Disconnect the ignition switch from the main wiring loom and check for continuity between the brown and white terminals on the switch side of the wiring. When the switch is in the ON position there should be continuity between the two, and when the switch is in the OFF position there should be an open circuit. If this is not the case, the switch is faulty and must be either repaired or renewed.

5   On ZX900 and ZX1000 A models the main relay is also in the temperature gauge circuit. On US models the main relay is the top right-hand of the three circular relays situated in the centre of the junction box, and on UK models it is the uppermost of the two (the headlamp relay not being fitted). The relay is identical to the starter relay and can be tested as described in paragraph 6 of Section 8. If faulty, the relay must be renewed.

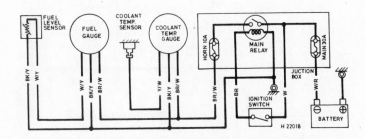

Fig. 7.12 Temperature and fuel gauge circuits – ZX900 and ZX1000 A models (Secs 13 and 15)

BK Black
BL Blue
BR Brown

R Red
W White
Y Yellow

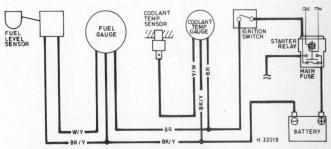

Fig. 7.13 Temperature and fuel gauge circuits – ZX1000 B and ZX1100 C models (Secs 13 and 15)

Fuel gauge circuit applies to ZX1000 B only

BK Black
BR Brown

W White
Y Yellow

6   If the switch and main relay (as applicable) are satisfactory and the wiring is known to be good, the gauge itself is at fault and it must be renewed. Refer to Section 20 of Chapter 5 for information on dismantling and reassembling the instrument panel.

14 Tachometer: testing

1   All models use an electronic tachometer which is operated by the ignition system. On ZX900 and ZX1000 A models the tachometer also doubles as a voltmeter which can be used to measure the battery and charging voltage. This is controlled by a button on the instrument panel.
2   If the tachometer malfunctions, yet the ignition system is still operating correctly, first check the horn and main fuses (ZX900 and ZX1000 A models) or main fuse (ZX1000 B and ZX1100 C models), then examine the relevant wiring for signs of broken wires and corroded connections. If no fault is found test the ignition switch (all models) and main relay (ZX900 and ZX1000 A models only) as described in paragraphs 4 and 5 of Section 13. If both the switch and relay (as applicable) are serviceable, the tachometer unit itself is defective and must be renewed as described in Section 20 of Chapter 5.

15 Fuel gauge circuit: testing – ZX900 and ZX1000 models

Note: *Petrol (gasoline) is extremely flammable, especially when in the form of vapour. Take all precautions to prevent the risk of fire and read the Safety first! section of this manual before starting work.*

1   The fuel gauge circuit consists of the sender unit inside the fuel tank, and the gauge assembly mounted in the instrument panel. If the system malfunctions check first that the battery is fully charged and that the horn and main fuses (ZX900 and ZX1000 A) or main fuse (ZX1000 B) are intact, then test the circuit using the following procedure.
2   Remove the fuel tank as described in Section 3 of Chapter 3 and turn the ignition switch ON. The fuel gauge needle should point to the E on the gauge. Using an insulated auxiliary wire, join the two terminals of the fuel level sender on the wiring side of the block connector. As the terminals are joined the needle on the gauge should immediately swing over to F on the gauge. Do not join the terminals for any longer than is necessary to take the reading or the gauge may be damaged. If the needle moves as described above, the sender unit is at fault and it should be removed and tested as described in paragraph 3 below. If the needle's movement is still faulty, or it does not move at all, the fault lies in either the wiring, the main relay (ZX900 and ZX1000 A models only), the ignition switch or the gauge itself. If this is the case, proceed as described in paragraph 4.
3   Drain the contents of the fuel tank into a clean metal container,

taking great care to avoid the risk of fire. Place the tank on its side on some soft cloth. Remove the sender unit cover (where fitted), release the four bolts which secure the sender unit to the underside of the tank, and carefully manoeuvre the sender unit out of the fuel tank. Check that the float moves up and down smoothly without any sign of binding, and that it always returns to the empty position under its own weight. Also check the sender unit wires for signs of damage as these can easily get trapped if the fuel tank is refitted incorrectly. If all is well, check the operation of the sender unit using a multimeter set to the appropriate scale. Connect the meter probes to sender unit block connector terminals and measure the resistance reading of the switch in both the full and empty positions. If the readings obtained are not within the limits given in the Specifications, or the readings do not change smoothly as the float is moved up and down, the sender unit is defective and must be renewed. On refitting, examine the sender unit gasket for signs of damage and renew it if necessary. Refit the sender to the fuel tank, tightening its retaining bolts securely, and refit the cover (where fitted).
4   Refer to either Fig. 7.12 or 7.13, as applicable, examine all the relevant wiring for broken or chafed wires or corroded connections. If no fault is found test the ignition switch (all models) and main relay (ZX900 and ZX1000 A models only) as described in paragraphs 4 and 5 of Section 13. If the ignition switch and relay (as applicable) are serviceable, the fuel gauge itself is defective and must be renewed. Refer to Section 20 of Chapter 5 for further information on dismantling and reassembling the instrument panel.

16 Fuel level warning lamp circuit: testing – ZX1100 C models only

Note: *Petrol (gasoline) is extremely flammable, especially when in the form of vapour. Take all precautions to prevent the risk of fire and read the Safety first! section of this manual before starting work.*

1   This circuit consists of a fuel level sensor which is mounted in the fuel tank, a fuel level warning lamp relay, a fuel level sensor relay, a diode and two warning lamps situated in the instrument panel. The fuel level warning lamps should come on whenever the ignition switch is in the ON position, or whenever there is less than 6.5 litres of fuel in the fuel tank. The warning lamps should go out as soon as the engine is started, providing there is sufficient fuel in the tank.
2   If the warning lamps fail to light, first check the bulbs and renew them if blown. Note if only one bulb has blown the remaining bulb will flash on and off more frequently. If not, check that the oil pressure warning lamp is lit. If the oil pressure lamp is not lit, examine the oil pressure warning lamp circuit as described in Section 10. If the oil pressure lamp is functioning correctly proceed as follows.
3   Referring to the accompanying circuit diagram, examine all the wiring for signs of broken or chafed wires and corroded connections. If no fault can be found in the wiring, it will be necessary to test the fuel level warning lamp and sensor relays.
4   Both the fuel level warning lamp relay and the sensor relays are

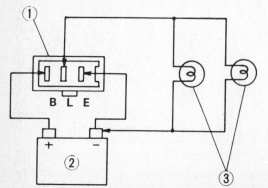

Fig. 7.14 Fuel level sensor unit relay test – ZX1100 C models (Sec 16)

1   Connector block   3   Warning lamp bulbs
2   12 volt battery

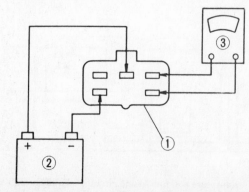

Fig. 7.15 Fuel level warning lamp relay test – ZX1100 C models
(Sec 16)

1   Connector block   3   Multimeter
2   12 volt battery

Fig. 7.16 Fuel level warning lamp circuit – ZX1100 C models (Sec 16)

1   Warning lamps
2   Warning lamp relay
3   Circuit relay
4   Level sensor
5   Oil pressure switch
6   Diode
7   Ignition switch
8   Main fuse
9   Starter relay
10 Battery

BK Black
BL Blue
BR Brown
P   Pink
R   Red
W   White
Y   Yellow

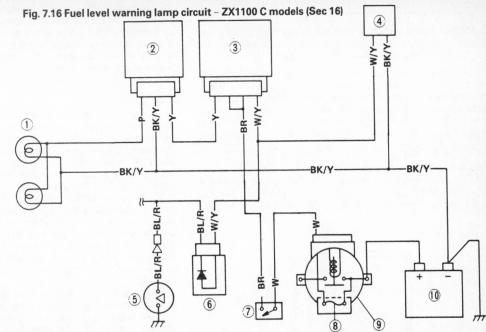

situated behind the left-hand sidepanel where they are mounted onto the rear of the frame. The fuel level warning lamp relay is the front one of the two relays and is easily identified by its 3-pin block connector.

5   To test the fuel level warning lamp relay a fully charged 12 volt battery, two 12 volt 3 watt bulbs and some insulated auxiliary wires will be needed. Connect the battery and two bulbs to the relay as shown in the accompanying figure, and then count how many times the bulbs flash in one minute. Then disconnect one of the bulbs and again count the number of times the single bulb flashes in one minute. With the two bulbs connected to the relay the bulbs should flash between 70 and 100 times in a minute, and when only the single bulb is connected between 140 and 200 times. If this is not the case, the relay is faulty and must be renewed.

6   To test the fuel level sensor relay a multimeter, a fully charged 12 volt battery and two insulated auxiliary wires will be needed. Remove the relay from the machine, set the meter to the ohms x 1 scale and connect the battery and meter to the relay as shown in the accompanying diagram. When the battery is connected to the relay a reading of 0 ohms should be shown on the meter, yet when the battery is disconnected there should be an open circuit. If this is not the case, the relay is defective and must be renewed.

7   Remove the fuel level circuit diode which is located just to the rear

of the junction box. Note that on US models there are two diodes, the fuel level circuit diode being connected to the blue/red and white/yellow wires. Using a multimeter set to the appropriate ohms scale, measure the resistance between its terminals in both directions. If the relay is serviceable, one of the resistance readings will be low and the other at least ten times higher. If this is not the case, renew the diode.

8   If the relays and diode are serviceable, remove the fuel tank as described in Section 3 of Chapter 3 and drain its contents into a clean metal container. Place the tank on some soft cloth, release the two screws which secure the fuel sensor and remove it from the tank. Reconnect the sensor block connector to the main wiring loom.

9   Turn the ignition switch to the ON position. With the switch on and the sensor unit held in the open air both fuel lamps should be flashing. Then taking great care to avoid the risk of fire, submerge the cylindrical thermistor at the top end of the sensor in the fuel which has been drained from the tank. As soon as the thermistor is submerged in the fuel both the fuel lamps should extinguish. Remove the sensor from the fuel and leave it in the open air. After the sensor has been left in the air for some time both warning lamps should again begin to flash, noting that it could take up to three minutes for the sensor to warm up. If the fuel warning lamps do not perform as expected the sensor unit is defective and must be renewed.

16.4 Location of fuel level warning lamp relay (A) and sensor relay (B)

16.8 Fuel level sensor unit is retained by two screws

17   Fuel pump circuit: testing – ZX1000 B and ZX1100 C models

Note: *Petrol (gasoline) is extremely flammable, especially when in the form of vapour. Take all precautions to prevent the risk of fire and read the Safety first! section of this manual before starting work.*

1   The fuel pump should operate whenever the starter button is pressed or the engine is running, providing the fuel level in the carburettors is low. When the fuel level in the carburettors is correct the pressure in the fuel line rises and the pump will automatically shut off. If the fuel pump fails to operate correctly first refer to the accompanying circuit diagram checking all the wiring and connections before proceeding further.

Fuel pump relay – ZX1100 C models only
2   The fuel pump relay is situated inside the tail section where it is mounted to the rear mudguard just in front of the rear lamp assembly. Remove the left-hand sidepanel, disconnect the relay block connector

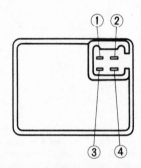

Tester (−) Lead	Tester (+) Lead Connection			
Connection	1	2	3	4
1	–	∞	∞	∞
2	∞	–	∞	∞
3	∞	10~100	–	∞
4	∞	20~200	1 ~ 5	–

Fig. 7.17 Fuel pump relay test – ZX1100 C models (Sec 17)

and remove it from the machine. Check the resistances between the various relay terminals using the accompanying diagram and table of results. *Never use a meter with a large capacity battery to test the fuel pump relay as this will almost certainly damage it.* Kawasaki also state that only their own meter, Part Number 57001-983, should be used to test the relay as another meter could produce different values. If the readings obtained differ greatly from those given in the table, the relay is faulty and must be renewed.

Fuel pump
3   Remove the fuel pump and filter assembly from the machine as described in Chapter 3. The fuel pump can then be tested using a 12 volt battery, some insulated auxiliary wires and a container of paraffin (kerosene). Submerge the filter inlet hose into the paraffin (kerosene) and hold the pump outlet hose above the surface of the liquid. On ZX1000 B models use the auxiliary wires to connect the positive terminal of the battery to both the red and yellow wires, and the negative terminal to the black/yellow wire. On ZX1100 C models connect the positive terminal to the red wire, and the negative terminal to the black wire. With the pump connected thus, it should function and paraffin should be pumped out of the outlet hose. If not, the pump is faulty and must be renewed. With the pump functioning, block the end of the outlet hose to stop the flow of liquid. The pump should cut out as soon as the hose is blocked, if not the pump is defective and must be renewed.
4   If a pressure gauge capable of reading approximately 0 – 5 psi is available, the pump operating pressure can be checked as follows. Fit the pressure gauge to the outlet hose of the pump and set up the circuit described above. With the pump functioning, block the end of the outlet pipe to stop the flow of the paraffin (kerosene) and note the pressure reading obtained on the gauge. If the pump is serviceable this reading should be between 1.6 – 2.3 psi. If any of the above tests show the pump to be faulty, it must be renewed.

18   Headlamp relay and reserve lighting system: testing – US models only

1   The US models are fitted with a headlamp relay. The headlamp remains off when the ignition switch is first switched on, and does not light until the starter button is pressed. The headlamp then stays on until the ignition switch is turned off. Note that the headlamp will go out temporarily if the starter button is pressed to restart the engine after it has stalled.
2   US ZX900 and ZX1000 A models are also fitted with a reserve

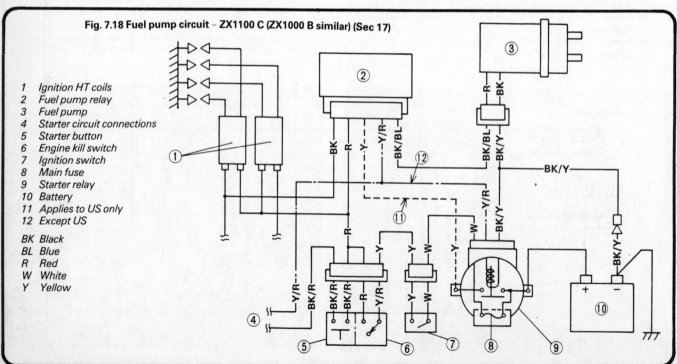

Fig. 7.18 Fuel pump circuit – ZX1100 C (ZX1000 B similar) (Sec 17)

1   Ignition HT coils
2   Fuel pump relay
3   Fuel pump
4   Starter circuit connections
5   Starter button
6   Engine kill switch
7   Ignition switch
8   Main fuse
9   Starter relay
10   Battery
11   Applies to US only
12   Except US

BK   Black
BL   Blue
R   Red
W   White
Y   Yellow

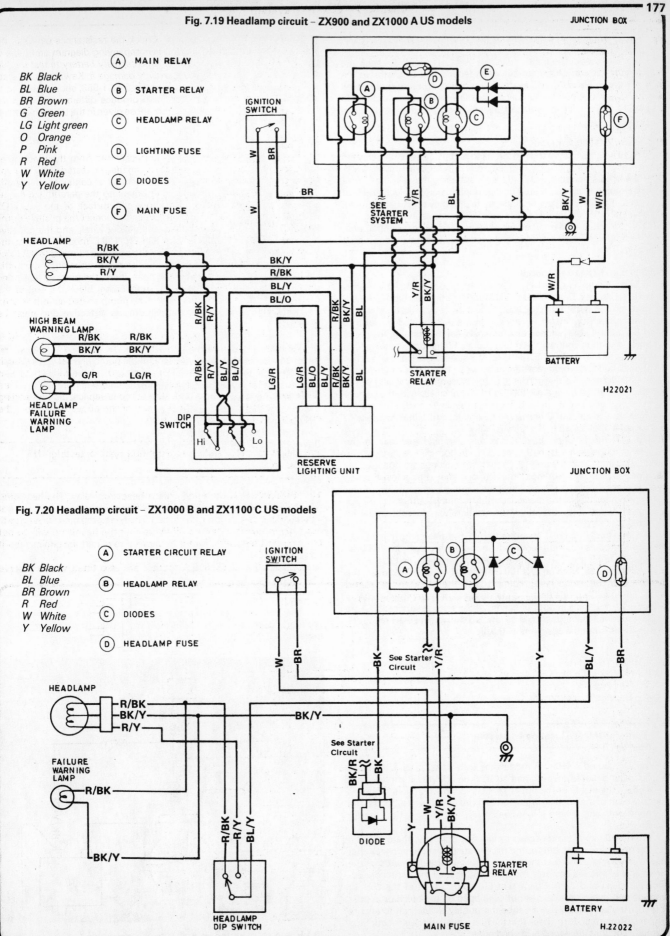

Fig. 7.19 Headlamp circuit – ZX900 and ZX1000 A US models

BK Black
BL Blue
BR Brown
G Green
LG Light green
O Orange
P Pink
R Red
W White
Y Yellow

A MAIN RELAY
B STARTER RELAY
C HEADLAMP RELAY
D LIGHTING FUSE
E DIODES
F MAIN FUSE

JUNCTION BOX

H22021

Fig. 7.20 Headlamp circuit – ZX1000 B and ZX1100 C US models

BK Black
BL Blue
BR Brown
R Red
W White
Y Yellow

A STARTER CIRCUIT RELAY
B HEADLAMP RELAY
C DIODES
D HEADLAMP FUSE

JUNCTION BOX

H.22022

lighting system and headlamp bulb failure warning lamp, the operation of which is shown in Fig. 7.19.

3   If on any model the lighting system malfunctions, first check the bulbs are intact and of the correct wattage, and that all the fuses are intact. Refer to Fig. 7.20 and examine the wiring for broken or chafed wires and corroded connections, and check the switches as described in Section 11. If no fault can be traced, test the headlamp relay and diodes as follows.

ZX900 and ZX1000 A models

4   The headlamp relay is the top left-hand of the three circular relays in the centre of the junction box, and the diode is located directly below it. Both the headlamp relay and diode are identical to those in the starter switch circuit and can be tested as described in paragraphs 6 and 8 of Section 8. If either the relay or diode are faulty, they must be renewed. However, if both are found to be serviceable, the reserve lighting unit must be defective. The only means of testing the reserve lighting unit, which is situated in the upper fairing section, is to substitute it with a new item.

ZX1000 B and ZX1100 C models

5   The headlamp relay and all but one of the diodes are an internal part of the junction box. Disconnect the junction box from its block connectors and remove it from the machine. To test the relay a multimeter, a 12 volt battery and two insulated auxiliary wires will be needed. Refer to Fig. 7.5 to identify the junction box terminals, set the meter to the ohms x 1 scale, and then connect the meter probes first to terminals 7 and 8, and then to terminals 7 and 13. If the relay is serviceable there should be an open circuit (very high resistance) between both pairs of terminals. Then connect the positive terminal of the battery to terminal 9 of the junction box, and the negative terminal to terminal 13. With the battery connected check for continuity between terminals 7 and 8. If the relay is serviceable a reading of 0 ohms will be obtained. If either test fails to produce the above results the relay is faulty.

6   To test the junction box diodes use a multimeter, set to the resistance range, to measure the resistance in both directions between terminals 8 and 13, and 9 and 13, so that two readings are obtained for each pair. Of the two readings obtained, one should be a low reading and the other should be at least ten times larger. If this is not the case for either pair of terminals, the diode assembly is faulty. If either the relay or diodes are found to be defective, the junction box assembly must be renewed.

7   An additional diode is incorporated in the headlamp circuit. On ZX1000 B models it is situated between the battery and junction box, and on ZX1100 C models it is situated beneath the seat, just to the rear of the junction box. Note on ZX1100 C models there are two diodes, the headlamp circuit diode being connected to the black and black/red wires. Remove the diode from the machine and measure the resistance between its terminals in both directions. If the relay is serviceable, one of the resistance readings should be low and the other at least ten times higher. If this is not the case, renew the diode.

19 Turn signal relay: location and testing

1   On ZX900 and ZX1000 A models the turn signal relay is the large square relay situated in the junction box, on ZX1000 B models it is situated on the inside of the upper fairing section where it is mounted just to the left of the headlamp, and on ZX1100 C models it is behind the left-hand sidepanel where it is mounted just to the rear of the starter relay.

2   If the turn signal lamps cease to function correctly, there may be several possible causes before the relay is suspected. First check that the fuses are intact and that the battery is fully charged. Check that the turn signal lamps are securely mounted and that all the earth connections are clean and tight. Check that the bulbs are all of the correct wattage and that corrosion has not developed on the bulbs or in their holders. Any such corrosion must be thoroughly cleaned off to ensure proper bulb contact. Also check that the turn signal switch is functioning correctly and that the wiring is in good order.

19.1 On ZX1100 C models turn signal relay is situated next to starter relay

3   Faults in any one of the above items will produce symptoms for which the turn signal relay may be unfairly blamed. If the fault persists even after the preliminary checks have been made the relay is at fault and must be renewed, no further test details are available.

4   All US models are fitted with hazard warning lights, operated from a switch on the left-hand handlebar cluster. With the hazard switch in the ON position and the ignition switch in the ON or PARK positions, all four turn signal lamps, plus the warning lamps, should flash. If a fault develops check the turn signal circuit and relay as described above. If this fails to cure the problem, the hazard switch itself must be at fault. Identify the switch wires using the appropriate wiring diagram at the end of this chapter, disconnect the handlebar switch block connector and check for continuity across the pairs of switch terminals as shown in the switch boxes at the base of the diagram.

20 Horns: location and testing

1   The horns are mounted inside the fairing on each side of the radiator. To gain access to the horns it will be necessary to remove the lower and side fairing sections as described in Chapter 5.

20.1 Horns are mounted on each side of the radiator

2   If the horns fail to work, first check that the fuses are intact. Check that power is reaching the horns by disconnecting their wires and connecting them to two 12 volt bulbs. Switch on the ignition and press the horn button. If the bulbs light, the horn circuit is proved good and the horn is at fault. If not, there is a fault in either the wiring or horn button which must be found and rectified.

3   To test a horn, connect a fully charged 12 volt battery directly to the horn itself. If it does not sound, a gentle tap on the outside of the horn may free the internal contacts. If this fails the horn must be renewed; repairs are not possible.

21 Bulbs: renewal

Headlamp and parking lamp

1   The headlamp bulb is of the quartz-halogen type with a conventional H4 fitting. Do not touch the bulb's glass envelope as skin acids will shorten the bulb's service life. If the bulb is accidentally touched, it should be wiped carefully when cold with a rag soaked in methylated spirits (stoddard solvent) and dried before being refitted.

2   To renew the headlamp bulb it will probably be necessary to remove the fairing, however, some owners might find it possible to renew the bulb with the fairing still fitted to the machine. Due to the amount of work necessary to remove the fairing it is therefore recommended that an attempt be made to carry out the operation with the fairing on the machine. If this proves unsuccessful, the fairing should be removed as described in Chapter 5. The same applies to the parking/pilot lamp bulb although this will be considerably easier to renew. On ZX900 and ZX1000 A models both operations can be made easier by removing the small cover situated below the headlamp on the underside of the upper fairing section.

3   Unplug the headlamp bulb connector and remove the rubber bulb cover from the back of the headlamp unit noting its correct position. On ZX900 models remove the bulb holder by pushing it in towards the headlamp unit and turning it anticlockwise, and on ZX1000 and ZX1100 C models disengage the bulb retaining spring clip from the headlamp unit. On all models withdraw the headlamp bulb. On refitting, note that the locating tangs on the metal bulb collar are offset so that the bulb can only be fitted one way. Secure the bulb with its holder or clip (as applicable) and fit the rubber bulb cover ensuring that it is fitted in its original position and is correctly seated. Refit the headlamp connector. Check the headlamp beam setting as described in Routine maintenance.

4   The parking/pilot lamp bulb holder is a push fit in the headlamp assembly. The bulb is a bayonet fit into the holder and can be removed by pressing it in and turning it anticlockwise.

Stop and tail lamp

5   All models are fitted with twin stop/tail lamp bulbs which can be accessed from inside the tail section once the seat has been removed. Remove the bulb holders from the back of the tail lamp assembly by turning them anticlockwise. The bulbs are a bayonet fit and can be removed from their holders by pressing them in and turning them anticlockwise. The bulbs are refitted by a reversal of the removal procedure noting that the pins on each bulb are offset to prevent it from being incorrectly fitted.

Turn signal lamps

6   To renew the turn signal bulbs on ZX900 models remove the screw from the back of the lamp and remove the lens and bulbholder assembly. Release the two small screws which secure the bulbholder to the lens and remove the lens. The bulb can then be removed by pressing it in and turning it anticlockwise. On refitting ensure the rubber lens gasket is correctly positioned and take care not to overtighten the lens retaining screws.

7   On ZX1000 A models to renew the front bulbs, lever out the two plugs from the turn signal assembly and remove the two screws which secure each unit to the fairing. Partially withdraw the turn signal, remove the bulb holder by turning it anticlockwise, and lower the assembly away from the machine. The bulb can then be removed from its holder by pressing it in and turning it anticlockwise. The bulb is refitted by a reversal of the removal procedure ensuring that the rubber

21.3a Fit the bulb to the headlamp unit ...

21.3b ... and secure it with the retaining clip (or holder)

21.3c Ensure rubber bulb cover is correctly installed and refit the headlamp connector

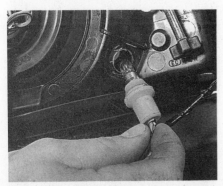

21.4a Parking lamp bulbholder is a push fit in the headlamp unit ...

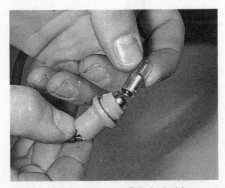

21.4b ... bulb is a bayonet fit in its holder

21.5a Stop/tail lamp bulbholders are removed from inside the tail section

21.5b Note offset pins on bulb to prevent incorrect installation

21.6a On ZX900 models release screw from the back of the lamp ...

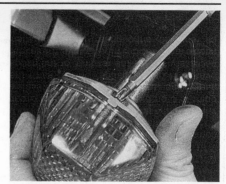

21.6b ... remove lens assembly and slacken two screws which secure lens to the bulbholder

21.6c On refitting do not omit the lens gasket

21.9a On ZX1100 C models remove the retaining screw and pull the lamp out of position

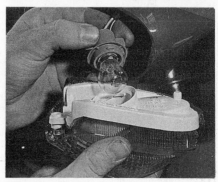

21.9b Bulbholder is a screw fit into the lamp

21.10 Instrument panel bulbs are of the capless type

damper is correctly positioned between the turn signal and the fairing.

8   To gain access to the front bulbs on ZX1000 B models it will first be necessary to remove the inner fairing sections as described in Chapter 5. The bulb holder can then be reached from inside the fairing and removed from the back of the turn signal lamp by turning it anticlockwise. The bulb can then be removed by pressing it in and turning it anticlockwise, and is refitted by reversing the removal sequence.

9   Both front and rear turn signal bulbs on ZX1100 C models, and the rear bulbs on ZX1000 models are renewed by removing the screw(s) which secure the lamp, and withdrawing the lamp from the bodywork. Remove the bulb holder and bulb as described above. On refitting do not overtighten the lamp retaining screw(s).

Instrument panel bulbs

10   Remove the instrument panel from the machine as described in Section 20 of Chapter 5. All instrument panel bulbs are of the capless type being pressed into their holders, which are also a push fit into the underside of the instrument panel. Be careful not to damage the delicate wire terminals of the bulbs when removing or refitting them.

Chapter 8 The ZX1100 D model

Contents

Specifications

Refer to the specifications for the ZX1100 C model in all previous chapters, unless given here.

Specifications relating to Routine maintenance

Engine

Idle speed:

UK and US 49-state models .... 950 – 1050 rpm

California models .... 1150 – 1250 rpm

Cycle parts

Brake pad friction material thickness .... 4.0 mm (0.157 in)

Service limit .... 1.0 mm (0.039 in)

Front forks:

Oil capacity per leg – at oil change .... 410 cc (14.4 Imp fl oz, 13.9 US fl oz)

Fork oil level* .... 133 ± 2 mm (5.2 ± 0.08 in)

*Measured with fork fully compressed and without spring

Specifications relating to Chapter 1

Piston

Second compression ring groove width .... 0.82 – 0.84 mm (0.032 – 0.033 in)

Service limit .... 0.92 mm (0.036 in)

Second compression ring/groove clearance .... 0.03 – 0.07 mm (0.001 – 0.003 in)

Service limit .... 0.17 mm (0.007 in)

Piston rings

Second compression ring thickness .... 0.77 – 0.79 mm (0.030 – 0.031 in)

Service limit .... 0.70 mm (0.027 in)

Torque settings	kgf m	lbf ft
Main engine mounting bolts	4.5	33.0
Frame cradle retaining bolts	4.5	33.0
Rear mounting bolt collar Allen screws	2.0	14.5

Specifications relating to Chapter 2

Torque settings

Coolant drain plug .... 1.0 kgf m (7.0 lbf ft)

Specifications relating to Chapter 3

Fuel tank capacity
Overall .... 24 litres (5.28 Imp gal, 6.34 US gal)
Reserve .... 6.5 litres (1.43 Imp gal, 1.72 US gal)

Carburettors
Make .... Keihin
Type CVKD40
Main jet:
    Cylinders 1 and 4 .... 160 (158*)
    Cylinders 2 and 3 .... 158 (155*)
Main air jet 70
Jet needle N96X
Pilot jet 38 (35*)
Pilot air jet:
    UK models 130
    US models 120
Starter jet 58
Pilot screw – turns out:
    UK models 2
    US models .... Preset
Fuel level – below mark .... 4.5 ± 1 mm (0.177 ± 0.040 in)
Float height .... 13 ± 2 mm (0.512 ± 0.080 in)
Idle speed:
    UK and US 49-state models .... 950 – 1050 rpm
    California models .... 1150 – 1250 rpm
Note: specifications denoted by the asterisk (*) apply when machine is used at high altitude

Specifications relating to Chapter 5

Front forks
Wheel travel .... 120 mm (4.72 in)
Fork spring standard free length .... 295 mm (11.6 in)
Fork spring free length service limit .... 289 mm (11.4 in)
Fork oil capacity per leg – after reassembly .... 465 ± 4 cc (16.4 ± 0.14 Imp fl oz, 15.7 ± 0.13 US fl oz)
Fork oil capacity per leg – at oil change .... 410 cc (14.4 Imp fl oz, 13.9 US fl oz)
Fork oil level* .... 133 ± 2 mm (5.2 ± 0.08 in)
Recommended fork oil .... SAE10W/20 fork oil
Measured with fork fully compressed and without spring

Rear suspension
Wheel travel .... 112 mm (4.41 in)
Air pressure .... Not applicable

Specifications relating to Chapter 6

Tyre sizes
Front 120/70ZR17
Rear 180/55ZR17

Rear brake
Brake pad service limit .... 1 mm (0.04 in)
Pedal height .... 45 mm (1.77 in)
Master cylinder pushrod standard length .... 80 ± 1 mm (3.15 ± 0.04 in)

Torque settings	kgf m	lbf ft
Wheel spindles:		
Front	15.0	110.0
Rear	11.0	80.0
Brake disc bolts:		
Front	2.3	17.0
Rear	2.5	18.0
Front brake caliper:		
Mounting bolts	3.5	25.0
Joining bolts	2.1	15.0
Rear brake caliper:		
Mounting bolts	2.5	18.0
Joining bolts	Not available	

Specifications relating to Chapter 7

Battery
Capacity .... 12 Ah

Fuel gauge sender unit resistances
In full position .... 4 – 10 ohms
In empty position .... 90 – 100 ohms

Fuses

Main	30A
Headlamp	10A
Tail lamp	10A
Fan	10A
Accessory	10A

Bulbs

Headlamp	12V 60/55W
Parking lamp – UK models only	12V 5W
Stop/tail lamp:	
UK models	12V 21/5W
US models	12V 27/8W
Turn signal lamps:	
UK models	12V 21W
US models	12V 23/8W (front), 12V 23W (rear)
Instrument and gauge illuminating lamps	12V 1.7W
Warning lamps	12V 3.4W
Licence plate lamp	12V 5W

1 Introduction

This Chapter provides specifications and revised procedures for the ZX1100 D where they differ from that given for its predecessor, the ZX1100 C, in previous Chapters. If the information cannot be found in this Chapter, refer back to that given for the ZX1100 C in the main part of this book.

The ZX1100 D1 (ZZ-R1100 or ZX-11D) was introduced in December 1992 in the UK to supersede the ZX1100 C3. In the US the ZX1100 D1 ran alongside the ZX1100 C4 for 1993, with the C4 being discontinued at the end of that year. For 1994 both UK and US have the ZX1100 D2. See the engine and frame number details in the main introductory text at the beginning of this Manual for a means of model identification.

The main differences between the ZX1100 D and C models lie in the intake system, fairing and frame. The ZX1100 D has a twin Ram Air intake system, a redesigned fairing, modified frame and rear engine mountings, a new rear brake caliper and a fuel gauge. Differences between the D1 and D2 models are cosmetic.

2 Routine maintenance

Cooling system – level check

1   The expansion tank is situated beneath the tail section on the right-hand side. Its coolant level can be checked by observing the level marks on the front portion of the tank once the seat has been removed. If the marks are indistinct, remove the tail section for a better view.
2   Check the coolant level with the engine cold and the machine held upright. The level should be between the Upper and Lower lines. To top up the coolant, unscrew the tank cap and add the specified coolant mixture (see *Routine maintenance*) to replenish the level. In an emergency, distilled water alone can be used, but remember that this will dilute the coolant and reduce its protection against freezing.
3   Do not overfill the reservoir tank otherwise excess coolant will be expelled via the breather hose when the engine has warmed up; siphon some off if overfilled. **Warning**: *Antifreeze is poisonous – don't siphon by mouth.*

Air filter element – removal, cleaning and refitting

4   Remove the fuel tank as described in Section 5.
5   Remove its seven screws and lift off the air filter housing cover, noting its sealing ring. Lift out the element and its support frames.
6   Separate the element from its support frames and inspect it for damage. If torn or excessively dirty, renew it. Clean the element by soaking it in a high flash-point solvent such as white spirit (stoddard solvent); do not use petrol (gasoline) due to the fire risk. Squeeze the element gently to remove all old oil and dirt, but do not wring it otherwise it will be damaged.
7   Dry the element thoroughly and leave it awhile to allow the excess solvent to evaporate. When dry, soak it in fresh SE class SAE30 motor oil, then carefully squeeze out the excess oil. When it is slightly oily to the touch it can be refitted.
8   Make sure the housing is clean, then install the element (grey foam side upwards, yellow side downwards) complete with support frames. Check that the air screen is correctly installed (protrusion facing the carburettor air intakes) and that the seal is in position, then fit the housing cover. Tighten the cover screws securely and refit the fuel tank.

Air vent filter and oil reservoir – cleaning

9   Clean the air vent filter and drain the transparent oil reservoir as described in *Routine maintenance*. The air vent filter can be accessed after removing the fairing inner panel (see Section 7).

Evaporative Emission Control System – check (California models)

10   In addition to the check of the system lines described under the 3000 mile (5000 km) service interval in *Routine maintenance*, check the transparent reservoir on the left-hand side of the engine. It lies next to the air filter oil reservoir and runs from the T-piece connection between the vacuum valve and canister. Remove the plug from the pipe end and drain off any fluid from the reservoir.

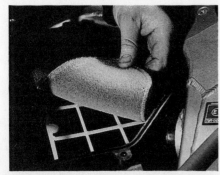
2.8a Install the air filter element with its grey foam side uppermost

2.8b Place the support frame over the element

2.8c Protrusion on air screen must face the carburettor intakes

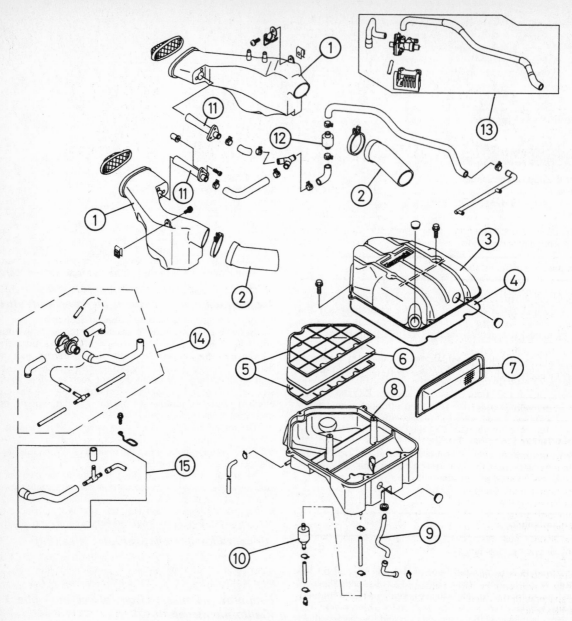

Fig. 8.1 Air filter (Sec 2)

1	Air intake ducts	5	Element support frames
2	Connecting hoses to filter housing	6	Air filter element
3	Housing cover	7	Air screen
4	Seal	8	Housing

9	Crankcase breather hose
10	Oil reservoir
11	Carburettor air intakes
12	Air vent filter

13	Vacuum valve – California only
14	Air suction vacuum switch valve
15	Alternative connections for California

Rear suspension settings – check

11   The method of adjusting spring preload and damping is the same as described for the ZX1100 C model in Routine maintenance.

12   The standard setting for spring preload is 19.5 mm (0.76 in), although a usable range of 19 – 31 mm (0.75 – 1.22 in) provides a degree of flexibility for riding style and load.

Rear brake caliper – brake pad wear check and renewal

Note: *Take care not to inhale any brake dust during this operation, and read the notes given in 'Safety first!' concerning asbestos.*

13   It is possible to remove the pads without removing the caliper from its mountings, but access is difficult due to the caliper's location. Remove the caliper as follows, or proceed to Step 15.

14   To remove the caliper, extract the split pin and unscrew the nut from the torque arm rear bolt. Displace the bolt and free the torque arm. Remove the two Allen-head bolts which retain the caliper to its mounting bracket. There is no need to disconnect the fluid hose, just make sure no strain is placed on it.

15   Pry free the black plastic cover from the base of the caliper and using pliers, extract the two R-pins (pad retaining pin clips). While releasing pressure from the pad springs, pull the pad retaining pins from the caliper and lift out the brake pads.

16   Measure the thickness of each pad's friction material; if worn to or beyond the service limit, both pads must be renewed as a set. The pads fitted as original equipment have a slot between the pad material and metal backing which when exposed indicates the need for pad renewal. Renewal is also required if they are fouled with oil or grease, badly scored or damaged.

2.18a Install the pads in the caliper ...

2.18b ... slide one pad retaining pin into place, then install the pad springs and fit the other retaining pin ...

2.18c ... secure with the R-pins (retaining pin clips)

17   If the pads are in good condition, clean them with a fine wire brush (which itself is not oily or dirty) and remove any glazed areas with emery cloth.

18   If new pads are being fitted you will have to push the pistons back into their bores to allow clearance for the thicker friction material. Refit the pads in the caliper, and with the pad springs in position, fit the pad pins (requires some perseverance if being done with the caliper in situ). Secure the pad pins with the R-pins (retaining pin clips). Install the plastic cover.

19   If removed, install the caliper on its mounting bracket and tighten the bolts to the specified torque. Remake the torque arm connection and tighten the nut to the specified torque; secure with a new split pin.

20   Check the operation of the rear brake before riding the machine.

3   Engine, clutch and gearbox

Removal and refitting procedure

1   Follow the procedure given in Chapter 1, Section 4 for the ZX1100 C model up to the point where the engine is only retained by its mounting bolts. Note also the revised procedures for fairing, air filter and fuel tank removal contained in this Chapter.

2   Prior to removing the rear mounting bolts, slacken the Allen screw on each supporting collar, inboard of the frame on the left-hand side. Access to the top Allen screw can be made from above, whereas the lower Allen screw must be accessed from below and to the rear. Removal of ail engine mountings can then continue as described in Chapter 1, Section 4 .

3   When refitting the two rear engine mounting bolts, install the collar on the left-hand side, with its flanged head facing the right-hand side. Clamp the spacer with the Allen screw, noting the torque setting given in the Specifications.

4   Cooling system

Draining and filling

1   Refer to Chapter 2, Section 2, noting that the seat and tail section

must be removed to gain access to the expansion tank as described in Section 7 of this Chapter.

2   To drain the expansion tank, remove its two mounting bolts and invert the tank to expel the coolant .

Radiator – removal, cleaning, examination and refitting

3   Refer to the information in Chapter 2, Section 5 for the ZX1100 C model. The ZX1100 D radiator assembly is shown in Fig. 8.2.

Thermostat – removal, testing and refitting

4   Refer to paragraphs 1 and 2 of Chapter 2, Section 8 concerning thermostat operation. To remove the thermostat proceed as follows.

5   The thermostat/pressure cap assembly is mounted on a bracket attached to the front right-hand side of the frame, just to the rear of the air intake duct. Remove the fairing for access (see Section 7).

6   If only the thermostat is being removed, there is no need to disconnect any of the hoses or electrical connections, although be prepared for a small amount of coolant loss. Remove the four screws and separate the thermostat housing from the pressure cap neck. Lift the thermostat out of its housing .

7   To remove the housing completely, disconnect the electrical connector to the temperature sensor switch, the earth wire, and the main coolant hose. Similarly, if the pressure cap neck requires removal, disconnect the reservoir tank hose and main coolant hose, followed by the bolts retaining it to its bracket.

8   The thermostat opening temperature and lift can be checked as described in Chapter 2, Section 8.

9   When refitting the thermostat in its housing note that it must be positioned with the bypass hole at the top. Replenish any lost coolant.

Water pump – removal, examination and refitting

10   Follow the procedure given in Chapter 2, Section 9 for the ZX1100 C model. Removal of the fairing left-hand side section will be necessary for access to the water pump, but there is no need to remove the gearchange linkage, clutch slave cylinder and engine sprocket cover.

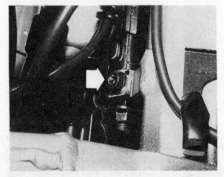

3.2 Upper rear engine mounting bolt Allen screw location (arrow)

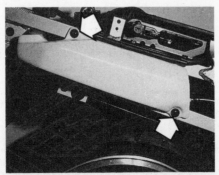

4.2 Coolant expansion tank mountings (arrows)

4.6 Thermostat/pressure cap assembly. Thermostat housing outer screws (A)

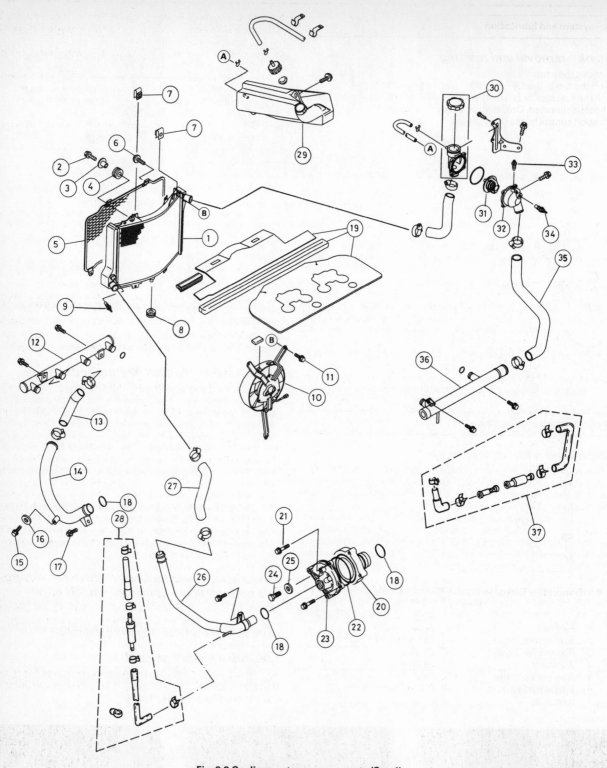

Fig. 8.2 Cooling system components (Sec 4)

1	Radiator	10	Fan	20	Water pump	29	Expansion tank
2	Bolt – 2 off	11	Bolt – 3 off	21	Air bleed bolt	30	Pressure cap neck
3	Spacer – 2 off	12	Front coolant pipe	22	O-ring	31	Thermostat
4	Mounting rubber – 2 off	13	Lower hose	23	Water pump cover	32	Thermostat housing
5	Radiator guard	14	Lower metal pipe	24	Drain plug	33	Bleed valve
6	Screw – 4 off	15	Drain plug	25	Sealing washer	34	Temperature sensor switch
7	Nut – 7 off	16	Sealing washer	26	Water pump to cylinder metal pipe	35	Upper hose
8	Mounting rubber	17	Bolt	27	Water pump to cylinder hose	36	Upper metal pipe
9	Fan switch	18	O-rings	28	Carburettor warmer pipe check valve assembly – UK only	37	Carburettor warmer pipe filter assembly – UK only
		19	Insulators				

5 Fuel system and lubrication

Fuel tank – removal and refitting

1   Remove the seat.

2   With the tap in the OFF position, squeeze the clamp ears together and pull the fuel supply hose off the lower union on the tap; leave the other hoses connected. On California models, label and then disconnect the emission control hoses from the rear of the tank.

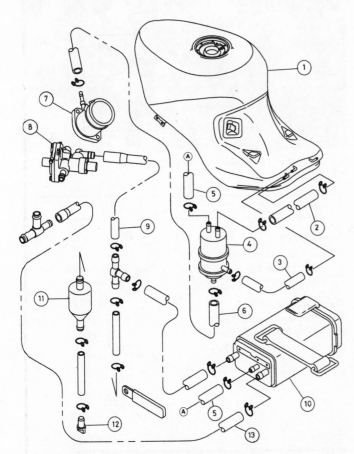

Fig. 8.3 Evaporative Emission Control System – California models (Sec 5)

1	Fuel tank	8	Vacuum valve
2	Blue-marked hose	9	Yellow-marked hose
3	Red-marked hose	10	Canister
4	Separator	11	Catch reservoir
5	Blue-marked hose	12	Plug
6	White-marked hose	13	Green-marked hose
7	Inlet stub		

3   Remove the two mounting bolts at the rear and two at the front, and lift the tank sufficiently to disconnect the level gauge wiring and pull free the fuel breather pipe (where fitted).

4   Refer to the information in Chapter 3, Section 3 concerning fuel tank repair and contamination problems.

5   There are two fuel filters inside the tank, which can be reached once the ON and RES hose links are detached from the tank underside. Remove the filters and flush them through with clean fuel whilst observing the necessary fire precautions.

6   Refit the tank in a reverse of the removal sequence, making sure that all hoses are routed correctly. The emission control hose connections are given in Fig. 8.3. Check that there is no sign of fuel leakage before riding the machine.

Fuel tap – removal and refitting

7   Remove the fuel tank as described above.

8   Move the lever to the RES position and drain the fuel into a suitable container. Remove the two bolts retaining the tap to the tank and disconnect the short ON and RES hoses from the tap to the tank underside.

9   To dismantle the tap, remove the central screw and remove the operating lever – note the spring and steel ball which will drop free. Remove the disc, O-ring and seal from the tap body.

10   Clean the tap body thoroughly and renew the seal if leakage has been noted or signs of deterioration are apparent. Renew the large O-ring. Ensure that the steel ball is correctly located in its detent when refitting the operating lever.

11   Refit the fuel tap and tank in a reverse of the removal procedure.

Carburettors – removal and refitting

12   Refer to Chapter 3, Section 7 for the ZX1100 C models, noting the following.

13   Remove the air filter element as described in Section 2.

14   To remove the air filter housing, first remove the eight bolts from around the carburettor intakes, noting that access to one of them is made by removing the plug in the rear of the filter housing. You will notice that the housing is only held to the carburettors by four of these bolts, the other four just retain the plate between the carburettor bank and housing.

15   Push the air intake ducts out of the front of the housing and pull the large diameter crankcase breather hose out of the housing at the rear. Raise the housing slightly, and pull off the small diameter breather pipes at the front, the oil reservoir pipe at the rear, and the air suction valve hose at the centre. Lift the air filter housing free, and remove the plate from the carburettors.

Evaporative Emission Control System – description and examination – California models only

16   Refer to the text in Chapter 3, Section 13 for description and examination of the system components. The system fitted to ZX1100 D models is shown in the accompanying illustration.

Clean air system – general

17   Previously only fitted to US models in the range, the system is now fitted to the UK ZX1100 D models. Its purpose and component parts are described in Chapter 3, Section 16.

5.5 Detach the hose link and unscrew each filter for cleaning

5.8 Disconnect the ON and RES hose links from the rear of the tap

5.14 One of the air filter housing bolts must be accessed from side of housing

18 Although entirely automatic in its operation, it is necessary to perform a check of the valves on the cylinder head cover at the 3000 mile (5000 km) service interval – see *Routine maintenance* for details.
19 To gain access to the valves on all ZX1100 D models, remove the fairing side sections and air filter housing.

6 Ignition system

Ignition coils – location

1 The ignition coils are mounted inboard of the frame top rails, near the steering head. To gain access to them, remove the fuel tank and fairing inner panel (removal of the air filter housing will improve access greatly).
2 The coil for cylinders 1 and 4 is mounted on the left frame section, and that for cylinders 2 and 3 on the right; two bolts secure each coil.
3 Testing can be carried out as described in Chapter 4, Section 6 for the ZX1100 C model.

IC Ignitor unit – testing

4 The ignitor is mounted to the rear mudguard by two bolts. Remove the seat for access .
5 A test of the ignitor's internal resistance can be made by making the connections shown in Fig. 8.4. Note that Kawasaki advise the use of their multimeter, Part No. 57001-983 for making these tests since other meters might produce different readings. It should, however, be possible to gain an indication of the unit's condition with another type of meter, and then have your findings confirmed by a Kawasaki dealer. *Do not use a meter with a large capacity battery as this will almost certainly damage the unit.*
6 Make sure the ignition is switched off and disconnect the multi-pin connector, then remove the two mounting bolts and lift the unit from the machine. Make the meter connections shown in the test table. If your results do not closely resemble those in the table, the ignitor should be renewed.

6.4 IC ignitor is retained by two bolts (A). Disconnect at connector (B) for testing

7 Frame and forks

Front forks

Preload and damping adjustment

1 Refer to the information given in *Routine maintenance* for the ZX1100 C models.

Removal and refitting

2 Refer to Chapter 5, Sections 2 and 5, noting the following differences from the ZX1100 C model.

Unit : kΩ

Lead		Tester (+) Lead Connection								
	Terminal	**R**	**BK/Y**	**Y**	**BK/W**	**BK**	**G**	**G/BK**	**R/W**	**BK/R**
(−)*	**R**	–	2.8 ~ 12	4.9 ~ 20	2.8 ~ 12	6.7 ~ 28	6.7 ~ 28	8.5 ~ 34	3.1 ~ 13	8.1 ~ 33
	BK/Y	40 ~ 170	–	1.4 ~ 5.7	0	1.7 ~ 7.2	1.7 ~ 7.2	3.9 ~ 16	0.2 ~ 0.8	2.2 ~ 9.0
	Y	42 ~ 170	1.4 ~ 5.7	–	1.4 ~ 5.7	3.7 ~ 15	3.7 ~ 15	5.2 ~ 21	1.6 ~ 6.4	4.3 ~ 18
	BK/W	40 ~ 170	0	1.4 ~ 5.7	–	1.7 ~ 7.2	1.7 ~ 7.2	3.9 ~ 16	0.2 ~ 0.8	2.2 ~ 9.0
	BK	∞	∞	∞	∞	–	∞	∞	∞	∞
	G	∞	∞	∞	∞	∞	–	∞	∞	∞
	G/BK	46 ~ 190	4.2 ~ 17	5.6 ~ 23	4.2 ~ 17	7.5 ~ 30	7.5 ~ 30	–	8.1 ~ 33	4.4 ~ 18
	R/W	42 ~ 170	0.2 ~ 0.8	1.5 ~ 6.3	0.2 ~ 0.8	2.0 ~ 8.2	2.0 ~ 8.2	4.0 ~ 17	–	2.5 ~ 10
	BK/R	70 ~ 280	30 ~ 120	30 ~ 130	30 ~ 120	42 ~170	42 ~ 170	34 ~ 140	30 ~ 120	–

(−)*: Tester (−) Lead Connection

Fig. 8.4 IC Ignitor unit test table (Sec 6)

See wiring diagrams for wire colour key

7.4a Front mudguard rear section lower screw ...

7.4b ... and top screws (only one shown)

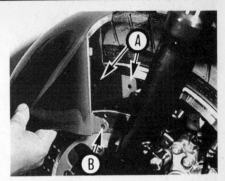

7.4c Front mudguard front section inner (A) and outer mountings (B) on fork leg

7.5a Install plain washer on top of fork spring ...

7.5b ... followed by spacer and special washer ...

7.5c ... then install top bolt

3   There is no requirement to remove the handlebar castings from the top yoke unless you intend dismantling the forks, in which case it is good practice to slacken off the top bolts whilst firmly held in the yokes. When sliding the forks back into place, the top surface of the top bolt hex should be level with the top surface of the handlebar clamp.

4   To remove the front mudguard, first remove the single screw on each side, followed by the two screws at the join of the front and rear sections at the top. Unscrew the speedometer cable knurled nut at the wheel end and pull the cable through the guide on the mudguard. Free both brake hydraulic hoses from their guide clips, then manoeuvre the mudguard rear section free. To remove the front section, remove the two bolts from each fork lower leg and the single screw on each outer face. Make sure that the brake hoses and speedometer cable are correctly located after refitting the mudguard.

Dismantling and reassembly

5   Refer to the procedure in Chapter 5, Section 3 and Fig. 5.2, noting that there is a special washer, spacer and plain washer situated on top of the fork spring. Apart from this, all procedures for fork overhaul are unchanged from that given for the ZX1100 C model.

Fig. 8.5 Suspension linkage (Sec 7)

1   Tie-rods
2   Tie-rod-to-swinging arm through-bolt
3   Inner sleeves
4   Dust seals
5   Needle roller bearings
6   Nuts
7   Dust seals
8   Relay arm
9   Tie-rod-to-relay arm through-bolt
10 Relay arm-to-frame through-bolt
11 Grease nipples

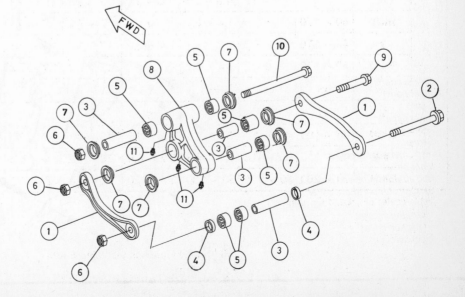

Fig. 8.6 Fairing (Sec 7)

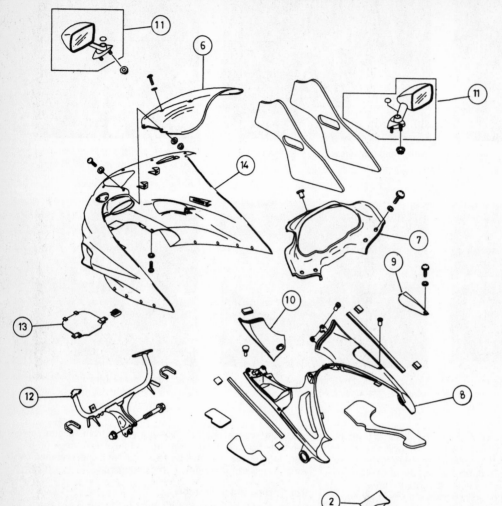

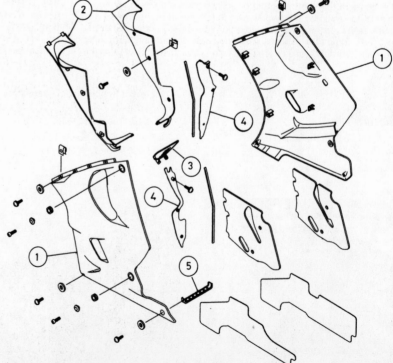

1 Side sections
2 Inner panels
3 Guard
4 Inner panels
5 Joining strut
6 Screen
7 Instrument panel cover
8 Inner panel
9 Radiator pressure cap access cover
10 Storage compartment cover
11 Mirrors
12 Mounting bracket
13 Inspection cover
14 Main fairing

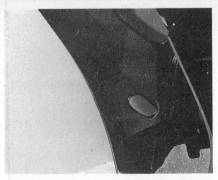

7.13a Remove the three screws on the fairing side section front inner edge ...

7.13b ... and the single screw at the lower corner

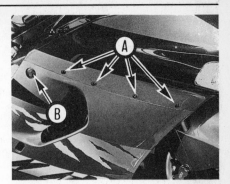

7.14a Remove the four screws (A) along the main fairing bottom edge, the single Allen screw (B) ...

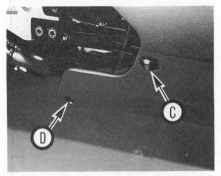

7.14b ... followed by the single Allen screw (C) and strut mounting screw (D)

7.18 Instrument panel cover is retained by two screws (arrows) on each side

7.22a Pull the hose off the air vent filter ...

7.22b ... and slacken the screw on each air intake duct clamp

7.23 Main fairing is retained to its mounting bracket at the mirror mountings

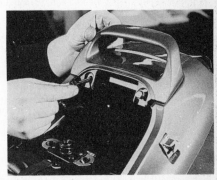

7.26 Grab rail is retained by two bolts

7.27 Flip up luggage hooks to reveal their retaining screws

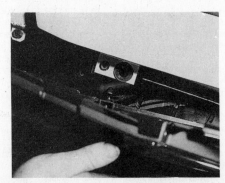

7.29a Ensure that panel stub engages grommet on refitting

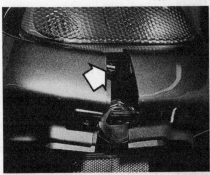

7.29b Tab must engage properly where two panels meet under tail lamp (arrow)

Rear suspension unit – removal and refitting

6   Refer to Chapter 5, Sections 11 and 13 for the ZX1100 C model. Ignore the reference to the remote oil reservoir.

Suspension linkage – removal and refitting

7   Place a suitably-sized block of wood under the rear wheel to prevent the wheel dropping when the suspension bolts are removed. Detach the torque arm from the brake caliper and swing it downwards out of the way.
8   The tie-rods can be released after removing the through-bolts at their upper and lower ends. The right-hand exhaust pipe silencer prevents access to the tie-rod-to-swinging arm bolt, and will thus require removal first.
9   To release the relay arm first detach the right-hand exhaust pipe silencer for access. Remove the suspension unit lower mounting bolt, the tie-rod lower end through-bolt (if not already done), and the relay arm-to-frame through-bolt.

Seat mechanism

10   The seat latch is operated by a short cable from the seat lock. To gain access to the cable, first remove the seat and trace the cable's route.
11   To remove the cable, first remove the latch mechanism bolts and invert the latch to allow the cable end to be disconnected. Turning attention to the seat lock, remove the two bolts from its mounting bracket and manoeuvre the bracket so that access can be gained to the cable connection on its reverse side. Release the outer cable from its stay and free the cable trunnion from the lock lever.

Fairing – removal and refitting

Side sections

12   While it may be possible to remove the fairing side sections as a complete assembly, the following procedure is advised to avoid the likelihood of damage. This involves removing each panel separately, and may well be preferable if work is only required on one side of the machine.
13   Start by removing the four screws from the front edge of one of the side sections (three are accessed from inside the panel, and the fourth, or lower screw, from the outside face).
14   Remove the four screws along the main fairing bottom edge on each side, and the single Allen screw at the top and bottom rear corners on each side. Also remove the screw securing the panel to the strut on the underside at the rear. The side section is now free.
15   Having removed one side section, you can either perform the same procedure on the other side section which will allow the delicate inner panels to be freed separately, or just the steps in paragraph 14, which will retain the inner panel with the side section. If you choose the latter, however, be very careful not to break the inner panel as it is withdrawn.
16   Refit the fairing side sections in a reversal of the removal procedure, but install the main fasteners only finger-tight during installation. When you are satisfied with the final fit of the panels secure all fasteners.

Screen and inner panels

17   Remove the six screws which retain the windscreen to the fairing and lift the screen free. The two outer screws have nuts on the inside of the fairing.
18   Having removed the screen, detach the instrument panel cover by removing its four retaining screws. Manoeuvre the panel off the instruments .
19   The fairing inner panel is held by the four instrument panel cover screws described above, two bolts on the fuel tank front mounting and the single Allen screw at the top corner of each fairing side section. With care, the inner panel can be manoeuvred over the fuel tank, although if in doubt about doing this safely remove the tank first.
20   When refitting the inner panel, make sure that its front ends rest on the two cushioned support brackets and that the inner panel and instrument panel cover mesh properly together before tightening the screws. Note that apart from the two outer screws, the main screen retaining screws thread into nuts held in the instrument panel cover; check that all threads are visible and correctly aligned before fitting the screen and do not overtighten them.

Main section

21   Remove the side sections, screen and inner panels as described above. The main fairing is removed complete with the headlamp, turn signals and air ducts, leaving the instruments attached to the mounting bracket.
22   Working from inside the fairing, pull the hose off the air vent filter and free it from its clip on the right-hand air intake duct. Slacken the clamps of both air intake ducts.
23   Remove the two nuts on each mirror mounting to release the mirrors and main fairing from the mounting frame. Ease the fairing forwards until the 6-pin wiring connector (coloured black) can be disconnected, then remove the fairing fully.
24   Refit all components in the reverse of the removal procedure, paying particular attention to the correct location of any spacers and damper strips.

Tail unit – removal and refitting

25   Remove the seat.
26   Remove its two bolts and detach the grab rail. Remove the two screws directly under the grab rail.
27   Working on one panel at a time, release the screw from the front portion, then flip up the luggage hooks and release the screws retaining them.
28   There is a further screw at the joint of the two panels, just under the tail lamp. Once removed, unhook the two sidepanels at the rear joint and gently pry them off the mounting stub on the frame. The rear turn signals are detached with the panel, but reach behind and twist out the bulbholder as the panel is withdrawn. The fillet between both sections at the top can be lifted free.
29   Refit in the reverse of the removal procedure, noting that the rear joint hook should be engaged before the retaining screws are secured. Take care not to overtighten the screws and ensure that all grommets and damping rubbers are correctly located.

---

8   Wheels, brakes and tyres

Rear brake caliper – removal, overhaul and refitting

Note: *Brake fluid will discolour or remove paint if contact is allowed. Avoid this where possible and remove accidental splashes immediately. Similarly, avoid contact between the fluid and plastic parts.*

Removal

1   Extract the split pin and unscrew the nut from the torque arm rear bolt. Displace the bolt and let the torque arm drop free. Remove the two Allen-head bolts which retain the caliper to its mounting bracket.
2   If caliper overhaul is intended, remove the hose banjo bolt and allow the fluid to drain into a container. Wrap a plastic bag around the end of the hose to prevent the entry of dirt into the system and prevent further fluid loss. Manoeuvre the caliper off the disc.

Overhaul

3   Refer to Section 2 and remove the brake pads from the caliper.
4   To extract the pistons the caliper halves must be separated by removing the two hex-head bolts. To enable the assembly to be held firmly whilst the bolts are slackened it is advised that the caliper be remounted on its bracket.
5   Separate the caliper halves and mop up any lost fluid. The pistons must be removed from their bores using air pressure; attempts at prying them from position will almost certainly damage the bore and piston surface. When working on the inner half of the caliper apply air pressure via the fluid passage to force the piston free. On the outer half, use a block of wood with one side faced with a rubber pad to seal the fluid passage and allow air pressure to force the piston out (see Fig. 6.3 in Chapter 6). Make sure each piston leaves its bore squarely and take care to avoid trapped fingers as it emerges.
6   Remove the fluid and dust seals from the piston bores and the O-ring from the fluid passage.
7   Inspect each piston and its bore for signs of extreme wear and damage. Keep each piston with its matched bore. Inspect the bearing and dust seals in the torque arm mounting.
8   Install new fluid and dust seals in the caliper bore and using only new hydraulic fluid, install the pistons.

8.4 Caliper hex-head joining bolts (arrows)

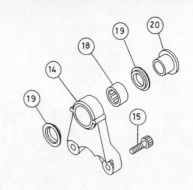

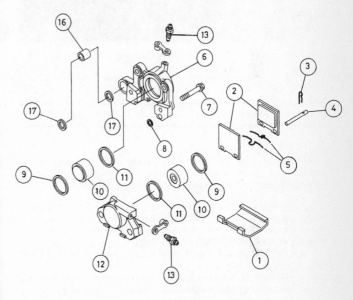

Fig. 8.7 Rear brake caliper (Sec 8)

1	Plastic cover	11	Fluid seals
2	Brake pads	12	Caliper inner half
3	R-pin – 2 off	13	Bleed valves
4	Pad retaining pin – 2 off	14	Caliper mounting bracket
5	Anti-rattle springs	15	Allen-head mounting bolt
6	Caliper outer half		– 2 off
7	Hex-head caliper joining	16	Torque arm bearing
	bolt – 2 off	17	Sealing washers
8	O-ring	18	Needle roller bearing
9	Dust seals	19	Grease seals
10	Pistons	20	Spacer

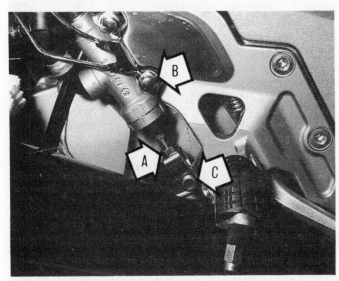

8.16 Pedal height adjustment locknut (A), bottom mounting (B) and clevis pin (C)

9   Using a new O-ring around the fluid passage join the two caliper halves together. Install the hex-head bolts and tighten them securely.
10   Refer to Section 2 and refit the brake pads.

Refitting

11   Offer the caliper up to the disc, if necessary pushing the pistons further into their bores to create enough clearance for the disc. Install the Allen-head mounting bracket bolts and tighten to the specified torque.
12   Position the caliper so that it aligns with the torque arm fork and install the bolt and nut, tightening them to the specified torque. Install a new split pin.
13   Using new sealing washers each side of the hose union, refit the banjo union bolt, tightening it to the specified torque.
14   Fill the system with fresh brake fluid and bleed it of air as described in Chapter 6, Section 13. Check for correct operation of the brakes before taking the machine out on the road.

Rear brake pedal height and freeplay adjustment

15   The pedal height should not normally require adjustment unless the master cylinder pushrod length has been disturbed. With the pedal in the 'at rest' position, measure the vertical height from the pedal pad to the top surface of the footrest. The standard measurement is given in the Specifications.
16   Adjustment of the pedal height is made by slackening the locknut at the pushrod link and turning the pushrod in or out to alter its length. Note the standard length for the pushrod in the Specifications – measured from the centre of the bottom mounting for the master cylinder body to the centre of the clevis pin .

Rear brake light switch setting

17   The brake light should illuminate after the brake pedal has been depressed approximately 10 mm (0.4 in). To adjust, slacken the switch locknut and turn the adjusting nut to either raise or lower the switch body relative to its bracket.

9.5 Fuel level sender unit is retained by six screws

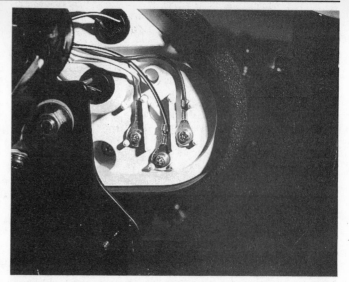

9.8 Make note of wire connections to fuel gauge before disconnection

9   Electrical system

Fuel gauge circuit – testing

Note: *Petrol (gasoline) is extremely flammable, especially when in the form of vapour. Take all precautions to prevent the risk of fire and read the Safety first! section of this manual before starting work.*

1   The fuel gauge circuit consists of the sender unit inside the fuel tank, and the gauge assembly mounted in the instrument panel. If the system malfunctions, first check that the battery is fully charged and that the main fuse (situated in the starter relay) is intact.
2   To test the sender unit first remove it from the tank as described below.
3   Using a test meter, measure the resistance across the yellow/white and black/yellow wires with the float fully raised (full position) and fully lowered (empty position). Compare the readings with the figure given in the Specifications. If the meter reading does not change gradually through the movement of the float, or the resistance figures differ widely from that specified, the sender unit should be renewed.
4   No test details for the fuel gauge are available. If the fault cannot be traced to the sender unit or the circuit wiring and connections, the gauge must be considered defective.

Fuel level sender unit – removal and refitting

5   Remove and drain the fuel tank as described in Section 5 of this Chapter. Displace the cap from the base of the sender unit and remove the six screws to release the sender unit from the tank. Be very careful not to bend the float arm as the sender unit is manoeuvred out of the tank.
6   Refit in the reverse of the removal procedure, noting that a new seal should be installed between the tank and sender unit. Note that while the tank is drained of fuel it is a good opportunity to clean its internal filters (see Section 5).

Fuel gauge – removal and refitting

7   Refer to Section 7 and remove the main fairing. Disconnect both wiring block connectors to the instruments and unscrew the speedometer drive cable, then remove the three nuts and two bolts to free the instrument panel from the fairing mounting bracket. **Note:** *Always keep the instruments facing the correct way up otherwise damage to their movement will occur.*
8   Identify the three wiring connections to the rear of the fuel gauge and unscrew them. Remove all screws retaining the instrument top and bottom halves and separate them to gain access to the fuel gauge.
9   Refit in a reverse of the removal procedure, making sure that the wiring connections are made correctly.

9.13 Main fuse (A) on starter relay can be accessed from above. Note fuel pump relay location (B)

9.15 Turn signal relay location on rear frame rails

Licence plate lamp – *bulb renewal*

10   Access is limited to the two lens retaining screws with the tail unit in place, necessitating either removal of the tail unit or removal of the lamp mounting bolts so that the lamp can be angled down to provide access.

11   Remove the two screws and carefully separate the lens from the reflector, taking care not to tear the seal. To remove the bulb push it in and twist it anticlockwise.

12   To install a new bulb, push it in and turn clockwise. Refit the seal and lens, taking care not to overtighten its screws.

Relay locations

Starter relay

13   The relay is mounted just to the left of the battery, under the frame cross-member. It can be accessed from above, once the seat has been removed, or from underneath after removing the tail unit. The main fuse is incorporated in the starter relay.

14   Refer to Chapter 7, Section 8 for test details.

Turn signal relay

15   The relay is mounted on the left-hand rear frame rails. Remove the seat and tail unit as described in Section 7 of this Chapter for access. Unplug its wiring connector and pull the relay out of its mounting.

16   Refer to Chapter 7, Section 19 for test details.

Fuel pump relay

17   The relay is positioned to the left of the battery and forward of the starter relay; remove the seat for access.

18   Refer to Chapter 7, Section 17 for test details.

Wiring diagram component key

1	Front right-hand turn signal (running lamp – US models)		34	Tail/stop lamp
2	Cooling fan switch relay		35	Rear right-hand turn signal
3	Right-hand turn signal warning lamp		36	Rear brake lamp switch
4	High beam warning lamp		37	Alternator
5	Oil pressure warning lamp		38	Ignitor unit
6	Side stand warning lamp		39	Pick-up coil(s)
7	Neutral lamp		40	Spark plugs
8	Instrument illuminating lamps		41	Ignition HT coils
9	Tachometer/voltmeter		42	Cooling fan switch (110°C)
10	Coolant temperature gauge		43	Coolant temperature sender unit
11	Fuel gauge		44	Fuel gauge sender unit
12	Left-hand turn signal warning lamp		45	Engine kill switch
13	Headlamp		46	Starter button
14	Parking lamp		47	Headlamp switch
15	Front left-hand turn signal (running lamp – US models)		48	Front brake lamp switch
16	Horns		49	Ignition switch
17	Oil temperature switch		50	Cooling fan switch (97°C)
18	Headlamp flash button		51	Headlamp failure warning lamp
19	Horn button		52	Reserve lighting unit
20	Headlamp dip switch		53	Hazzard warning lights switch
21	Turn signal switch		54	Cooling fan switch
22	Cooling fan		55	Tachometer
23	Starter lockout (clutch) switch		56	Turn signal relay
24	Side stand switch		57	Main fuse
25	Oil pressure switch		58	Fuel pump
26	Neutral switch		59	Diode
27	Cooling fan relay		60	Fuel level warning lamps
28	Starter relay		61	Fuel level warning lamp relay
29	Starter motor		62	Fuel level warning circuit relay
30	Battery		63	Fuel pump relay
31	Junction box		64	Fuel level sensor
32	Rear left-hand turn signal		65	Accessory terminals
33	Licence plate lamp			

Colour key

BK	Black		O	Orange
BL	Blue		P	Pink
BR	Brown		R	Red
G	Green		W	White
GY	Grey		Y	Yellow
LG	Light green			

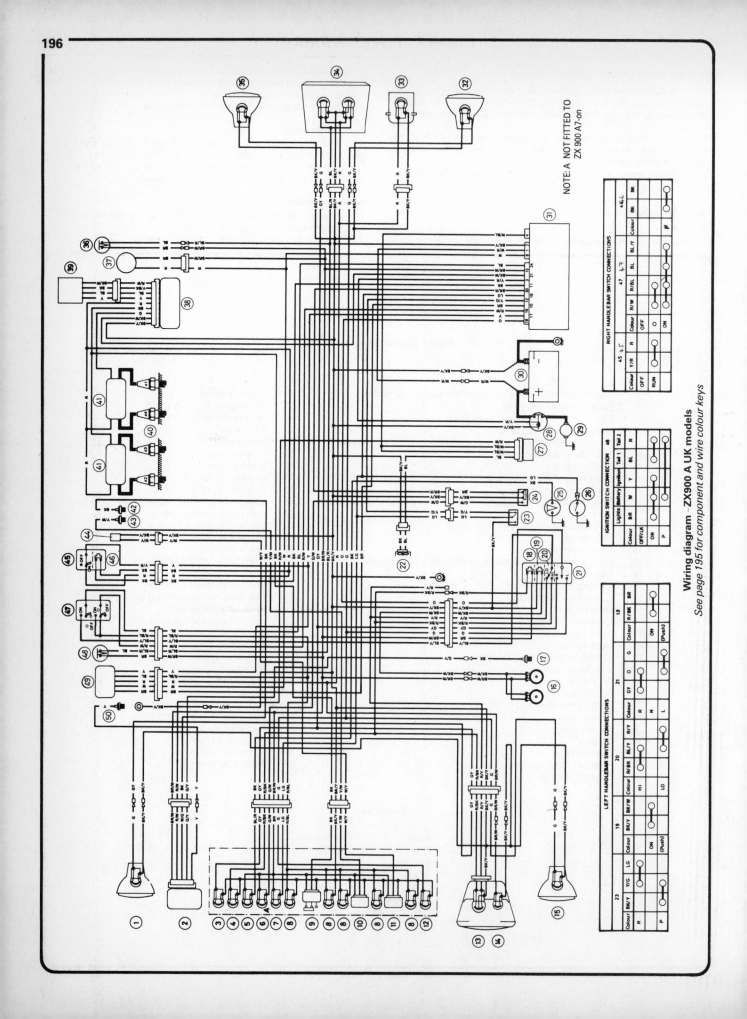

Wiring diagram – ZX900 A UK models
See page 195 for component and wire colour keys

NOTE: A NOT FITTED TO ZX 900 A7-on

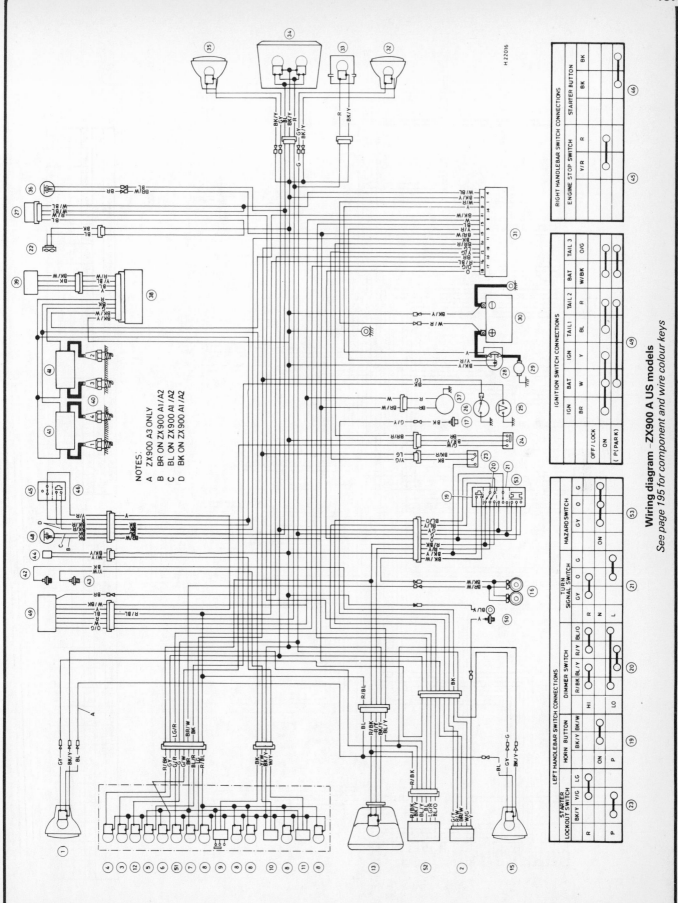

H-22016

Wiring diagram – ZX900 A US models
See page 195 for component and wire colour keys

NOTES:
A ZX900 A3 ONLY
B BR ON ZX900 A1/A2
C BL ON ZX900 A1/A2
D BK ON ZX900 A1/A2

Wiring diagram – ZX1000 A UK models

See page 195 for component and wire colour keys

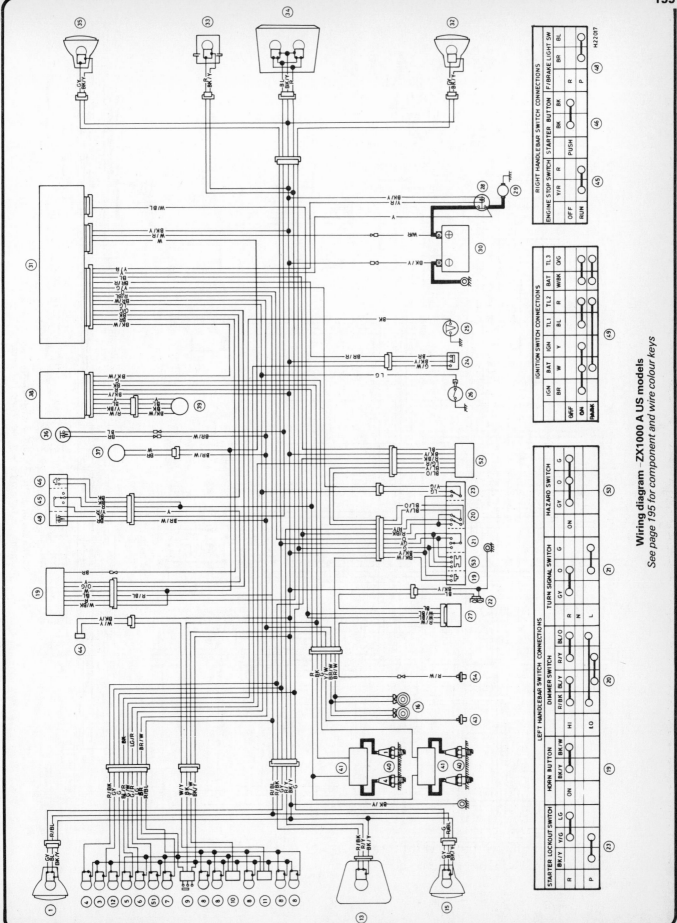

Wiring diagram – ZX1000 A US models
See page 195 for component and wire colour keys

Wiring diagram – ZX1000 B UK models
See page 195 for component and wire colour keys

IGNITION SWITCH CONNECTIONS 49

Color	Light BR	Battery W	Ignition Y	Tail 1 BL	Tail 2 R
OFF, LOCK					
ON					
P (PARK)					

RIGHT HANDLEBAR SWITCH CONNECTIONS

48 Color	BK/R	BK
Released		
Pulled in		

46 Color	BK/R	BL/Y	BL	R/BL	R/W
Push					

47 Color	OFF	O	ON
OFF			
RUN			

45 Color	Y/R	R
OFF		
RUN		

LEFT HANDLEBAR SWITCH CONNECTIONS

18 Color	R/BK	BR

21 Color	GY	O	G	N	L

20 Color	R/BK	BL/Y	BK/W
HI			
LO			

19 Color	BK/Y	GY
ON (Push)		

23 Color	Y/G	LG	BK/Y	GY	BK/Y	G
Released						
Pulled in						

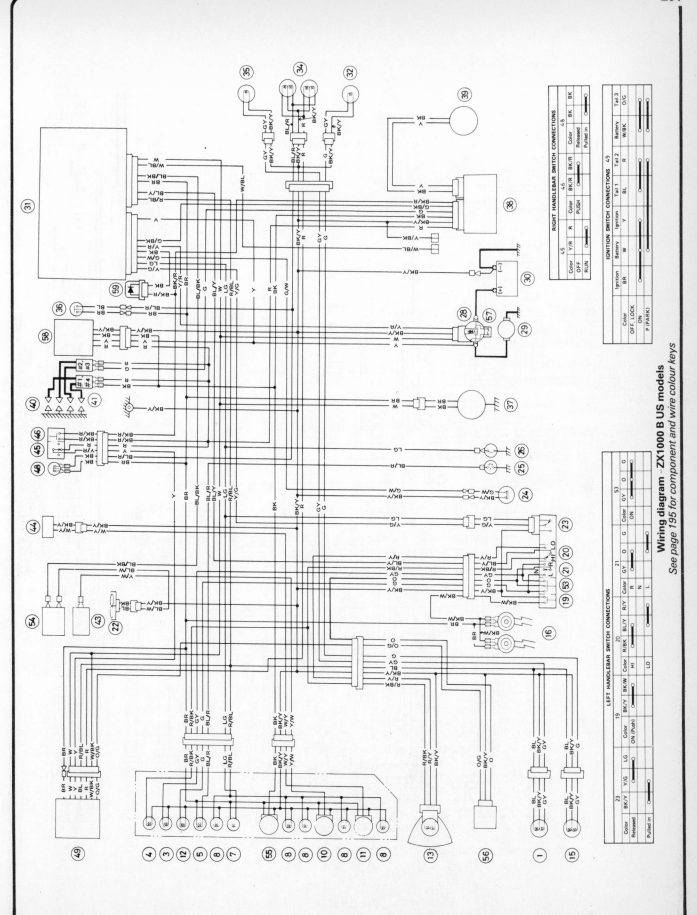

Wiring diagram – ZX1000 B US models
See page 195 for component and wire colour keys

Wiring diagram – ZX1100 C UK models
See page 195 for component and wire colour keys

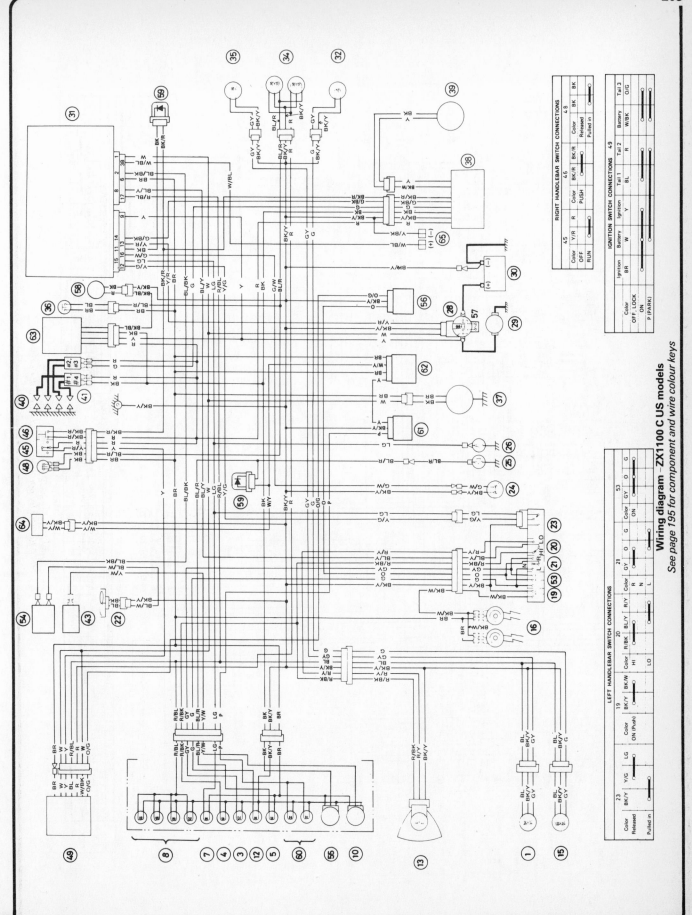

Wiring diagram – ZX1100 C US models
See page 195 for component and wire colour keys

Pickup Coil

I.C. Igniter

Turn Signal Relay

Rear Right Turn Signal Light 12V21W

Tail/Brake Light 12V5/21Wx2

Licence Light 12V5W

Rear Left Turn Signal Light 12V21W

Junction Box
1. Starter Circuit Relay
2. Taillight Fuse 10A
3. Headlight Fuse 10A
4. Fan Fuse 10A

Battery 12V12Ah

Main Fuse 30A

Starter Motor

Fuel Pump

Fuel Pump Relay

Rear Brake Light Switch

Alternator

IC REG

Spark Plugs

Ignition Coil

Right Handlebar Switch
1. Headlight Switch
2. Front Brake Light Switch
3. Engine Stop Switch
4. Starter Button

Fuel Level Sensor

6. Side Stand Switch
7. Oil Pressure Switch
8. Neutral Switch
(I) Italian Model

Left Handlebar Switch
1. Horn Button
2. Turn Signal Switch
3. Dimmer Switch
4. Starter Lockout Switch
5. Passing Button

Cooling Fan Switch

Water Temperature Sensor

Horn 12V2.5Ax2

Cooling Fan

Ignition Switch

Neutral Indicator Light 12V3.4W

Tachometer Light 12V1.7W

Tachometer

Speedometer Light 12V1.7W
Fuel Gauge Light 12V1.7W

Water Temperature Gauge

Water Temp. Gauge Light 12V1.7W

High Beam Indicator Light 12V3.4W
Right Turn Signal Indicator Light 12V3.4W
Left Turn Signal Indicator Light 12V3.4W
Oil Pressure Warning Light 12V3.4W

Fuel Gauge

Head Light 12V60/55W

City Light 12V5W

Front Right Turn Signal Light 12V21W

Front Left Turn Signal Light 12V21W

RIGHT HANDLEBAR SWITCH CONNECTIONS

Headlight Switch			Front Brake Light Switch		Engine Stop Switch		Starter Button	
Color	BL/Y	BL	Color	R/BL/R/W	Color	Y/R	Color	BK/R	BK/BK
OFF			Brake Lever		OFF		OFF		
ON			Pulled In		RUN		RUN		
							Push		

IGNITION SWITCH CONNECTIONS

	Ignition	Battery	Ignition	Tail1	Tail2
Color	BR	W	GY	BL	R
OFF,LOCK					
ON					

LEFT HANDLEBAR SWITCH CONNECTIONS

Horn Button		Turn Signal Switch			Dimmer Switch			Starter Lockout Switch		Passing Button	
Color	BK/WBK/Y	Color	G	O	GY	Color	BK/Y/R	BK	Color	BR/BK	Color	BR
Push		L				HI			Clutch Lever		Push	
		R (Push)				LO			Released			
									Pulled In			

Wiring diagram – ZX1100 D UK models
See page 195 for wire colour key

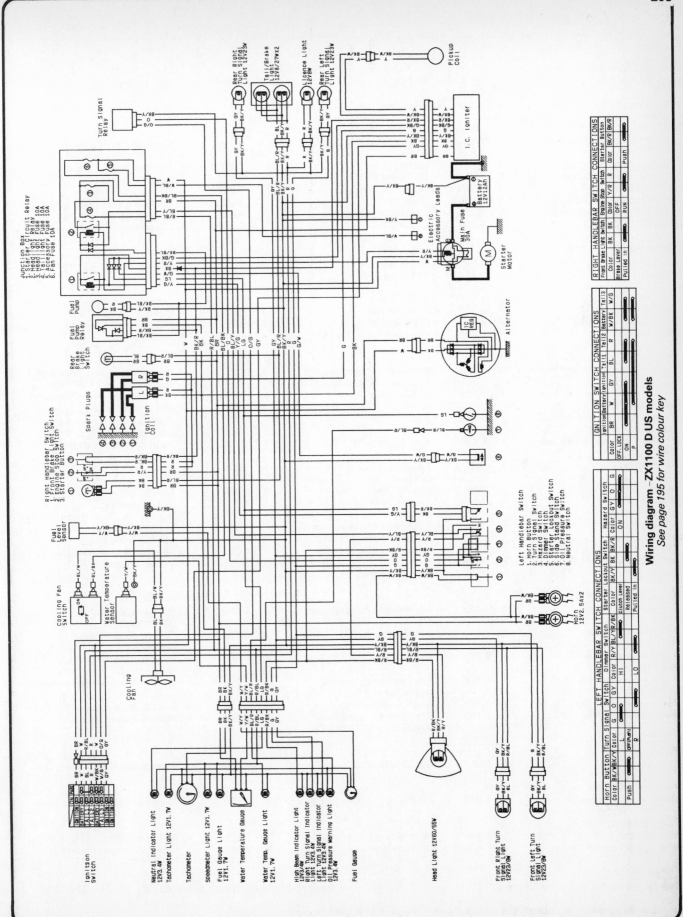

Wiring diagram – ZX1100 D US models
See page 195 for wire colour key

Conversion factors

Length (distance)

Inches (in)	X	25.4	= Millimetres (mm)	X 0.0394	= Inches (in)
Feet (ft)	X	0.305	= Metres (m)	X 3.281	= Feet (ft)
Miles	X	1.609	= Kilometres (km)	X 0.621	= Miles

Volume (capacity)

Cubic inches (cu in; in³)	X	16.387	= Cubic centimetres (cc; cm³)	X 0.061	= Cubic inches (cu in; in³)
Imperial pints (Imp pt)	X	0.568	= Litres (l)	X 1.76	= Imperial pints (Imp pt)
Imperial quarts (Imp qt)	X	1.137	= Litres (l)	X 0.88	= Imperial quarts (Imp qt)
Imperial quarts (Imp qt)	X	1.201	= US quarts (US qt)	X 0.833	= Imperial quarts (Imp qt)
US quarts (US qt)	X	0.946	= Litres (l)	X 1.057	= US quarts (US qt)
Imperial gallons (Imp gal)	X	4.546	= Litres (l)	X 0.22	= Imperial gallons (Imp gal)
Imperial gallons (Imp gal)	X	1.201	= US gallons (US gal)	X 0.833	= Imperial gallons (Imp gal)
US gallons (US gal)	X	3.785	= Litres (l)	X 0.264	= US gallons (US gal)

Mass (weight)

Ounces (oz)	X	28.35	= Grams (g)	X 0.035	= Ounces (oz)
Pounds (lb)	X	0.454	= Kilograms (kg)	X 2.205	= Pounds (lb)

Force

Ounces-force (ozf; oz)	X	0.278	= Newtons (N)	X 3.6	= Ounces-force (ozf; oz)
Pounds-force (lbf; lb)	X	4.448	= Newtons (N)	X 0.225	= Pounds-force (lbf; lb)
Newtons (N)	X	0.1	= Kilograms-force (kgf; kg)	X 9.81	= Newtons (N)

Pressure

Pounds-force per square inch (psi; lbf/in²; lb/in²)	X	0.070	= Kilograms-force per square centimetre (kgf/cm²; kg/cm²)	X 14.223	= Pounds-force per square inch (psi; lbf/in²; lb/in²)
Pounds-force per square inch (psi; lbf/in²; lb/in²)	X	0.068	= Atmospheres (atm)	X 14.696	= Pounds-force per square inch (psi; lbf/in²; lb/in²)
Pounds-force per square inch (psi; lbf/in²; lb/in²)	X	0.069	= Bars	X 14.5	= Pounds-force per square inch (psi; lbf/in²; lb/in²)
Pounds-force per square inch (psi; lbf/in²; lb/in²)	X	6.895	= Kilopascals (kPa)	X 0.145	= Pounds-force per square inch (psi; lbf/in²; lb/in²)
Kilopascals (kPa)	X	0.01	= Kilograms-force per square centimetre (kgf/cm²; kg/cm²)	X 98.1	= Kilopascals (kPa)
Millibar (mbar)	X	100	= Pascals (Pa)	X 0.01	= Millibar (mbar)
Millibar (mbar)	X	0.0145	= Pounds-force per square inch (psi; lbf/in²; lb/in²)	X 68.947	= Millibar (mbar)
Millibar (mbar)	X	0.75	= Millimetres of mercury (mmHg)	X 1.333	= Millibar (mbar)
Millibar (mbar)	X	0.401	= Inches of water (inH₂O)	X 2.491	= Millibar (mbar)
Millimetres of mercury (mmHg)	X	0.535	= Inches of water (inH₂O)	X 1.868	= Millimetres of mercury (mmHg)
Inches of water (inH₂O)	X	0.036	= Pounds-force per square inch (psi; lbf/in²; lb/in²)	X 27.68	= Inches of water (inH₂O)

Torque (moment of force)

Pounds-force inches (lbf in; lb in)	X	1.152	= Kilograms-force centimetre (kgf cm; kg cm)	X 0.868	= Pounds-force inches (lbf in; lb in)
Pounds-force inches (lbf in; lb in)	X	0.113	= Newton metres (Nm)	X 8.85	= Pounds-force inches (lbf in; lb in)
Pounds-force inches (lbf in; lb in)	X	0.083	= Pounds-force feet (lbf ft; lb ft)	X 12	= Pounds-force inches (lbf in; lb in)
Pounds-force feet (lbf ft; lb ft)	X	0.138	= Kilograms-force metres (kgf m; kg m)	X 7.233	= Pounds-force feet (lbf ft; lb ft)
Pounds-force feet (lbf ft; lb ft)	X	1.356	= Newton metres (Nm)	X 0.738	= Pounds-force feet (lbf ft; lb ft)
Newton metres (Nm)	X	0.102	= Kilograms-force metres (kgf m; kg m)	X 9.804	= Newton metres (Nm)

Power

Horsepower (hp)	X	745.7	= Watts (W)	X 0.0013	= Horsepower (hp)

Velocity (speed)

Miles per hour (miles/hr; mph)	X	1.609	= Kilometres per hour (km/hr; kph)	X 0.621	= Miles per hour (miles/hr; mph)

Fuel consumption*

Miles per gallon, Imperial (mpg)	X	0.354	= Kilometres per litre (km/l)	X 2.825	= Miles per gallon, Imperial (mpg)
Miles per gallon, US (mpg)	X	0.425	= Kilometres per litre (km/l)	X 2.352	= Miles per gallon, US (mpg)

Temperature

Degrees Fahrenheit = (°C x 1.8) + 32   Degrees Celsius (Degrees Centigrade; °C) = (°F - 32) x 0.56

*It is common practice to convert from miles per gallon (mpg) to litres/100 kilometres (l/100km),
where mpg (Imperial) x l/100 km = 282 and mpg (US) x l/100 km = 235*

English/American terminology

Because this book has been written in England, British English component names, phrases and spellings have been used throughout. American English usage is quite often different and whereas normally no confusion should occur, a list of equivalent terminology is given below.

English	American	English	American
Air filter	Air cleaner	Number plate	License plate
Alignment (headlamp)	Aim	Output or layshaft	Countershaft
Allen screw/key	Socket screw/wrench	Panniers	Side cases
Anticlockwise	Counterclockwise	Paraffin	Kerosene
Bottom/top gear	Low/high gear	Petrol	Gasoline
Bottom/top yoke	Bottom/top triple clamp	Petrol/fuel tank	Gas tank
Bush	Bushing	Pinking	Pinging
Carburettor	Carburetor	Rear suspension unit	Rear shock absorber
Catch	Latch	Rocker cover	Valve cover
Circlip	Snap ring	Selector	Shifter
Clutch drum	Clutch housing	Self-locking pliers	Vise-grips
Dip switch	Dimmer switch	Side or parking lamp	Parking or auxiliary light
Disulphide	Disulfide	Side or prop stand	Kick stand
Dynamo	DC generator	Silencer	Muffler
Earth	Ground	Spanner	Wrench
End float	End play	Split pin	Cotter pin
Engineer's blue	Machinist's dye	Stanchion	Tube
Exhaust pipe	Header	Sulphuric	Sulfuric
Fault diagnosis	Trouble shooting	Sump	Oil pan
Float chamber	Float bowl	Swinging arm	Swingarm
Footrest	Footpeg	Tab washer	Lock washer
Fuel/petrol tap	Petcock	Top box	Trunk
Gaiter	Boot	Torch	Flashlight
Gearbox	Transmission	Two/four stroke	Two/four cycle
Gearchange	Shift	Tyre	Tire
Gudgeon pin	Wrist/piston pin	Valve collar	Valve retainer
Indicator	Turn signal	Valve collets	Valve cotters
Inlet	Intake	Vice	Vise
Input shaft or mainshaft	Mainshaft	Wheel spindle	Axle
Kickstart	Kickstarter	White spirit	Stoddard solvent
Lower leg	Slider	Windscreen	Windshield
Mudguard	Fender		

Index